WITHDRAWN FROM
TSC LIBRARY

W9-CZY-251

TALLAHASSEE
LIBRARY

Tolerance and intolerance in the European Reformation

This volume of essays offers a new interpretation of the role of tolerance and intolerance in the European Reformation. It questions the traditional view, which has claimed a progressive development towards greater religious toleration from the beginning of the sixteenth century to the end of the seventeenth. Instead, it places incidents of religious tolerance and intolerance in their specific social and political context. Fifteen leading scholars present a comprehensive examination of this subject in all the regions of Europe which were directly affected by the Reformation in the crucial period between 1500, when northern humanism had begun to make an impact, and 1648, the end of the Thirty Years War. In this way, *Tolerance and intolerance in the European Reformation* provides a dramatically different view of how religious toleration and conflict developed in early modern Europe.

Tolerance and intolerance in the European Reformation

Edited by
Ole Peter Grell and Bob Scribner
University of Cambridge

CAMBRIDGE
UNIVERSITY PRESS

Published by the Press Syndicate of the University of Cambridge
The Pitt Building, Trumpington Street, Cambridge CB2 1RP
40 West 20th Street, New York, NY 10011-4211, USA
10 Stamford Road, Oakleigh, Melbourne 3166, Australia

© Cambridge University Press 1996

First published 1996

Printed in Great Britain at the University Press, Cambridge

A *catalogue record for this book is available from the British Library*

Library of Congress cataloguing in publication data

Tolerance and intolerance in the European reformation / edited by Ole Peter Grell
and Bob Scribner.
    p.   cm.
Papers from a conference held at Corpus Christi College, Cambridge in September
1994.
Includes bibliographical references and index.
ISBN 0 521 49694 2 (hardcover)
1. Reformation–Congresses. 2. Religious tolerance–Europe–History–16th century–Congresses. 3. Religious tolerance–Europe–History–17th century–Congresses. I. Grell, Ole Peter.
II. Scribner, Robert W.
BR3000.T65 1996
261.7′2′09409031–dc20 95-40174 CIP

ISBN 0 521 496 942 hardback

w v

Contents

Contributors

LORNA JANE ABRAY, Division of Humanities, Scarborough Campus, University of Toronto, Canada

PHILIP BENEDICT, Department of History, Brown University, Providence, RI, USA

EUAN CAMERON, Department of History, University of Newcastle upon Tyne, England

NORAH CARLIN, Faculty of Humanities, Middlesex University, London, England

BRUCE GORDON, St. Andrews Reformation Studies Institute, University of St. Andrews, Scotland

OLE PETER GRELL, Wellcome Unit for the History of Medicine, University of Cambridge, England

✠HANS R. GUGGISBERG, formerly Historisches Seminar, University of Basle, Switzerland

DIARMAID MacCULLOGH, Faculty of Theology, University of Oxford, England

WILLIAM MONTER, Department of History, Northwestern University, Evanston, Illinois, USA

MICHAEL G. MÜLLER, Department of History, European University Institute, San Domenico di Fiesole, Italy

HEIKO A. OBERMAN, Division for Late Medieval and Reformation Studies, University of Arizona, Tucson, Arizona, USA

JAROSLAV PANEK, Folia Historica Bohemica, Charles University, Prague, Czech Republic

KATALIN PÉTER, Institute of History, Hungarian Academy of Sciences, Budapest, Hungary

ANDREW PETTEGREE, St. Andrews Reformation Studies Institute, University of St. Andrews, Scotland

BOB SCRIBNER, Clare College, University of Cambridge, England

Preface

This volume springs from a conference held at Corpus Christi College, Cambridge in September 1994 which was organised under the auspices of the William and Mary History of Toleration Committee. As such it forms a companion volume to O. P. Grell, J. I. Israel and N. Tyacke (eds.), *From Persecution to Toleration. The Glorious Revolution and Religion in England*, published in 1991, which originated from a conference held in London in 1988 in connection with the William and Mary Tercentenary.

It explores the role and significance of tolerance and intolerance in Reformation Europe. Geographically, as wide a coverage as possible has been sought by the editors, including all the northern and central European countries which were directly affected by the Reformation.

Similarly, it has been considered imperative to emphasise the role of specific areas and cities such as Basle and Strassburg which provide particularly interesting examples of religious toleration. Chronologically this volume focuses on the period from the start of the sixteenth century, when northern humanism had begun to make an impact until the middle of the seventeenth century when the Thirty Years War had come to an end and the long term effects of the Reformation were drawing to a close. In three cases these chronological parameters have been extended in order to provide a fuller and more satisfying interpretation. In the case of France this has meant taking the story up to the Revocation of the Edict of Nantes in 1685, and in the case of toleration for English Catholics it has meant that the parameters needed to be extended into the 1650s, while in the case of Bohemia and Moravia the story had to begin with the Hussites in the fifteenth century.

This volume offers new and revisionist interpretations of the role and place of tolerance and intolerance in the European Reformation, setting the specific historic developments in their local, social and political context. As such it questions the validity of the hitherto dominant scholarly view of religious toleration in the early modern period as having seen a steady expansion between the late fifteenth and the seventeenth centuries, both theoretically and practically, apart from the brief period of persecution which followed the emergence of Protestantism in the 1520s.

Bearing in mind the horrific examples of intolerance and ethnic and religious conflict we have witnessed in former Yugoslavia in general and Bosnia in particular over the last three years, the relevance and actuality of this volume's concern for tolerance and intolerance needs no justification. Watching the television pictures of the civil war in Bosnia one wonders whether any progress towards greater tolerance has really been achieved in Europe since the sixteenth century, and whether the liberal tradition of tolerance and respect for others which we consider a central part of our cultural heritage is, in fact, only a paper-thin veneer which given the right, or rather wrong, social and political conditions might quickly be discarded and replaced by violence and bigotry.

A number of scholars have provided us with the valuable advice and we should like to thank Professor Robert Evans, Brasenose College, Oxford and Dr Robert Frost, King's College, London, for their assistance.

We are also grateful to the Herzog August Bibliothek Wolfenbüttel for permission to reproduce the print used on the cover of this book, showing Luther, the Pope and Calvin engaged in a 'spiritual brawl'.

Without the financial support we received for the conference none of this would have been possible and we are indebted to The William and Mary Tercentenary Trust and The British Academy for their generosity.

O. P. GRELL
R. W. SCRIBNER
July 1995 Cambridge

The editors were saddened to hear of the sudden death of Hans Guggisberg as the proofs for this volume were being collated. Guggisberg was one of the great historians of toleration of our age and we wish to dedicate this volume to him as a fitting memorial to his pre-eminent contribution to the subject.

O.P.G.
R.W.S.
January 1996.

In memoriam Hans R. Guggisberg

1   Introduction

Ole Peter Grell

Within the historiography of religious tolerance the Reformation era has always been considered of paramount importance for the developments which led to the achievement of 'a liberal and tolerant society'. This was, of course, a highly valued goal for the educated elite in nineteenth-century Western Europe and has subsequently influenced a later period's scholars in their inquiries and judgements. Evidently the break-up of the near monolithic structure of medieval Western Christianity for the first time presented contemporary lay and ecclesiastical rulers with the practical problem of how to deal with religious plurality. Likewise, this fragmentation gave rise to a growing debate about aspects of religious toleration, such as freedom of conscience and freedom of worship.

Not surprisingly this field of research has been dominated by historians of ideas who have promoted the view that religious tolerance in Europe witnessed an organic growth from the late fifteenth to the late seventeenth century. With regard to the Reformation period, starting with the Christian humanists at the beginning of the sixteenth century and concluding their story in the seventeenth century, historians such as W. K. Jordan and Joseph Lecler have portrayed the period as one beginning with the tolerance of humanists, such as Erasmus and Thomas More. This brief interlude was then followed by the bigotry and intolerance of the first decades of the Reformation, especially by reformers such as Calvin, Knox and Beza. Eventually the resulting religious wars and a gradual tiredness of constant religious confrontations caused religious fervour to evaporate towards the end of the sixteenth century, thus making way for a common-sense tolerance of religious differences.[1] Within this rather 'whiggish' interpretation of the development of toleration in early modern Europe two variations on the general theme deserve to be mentioned. One focuses on the role and significance of scepticism in promoting religious toleration from the second half of the sixteenth

---

[1] See W. K. Jordan, *The Development of Religious Toleration in England*, 4 vols. (London, 1932–40), and J. Lecler, *Toleration and the Reformation*, 2 vols. (London, 1960).

1

century onwards and has won particular favour among historians of ideas.[2] The other variation has been concerned with the significance of free trade and mercantilism in promoting greater religious liberty, often claiming that the Reformation period led to increased tolerance, not as a consequence of Protestantism, but, despite the reformers, as a product of predominantly economic considerations.[3]

Among the first historians to question this generally accepted interpretation of the development of toleration in the early modern period was Geoffrey Elton. In an article from 1984 concerned with England in general and comparing the approaches to toleration and persecution of Thomas More and John Foxe in particular, Elton rejected the accepted 'model'. In fact, in the cases of More and Foxe he turned it upside down. He portrayed the humanist More not only as intolerant, but as a firm believer in religious persecution, while the Calvinist Foxe is shown to have had a deep faith in religious toleration which had direct practical implications for his actions. Thus Foxe actively intervened to try to prevent the execution of the Catholic Edmund Campion as well as five Dutch Anabaptists who had been sentenced to be burned for heresy in 1575.[4]

Similarly, the view that it was late sixteenth century scepticism which was responsible for promoting the move towards greater tolerance has also been seriously questioned recently. Thus a leading sceptic and irenicist in post-Reformation Europe, the Leiden professor, Justus Lipsius, has been shown to have been a firm supporter of religious persecution. According to Lipsius, religious pluriformity would lead to civil strife and encourage religious fanatics who in turn would destabilise society, something which had to be prevented at all costs. Only if repression turned out to be politically too costly should toleration be contemplated. In his work, *Politicorum libri sex*, published in 1589, Lipsius argued for the repression of religious dissenters, pointing out that they were to be shown no clemency, but to be burned, since it was better to sacrifice one member rather than risk the collapse of the whole commonwealth.[5]

Lipsius's advocacy of persecution was quickly attacked by the Spiritualist Dirck Coornhert who served as secretary to the States of Holland. Coornhert published an eloquent defence of religious toleration, based on his non-

---

[2] See for instance Q. Skinner, *The Foundations of Modern Political Thought*, vol. 2 (Cambridge, 1978), 247–50.

[3] See H. Kamen, *The Rise of Toleration* (London, 1967).

[4] G. R. Elton, 'Persecution and Toleration in the English Reformation', in W. J. Sheils (ed.), *Persecution and Toleration* (Oxford, 1984), 163–87. For the role played by the exiled Dutch community in London in the conviction and execution of the Dutch Anabaptists in 1575, see also chapter 10 below.

[5] R. Tuck, 'Sceptism and Toleration in the Seventeenth Century', in S. Mendus (ed.), *Justifying Tolerance: Conceptual and Historical Perspectives* (Cambridge, 1988), 21–35, especially 21 and 26. See also R. Tuck, *Philosophy and Government 1572–1651* (Cambridge, 1993), 58.

dogmatic piety and firm belief that ultimate truth could be found in the Scriptures. As opposed to Lipsius he was convinced that toleration would not create religious and by implication political strife. Instead, free access to the Gospel would eventually bring harmony and concord and serve to enhance political and social stability.[6]

In some respects Coornhert differed in his religious views from other major advocates of toleration in the early modern period, but neither he nor those with whom he differed such as the Anabaptist-Spiritualist, David Joris, and the 'libertine' Reformed, Sebastian Castellio and Jacobus Acontius, can be described as sceptics.[7] All of them were firmly anchored in a non-dogmatic, Scripturally-based type of Christianity, which owed most of its inspiration to Christian humanists such as Erasmus and Protestant theologians such as Luther. Apart from Coornhert, whose writings were published in Holland during the 1590s, it is noteworthy that all the other authors, who at some time had found refuge in Basle, chose to publish their works on toleration in that city.[8] There was undoubtedly a concerted campaign for toleration in Basle around the middle of the sixteenth century as emphasised by Hans Guggisberg.[9] The role and significance of foreign immigrants in this campaign would appear to have been significant. Castellio, Joris, and briefly Acontius, had all settled in Basle together with other exiled advocates of some form of religious toleration, such as Bernardino Ochino and Mino Celsi.[10] For Protestant individuals like these, and others such as John Foxe,[11] the personal experience of persecution and exile may well have been a formative influence on their intellectual development. To try and take this analogy further, however, would seem dangerous. In fact, the attitude of the exiled Dutch and Walloon communities in London to religious toleration in the second half of the sixteenth century would seem to argue for a reverse

[6] See G. Güldner, *Das Toleranz-Problem in den Niederlanden im Ausgang des 16. Jahrhunderts* (Lübeck, 1968), especially 66–90 and Tuck, 'Sceptism and Toleration'. For Coornhert, see also J. I. Israel, *The Dutch Republic: Its Rise, Greatness, and Fall 1477–1806* (Oxford, 1995), 97–9 and 372–4.

[7] For Joris, see Lecler, *Toleration and the Reformation* 1, 216–22; for Castellio, see chapter 9 below and F. Buisson, *Sébastien Castellion, sa vie et son oeuvre*, 2 vols (Paris, 1892); for Jacobus Acontius, see E. R. Briggs, 'An Apostle of the Incomplete Reformation: Jacopo Aconcio (1500–1567)', *Proceedings of the Huguenot Society of London*, 22 (1970–76), 481–95 and J. Jacquot, 'Acontius and the Progress of Tolerance in England', *Bibliothèque d'Humanisme et Renaissance*, 16 (1954), 192–206.

[8] S. Castellio, *De haereticis an sint persequendi* (Basle, 1554); D. Joris, *Christelijcke Waerschouwinghe aen allen Regenten unde Ouvericheden . . . : Datmen niemeant om sijn Gheloof en behoort te . . . vervolghen, veele min te dooden* (1554); J. Acontius, *Santanae Stratagemata* (Basle, 1565).

[9] See chapter 9 below.

[10] For Bernardino Ochino and Mino Celsi, see Lecler, *Toleration and the Reformation*, 1, 367–9 and 377–80. For Castellio, see chapter 9 below.

[11] For the significance of Foxe's personal experience in this respect, see Elton, 'Persecution and Toleration', 179.

relationship, namely one between persecution/exile and intolerance, as can be seen from the incidents discussed by Ole Peter Grell.[12]

Undoubtedly, toleration in the early modern period was either a loser's creed as argued by Andrew Pettegree or a belief only advocated by outsiders in both religious, political and social terms.[13] In this connection it is significant that many of those who otherwise naturally inclined towards some form of religious tolerance argued strongly against it for political reasons. The reason of state which made Justus Lipsius argue for persecution for the sake of unity also served to limit the toleration Hugo Grotius was prepared to allow his fellow citizens. Even while in exile, post-1618, Grotius continued to argue for a strong state church which in the interest of the commonwealth should control the religious life of the bulk of the nation. The only difference, but admittedly a significant one, between Grotius and his Calvinist opponents was that Grotius perceived his model for a national church to be inclusive and based on a minimum of doctrine, as opposed to the exclusive and dogmatic ideal of his Counter-Remonstrant opponents.[14]

The problem of how to reconcile the idea of some form of religious tolerance with the political realities of the day is potently demonstrated in the changing attitude to this issue by Martin Luther. In his early writings Luther had argued strongly against any use of force or direct intervention by lay authorities in matters of faith. Undoubtedly this was a typical position taken by most 'religious outsiders' in the sixteenth century. Thus, in 1523 when Luther published his now classic statement on religious toleration *On Secular Authority (Von Weltlicher Oberkeit)* he argued from a position of weakness, wanting to reform a Church which had already excommunicated him, while simultaneously being infused with religious optimism, believing that a reformation would quickly follow upon unadulterated Scripture being made available to the laity through vernacular preaching and texts. Only God could generate true, evangelical faith in man and accordingly:

Each must decide at his own peril what he is to believe, and must see to it that he believes rightly. Other people cannot go to heaven or hell on my behalf, or open or close (the gates to either) for me. And just as little can they believe or not believe on my behalf, or force my faith or unbelief. How he believes is a matter for each individual's conscience, and this does not diminish (the authority of) secular governments. They ought therefore to content themselves with attending to their own business, and allow people to believe what they can, and what they want, and they must use no coercion in this matter against anyone.[15]

---

[12] See chapter 10 below.
[13] See chapter 11 below.
[14] See Israel, *The Dutch Republic*, 499–505.
[15] The translation used here is that of Harro Höpfl (ed.), *Luther and Calvin on Secular Authority* (Cambridge, 1991), 3–43, see especially 25. For the original German text, see O. Clemen (ed.), *Luthers Werke in Auswahl* (Berlin, 1967), 2, 360–94.

Luther went on to point out that lay authorities should under no circumstances try to fight heresy with the sword. This was a matter solely for the Word of God. To use force in matters of faith would according to Luther only make matters worse.[16]

For people take it for granted that force is not being used in the cause of right, and that those who use it are acting unjustly, precisely because they are acting without God's Word and because they cannot think of any other way of furthering their aims except by mere force, like animals that have no use of reason. Even in secular matters force cannot be used unless guilt has first been established by reference to the law. And it is all the more impossible to use force without right and God's Word in such high spiritual matters (as heresy).[17]

A couple of years later, however, social, political and religious realities forced Luther to limit his original tolerant stance, not least because of the increasingly serious challenge mounted by the more radical reformers such as Müntzer and Karlstadt and their growing number of followers and the outbreak of the Peasants' War in Germany in 1524. These experiences led Luther to believe that his rigid distinction between the two kingdoms – the spiritual and the temporal – could not be upheld in extreme cases. Instead, lay authority had an obligation to step in to prevent blasphemy, an act which according to Luther could have serious implications for the peace and stability of society in general. Similarly, he expected lay authority to take action against sedition; in both cases civil authority had an obligation to intervene against 'outward' manifestations of false belief to prevent civil disorder and protect the new evangelical churches. By establishing these categories Luther was able to justify suppression of the mass and persecution of Anabaptists, while he increasingly sought to encourage the princes to intervene in order to protect and promote the evangelical cause.[18] Within less than a decade Luther had moved from an outsider's position, hoping and wanting to reform the whole Church to that of an insider who sought to protect and secure the existence of the Protestant churches already established. Political considerations had forced him to modify his theology on this point. In other words, the reason of state which later determined the views on toleration of Justus

---

[16] For Luther's attitude to toleration, see W. D. J. Cargill Thompson, *The Political Thought of Martin Luther* (Sussex, 1984), 155–62. I should however emphasize that I disagree with Cargill Thompson's conclusion that Luther's support for toleration in the early 1520s was essentially based on negative principles, namely that repression was counterproductive. I think Luther's statement that 'the faith is free and no one can be compelled to believe' is a positive belief in freedom of conscience and as such an essential part of his theology of faith and grace.

[17] See Höpfl, *Luther and Calvin*, 30–1.

[18] For this development, see Cargill Thompson, *Political Thought*, 158–62 and Lecler, *Toleration and the Reformation*, 1, 152–64. See also C. Hinrichs, *Luther und Müntzer ihre Auseinandersetzung über Obrigkeit und Widerstandsrecht* (Berlin, 1962).

Lipsius and Hugo Grotius also served to change the views of Luther more than half a century earlier. However, Luther's original, more tolerant views from the early 1520s found an extra lease of life when they were taken over by Sebastian Castellio, who included a translation of a substantial part of Luther's tract, *On Secular Authority*, in his, *De Haereticis an sint persequendi* . . . (1554).[19] Thus, it was not only the ideas of Erasmus who inspired the writings of Castellio and others towards the middle of the sixteenth century. Moreover, the debate on freedom of conscience in France between 1559 and 1561, which according to Philip Benedict was so innovative, undoubtedly had roots in the writings of Luther and Erasmus from the beginning of the century.[20]

It is significant that most, if not all, of this period's writers on toleration, at least until the third decade of the seventeenth century, only argued for freedom of conscience and occasionally for some limited freedom of worship out of the conviction that this tolerance would eventually serve to establish true peace and concord. For all of them religious diversity was nothing positive in itself and was only to be tolerated in the short run, in order that true faith might eventually be victorious. This concord could be based on a limited dogmatic formula as was the case for Castellio and Acontius, or be founded on the firm belief that everyone would eventually see the light through evangelical instruction and preaching, as was the case for Luther until 1525.

It was, however, not until the publication of the writings of Dutch Remonstrants, such as Johannes Uyttenbogaert and Simon Episcopius who had found themselves marginalised after their Arminian theology had been rejected at the Synod of Dort in 1618 that this inherently negative view of religious diversity changed. Confronted with the intolerance of their victorious Counter-Remonstrant opponents, the leading Remonstrant theologians became forceful promoters of religious toleration. Considering the ruthlessness with which they had pursued their original political advantage in the years before the Synod of Dort and suppressed their Calvinist opponents, as pointed out by Andrew Pettegree, this was a significant transformation.[21] According to Uyttenbogaert and Episcopius religious persecution was detrimental not only to human freedom but also to economic prosperity.

Episcopius developed his view on toleration from the principles of his theology. In two tracts from the late 1620s *Vrye Godes-dienst* (1627) and *Apologia pro Remonstrantium* (1629) he pointed out that most theological disputes were about adiaphora, non-essential questions, for which no consensus was needed. A wide variety of views could, according to Episcopius, be

[19] Höpfl, *Luther and Calvin*, xi and xxiv–xxv.
[20] See chapter 5 below.
[21] See chapter 11 below.

deducted from Scripture. Accordingly diversity of belief was a positive thing which might contribute to greater insight and strengthen true faith.

However, of greater significance were Episcopius's and Uyttenbogaert's economic and political arguments in favour of toleration. They pointed to the severe recession which had affected the provinces of Holland and Zeeland in particular during the 1620s as indisputable evidence of the damage caused by religious persecution. In this instance it was seen to have been caused by the repression of Arminian merchants and craftsmen, many of whom had chosen to emigrate. Instead, Episcopius and Uyttenbogaert argued that religious toleration, even of Catholics, whom many considered to be potentially dangerous to the Republic, would benefit society economically as well as politically.[22] Evidently where 'reason of state' had hitherto provided ample justification for repression, by the third decade of the seventeenth century predominantly economic considerations had caused some writers to reverse such arguments, providing a strong political rationale for religious toleration.

By then the practical experience of successful and peaceful co-existence of several confessions within a number of cities would have provided considerable support for this change in political thinking. Excluded from the *cuius regio eius religio* clause of the Peace of Augsburg in 1555 the imperial cities had been left to pursue a policy of *pax et concordia* in the interest of trade and prosperity which had characterised most of them since the late medieval period,[23] The result had been that a peaceful bi-confessionalism had been allowed to develop in several imperial cities in Swabia, such as Ulm, Ravensburg and Augsburg. Even in confessionally Lutheran cities, such as Nuremberg and Frankfurt-on-Main, both amongst the most prosperous mercantile centres of the Empire, a pluriformity of confessions were quietly 'tolerated' or allowed to exist. In fact, the magistrates of both these cities actively encouraged exiled Calvinist merchants and artisans from the southern Netherlands to settle during the second half of the sixteenth century, in the case of Nuremberg the immigrants were offered economic inducements, such as tax exemption.[24]

Further evidence of this change in contemporary political and economic thinking, based on 'reason of state', with regard to religious tolerance can

---

[22] Israel, *The Dutch Republic*, 502–3; see also D. Nobbs, *Theocracy and Toleration: A Study of the Disputes in Dutch Calvinism from 1600 to 1650* (Cambridge, 1938), 102–7.

[23] See M. Heckel, *Deutschland im konfessionellen Zeitalter, Deutsche Geschichte 5* (Göttingen, 1983), 33–99.

[24] R. Po-Chia Hsia, *Social Discipline in the Reformation: Central Europe 1550–1750* (London, 1989), 73–88; for Nürnberg, see G. Pfeiffer, *Nürnberg – Geschichte einer europäischen Stadt* (Munich, 1971) and H. Neiddiger, 'Die Entstehung der evangelischer-reformierten Gemeinde in Nürnberg als rechtsgeschichtliches Problem', *Mitteilungen des Vereins für Geschichte der Stadt Nürnberg*, 43 (1952), 225–340; for Frankfurt, see A. Dietz, *Frankfurter Handelsgeschichte*, 4 vols. (Frankfurt, 1910–25).

be seen in the number of foundations of new cities in the German-speaking world offering religious toleration, including freedom of worship, to prospective settlers, which came into existence from the second half of the sixteenth century onwards. Among the first was Frankenthal in the Palatinate which in 1562, when the country turned Reformed, among others attracted a considerable number of Dutch and Walloon immigrants who had previously settled in Frankfurt-on-Main; Neu-Hanau, which was founded in 1595 in order to attract many of the Calvinist refugees who had recently settled in Frankfurt-on-Main where the city's Lutheran clergy had become increasingly antagonistic towards the growing number of foreign residents within its walls; or the two new cities Altona and Glückstadt founded in 1602 and 1617 in order to attract some if not all of the growing number of Reformed, Mennonite refugees or Jews who had settled in Lutheran Hamburg where the toleration granted them was often tentative at best due to the hostility of the city's Lutheran clergy.[25]

A similar mercantilist 'reason of state' lies behind the actions of the government of Elizabeth I of England. It was economic not religious considerations which moved Elizabeth and her chief adviser and Secretary of State, William Cecil, to renew the charter of the Dutch and Walloon Reformed communities in London in 1560. They had no need of a model Protestant congregation, as had been the case ten years earlier in the reign of Edward VI.[26] However, even in 1550 different motives were at play among the foreign communities's English supporters, as Diarmaid MacCullogh demonstrates in the case of Archbishop Cranmer. Cranmer's motive for backing the strangers was not rooted in theological agreement with them, but was based on his ambition to achieve concord and toleration within Protestantism through dialogue and persuasion.[27]

Elizabeth was not the only European ruler who pursued such policies around 1560. One of her suitors, Erik XIV of Sweden, also tried to encourage Reformed refugees to settle in his kingdom. In his case the role of his Huguenot advisors and Reformed tutors may well have caused him to undertake what eventually proved an unsuccessful attempt to encourage Reformed immigration into Sweden.[28]

In the case of France, where bi-confessionalism was legally guaranteed by the Edict of St Germain in 1592, the toleration introduced was the consequence of the growing political and popular strength of the Reformed religion. As such it was in tune with the political thinking of Justus Lipsius

---

[25] Hsia, *Social Discipline*, 85–8, for Hamburg, see J. Whaley, *Religious Toleration and Social Change in Hamburg 1529–1819* (Cambridge, 1985).
[26] See O. P. Grell, *Dutch Calvinists in Early Stuart London* (Leiden, 1989), 10–11.
[27] See chapter 12 below.
[28] See chapter 10 below.

and others who argued that tolerance should only be granted as a temporary, political measure of containment. As Philip Benedict points out, such an interpretation explains the many shifts of peaceful co-existence between Reformed and Catholics interchanged with periods of religious wars and bloody persecution which eventually led to the Revocation of the Edict of Nantes in 1685.[29]

As an example of religious toleration being granted as a purely political concession developments in France bear many similarities to events in Hungary, Bohemia, Moravia, and Poland, in spite of the obvious political, economic and social differences, not to mention the significant variations in chronology. Thus Jaroslav Pánek emphasises that the *Compacta of Jihlava* in 1436, which provided the legal framework for bi-confessionalism in Bohemia and Moravia, granting freedom of conscience and worship to both Catholics and Hussites/Utraquists, was a purely political concession. The toleration granted was a natural consequence of the political and social strength of Utraquism. Similarly, it is noteworthy that the more radical Bohemian Brethren or Unity of Brethren remained outlawed until 1609 when the charter which legalised the Bohemian Confession was issued. By then, however, active persecution of the Brethren was more or less non-existent due to the significant support they had been able to mobilise among the Estates since the beginning of the sixteenth century. Despite religious tolerance and pluriformity being firmly ensconced in Bohemia and Moravia well before the advent of the Reformation, it was neither unlimited nor secure but always remained dependent on political factors.[30]

Similarly, in the case of Hungary in the sixteenth century Katalin Péter underlines the delicate political balance between rulers and Estates, which made it possible for individual nobles and cities to pursue a policy of toleration of evangelical preachers and communities via their roles as patrons of the parishes and churches on their estates. This policy had already commenced well before the Reformation in order to accommodate subjects of the Orthodox Church. Moreover, Péter, while rejecting the traditional view within Hungarian historiography that the Turks were more positively inclined towards Protestantism than Catholicism, points to the indirect positive effects the Ottoman threat had for Protestantism in Hungary, in effect making it difficult, if not impossible, for the country's secular rulers to take action against their evangelically inclined subjects, had they wished to do so.[31]

Likewise, religious toleration in Poland developed along lines which had already been introduced by the monarchy in the fifteenth century in order to secure the integration of feudal elites from Catholic as well as Orthodox

[29] See chapter 5 below.
[30] See chapter 14 below.
[31] See chapter 15 below.

areas. Furthermore, the success and failure of Protestantism in Poland depended totally on the degree of toleration the magnates who supported the new faith were able to extract from the country's rulers. Lack of institutional and political power towards the end of the sixteenth century saw Protestantism in retreat in most rural areas and smaller towns, while the growing confessionalisation of the late sixteenth and early seventeenth centuries eventually caused a total break-down of the religious co-existence and practical tolerance between Catholics, Reformed and Lutherans in the major towns such as Danzig. Here German-speaking Lutheranism came to dominate with the resulting loss of a religious tolerance which had been based on an older socially and politically determined tradition of *pax et concordia*, as pointed out by Michael Müller.[32]

Securing peace and co-existence in the local community had been of paramount importance to most city magistracies long before the Reformation, as emphasised in several of the chapters in this volume such as those by Lorna Abray, Hans Guggisberg, Bruce Gordon and Bob Scribner.[33] However, the need to establish religious concord added a new and difficult dimension in the Reformation period to this traditional area of magisterial concern; and it is noteworthy that where and when some form of religious toleration was granted, it was never offered as a policy of choice but as a pragmatic, 'politique' solution, as was the case in Erfurt and Strassburg.

In this connection the legal context often proved important. The significance of the rule of law in both secular and ecclesiastical matters, as emphasised by Luther in 1523, was of the highest importance in guaranteeing some form of tolerance in a number of places, even in times of crisis, as can be seen from the chapters of Heiko Oberman and Philip Benedict.[34] However, even if the law appears to have been applied and to have protected heterodox individuals and groups in certain areas at certain times, it may not have been as decisive in securing and promoting religious toleration in the longer term as argued by some contributors to this volume. The examples of Basle and the Dutch Republic, two of the most successful cases of peaceful co-existence between religiously heterodox groups in the sixteenth and early seventeenth centuries, owe little or nothing to the legal protection provided. Instead, a mixture of the medieval ambition to secure *pax et concordia*, political pragmatism, and what Bob Scribner has termed 'the tolerance of practical rationality' was what mattered.

In a period where politics and religion were closely interwoven some groups found toleration more difficult to come by than others. This was cer-

---

[32] See Müller, *Zweite Reformation und städtische Autonomie im Königlichen Preussen: Danzig, Elbing und Thorn in der Epoche der Konfessionalisierung 1557–1660* (forthcoming) and chapter 16 below.
[33] See chapters 3, 6, 8 and 9 below.
[34] See chapters 2 and 5 below.

tainly the case for the Anabaptists who after the 'Kingdom of Münster' found themselves persecuted and marginalised in most of Europe throughout the sixteenth century. Likewise, the strong political connotations of Catholicism in Britain and the United Provinces in the late sixteenth century and the early seventeenth excluded Catholics, often perceived as a papal/Spanish fifth column, from both the official and practical toleration accorded to other Christian denominations in these countries, as can be seen from the chapters by Norah Carlin and Andrew Pettegree.[35]

The aggressive religious polemic which characterised the Reformation period should not always be taken at face value, as pointed out by Euan Cameron with regard to the inter-Protestant confessional divisions during the second half of the sixteenth century. Bitter confessional strife proved no barrier to Protestant solidarity when faced with a common enemy such as the Catholic Church. Cameron finds proof for this interpretation in the non-confessional attitude to the education of Protestant ministers, many of whom attended universities which differed confessionally from the creed of their own region or country. Likewise, he finds considerable and often contradictionary differences between the dogmatic and historical writings of Reformed and Lutheran clergy, the latter demonstrating a far more accommodating attitude to fellow-Protestants than the former. Bob Scribner, on the other hand, sees the negative influence of the aggressive polemical discourse of the reformers as contributing significantly in arousing popular religious passion and violence, causing the 'virus of intolerance and persecution' to be kept alive.[36]

Apart from William Monter's chapter on the heresy executions in Reformation Europe, which highlights the years between 1520 and 1560/5 as the period of persecution and repression par excellence, and thus indirectly supports the traditional view of toleration as growing gradually between the fifteenth and seventeenth centuries, interrupted only by an interlude of extreme intolerance during the first three or four decades of the Reformation, most of the chapters in this volume have followed the line taken by Heiko Oberman, offering a revisionist interpretation of religious toleration in this period. This places toleration and persecution firmly in the proper local, social, religious and political context. Consequently, a far less homogeneous and less idealistic picture, of how tolerant European societies were during the reformation periode, emerges in chronological, as well as, geographical terms.

Most of the contributors to this volume will undoubtedly find it difficult to accept without qualifications the liberal tradition of the nineteenth and twentieth centuries which has portrayed the advent of Protestantism as a

[35] See chapters 11 and 13 below.
[36] See chapters 3 and 7 below.

major step towards creating the tolerant society it cherished. Thus, Elton's statement from 1984, that Protestantism 'did not preclude genuine toleration for varieties of the faith, whereas the attitude of Catholics did',[37] will only be accepted with modifications by most of the present contributors. However, the example of cities such as Strassburg and Basle would indicate that Protestant authorities were more likely to grant freedom of belief to individuals than were their Catholic counterparts. But perhaps the significance of the Reformation for religious toleration does not lie primarily in its insistence on the right of individuals to exercise private judgement, an ideal which, after all, belongs to the intellectual baggage of nineteenth-century rationalists such as Lecky,[38] but in its questioning of authority and blind obedience.

[37] Elton, 'Persecution and Toleration', 185.
[38] W. E. H. Lecky, *History of the Rise and Influence of the Spirit of Rationalism in Europe*, 2 vols. (London, 1865).

2   The travail of tolerance: containing chaos in early modern Europe

Heiko A. Oberman

The natural habitat of intellectual history

The history of tolerance and toleration is one of the last preserves still firmly in the grasp of the intellectual historians. In their saga the sixteenth century plays a pivotal role, and in their ranks the Protestant Reformation was long the uncontested avant-garde, battling for individual liberty and public toler-ance.[1] When the Jesuit scholar Joseph Leclcr published his impressive and widely hailed *Histoire de la tolérance au siècle de la Réforme*[2] in 1955, the confession of some key players had changed but thc perimeters of the intel-lectual playing field remained fixed. His saga has a new beginning and a fresh ending: the curve of progress is now traced from the scholastic debate about the rights of the erring conscience to the climate of toleration in Cath-olic Poland. Notwithstanding his awareness of the importance of political realities, Lecler concentrated on tracts and treatises, on publishers and prin-ters. The ensuing critique of Lecler refocused on the creative triangle Basle–London–Amsterdam and turned with vigour to the new climate of scepticism emerging in the transition from the sixteenth century to the seventeenth. However, as in the case of Lecler and his predecessors, the debate continued to be a discourse in intellectual history.

In the English-speaking world, Henry Kamen raised his independent voice. Though granting that the Reformation brought greater religious liberty, he insisted that it did so 'despite the reformers' and merely 'as a concomitant of free trade'.[3] This intriguing observation evolves into a general thesis: in Protestant countries 'toleration tended to increase in proportion to the

---

[1] The most useful bibliographies can be found in: Massimo Firpo, *Il Problema della Tolleranza Religiosa nell' Età Moderna. Dalla Riforma Protestante a Locke* (Turin, 1978); Manfred Hoff-man (ed.), *Toleranz und Reformation* (Gütersloh, 1979); Hans R. Guggisberg (ed.), *Religiöse Toleranz. Dokumente zur Geschichte einer Forderung* (Stuttgart, 1984). For England see W. K. Jordan, *The Development of Religious Toleration in England*, 4 vols. (London, 1932–1940); for the 'Left Wing' of the Reformation see Meinulf Barbers, *Toleranz bei Sebastian Franck* (Bonn, 1964).

[2] (Paris, 1955), 2 vols., with extensive bibliography in volume 1, 11–39.

[3] Henry Kamen, *The Rise of Toleration* (New York, 1967), 224, 240.

decrease of dogmatic belief'.[4] Before we have time to realise that he thus embraces a fundamental conviction of John Calvin, he goes on to confess that for him as an historian of toleration 'the position of the Roman Church is intrinsically more interesting than that of the Protestant churches', because in the deliberations of the Second Vatican Council and in the encyclical of Pope John XXIII, *Pacem in Terris* (1963), the 'acceptance of universal toleration has not been accompanied by any repudiation of dogma'.[5] Turning to a region long considered too arid to germinate the seeds of tolerance, Kamen finds evidence in sixteenth-century Spain of an 'alternative tradition' of toleration and dissent. The terror of Duke Alva in the Netherlands 'was criticized strongly both in Madrid and in Brussels'. Spain's mid-century persecution of Protestants should be regarded as 'the harsh reaction' typical of a crisis period. Insofar as Spain was a repressive, intolerant society, this was due to a crisis of but short duration: beyond the 1560s 'censorship was attenuated and cultural contacts continued fairly freely'.[6]

As Lecler before him, Kamen combats a Protestant triumphalistic reading of the sources, presenting a view perhaps best described as the antithesis to a thesis in that awkward phase of unclarity and suspense before a new synthesis has been reached. This is not a critique specifically directed at the revisionism of Henry Kamen; rather, it characterises the general state of toleration studies today. It is important to note that when Kamen leaves the area of his special competence – the close study of the interdependence of early modern society, politics, and religion on the Iberian peninsula[7] – he too retreats to the well-travelled territory of intellectual history. Here we encounter again its traditional *pièce de résistance*: John Locke (1632–1704) stands at the apogee of the saga of toleration in early modern Europe; and the *Letter concerning Toleration* (1689) is its 'classic statement'.[8] Faced with such a consensus, we must take our point of departure from this supposedly high ground.

The creed of John Locke

Even the more cautious historians of tolerance hold one common conviction as an unassailable article of faith: John Locke's first letter *De tolerantia*,

[4] *Ibid.*, 55.
[5] *Ibid.*, 240f.
[6] 'Toleration and Dissent in Sixteenth-Century Spain: The Alternative Tradition', *The Sixteenth Century Journal*, 19 (1988) 3–23; 18f. Republished in H. Kamen, *Crisis and Change in Early Modern Spain* (London, 1993). Cf. Kamen, *Spain 1469–1714. A Society of Conflict* (New York, 1983), 138.
[7] See Kamen's comprehensive and yet compact survey 'The Habsburg Lands: Iberia', in Thomas A. Brady Jr., Heiko A. Oberman and James D. Tracy (eds.), *Handbook of European History 1400–1600. Late Middle Ages, Renaissance and Reformation* vol. 1 (Leiden, 1994), 467–98.
[8] Kamen, *The Rise of Toleration*, 234.

published 1689 in Gouda, marks a new era in the history of civilisation. Showing Europe how to escape the age of religious wars, Locke enunciated the principle of the separation of church and state while declaring religion a private matter 'between the individual soul and his Creator'.[9] Indeed, the importance of this document cannot be denied. Thoroughly familiar with the works of Sebastian Castellio and his insight that no human being can be certain to have the full truth, Locke's impact on the eighteenth-century Enlightenment cannot easily be overestimated. At the same time his was not an isolated voice, out of tune with his time. As the eminent historian of tolerance Hans Guggisberg has pointed out, in the political climate after the Glorious Revolution both Tories and Whigs were open to his views, in keeping with the principles underlying the Toleration Act of 1689.[10] After all, Locke excluded both 'Popery' and 'Atheism' from the social contract.[11]

Whereas Locke's principles have been hailed as the blueprint for modern secular society, the limits of his version of tolerance have been condoned as merely inconsistent in their 'practical application'.[12] Locke's manifesto has functioned explicitly or implicitly as a yardstick to measure 'degrees' of civilisation in its light: late medieval and early modern Europe has been found wanting, unmasked as a persecuting society. Hence, Locke's 'civilised' principles deserve a hard second look.

The very point of departure of the *Epistola* as well as its announced theme is the *mutua inter Christianos tolerantia*, the tolerance of Christians for each other. For tolerance is the 'most important mark of the true church', the *praecipuum verae ecclesiae criterium*.[13] From the very beginning, therefore, both atheism and dissent are eliminated from consideration, especially the sort of dissent which calls the true church into question.

From here we turn to Locke's central definition of tolerance, formulated in one simple Latin sentence which has hitherto not received the attention it deserves. The Latin text reads: *Tolerantia eorum qui de rebus religionis diversa sentiunt, Evangelio et rationi adeo consona est, ut monstro simile videatur homines in tam clara luce caecutire.* The translator, Emeritus Fellow of Oriel College, has not done full justice to his fellow Oxfordian (Christ

---

[9] See J. W. Gough in the introduction to his translation in *John Locke. Epistola de Tolerantia. A Letter on Toleration*, ed. Raymond Klibansky (Oxford, 1968), 23. Henceforth quoted as *Epistola*.

[10] Guggisberg (ed.), *Religiöse Toleranz*, 179. See also O. P. Grell, Jonathan I. Israel and N. Tyacle (eds.), *From Persecution to Toleration: The Glorious Revolution and Religion in England* (Oxford, 1991), especially F. Dunn, 'The Claim to Freedom of Conscience: Freedom of Speech, Freedom of Thought, Freedom of Worship?', 171–93.

[11] For 'the threat of atheism' see the well-documented article by Ernestine van der Wall, 'Orthodoxy and Skepticism in the Early Dutch Enlightenment', in Richard A. Popkin and Arjo Vanderjagt (eds.), *Skepticism and Irreligion in the Seventeenth and Eighteenth Century* (Leiden, 1993), 121–41; for further bibliography see here 122, footnote 3.

[12] See J. W. Gough in *Epistola*, 23.

[13] *Epistola.*, 58.

Church), rendering Locke's lucid Latin as: 'The toleration of those who hold different opinions on matters of religion is so agreeable to the Gospel and to reason, that it seems monstrous for men to be blind in so clear a light.'[14] Locke actually claims that toleration of those who hold deviant opinions is not merely 'agreeable' but completely 'in keeping' with the Gospel and 'co-extensive' with reason. We note in passing that he is not prepared to grant his opponent the right to his own understanding of the truth: he does not hesitate to hurl the harshest Latin term conceivable, namely *monstrum*, at the subhuman creature who would dare to question this truth.

Locke's main point is, however, that the rule of tolerance is not only in keeping with the Gospel truth – hence, excluding atheism from the very start – but also fully consonant with sound reason. Judged from this lofty view, the sixteenth century tends to be regarded as an extension of the 'Dark Ages', driven by irrational fear and the tyrannical concept of an indivisible truth. Questioning this assumption, I intend to tackle the daunting task of presenting a whole century of European history with all its temporal and regional differences. Three test cases will, I trust, provide sufficient evidence to revise those assumptions which obscure the clear profile of sixteenth-century historical 'reality'.

Allow me one more preliminary observation. Within the last two decades a marked advance in toleration studies has led to a better grasp of the wide-spread late medieval and early modern call for *pax* and *concordia*. Today this is increasingly understood as a limited programme for the consolidation of Christian society, clearly excluding dissidents and non-Christian confessions, not to be confused with the later quest for the freedom of conscience and religious liberty.[15] John Locke's point of departure in his *Epistola* and his very definition of tolerance make clear that he belongs to this earlier limited phase, even though he ventures to draw a demarcation line between church and state, extending the authority of secular power at the expense of the spiritual sword.

True enough, the Declaration on Tolerance was sufficiently novel, even in the Netherlands, to make it seem advisable to publish it anonymously, or rather under the cover of a cryptogram of seven letters, P.A.P.O.I.L.A. When after Locke's death its secret was revealed by his close friend and its addressee Philip van Limborch, Professor of Divinity at the Arminian Seminary at Amsterdam, the last three letters proved to signify the author's name

---

[14] *Ibid.*, 64f.

[15] See Mario Turchetti, 'La liberté de conscience et l'autorité du magistrat au lendemain de la Révocation. Aperçus du débat touchant la théologie morale et la philosophie politique des Réformés: Pierre Bayle, Noël Aubert de Versé, Pierre Jurieu, Jacques Philipot et Elie Saurin', in Hans R. Guggisberg, Frank Lestringant, et Jean-Claude Margolin (eds.), *La liberté de conscience (XVIᵉ–XVIIᵉ siècles). Actes du Colloque de Mulhouse et Bâle* (1989) (Geneva, 1991), 289–367.

and origin, *Ioanne Lockio Anglo*, John Locke the Englishman. The first four epitomised his programme: *Pacis Amante, Persecutionis Osore.*[16] Whereas the last two words, 'The Hater of Tyranny', have drawn the full attention of later scholarship, the first part, 'The Lover of Peace', must have seemed less exciting. For this phrase encapsulates the sixteenth-century search for unity, understood as that cohesion of the Christian commonwealth, which alone deserves to be protected and enforced by the increasingly sovereign state, represented by emperor, king, prince, or city council.

In an effort to repossess the territory of toleration so long held by the intellectual historian, the practice of sixteenth-century 'sound reason' will have to be tested in real and realistic circumstances. We must replace a timeless, immutable and therefore ahistorical principle of rationality with actual historical situations and specific events. John Locke himself did not develop his platform in the splendid isolation of his Dutch exile, or by studying works of a Castellio from behind his desk. Rather, he could characterise himself as the 'Hater of Tyranny', because he responded to a Europe torn by religious factionalism. He was so well received in England because he had fashioned the principles of 'Reason' to serve the needs of the established church in the wake of the Glorious Revolution.

In order to probe the profile of pre-Lockean rationality in sixteenth-century Europe I am going to look at three test cases from different times and differing areas, all three of them challenges to the cohesiveness of a society long held to be unified under the designation of *Christianitas*. On the assumption that the degree of tolerance in a society can best be tested at its margins, I will deal successively with the threat of witchcraft, with the perception of Jewish subversion, and with the challenge of early Protestant dissent.

The test case of the witch

The first case brings us to southern Germany, to Ringingen, a small village between Ulm and Ehingen some four miles north of the Danube. Here in the year 1505 dramatic events unfolded, beginning with suspicion of sorcery, and leading to the accusation of Anna Spülerin as a witch. She was incarcerated and, despite repeated torture, released after she successfully defended her innocence. This young mother's request for reparation of 2,000 florins, presented to the court of Ulm in December 1508, contains a detailed record of her experience – the charge of witchcraft and the prosecution of her case. In the past I have looked at the brief for the defence of Anna Spülerin because it provides a unique description of torture and trial from a woman's point of

---

[16] *Epistola*, iv.

view, a perspective demanded but not pursued in modern witchcraft studies. This time I will present extensive quotations from her recorded account and then measure her case by the test question before us.[17]

The calamities of Anna Spülerin began some time in the year 1504. Upon the accusation of unidentified inhabitants in Ringingen, the bailiff of Blaubeuren arrested her mother together with some other women and charged them with sorcery. Shocked to see her mother taken away, Anna had vented her anger, as she reports, with some rude words, perhaps with a curse or even a 'may the Devil get you'. She was reprimanded and warned that her shrill reaction could implicate her in the crime. Thus one morning, a year later, a threatening crowd gathered around her house; she escaped through the back door but, overtaken in the fields, was brought to the prison in Blaubeuren. Whereas she expected to be released forthwith, she was in for a surprise:

Who should appear that evening but the official investigator and torturer of the city of Ulm. He treated her harshly, cruelly, inhumanely and unwomanly [*unmenschlich und unweyblich*], interested only in extracting the confession that she was a witch. But she maintained her innocence; she refused to incriminate herself and to admit to a falsehood; instead she placed her hope in God Almighty.

Thereafter she was taken into another cell and not once or twice, but more than four times inhumanely and gruesomely tormented: all her limbs were mutilated until she lost her mind and the use of her five senses – so much so that she never fully recovered her sight and hearing. Afraid that she would die in that miserable cell, her agony increased to such an unbearable level that she was overcome by terror. Deprived of her sight, she was unable to realise the full extent of her mutilation.

Yet severe torture did not bring the expected confession. The bailiff brought in another torturer from Tübingen, who encouraged her to confess and thus put an end to her torment. The bailiff addressed her amicably and asked why she resisted so stubbornly – she should really confess her guilt; for after her death the inhabitants of Ringingen, every single one of them, would endow a mass for her eternal salvation. To this she answered: she was sincerely grateful for the bailiff's concern, but she was completely certain of her own innocence.

When even the offer of an endowed mass failed to move her, the bailiff turned to another tactic, explaining how her mother had admitted Anna's guilt and confessed that Anna, too, was a witch. But Anna countered this charge knowing very well that her mother would not have spoken so wickedly of her and, therefore, had certainly not done so. She held to her complete innocence of all charges and unwaveringly stuck to the truth. When her interrogators noted this, they redoubled their efforts and confronted her with so-called confessions of her mother while threatening to break every bone in her body. More than once she politely asked why they continued to accuse her; did they really want to drive her to falsehood?

---

[17] *Werden und Wertung der Reformation. Vom Wegestreit zum Glaubenskampf* (1977; 3rd edn Tübingen, 1989), 202–6; English version, *Masters of the Reformation: The Emergence of a New Intellectual Climate in Europe* (Cambridge, 1981), 160f.; cf. W. G. Soldan, H. Heppe, *Geschichte der Hexenprozesse*, ed. M. Bauer, 2 volumes (1911; Hanau, 1968), vol. 1 482–6.

Why did they refuse to hear and to accept her words? Instead, they continued to call her a witch and would accept nothing short of her full confession; and this without a single scrap of evidence.

Confronted with the plaintiffs from the village, she was then asked where the shirt of Our Lady could be found, which had disappeared from the church of Ringingen, and had been subsequently shredded. 'Do I stand accused of this act', she inquired. The bailiff replied that he simply knew what had happened; his little finger had told him. Once more, she portrayed herself as a victim of injustice and continued to maintain her full innocence. If someone would come forward to swear that she had committed such a crime, she would be perfectly prepared to pay for it with her life. But no one could possibly desire to accuse her of such a crime. Thereupon they left her, threatening to return the next morning and to interrogate her with even greater cruelty and torture. She was thereafter transferred to an even harsher and more intolerable prison.

When her interrogators had all departed, she decided to take refuge in Him who possessed the power to aid her, namely God Almighty and the Mother Mary, Queen of Heaven. From the depths of her heart she called on both to deliver her in view of her innocence, and for the sake of justice and truth to liberate her from this harsh prison and to prevent her from speaking a falsehood. This her prayer together with vows to undertake pilgrimages were heard by God Almighty: between the tenth and eleventh hour of that same night she was released from prison.

Yet this was not the end of Anna's misery. She had endured denunciation by the people of Ringingen and a gruesome and barbaric torture. Anna was maimed in body and stripped of her mental powers and physical senses. Robbed of her good reputation and good health, she fell into a great and bottomless pit of sorrow; she could no longer feed herself or nurse her babies, nor could she resume marital intercourse with her husband. Therefore Anna now demanded recompense. The inhabitants of Ringingen should be obliged to compensate her for her pain, agony, humiliation, and injury in keeping with her destitution and her dignity. If she could not prompt this recompense amicably, then Anna expected that the courts would execute justice to accede to her reasonable demands.

And, indeed, the case of Anna Spülerin was adjudicated from 1508 through 1518 with a final appeal to the Reichskammergericht, the highest judiciary in the Empire. Whereas the final outcome of Anna's litigation is unknown, her brief does not leave any doubt as to the two pivotal principles of law underlying her defence: unforced confession and reliable evidence. Accordingly, the famous article 22 of the *Carolina*, the imperial law of 1539, more carefully defines the *indicia*, the type of evidence required before the use of torture is permitted.[18]

Notwithstanding the horrors described so graphically, Anna lived in relatively favorable times. Fifty years later, she would not have been released from prison and her appeals would have gone unheard.[19] In the mirror of the

[18] See John Langbein, *Torture and the Law of Proof: Europe and England in the Ancien Régime* (Chicago, 1977), 49f. For the English translation of article 22 of the *Carolina* see here 168.

[19] See H. C. Erik Midelfort, *Witch-Hunting in Southwestern Germany, 1562–1684: The Social and Intellectual Foundations* (Stanford, 1972); cf. Midelfort, 'Witch-Hunting and the Domino

great witch-hunt we detect a significant disjunction. There is no uninterrupted line of organic growth in the 'civilising process' from the 'superstitious middle ages' to the 'safe shores of religious tolerance' at the time of John Locke. Even the standard of rationality, as proclaimed in *De tolerantia*, would not have withstood the witch-craze. For no threat to greater public welfare and, therefore, no form of *maleficium* could command the protection of Locke's law of liberty. In the period before torture was proscribed as a legal method of investigation, only one effective way to escape prosecution for witchcraft remained to the accused. The accused had to insist on the quality of the *indicia*, on the type of evidence which justified this extreme means of torture or *peinliche Befragung*.

A quarter of a century before the famous *Carolina* a simple woman insisted on exactly this criterion of justice . . . and was successful. The case of Anna Spülerin clearly belongs to that first phase in the European witch-hunt when the indictment is shifting from sorcery to witchcraft: Anna's mother was still accused as a sorceress whereas Anna was pressed to confess to being a witch. After about 1560 we see a sharp increase in witchcraft prosecutions; the safety-belt of the conditions of article 22 of the *Carolina* could no longer contain the fury which in 100 years would take more than 100,000 lives. In the rich harvest of recent witchcraft studies this phenomenon has been explained in terms of economic recession, misogyny, the mobilisation of high against low culture, or the harsh discipline of the early modern state. None of these factors plays a role in Ringingen – with the exception of gender. All the accused are women; Anna Spülerin is particularly mutilated in her female parts; she herself proves to be fully aware of the unfeminine, the *unweibliche* dimension of the procedure.

Yet in our search for societal explanations of the craze, we should not ignore society's legal resources: Anna was set free and lived to plead her case before the courts. She defended her rights and refused to settle without the payment of 2,000 guilder for loss in body and soul, the equivalent of some forty years salary for a German university professor. She sought and found protection in a legal system which contrasted sharply with the superstition of the accusing common folk and the prosecuting elite. Her case illumines and foreshadows the only form of rationality that would ultimately check and curb the witch-hunt.

The test case of the Jews

In our second test, probing the curve of tolerance and toleration from the fifteenth century to the seventeenth, we remain focused on the margins of

Theory', in James Obelkevich (ed.), *Religion and the People 800–1700* (Chapel Hill, NC, 1979), 277–325; Bob Scribner, 'Witchcraft and Judgement in Reformation Germany', *History Today* 40 (1990), 12–19.

society. We now move from the witches to the Jews. For Jews living under the conditions of the diaspora in Christian Europe, the degree of toleration varied widely in time and space, thus making the task of the microhistorian extremely hazardous when extracting applicable insights for all of Europe from one single case. From a singular event in Ringingen, overlooked in modern scholarship, we turn therefore to an event which is widely studied, well known, and generally regarded as a dramatic turning point in the relation between Christians and Jews in sixteenth-century Europe: Reuchlin's defence of the civic rights of Jewish citizens.

To begin with, our perception of Reuchlin as a 'friend of the Jews' is strongly coloured by Enlightenment historiography.[20] It is safe to say that for Reuchlin there is no place for the Jews as Jews in Christian society. As long as they are not baptised they live in the 'prison of the Devil' (*gefencknüs des Düfels*), to remain there 'as long as they are Jews' (*so lang sie Iuden sind*).[21] When on 26 July 1510, Emperor Maximilian I entrusted Reuchlin with writing an expert opinion on the toleration of Jewish books – which the converted Jew Johannes Pfefferkorn wanted to see destroyed – Johannes Reuchlin of Pforzheim (d. 1522) gave a more lucid defence of Jewish books than of their Jewish owners. He characterised them not as *cives*, full citizens, but as *concives*, perhaps best translated as 'resident aliens'.[22] Imperial censorship should not establish whether but which Jewish books should be burned, while those books passing inspection should be retained as a resource for the conversion of the Jews.

Today it is clear that Reuchlin's view of the Jews is more complex than earlier scholarship had led us to believe. Yet, in order to discern his exact position in relation to early modern anti-Semitism we must realise that this phenomenon has no fixed coordinates. It appears in variable modes and disguises, much like a snake which sheds its skin only to reappear in an ever new *Gestalt*, skillfully adjusted to the new environment provided by cultural change. The full implications of Reuchlin's position *vis-à-vis* the Jews can only be assessed properly within the context of the general escalation of anti-Semitism in the fifteenth and sixteenth centuries. Within this frame of reference there are four sensitive test areas for a proper diagnosis of late medieval and early modern anti-Semitism: (1) the criminalisation of the Jews; (2) the polemic against usury; (3) the suspicion of baptised Jews; and (4) the charge of falsifying Holy Scripture.

[20] Cf. Heiko A. Oberman, *The Impact of the Reformation* (Grand Rapids, 1994), 141–70.
[21] See my *Roots of Anti-Semitism in the Age of Renaissance and Reformation* (Philadelphia, 1984), 24–31; 28.
[22] For a concise description of the status of Jews in Christendom see Robert Bonfil, 'Aliens Within: The Jews and Anti-Judaism', in *Handbook of European History 1400–1600*, I, 263–302; 276–9.

The criminalisation of the Jews

The myth of Jewish well poisoning emerged in the wake of the plague which had scourged Europe since 1348. This superstition was by no means confined to the common man or to the naive piety of the uneducated. The influential Swiss humanist and admirer of Reuchlin, Joachim von Watt (Vadianus) (d. 1551), inserted horrifying stories in his chronicles, presenting them as factual reports: Many Jews in Zurich, Schaffhausen, Winterthur, and St Gallen 'were burned as punishment for their terrible deeds – the poisoning of wells'.[23]

Equally widespread were reports of Jews desecrating the host. This libel, punishable by burning, was given renewed credibility by the avant-garde publisher of humanist works, Hieronymus Höltzel of Nuremberg. In 1510, the very year Reuchlin submitted his expert opinion concerning Jewish books, Höltzel's Nuremberg press reported in gruesome detail a shocking account under the headline *Ein wunderbarlich geschichte*: thirty-eight Jews had desecrated the host and were therefore burned at the stake.[24]

Belief in Jewish ritual murder extended to all social strata in Reuchlin's day – including leading scholars such as Johannes Eck, Reuchlin's host in Ingolstadt.[25] In 1267, residents of Reuchlin's birthplace, Pforzheim, had accused the Jews of the outrageous crime of kidnapping a young girl named Margaretha, draining her blood, and discarding her body in the river. In Reuchlin's own lifetime, in 1507, Dominican sisters opened Margaretha's grave and, with Cardinal Bernardino Carvajal as authenticating witness, reported that Margaretha's corpse had not yet decomposed – full proof of her saintly martyrdom at the hands of the Jews.[26] Such a 'miracle' encouraged ever new accusations of ritual murder – even until 1932 in Paderborn.

The polemic against usury

Recent research has shown how the sermons of the mendicant friars, in particular the Franciscans of the fourteenth and fifteenth centuries, spread

---

[23] Joachim von Watt (Vadian), *Deutsche Historische Schriften*, ed. E. Götzinger, vol. 1 (St. Gallen, 1875), 389–90 and 447; cf. C. Bonorand, 'Bücher und Bibliotheken in der Beurteilung Vadians und seiner St. Galler Freunde', *Zwingliana*, 14 (1974–78), 94.

[24] See my *Roots of Anti-Semitism*, 97–9, 147–9.

[25] *Roots of Anti-Semitism*, 36–7.

[26] Siegmund Friedrich Gehres, *Pforzheims kleine Chronik: Ein Beytrag zur Kunde deutscher Städte und Sitten* (Memmingen, 1792), 19–23; cf. L. Geiger, *Johann Reuchlin: Sein Leben und seine Werke* (1871; Nieuwkoop, 1964), 5. Cardinal Carvajal was papal legate to the court of Emperor Maximilian from 1507 to 1508.

anti-Jewish propaganda to a European-wide audience.[27] Poisoned wells, desecrated sacraments, and ritual murders became living legends which grew ever deeper in the soil of popular piety. It is thus tempting to assume that these legends rose from 'below' to the 'top' of society. This model, however, does not do justice to the evidence. The educated elite not only disseminated such 'evidence' uncritically, but also embraced it as part of their own basic convictions; in unison the civic elite and the common man charged the Jews with extortionate money-lending practices – the vicious crime of usury. The leading humanists were proud to be laymen no longer living under monastic vows. Yet a great many of them, especially the humanists north of the Alps, observing the 'hours' in their libraries, retained basic perceptions of their mendicant predecessors, perpetuating their animosity toward the Jews. The expulsion of the Jews was supported by all classes of society, including the educated.

The Marranos: suspicion of the baptised Jew

Two new developments emerge at the beginning of the sixteenth century. After the expulsion of unconverted Jews from Spain (1492), those 'prepared' to be baptised, the Marranos, fell increasingly under suspicion. Baptised Jews were accused of hypocrisy; they concealed their opportunistic and diabolical motives. By secretly reverting to their previous faith, they returned to their own 'vomit' because they had 'swallowed' the Christian faith unwillingly. This caricature can be found among Reuchlin's opponents and allies; Reuchlin himself subscribed to this view. Erasmus of Rotterdam offered a variant of the same malicious charge when he suggested that countless unbaptised Jews would spring forth if the militant convert Johannes Pfefferkorn were to be split open.[28]

Here we encounter not religious anti-Judaism, as Erasmus scholars prefer to put it, but one of the deep roots of anti-Semitism. Gavin I. Langmuir's psychologising definition of 'anti-Semitism' must surely be handled with caution but he rightly rejects the view of Hannah Arendt that anti-Semitism replaced anti-Judaism only in the modern era.[29] The fatal shift from anti-

---

[27] Jeremy Cohen, *The Friars and the Jews: The Evolution of Medieval Anti-Judaism* (Ithaca, 1982). Cf. František Graus, 'Randgruppen der städtischen Gesellschaft im Spätmittelalter', *Zeitschrift für Historische Forschung*, 8 (1981), 385–437; F. Graus, *Pest-Geissler-Judenmorde: Das 14. Jahrhundert als Krisenzeit* (1987; rev. edn. Göttingen, 1988), 155–389; cf. F. Graus, 'The Church and its Critics in Time of Crisis', in P. Dykema (ed.), *Anticlericalism in Late Medieval and Early Modern Europe* (Leiden, 1993), 65–81.

[28] *Opus Epistolarum Des. Erasmi Roterodami*, ed. P. S. Allen (Oxford, 1906–58), vol. 3, 127, line 24.

[29] See Hannah Arendt, *The Origins of Totalitarianism* (New York, 1951), 8–10; cf. Gavin I. Langmuir, *Toward a Definition of Antisemitism* (Berkeley, 1990), esp. 314.

Jewish sentiment to racial anti-Semitism can already be discerned when, in the later Middle Ages, the cleansing waters of baptism are no longer believed to purify the sinful Jew. Hence Holy Baptism is no longer 'colour blind'. This view applies to Reuchlin as well.

The truth of the Hebrew Bible and the lies of the rabbis

A fourth factor in the escalation of anti-Semitism during the later Middle Ages has not yet been identified as such and deserves closer consideration. When speaking about his own place in history, Reuchlin points to his discovery of the *veritas hebraica* as his greatest service to posterity. And indeed, Reuchlin's grammar was intended to make the self-study of the Hebrew Bible possible – and Jewish instruction redundant.

Yet, Reuchlin's achievement unleashed two kinds of polemic, one defending Christian 'orthodoxy', the other attacking Jewish religion. The first assault Reuchlin expected. He had anticipated the reaction of the theological establishment to his insistence on the literal meaning of the Hebrew text: 'They will condemn this as the most heinous crime conceivable.' This forecast proved to be more true than even Reuchlin foresaw. With his insistence on the authority of the Hebrew text the stage was set for the fundamental conflict between the new exegesis and the old church.[30] This daring advance into the virgin territory of God's original revelation is the basic thrust of Reuchlin's work. It is the dominant theme, ultimately transforming the 'Reuchlin dispute' into the 'Reuchlin case', concluded by his condemnation in 1520.

But this very advance in biblical studies, the discovery of the authority of the Hebrew text, had unexpected implications for the development of anti-Semitism. The enthusiastic recovery of the most ancient biblical language opened up a new front against the Jews. Apparently the rabbis had been untrustworthy guardians of the treasures entrusted to them; though knowing the *veritas hebraica*, they had been intentionally withholding 'the truth' from Christendom by manipulating the holy writings and mysteries entrusted to them. Martin Luther expressed this view in particularly harsh fashion in his 1543 treatise, *The Jews and their Lies*.[31] The 'Obscure Men' are this time not the scholastics, but the rabbis who distorted the text of the Old Testament. Thus, Luther advocated a severe restriction of tolerance for the Jews. He supported both the burning of synagogues and, though not the burning, the confiscation of rabbinic books in order to eliminate the centres from which

[30] See Heiko A. Oberman, 'Gansfort, Reuchlin and the "Obscure Men": First Fissures in the Foundations of Faith', in Johannes Helmrath and Heribert Müller (eds.), *Studien zum 15. Jahrhundert* (Munich, 1994), 717–35.

[31] *WA* 53. 417–552.

the Jewish lies were spread.[32] Luther justifiably considered himself Reuchlin's pupil by insisting on the original meaning of the Hebrew text. However,
Luther's recommendations clearly separate him from Reuchlin. Although
Luther never shared Pfefferkorn's hope for Jewish mass-conversion, like
Pfefferkorn he did propose a pogrom-like policy for the Jews, and at the end
of his life called for a silencing of the rabbis. It was the Christian discovery
of the *veritas hebraica* which thus led to the vilification of the rabbis.

With these four characteristics of early modern anti-Semitism before us,
we can now establish the relation of Reuchlin to that tradition with more
precision.

1 Traditional accusations against the Jews – the poisoning of wells, desecration of the host, and ritual murder – were rife among the educated elite.
Of these charges no trace appears in Reuchlin's work.

2 The fear of the Jews, propagated by the preaching mendicants, spread
like wildfire. This is not echoed by Reuchlin. But widespread approval of
Jewish expulsion touches on a sensitive point, which until now has not been
properly acknowledged. Reuchlin, long hailed as the defender of the Jews,
did indeed support a policy of forced expulsion. In his famous *Augenspiegel*
of the year 1511, Reuchlin takes up the problem that Jewish usury damages
the common good. Far from questioning this assumption, he makes it the
basis for the awesome alternative: the Jews must mend their ways or face
expulsion – *essent . . . reformandi seu expellendi.*[33]

Yet in determining the grounds for expulsion, Reuchlin advocates a vital
legal principle: in each case, individual guilt should be established since Jews
are legally *concives*; just as the Christians, they are subject to imperial law
and to the penalties based upon it. This form of 'equality before the law' is
a marked advance, even though the Jews are only given the status of 'resident
aliens,' and not the status of *cives*, as in Florence some three quarters of a
century before. Above all, when the charge of usury is documented and
expulsion of the guilty Jews is enacted, the true cause of Reuchlin's regret is
the loss of Hebrew expertise, of the key for decoding the sacred sources.

3 Insofar as Pfefferkorn's challenge brought home to Reuchlin the threat
posed by 'baptised Jews', he shared the suspicion of the Marranos, a view
likewise held by Reuchlin's humanist supporters. At the same time, it should
be granted that his personal bitterness toward Pfefferkorn is quite understandable; after all, Pfefferkorn's attack darkened the last ten years of his
life. But in his response he did not attack Pfefferkorn as a person but as the
Taufjuden, the damned Jew hiding under a Christian cloak.

---

[32] Cf. Heiko A. Oberman, *Luther: Man Between God and the Devil* (1989; London, 1992),
292–7.
[33] *Augenspiegel*, fol. 30v.

4 We find no evidence whatsoever that Reuchlin ever suspected the rabbis of consciously distorting the biblical text. Yet he is in full agreement with the view that the recovery of cabalistic truth not only confirms the superiority of the Christian faith, but also 'crushes the stubbornness of the Jews of our time, convicting them of their perfidy'.[34]

Against this background of Reuchlin's deep involvement in the anti-Semitic assumptions of his time, his achievements appear all the more clearly. Reuchlin's own claim to enduring fame did not prove to be lasting. His *Hebrew Grammar* was soon superseded and his daring cabalistic speculations never entered the mainstream of scholarship. Rather, Reuchlin's significance lies in his insistence that the policy of toleration must not only be *in* the books, but also *on* the books, by codification of human rights guaranteeing the existence of the Jews in a Christian Europe: their protection should not be dependent on Christian charity but on secular law. Indeed, the lasting legacy of Reuchlin's high views of Renaissance humanism is the insistence that 'humanism' is to be transferred from the realm of ideas to the rule of law.

Failing to correct the caricature of the Jew, Reuchlin's call for granting the Jews at least the status of 'resident aliens' found little resonance in the sixteenth and seventeenth centuries. The search for concord from Erasmus to Locke limits the purview of toleration to the Christian society. Erasmus of Rotterdam, in so many other respects the voice of reason, was so much committed to the quest for concord in the Christian commonwealth that he could not share in Reuchlin's cautious call for Jewish emancipation.

The eminent Belgian Erasmus scholar, Léon-E. Halkin, recently formulated his admiration for the 'Prince of Humanists' in the one melodious sentence: *Pour lui, tout ce qui est intolérant est intolérable.*[35] Whatever else can be said about such comprehensive words of praise, the validity of this statement stops short of the demarcation line between Christians and Jews: for Erasmus the biblical enemies of God continue to be an insufferable threat to society.[36] Reuchlin's programme was given the force of law and hesitantly enacted only after the Marranos found refuge in the Dutch Republic and thus became a conceptual, political and economic force in Amsterdam.[37] This new

[34] Letter to Willibald Pirckheimer, 18 February 1519; Geiger, *BW*, nr. 280, 313.

[35] Léon-E. Halkin, 'Érasme et la Troisième Voie', in *RHE* (1992), 405–16; 409.

[36] The most recent effort to 'salvage' Erasmus – Shimon Markish, *Erasmus and the Jews* (Chicago, 1986) – is convincingly criticized by Manfred Hoffman in *Erasmus Year Book*, 7 (1987), 135–42.

[37] See Arend H. Huussen, Jr., 'The Legal Position of Sephardi Jews in Holland, circa 1600', in Jozeph Michman (ed.), *Dutch Jewish History*, 3 (Assen, 1993), 19–41. Particularly revealing are the newly discovered minutes of the negotiations of the Haarlem city council with some Portugese merchants 'genaempt Joden', published in Appendix I to A. H. Huussen, Jr., 'De toelating van Sefardische joden in Haarlem in 1605', in *Haerlem Jaarboek 1991* (Haarlem, 1991), 48–62; 55f.

chapter in the history of toleration was not written in the sixteenth but in the seventeenth century.

The test case of religious dissent

Our third test case leads us from southern Germany to French-speaking Switzerland at the time of the Berne campaign to establish its authority and Protestant reform in the Pays de Vaud and particularly Lausanne. Almost a quarter of a century before Germany would agree to the regionally limited 'toleration' of the Peace of Augsburg under the guideline *cuius regio, eius religio* (1555), the Swiss had already established this form of religious settlement in the Second Peace of Kappel in 1531 by acknowledging the confessional division of the Swiss confederacy. The political clout of Zurich after the military defeat in the Second Kappeler War[38] was considerably curtailed. Its authority was so compromised that Zwingli's successor, Heinrich Bullinger, advised the city council to secede from the Swiss confederacy. The City Fathers felt that Berne had deliberately forsaken Zurich in its time of need, and their suspicion was confirmed by the rapid expansion of Berne in its increasingly aggressive western engagement. On 16 January 1536 Berne declared war on the Duke of Savoy, unleashing a campaign which would be of lasting importance for the history of the Reformation in western Switzerland.[39] In the first part of this campaign, culminating in the occupation of Yverdon, Berne seized its share of the collapsing Duchy of Savoy, today called the Canton de Vaud. She could only do so after securing the safety of Geneva against the successful advance of French troops who rapidly occupied Savoy all the way from Nice to before the city walls of Geneva. Without delay Berne had to secure vulnerable Geneva, now precariously wedged between expansionist France and a firmly Catholic Fribourg. Herewith the political and military hegemony of Berne over Geneva was established – determining its political 'space', just at the time John Calvin was drafted to serve Geneva as *lecteur*. As William G. Naphy has shown on the basis of Genevan archives, Calvin's opponents, assailed by the Reformer as immoral *Libertins*, *de facto* responded to the growing threat of foreign French import.[40] Intent on restricting the status of the Huguenot immigrants as *concives* and 'resident aliens', Calvin's opponents could count on finding open doors in Berne, during all the changing phases of that momentous inner-city struggle.

[38] Helmut Meyer, *Der Zweite Kappeler Krieg. Die Krise der Schweizerischen Reformation* (Zurich, 1976), 49, 314.

[39] Henri Vuilleumier, *Histoire de l'Église Réformée du Pays de Vaud sous le Régime Bernois*, 4 vols. (Lausanne, 1927–33), vol. 1, 93–121; Kurt Guggisberg, *Bernische Kirchengeschichte* (Bern, 1958), 192f.

[40] William G. Naphy, *Calvin and the Consolidation of the Genevan Reformation* (Manchester, 1994).

For our purposes the second phase of the war of 1536 is of special importance. When on 25 February Yverdon opened her gates the conditions of
capitulation stipulated that the mass could no longer be celebrated in the city.
Just as the campaign appeared finished and as the troops were disbanding,
new orders arrived from Berne: under the command of Hans Franz Nägeli,
1,000 soldiers marched on 11 March 1536 via Chillon to Lausanne. Before
these troops reached the city, the Bishop of Lausanne fled and took refuge in
Fribourg, never to return to his see. On the afternoon of 31 March Lausanne
was taken and the episcopal castle occupied. Unlike the one-sided settlement
in Yverdon, the citizens of Lausanne convened on 4 April 1536 and agreed
that everyone was to be at liberty either to participate in the Protestant service
or in the mass 'in accordance with the dictates of conscience'.[41]

The significance of this citizens' decree does not lie in its permanence.
Particularly due to the activity of the Reformed minister Pierre Viret, Lausanne was soon transformed into a Protestant stronghold. Together with
Farel's Neuchâtel and Calvin's Geneva, Lausanne came to form the staging
area for the export of Reformed Protestantism to France. The citizens' decree
does represent, however, an early document of religious freedom and marks
a significant stage on the road to the legalisation of confessional coexistence.
Hence, already in the sixteenth century this view was part of the arsenal
available to be applied to the volatile challenge of Protestant dissent.

The case of Lausanne is by no means isolated. We encounter the inverse
example five years earlier when, in the wake of the Second Kappeler War on
30 November 1531, Solothurn proclaims that 'in Saint Ursula a priest should
preach and read the mass, and in the Franciscan church a minister should
preach the Gospel and serve the mass in two kinds,' *wo es jedem gefällig*:
everyone should be at liberty to choose. Though religious freedom is here
formulated as a temporal arrangement rather than as a timeless principle, the
decree concludes with the general charge that each group should be tolerant
of the other and should not interfere with the other's form of service.[42] In
Solothurn, as in Lausanne, religious toleration endures for only a fleeting
moment, though this time on the reverse path: within weeks Solothurn is
thoroughly re-catholicised. Yet in the concerted effort to contain chaos,
momentary but momentous solutions were advanced, awaiting permanency
of law in later, more opportune times.

---

[41] Jean Barnaud, *Pierre Viret (1511–1571)* (1911; Nieuwkoop 1973), 129. For the early Berner
Ratschlag to pacify Neuchâtel in June 1531 – *bonne paix, unyon, transquilité et voysinance*,
see Gabrielle Berthoud, *Antoine Marcourt. Réformateur et Pamphlétaire du Livre des Marchants aux Placards de 1534* (Geneva, 1973), 10.

[42] Johannes Strickler (ed.), *Actensammlung zur schweizerischen Reformationsgeschichte in den
Jahren 1521–1532 im Anschluss an die gleichzeitigen eidgenössischen Abschiede*, vol. 3, no.
969, 249f.; vol. 4, (1881; Zurich, 1989) no. 1140, 377.

Conclusion

If we now venture the precarious jump from specific and therefore unique situations to general historical observations, it is important to point out that the three *exempla* were not shrewdly chosen in order to prove a preconceived thesis. Rather, genuine *test* cases were selected which may force us to 'tolerate' four unexpected conclusions. One preconceived thesis, however, should be made explicit at the outset.

1 In our reorientation from intellectual history to the social history of ideas we have been intent on complementing and correcting the grand saga of tolerance, with its traditional stages marked by Erasmus, Castellio and Locke. This does not imply that we disdainfully turn our back to the world of ideas in order to find 'reality' in social conditions, as if the realm of ideas were the domain of a ruling elite bent on legitimising the *status quo*. Actually, in each of the three test cases, ideas and convictions played an important and at times decisive role. Yet one heuristic axiom has been operative, namely that the limits of tolerance can best be measured on the margins of society.

2 The trial of Anna Spülerin of Ringingen has at least two larger implications. Anna insists on her unerring conscience against the joint pressure of the common villagers and her educated interrogators. We not only fail to find evidence of a marked contrast between popular and high belief systems, but there is also no proof for the conviction[43] that the great witch-hunt can be traced to the hegemony of the ruling class.

3 The very duration of Anna's appeal in the courts for over ten years points to that essential element in the history of toleration, signified by the protection of law. Regardless of the actual outcome of her appeal, the precious doctrine of *'indicia'* was already so well in place that Anna Spülerin lived to make an appeal and lodge a complaint which would have been inconceivable at the end of the century. The traditional view of the organic growth of toleration from the fifteenth century to the seventeenth will have to be revised.

4 The trial of Anna Spülerin has already suggested the importance of legal procedures; Johannes Reuchlin's defence of the rights of the Jews points us to the crucial importance of jurisprudence, defining the margins of a Christian society. Whereas our probing of the 'mentality' of Johannes Reuchlin established that he shared the basic anti-Semitic convictions of the common man and the ruling class of his time, as a legal expert he insisted on the rights of the Jews as *concives*. A general trend in social history has given precedence to the study of 'mentality' and the effect of societal conditions. But the astonishing progress we have made on our path of an increasingly sophisticated

---

[43] Brian P. Levack, *The Witch-hunt in Early Modern Europe* (London, 1987).

social history should not entice us to forget some of the major achievements of nineteenth-century scholarship. To these belong above all the history of law and legal institutions, a discipline not yet reduced to a field of marginal specialisation.

There was a time when it was obvious to all students of tolerance that the so-called 'law merchant' helped to pave the way for toleration. The eminent Wyndham Anstis Bewes may not have done us a service by entitling his study *The Romance of the Law Merchant*,[44] but in 1923 he could summarise an impressive scholarly tradition by tracing the important role of the law merchant and his 'fair', the equivalent of the term 'peace'. His involvement in long-distance trade stimulated the development of international law and the codification of the peace of the fairs, the merchants' safe conduct, and the tolerance of other religions on the open marketplace. Thus the law merchant became an effective agent in extending sanctuary from the cathedral to the fairgrounds.[45] The observation of Henry Kamen that the spread of toleration in seventeenth-century Netherlands is merely a 'concomitant of trade'[46] is seemingly innocuous. Actually, the Amsterdam merchant class and the exiled Sephardic Jews made a fundamental contribution to the Dutch ideal of toleration:[47] they deserve to be reinstated in the 'grand saga', next to Reuchlin, Castellio, and Locke.

5 The examples of Solothurn and Lausanne tend to confirm earlier findings[48] that a city council such as the *Rat* of Zurich chose the rational path of searching 'concord' and 'peace' in an effort to escape the calamity of confessional conflict. While in Zurich the political arena is 'Town-hall', in Lausanne we encounter the 'Town meeting' and its appeal to the freedom of conscience. Not explicitly claimed as a basic human right, this solution surfaces with a striking absence of ideological argumentation and with an equally surprising appeal to an 'obvious' common sense. Joseph Lecler may have been misled when pointing to scholasticism as the medieval matrix, yet it is not unreasonable to conclude that late medieval citizens' rights are here presupposed: individual 'self-determination' is here invoked as if this concept is already well established.

---

[44] (1923; London, 1988).
[45] Bewes, *The Romance of the Law Merchant*, 137; cf. W. Mitchell, *Essay on the Early History of the Law Merchant* (1904; New York, 1969); cf. Leon E. Trakman, *The Law Merchant: The Evolution of Commercial Law* (Littleton, Colorado, 1983).
[46] See note 3 above.
[47] The practical limits of this view should not be overlooked: 'Despite broad toleration, religious dissenters were largely or completely excluded from political influence and public office, and hence from the highest social rank and prestige.' Heinz Schilling, 'The History of the Northern Netherlands and Modernization Theory', in *Religion, Political Culture and the Emergence of Early Modern Society. Essays in German and Dutch History*, (Leiden, 1992), 341.
[48] *Masters of the Reformation* (note 17 above), 193f.

Looking back at the end of our path, we are well aware that the late medieval and early modern call for peace and concord was still a far cry from the religious tolerance of modern times. It served the consolidation of a Christian society mobilising all its resources to contain the centrifugal forces of chaos in early modern Europe. At the same time, it should be clear that at the beginning of the century essential legal institutions and ideological convictions were already in place. The sixteenth-century travail of tolerance is far more than a night battle with its superstitious heritage. In the concerted effort to contain perceived and actual chaos, old resources were mobilised and new solutions advanced, which mark the turn to that rationality which John Locke would proclaim as the foundation of a 'modern' tolerant society.

3   Preconditions of tolerance and intolerance in sixteenth-century Germany

Bob Scribner

Introduction

This chapter is intended to offer some broad reflections on the problem of tolerance and intolerance within the framework of German history which might serve as social-historical parameters for the major themes of this volume. It is my intention to raise issues for further exploration, rather than to provide answers, although many of the thoughts offered here first emerged in the course of my own research many years ago, while pondering the unique circumstances of the religious settlement achieved in the Thuringian city of Erfurt, which in 1530, by means of a treaty of state, allowed the exercise of divergent religious worship within the same polity, without implying any disobedience to the secular authority of the town's ruler. The example seemed to offer a paradigm of the conditions under which toleration was possible in the modern era: the separation of church and state and the acceptance of plurality of religions. It was immediately apparent, however, that the degree of toleration thus achieved was dependent not on any ideals about the philosophical or theological desirability of toleration, nor on any altruistic regard for the rights of minorities, but was a consequence of Erfurt's unusual constitution, political, social and economic situation, what we might call a 'pragmatic conjuncture', which overrode other, under different circumstances stronger, considerations tending towards intolerance and even fanaticism.[1]

From the Erfurt example we can readily identify two approaches to tolerance and intolerance: the idea of tolerance and its theoretical foundations; and the broad conditions under which any given period or society might be said to be tolerant or intolerant. For both approaches the nub of the question resides surely in the very nature of 'toleration' and what it involves, and I shall return to this shortly. The historiography of tolerance, however, has tended to emphasise the first approach and has largely focused on questions

---

[1] See R. W. Scribner, 'Reformation, Society and Humanism in Erfurt, c. 1450–1530' (PhD diss., University of London, 1972), 264–7, and more briefly in 'Civic Unity and the Reformation in Erfurt', in *Popular Culture and Popular Movements in Reformation Germany* (London, 1987), 185–216, esp. 212. See also Ulman Weiss, *Die frommen Bürger von Erfurt. Die Stadt und ihre Kirche im Spätmittelalter und in der Reformationszeit* (Weimar, 1988), 241–4.

of religious liberty, on how to deal with religious heterodoxy and dissent.[2] Moreover, it has always earmarked the Reformation era as a major stage in the attainment of a 'tolerant society'. Although historians such as Lord Acton admitted that 'Protestantism set up intolerance as an imperative precept and as a part of its doctrine', most liberal thinkers of the nineteenth and twentieth centuries would have agreed with Lecky's 1865 judgement that 'toleration is essentially a normal result of Protestantism, for it is the direct, logical and inevitable consequence of the exercise of private judgement'[3] This view has been heavily qualified by current scholarship, and neither Luther nor Erasmus can now be regarded unreservedly as champions of the modern concept of religious liberty.[4] More recent literature has directed more attention to the question of intolerance and has emphasised its sociological and anthropological context, seeking to establish just what constitutes a 'persecuting society'. That so much of this work focuses on medieval Europe also reflects a long-standing liberal consensus – that persecution (and by implication intolerance) was one of the leading characteristics of medieval society.[5] Yet newer approaches which highlight the social construction of intolerance and the labelling of deviant groups (religious dissidents, lepers, Jews and witches) tend to regard the early modern period as little different from the Middle Ages.[6] Indeed, we might be tempted to argue that the classification, exclusion and persecution of deviant groups as a response to problems caused by social or economic change is an issue that transcends both the Middle Ages and

[2] See for example Henry Kamen, *The Rise of Toleration* (London, 1967); Joseph Lecler, *Toleration and the Reformation*, 2 vols. (London, 1960); Heinrich Lutz (ed.), *Zur Geschichte der Toleranz und Religionsfreiheit* (Darmstadt, 1977); the selection of Reformation texts in Manfred Hoffman (ed.), *Toleranz und Reformation* (Gütersloh, 1979), and the extensive bibliographies in the latter two items.

[3] Lord Acton, in an essay of 1862, 'The Protestant Theory of Persecution', reprinted in *The History of Freedom and other Essays* (London, 1907), 150–87, the quotation on 187; W. E. H. Lecky, *History of the Rise and Influence of the Spirit of Rationalism in Europe*, 2 vols. (London, 1865), vol. 2, 78, although Lecky did agree with Acton that Protestantism as a dogmatic system was hostile to religious liberty, *ibid.*, vol. 2, 61.

[4] Manfred Hoffman, 'Reformation and Toleration', in Hoffman (ed.), *Martin Luther and the Modern Mind: Freedom, Conscience, Toleration, Rights* (New York, 1985), 85–123, here 114; most recently on Erasmus, James M. Estes, '*Officium principis christiani*: Erasmus and the Origins of the Protestant State Church', *Archiv für Reformationsgeschichte*, 83 (1992), 49–72.

[5] The most influential work has been R. I. Moore, *The Formation of a Persecuting Society: Power and Deviance in Western Europe 950–1250* (Oxford, 1987). Other works on the medieval period, while disagreeing with Moore's emphasis, agree with him on the essential features of such intolerance: see for example Jeffrey Richards, *Sex, Dissidence and Damnation: Minority Groups in the Middle Ages* (London, 1991), esp. 13, for whom the *leitmotiv* is sexual intolerance.

[6] See R. Po-chia Hsia, *The Myth of Ritual Murder: Jews and Magic in Reformation Germany* (New Haven and London, 1988); John Edwards, *The Jews in Christian Europe 1400–1700* (London, 1988), esp. 148–67; and the misleadingly titled book by William Monter, *Ritual, Myth and Magic in Early Modern Europe* (Brighton, 1983).

the early modern period to remain a major dilemma of our own age.[7] The question of the social construction of intolerance offers a different, albeit more pessimistic, way of understanding the historical problem of toleration, and leads us to ask to what degree the sixteenth century was a 'persecuting society' and in what forms and varieties toleration was possible in the age of the Reformation.

Forms of toleration

Before turning more specifically to the problem of a 'persecuting society', I want to specify more closely just what we mean when we speak of toleration as a historical phenomenon. The modern idea of tolerance is essentially permissive, allowing those with different beliefs and lifestyles to live together without any civil or economic disadvantage. The notion implies neutrality of attitude, or at least an absence of positive hostility (though I doubt that it owes much to Lockean rationality, more to a socio-cultural habitus that makes us indifferent to certain kinds of difference). It also transcends religious belief and encompasses, among other things, lifestyles, ethnicity, age difference and cultural otherness. The sixteenth-century idea of tolerance was rather different and entirely more complex. It was largely articulated in terms of religious belief, occasionally in terms of cultural or ethnic difference. Toleration in the matter of religious belief revolved around three separate but interrelated notions:

> claims to freedom of conscience, as advanced by Luther at the Diet of Worms, but also understood by all those of a humanist-erasmian orientation;
>
> separation of secular and spiritual authority inherent in Luther's Two Kingdom's doctrine (but also inherent in the medieval – and erasmian – distinction between those offences subject to ecclesiastical censure and those punishable by civil law);
>
> love of neighbour and patience with weaker brethren – an essentially erasmian notion, but one shared by many of the early reformers.

These three notions were all compromised or overridden in the course of the early Reformation. The imperative demands of the Word of God took precedence over claims of individual conscience (for example, the 'scandal' of tolerating the Mass led to its prohibition, even though celebrant and congregation may have regarded it as true worship); the urgent need to organise

---

[7] See the most recent discussion of such problems in Colin Sumner, *The Sociology of Deviance; An Obituary* (Buckingham, 1994).

new evangelical churches led to implicit (and often explicit) abandonment
of the separation of secular and spiritual authority; and the urgency to effect
immediate reform overrode love of neighbour and concern for weaker brethren.[8] What were the actual possibilities of religious toleration, and what forms
did they take? From my own knowledge of German sources and examples,
I can discern nine different manifestations of religious toleration during the
sixteenth century.

First, *freedom of belief was allowed, but only privately*, so that there was
to be no public proclamation or dissemination of dissident religious ideas and
certainly no public worship. This was the kind of limited toleration allowed to
Anabaptists in various circumstances, but most notably in Strassburg, where
magistrates came to regard religious dissidents, as Jane Abray put it, as 'individual eccentrics who could safely be tolerated'. Even if this was often more
a matter of moderation in the meting out of penalities, it was sufficient to
gain the city a reputation for toleration.[9] It was, perhaps, a form of tolerance
to which Protestant authorities were more inclined, in that it allowed freedom
of conscience while not permitting freedom of religious practices which
might be thought to be repugnant to the Word of God.[10]

Second, a *passive (or rather, covert) freedom of belief* and even of worship
was permitted, largely in circumstances in which a blind eye was turned to
the presence of dissident groups. This variation was common in towns which
contained a substantial following for Reformation ideas, but which were for
various reasons unwilling or unable formally and openly to adopt a reformed
church polity – prime examples were imperial free cities such as Speyer,
Worms and Regensburg. It can also be seen in practice in the case of rural
officials in territories such as Württemberg, Hesse and the Palatinate who
refused to implement or act more than minimally upon their government's
sterner prohibitions and penal mandates against Anabaptists.[11]

---

[8] These issues are neatly summed up in the 1530 debate in Nuremberg about whether the
application of religious conformity should involve repression of dissident religious belief,
most recently presented in James M. Estes (ed. and trans.), *Whether Secular Government has
the Right to Wield the Sword in Matters of Faith: A Controversy in Nuremberg 1530* (Toronto,
1994).

[9] Lorna Jane Abray, *The People's Reformation: Magisrates, Clergy and Commons in Strasbourg 1500–1598* (Oxford, 1985), 115, 183, the quotation on 115.

[10] On this distinction as a feature of the discussions surrounding the 1555 Peace of Augsburg,
see N. Paulus, 'Religionsfreiheit und Augsburger Religionsfriede', in Lutz (ed.), *Zur Geschichte der Toleranz*, 17–41, here 28–31.

[11] On Regensburg, L. Theobald, *Reformationsgeschichte der Reichsstadt Regensburg* (Munich,
1936), 107–200 passim; on Speyer, the dilemmas expressed in R. W. Scribner, 'Memorandum
on the Appointment of a Preacher in Speyer 1538', *Bulletin of the Institute of Historical
Research*, 48 (1975), 248–55; on Worms, Heinrich Boos, *Geschichte der rheinischen Städte-
kultur*, vol. 4 (Berlin, 1901), 266–76; on rural Anabaptism, C. P. Clasen, *Anabaptism: A
Social History 1525–1618* (Ithaca, 1972), 414.

Third, religious parity was sometimes accepted as an *enforced compromise* or what has been called 'licenced co-existence'.[12] The pre-eminent example, that of Erfurt, we have already mentioned, but the same was also true of the parity enforced in imperial cities by the Peace of Augsburg (Heiko Oberman's example of Lausanne perhaps belongs in this category). A similar politically determined tolerance was enforced in Protestant territories as a result of the imperial victory in the first Schmalkaldic War, so that, for example, the Elector Palatine Friedrich II was compelled to rescind the prohibition of the Mass and the compulsory attendance at evangelical sermons that he had issued in 1546.[13]

Fourth, toleration was allowed, but only *for ruling princes* (the principle of *cuius regio, eius religio*); in effect this allowed parity and equal rights for states. However, one must here remind Heiko Oberman that this arrangement was prefigured in the settlement of religious affairs achieved in independent German cities before 1530, and so was not a Swiss invention: it was what I have called a 'marsilian' religious settlement, in which the secular magistrates took control of the church and imposed upon it their own conditions and regulations.[14]

Fifth, toleration could be achieved *as an interim strategy* because the balance of contending groups allowed nothing else. This solution was quite common during the early period of the Reformation and was a situation frequently found in many independent towns. It could also be found in principalities such as the Margraviate of Baden in the 1520s, where evangelical tendencies were allowed to develop with minimal prohibitions of religious innovation, possibly because Margrave Philipp II was uncertain about which direction to follow.[15] Toleration as an interim measure also seems to have been a strategic principle which recommended itself to Protestant princes such as the Elector Palatine and the Elector of Brandenburg in the negotiations leading up to the 1555 settlement of Augsburg, and was clearly inspired by the hope of more easily winning over the subjects of Catholic princes. It could only ever have been a transitional solution, if only because a situation which allowed the practice of what Protestants regarded as the 'public idolatry' of the Mass was intolerable, in the same

---

[12] The term coined by N. M. Sutherland, 'Persecution and Toleration in Reformation Europe', in W. J. Sheils (ed.), *Persecution and Toleration* (Oxford, 1984), 153–61, here 159; her pre-eminent example was the French Edict of Toleration of January 1562, 160.

[13] H. Rott, *Friedrich II von der Pfalz und die Reformation* (Heidelberg, 1904), 57–9, 61.

[14] For the 'marsilian' variety, see Bob Scribner, *Varieties of Reformation* (London, 1993), 21–5.

[15] A summary of the situation in Baden is in Martin Brecht, Hermann Ehmer, *Südwestdeutsche Reformationsgeschichte* (Stuttgart, 1984), 88, 188; documents illuminating the prince's position are in R. Fester, 'Die Religionsmandate der Margrafen Philipp von Baden (1522–1533)', *Zeitschrift für Kirchengeschichte*, 11 (1980), 307–29.

way that the disruptive presence of open heresy was intolerable to Catholic princes.[16]

Sixth, we can speak of a form of *de facto toleration by virtue of pastoral latitudinarianism* (a stance of refusing to 'make windows into people's souls'). In essence, such a view permitted outward conformity by meeting basic religious needs and applying only the simplest doctrinal tests (such as the ability to recite the Ten Commandments, the Lord's Prayer, and the Creed). This form was found in territories such as Ernestine Saxony which espoused a gradual and conservative reform, and which sought to minimise doctrinal dispute on the grounds that it was socially divisive.[17] None the less, such a form of tolerance remained very minimal if there was no associated freedom of worship.

Seventh, and perhaps in practice not too far removed from the previous category, there was *toleration by dint of too few resources to enforce wider conformity*. This was undoubtedly the situation which, from the Catholic point of view, led to the declaration in the 1526 Recess of Speyer that each person and estate should be permitted to live according to their consciences in such ways as the Word of God and the law of the Empire allowed. In Habsburg territories it was the practical compromise accepted by a ruler faced with widespread disaffection of noble elites who could not be coerced without danger of serious upheaval.[18] It was also the *de facto* consequence of the powerlessness of secular authorities to enforce mandates against Anabaptism (unless recourse was had to the use of informers), so that apprehension of religious radicals relied very much on chance, as did the policing of other categories of the criminalised population.[19]

Eighth, we must mention *toleration on economic grounds*, most notably found in mercantile centres such as Hamburg, and which could also encompass Jews and (in a Lutheran city) those of Calvinist belief. This tolerance was very much the work of pragmatic magistrates faced with the continual and economically necessary presence of foreign merchants of different faiths, and was achieved only over several generations of struggle in the teeth

---

[16] N. Paulus, 'Religionsfreiheit und Augsburger Religionsfriede', 18–23.

[17] I have discussed some examples briefly in 'Pastoral Care and the Reformation in Germany', in James Kirk (ed.), *Humanism and Reform: the Church in Europe, England and Scotland. Essays in Honour of James Cameron* (Oxford, 1991), 92–4.

[18] See Günther R. Burkert, 'Protestantism and Defence of Liberties in Austrian Lands under Ferdinand I', in R. J. W. Evans and T. V. Thomas (eds.), *Crown, Church and Estates. Central European Politics in the Sixteenth and Seventeenth Centuries* (London, 1991), 58–69; Winfried Eberhard, 'Bohemia, Moravia and Austria', in Andrew Pettegree (ed.), *The Early Reformation in Europe* (Cambridge, 1992), 43.

[19] Clasen, *Anabaptism*, 360–1; for the weakness of sixteenth-century policing, R. W. Scribner, 'Police and the Territorial State in Sixteenth-Century Württemberg', in E. I. Kouri and Tom Scott (eds.), *Politics and Society in Reformation Europe. Essays for Sir Geoffrey Elton on his Sixty-fifth Birthday* (London, 1987), 103–20.

of strong resistance from the clergy, who took a typically severe line on the need for purity of doctrine to be reflected in confessional uniformity.[20]

Finally, as a ninth category, there was a largely unremarked but very widespread form of tolerance which was probably the most important of all, and which I shall call the *tolerance of practical rationality*. This was very much the tolerance of ordinary people, a tolerance found frequently in daily life which made little fuss about difference in belief and accepted it as a normal state of affairs. This attitude was found in both the rural and urban worlds, and was frequently manifested during the Reformation upheavals in a good-natured acceptance that common folk could hardly be expected to agree on matters of belief since theologians could not reach any form of agreement. It was summed up by a citizen of Strassburg who in 1557 maintained that the Anabaptist church was also a church of God; God had his church at Frankfurt, Geneva, Lausanne or Strassburg, at St Claus or St Andreas; neither Anabaptist nor Lutheran doctrine was wrong and everyone who believed in God would be saved.[21] Such doctrinal latitudinarianism could even manifest itself in positive and sometimes spectacular forms, such as attacking those who informed on Anabaptists or the judges who condemned them, or in the case of 52 villagers from the vicinity of Basle who made a compact to leave Anabaptists undisturbed (and suffered imprisonment for their pains).[22] I suspect that it is this form of tolerance which was at work in the example of Solothurn cited by Heiko Oberman. It was undoubtedly such expressions of practical rationality that a zealous reformer would strive to overturn in order to arouse awareness of confessional difference (Etienne François has documented both of these aspects for Augsburg in a later period[23]). But we should not be tempted to romanticise the mentality of popular culture – examples of the tolerance of practical rationality could be matched by examples of popular intolerance, and those skilled at arousing popular fears and prejudices could easily still this instinct and replace it by something altogether darker, amply illustrated by the popular anti-Jewish riots in Regensburg in 1519 and Frankfurt in 1614 (the Fettmilch disturbances) which provided intolerant endpapers for the century of the Reformation.[24]

---

[20] The essential study for the *longue durée* of development towards this limited form of tolerance is Joachim Whaley, *Religious Tolerance and Social Change in Hamburg 1529–1819* (Cambridge, 1985).

[21] Cited after Clasen, *Anabaptism*, 413.

[22] *Ibid.*, 412–13.

[23] Etienne François, *Die unsichtbare Grenze. Protestanten und Katholiken in Augsburg 1648–1806* (Sigmaringen, 1991), 140–4.

[24] On Regensburg, Philip M. Soergel, *Wondrous in his Saints: Counter-Reformation Propaganda in Bavaria* (Berkeley, 1993), 52–3, with further literature; on the Fettmilch rising, C. R. Friedrichs, 'Politics or Pogrom? The Fettmilch Uprising in German and Jewish History', *Central European History*, 19 (1986), 186–228.

All these manifestations of tolerance in practice were pragmatic in nature: in changed circumstances, toleration was a privilege that could be withdrawn; or it was no more than a working political compromise that could be altered if and when circumstances allowed. In essence, only a very meagre degree of toleration was possible in sixteenth-century Germany, and then it existed only on an ad hoc basis. This realisation points us in the direction of the more common phenomenon of intolerance and to the question why this appears to us nowadays to be such a defining characteristic of the age of the Reformation.

A 'persecuting society'?

It has been common to regard the sixteenth century as less tolerant than the later Middle Ages, as an age which 'sharpened all conflicts and augmented persecution'. As G. R. Elton put it, 'an era of moderation and tolerance gave way to one of ever more savage repression'.[25] Was it, therefore, the age of a 'persecuting society'? The notion of a 'persecuting society' as formulated by R. I. Moore for the Middle Ages involves three stages of development: classification, stigmatisation and persecution. *Classification* meant focusing on the alleged distinguishing peculiarities of specific groups of people – Moore cites heretics, lepers and Jews, who were characterised respectively by religious conviction, physical condition and race and culture (we might more appropriately say 'ethnicity'). In the stage of *stigmatisation*: these groups were so defined as to appear as enemies of society, and a myth was constructed about each group which identified them as a source of social contamination. *Persecution* moved this process to a final stage of intensification. The groups so identified were held to be sufficiently dangerous to warrant pursuit, denunciation and interrogation, exclusion from the community, deprivation of civil rights and loss of property. Their distinctiveness then became not the cause, but the result of persecution.[26]

In explaining the 'why' of this process, Moore rejects a Durkheimian view – there was no instinctive and collective determination to preserve social unity, nor was the persecutor merely an agent of society at large. Rather, Moore tends towards a Weberian view, finding the motor of such developments in bureaucratic agents, and seeing the development of legal processes and institutions for persecution as part of a process of 'bureaucratisation', as an aspect of the emergence of a 'bureaucratic state'. Moore also mentions,

---

[25] G. R. Elton, 'Persecution and Toleration in the English Reformation', in W. J. Sheils (ed.), *Persecution and Toleration* (Oxford, 1984), 163–87, 163.

[26] Moore does not quite so explicitly formulate the three-stage trajectory I offer here, although it is implicit in his three steps of 'the enemy defined', 'the enemy discovered' and 'the enemy destroyed', *Formation of a Persecuting Society*, 98–9, 118–21, 146–53.

without following the argument through, that a persuasive theoretical context might be found in Weber's view that the creation of ethical religions involved replacing a kinship-based society with a 'superior community of faith and a common ethical way of life.'[27] When Moore attributes some of the processes to the work of priests, prelates and magistrates generally, and even by implication of intellectuals, such persons may be seen ambiguously either as bureaucratic agents of the emergent state or else as those engaged in constructing that 'superior community of faith and common ethical way of life'.[28] In the end, however, Moore's analysis remains imprecise and theoretically simplistic. For example, he contrasts (Durkheimian) popular demand for persecution with (Weberian) bureaucratic impulse, without considering how the dynamics of classification and stigmatisation may have created popular demands to which agents of the state may only have responded; or that stigmatisation processes may independently have created popular stereotypes which remained beyond the reach of bureaucratic agents.

Let us none the less apply the problem to the sixteenth century. Groups mentioned by Moore as belonging to the classification of 'deviants' are fairly similar to those found in the age of the Reformation, but with significant and characteristic additions: Jews, heretics, witches, (female) prostitutes and (male) homosexuals, to which were added beggars, idlers, spendthrifts and the morally lax, as well as professional criminals (robber gangs, *Mordbrenner* or organised arsonists), demobilised soldiers (*Gartknechte*) and others of vagrant lifestyle (Gypsies, fake beggars, travelling folk).[29] A special category of classified situational deviance encompassed the clergy (when they stood outside secular control) and in evangelical polities, the priesthood and religious orders, especially mendicants. (Indeed, in Catholic polities, mendicants or nuns who stepped beyond secular or ecclesiastical control were also classified as deviant.) The operative criterion here seems to have been the notion that all social categories of person should belong to a sacral community (*Heilsgemeinschaft*), or at least be functionally integrated into a Christian civil society. Those who were not so integrated because they set themselves apart through a claim to special character or status were *ipso facto* perceived as deviant.[30]

---

[27] *Ibid.*, 106–12, esp. 112.

[28] *Ibid.*, 125–46. Here I assume that Moore is not arguing that Weber's 'superior community of faith' was a creation of the bureaucratic state.

[29] For an overview Bernd Roeck, *Außenseiter, Randgruppen, Minderheiten. Fremde in Deutschland der frühen Neuzeit* (Göttingen, 1993); for the later middle ages, Bernd-Ulrich Hergemöller (ed.), *Randgruppen der spätmittelalterlichen Gesellschaft* (Warendorf, 1990).

[30] On the importance of the *Heilsgemeinschaft* for the classification of deviance, Roeck, *Außenseiter*, 14, although he does not mention such dissident clergy. On the question of integration or otherwise of the clergy, and on the complexities of anticlericalism, see respectively, Thomas A. Brady, ' "You hate us priests": Anticlericalism, Communalism and the Control of Women at Strasbourg in the Age of the Reformation' and Bob Scribner, 'Anticlericalism

Not all of these groups were equally present as forms of 'otherness' at all times. For example, homosexuals were perceived as a form of otherness throughout the late-medieval and early modern periods, but they certainly were not a current issue in German consciousness of the sixteenth century as they seem to have been, for example, in Venice or Florence.[31] Nor were different kinds of 'otherness' always defined to the same degree – the spendthrift or the morally lax were seen as dangers to the moral health of the community, but they were not a threat to its peace or security (as were robber gangs, organised arsonists or *Gartknechte*), or to its ideological coherence (as were heretics). Here different modes of classification were at work – some groups were seen as socially dysfunctional (the morally lax such as adulterers or fornicators, because of the threat to patriarchy and inheritance), others as economically dysfunctional (spendthrifts and beggars, because they involved welfare expenditure for themselves or their indigent families); some were regarded as deviant simply because they were perceived as rootless and therefore out of control (vagrants, demobilised soldiers); others because they were socio-legal anomalies (the clergy under ecclesiastical jurisdiction).[32] The problem to be explained is why some types were thrust into the foreground at one moment in time, rather that at others, and therefore why they were specially subject to stigmatisation and persecution.

First, classification often brought stigmatisation simply by definition of 'otherness', and led to what we might call low-level intolerance, or at best conditional tolerance. Once the identity of outsiders had been established in common discourse, they became natural suspects and potential objects of fear or hostility; they were thus available as scapegoats at times of anxiety, or in moments of crisis in which explanations were sought and counter-action became imperative. Stigmatisation became more intense when it was linked to a process of *diagnosis* and *explanation*: that is, when a particular group could be associated in a causal manner with a specific threat or problem; and when the diagnosis was related to a wider form of ideological coherence. We can see an example of such diagnosis operating when serious outbreaks of fire-raising in the 1540s were traced first to vagrants and then to bands of beggar-arsonists who were held to be roaming the roads of virtually every

---

and the Cities', both in Peter A. Dykema and Heiko Oberman (eds.), *Anticlericalism in Late Medieval and Early Modern Europe* (Leiden, 1993), 167–207, 147–66.

[31] Gerd Schwerhoff, *Köln im Kreuzverhör. Kriminalität, Herrschaft und Gesellschaft in einer frühneuzeitlichen Stadt* (Bonn, 1991), 401 summarizes what little is known for this offence in Cologne, Nördlingen or Augsburg and draws the comparison with the Italian situation.

[32] See respectively Lyndal Roper, *The Holy Household. Women and Morals in Reformation Augsburg* (Oxford, 1989), esp. chs. 2–3; Thomas Fischer, *Städtische Armut und Armenfürsorge im 15. und 16. Jahrhundert* (Göttingen, 1979), 141–59; R. W. Scribner, 'Mobility: Voluntary or Enforced? Vagrants in Württemberg in the Sixteenth Century', in G. Jaritz, A. Müller (eds.), *Migration in der Feudalgesellschaft* (Frankfurt, 1988), 65–88.

part of Germany. Ideological coherence was found in ascribing the alleged work of these bands to some form of large-scale conspiracy, whether a papal conspiracy directed against the Protestant towns of Germany, or one inspired by the Emperor's main perceived enemy, the King of France.[33] This further level of ideological coherence is also exemplified in explanations for witchcraft which extrapolated from the notion of witchcraft as an expression of malevolence and ill-will to present it as a widespread satanic conspiracy. Diagnosis and explanation could then lead to a stronger degree of intolerance, essentially to what labelling theory calls a moral crusade – a concerted drive to counter the threat uncovered by the diagnosis and now provided with a coherent ideological explanation. It could even lead to the increased intensity expressed in a momentary (or sometimes prolonged) 'moral panic'. A further step is necessary to turn this development into persecution – a systematic procedure which entails unusual levels of violence or at least violation of personal rights (restrictions on individual or group freedom of action, surveillance, interrogation, imprisonment, punitive measures.).[34]

In the case of both the major examples I have cited here, arson panics and witchtrials, we could analyse and map the trajectories taken by such outbreaks of persecution in order to discern just how widespread and deep-rooted the phenomena were. Yet I suspect that such mapping in the case of witchcraft persecution would reveal not a general or widespread phenomenon, but something which was locally of very limited nature. I take my cue here from Wolfgang Behringer's work on Bavarian witchcraft accusations, which has revealed how few accusations actually resulted either in judicial proceedings or trials for witchcraft, and how few of these trials produced victims of persecution (in 81 per cent of trials there were no victims, while a mere 5 per cent of all trials accounted for 82 per cent of all victims). The conclusion to be drawn from such findings is that whatever the localised intensity of a few very large trials, the phenomenon of persecution for witchcraft, when viewed over nearly two centuries, was patchy and limited. We might even hazard a guess that the average villager or even town-dweller was more likely to encounter a trial for murder (in early modern Germany an exceptional event) than a trial for witchcraft.[35]

[33] An initial approach to the problem in Bob Scribner, 'The *Mordbrenner* Fear in Sixteenth Century Germany: Political Paranoia or the Revenge of the Outcast?' in Richard J. Evans (ed.), *The German Underworld. Deviants and Outcasts in German History* (London, 1988) 29–56.

[34] On moral panics, with a less than nuanced application to the witchcraze which alas does not take account of the complex relationships between magic and witchcraft, Erich Goode, Nachman Ben-Yehuda, *Moral Panics.' The Social Construction of Deviance* (Oxford, 1994), 144–84.

[35] W. Behringer, *Hexenverfolgung in Bayern* (Munich, 1987), 68; this amplifies the conclusion I had come to in my own view of the wider context of accusations for magic and witchcraft, and the possibility of short-circuiting judicial procedures before they may have run the full

If the trajectories of several forms of intolerance were analysed and mapped in a comparative manner, I suspect that it would become clear that sixteenth-century society was *not* a 'persecuting society' (nor, perhaps, when approached in the same manner, were the middle ages or the modern period). Rather there were moments or circumstances in which intensified persecution could be mobilised for various reasons, yet it was not possible for this to be continuous over time or across an entire society. Persecution which is both extensive and intensive is socially dysfunctional in the long or even medium term, and persecution may be more a matter of short-term political conjunctures or expedients. Undeniably sixteenth-century society was susceptible to moments of persecution, for reasons which are well known – a society based on transcendental sanctions is easily threatened by heterodoxy of belief. Moreover, contemporary belief in a 'moralised universe' entailed the view that individual or collective deviance could call down divine punishment on the community as a whole.[36] Moments of high ideological tension, when some aspect of the overall coherence of belief was under threat, could bring these matters to the fore and precipitate a phase of persecution. More pertinently, the Reformation also brought about a new and potent ideological input in the ideal of creating a reformed civic community, a classic exemplification of Weber's 'superior community of faith and common ethical way of life'. This ideal gave rise to a theological–political discourse which inevitably came to identify threats or alternatives to the creation of such a 'community of faith' as a moment of eschatological confrontation. The alternatives were between good and evil, Christ and Antichrist. Thus, what has been called 'sacral corporatism' or 'Reformation moralism' was by implication intolerant, even if it often seemed to permit survival spaces for dissenters or the 'confessional other'.[37]

Yet this eschatological moment was frequently counter-balanced by a secularised politics, which worked by means of a pragmatics of power (a 'machiavellian moment'?) and which was aware of dysfunctional as well as functional aspects of intolerance and persecution. In as far as all societies have the potential to be persecuting societies, the sixteenth century had the raw material in abundance; but we can also speak of societies having a loose or

course of building up to a stage of persecution: see 'Sorcery, Superstitition and Society: the Witch of Urach, 1529', in *Popular Culture and Popular Movements*, 257–76; 'Witchcraft and Judgment in Reformation Germany', *History Today* (April 1990), 12–19.

[36] By the 'moralized universe' I mean a belief that the state of the material world was affected by the moral quality of human behaviour, so that moral failings could call down divine punishment: see my essay 'Reformation and Desacralisation: from Sacramental World to Moralised Universe', in R. W. Scribner and R. Po-Chia Hsia (eds.), *Problems in the Historical Anthropology of Early Modern Europe* (forthcoming).

[37] On sacral corporatism, Thomas A. Brady, *Ruling Class, Regime and Reformation at Strasbourg 1520–1555* (Leiden, 1978), 270; on Reformation moralism Roper, *The Holy Household*, 56–7, 69–73, 254–5.

a tight weave in their inherent intolerance of dissent and deviance – and the sixteenth century was one with a distinctively loose weave. This was undoubtedly linked to the tolerance of practical rationality I perceive as the most common manifestation of toleration in an age of intensified religious belief, and which offered the ongoing possibility of the kind of 'pragmatic conjuncture' mentioned above. But it was also a consequence of two other, broadly sociological, features.

First, the advocates of intolerance by no means formed such an effective phalanx that they were always able to have their own way. This was partly a result of the manner in which popular opinion was formed, and which certainly could not be as directly influenced either by bureaucratic elites or by moral crusaders as Moore suggested for an earlier period. Not only was there quite a complicated dynamic between 'popular opinion' and moral crusades of various kinds, but active moral entrepreneurs were to be found well beyond the ranks of intellectual or bureaucratic elites. Indeed, a fuller discussion of the different kinds of moral entrepreneurs out and about in sixteenth-century Germany would reveal a complex range of social and personality types – including visionaries, millennialists, zealots, moral reformers, mere busybodies, men on the make (who might be political opportunists or even political virtuosi), townsfolk and peasants, cleric and laypeople, many of whom may not have belonged to intellectual or bureaucratic elites, or else existed on their fringes. The Württemberg vintner-prophet Hans Keil, so persuasively discussed by David Sabean, represented one such figure, a type common in the sixteenth and seventeenth centuries; Philip Schmidt, village pastor of Ringleben, north of Erfurt, in the early 1560s, represented another, in this case someone active as a moral crusader for over two decades without finding any official or popular approval.[38]

Secondly, despite evident tendencies towards stigmatisation and persecution, the labelling process by means of which deviants were identified was so loosely woven that it allowed moments of tolerance to slip through. Labelling depended on the creation, internalisation and manipulation of stereotypes, although it was neither continuous nor consistent in its operation. Within any culture, stereotypes are continually being formed, modified, forgotten, revived, revised and discarded. Sometimes they are applied only for

---

[38] David Warren Sabean, *Power in the Blood: Popular Culture and Village Discourse in Early Modern Germany* (Cambridge, 1984), 61–94; however, for a more nuanced and thorough evaluation of Hans Keil, see Norbert Haag, 'Frömmigkeit und sozialer Protest: Hans Keil, der Prophet von Gerlingen', *Zeitschrift für württembergische Landesgeschichte* 48 (1989), 127–41; for the wider phenomenon of popular prophets, Jürgen Beyer, 'Lutherische Propheten in Deutschland und Skandinavien im 16. und 17. Jahrhundert. Entstehung und Ausbreitung eines Kulturmusters zwischen Mündlichkeit und Schriftlichkeit', in Robert Bohn (ed.), *Europa in Skandinavien. Kulturelle und soziale Dialoge in der frühen Neuzeit* (Frankfurt, 1994), 35–55. On Phillip Schmidt, Scribner, 'Pastoral Care', 79–86.

short periods and may then lie dormant for a long time. What is important is their availability: once such social labels are created they remain present as a cultural fund to be drawn upon – they can be disseminated, appropriated, internalised, modified, even mutated – and so are available for mobilisation at any given moment when they might be thought appropriate. They provide an excellent example of cultural recycling or bricolage. The Reformation period was noteworthy for its attempt to present new religious and theological ideas as a recycling of old heresies in order to exploit the negative connotations of their associated stereotypes. This began with the attempt to depict Luther's ideas as a revival of Hussite heresy, but soon witnessed the polemical deployment (from all religious directions) of ancient heresies such as Pelagianism, Nestorianism, Arianism, Gnosticism. Zwingli provides the most interesting example here, because of the way in which he dug out some old Gnostic heresies and thereby managed successfully to label Anabaptists with the charge that they advocated community of women and practised libertine sexual relations, even distorting a doctrine of ascetic marriage without sexual relations into the very inverse. The label stuck to become a prime mark of Anabaptist deviance in the eyes of secular authorities.[39] Yet we do not know how far this stereotype was received and internalised by popular opinion; the kind of evidence of popular attitudes towards Anabaptists cited above seems to suggest the contrary, and reminds us that not all the stereotypes created by elites or moral entrepreneurs were capable of popular reception or internalisation. The most interesting example concerns cunning folk, whom secular and religious authorities consistently sought to associate with negative stereotypes of superstition or witchcraft. This proved no deterrent to their activities or to the positive evaluation in the popular mind of what they had to offer. On the other hand, popular opinion was capable of invoking and mobilising official action by bringing charges of malevolent witchcraft – perhaps based on popular stereotypes, perhaps influenced by the elite paradigm of satanic witchcraft.

Finally, we should also bear in mind the role played by what we might call cultural style and cultural modes of discourse. Here I particularly have in mind the question of violence, especially violence of language and how it may have been linked to recourse to physical violence. Hsia has written that the process of confessionalisation often brought about redirection or suppression of violence and anger. However, I am not so sure. The creation of religious identity founded on the inherent otherness of different faiths was inextricably tied up with the fostering of religious militancy, a militancy which expressed itself at the very least in aggressiveness of confessional

---

[39] The process is described in Bob Scribner, 'Practical Utopias: Pre-modern Communism and the Reformation', *Comparative Studies in Society and History*, 36 (1994), 743–74, esp. 747–52.

language. I suspect that such forms of militancy often lowered the threshold of violence, to the point where verbal aggression could be turned into action. One significant effect of classification and stigmatisation is that it depersonalises and dehumanises its subjects (Anne Kibbey has discerned a similar process in iconoclasm, leading to a depersonalisation and objectification of ethnic others).[40]

What is of importance here is the polemical style of religious dispute during the Reformation (although we should not ascribe it solely to religious polemic: humanist polemics set the tone of public debate on the eve of the Reformation, and the humanist promotion of rhetoric as the pre-eminent skill required for public discourse undoubtedly played its part). Religious reformers were none the less quick to adopt such forms of violent discourse as a means of arousing passions and provoking their audiences into positive decisions for the new religious ideas. There are numerous examples where the rhetoric of violence triggered physical violence, although to explore the matter further we would need to analyse under what conditions such triggering worked. It would be naive to ascribe religious riot merely to religious polemic: sometimes such violence was a form of political expediency, or fulfilled the need for scapegoats in acute moments of anxiety to which the input of religious passions supplied only an incidental spur.[41] Yet the polemical discourse of confessional allegiance quickly became a major cultural style, often inflammatory in tone and designed to arouse violent passions. I would like to suggest that attitudes of intolerance were closely linked to such violence of discourse. Was the incipient violence internalised (in Hsia's sense of being neutralised) or merely directed in legitimised ways against those now defined as the 'confessional other'? Many manifestations of violence were justified as expressions of an 'excess of pious zeal', whether anticlericalism, religious riot, iconoclasm and even religious rebellion or warfare.[42]

Summary

I have emphasised throughout that secular and political considerations often shaped policies of tolerance and intolerance. These included pragmatic atti-

---

[40] On confessionalization and suppression of violence R. Po-Chia Hsia, *Social Discipline in the Reformation* (London, 1989), 170; on violence and language Anne Kibbey, *The Interpretation of Material Shapes in Puritanism. A Study of Rhetoric, Prejudice and Violence* (Cambridge, 1986).

[41] For examples (and for the issue of political expediency), see Bob Scribner, 'Anticlericalism in the Cities', in 147–66, esp. 147–9 (Memmingen, 1524), 157 (Leisnig, 1522), 159 (Neustadt a.d. Orla, 1523), and Scribner, 'Ritual and Reformation', in *Popular Culture and Popular Movements* 106 (Magdeburg, 1524).

[42] The theme has been more frequently discussed in the context of the French Religious Wars rather than for Germany. See the magisterial work by Denis Crouzet, *Les guerriers de Dieu. La violence au temps des truobles de religion vers 1525–vers 1610*, 2 vols. (Paris, 1990).

tudes in the interests of economic prosperity, especially noticeable in the reluctance of commercial city states to get too closely involved in religious disputes, and their willingness to turn a blind eye to heterodoxy in their midst so long as this did not become socially disruptive. Equally, the desire for social stability and cohesiveness could also lead to an attitude of tolerance, through an acceptance of the view that disputes over religion could not be settled by secular magistrates, and that tolerance was a more fruitful mid-term reaction while the religious problems were resolved. Thus, the 'politique' attitudes that prevailed in several states only after prolonged periods of conflict were foreshadowed in the pragmatic politics of the early sixteenth century. However, commercial and political considerations could, under other circumstances, lead to intolerance – if it were thought politically expedient to single out a scapegoat group in the interests of distracting attention from more politically or socially divisive issues. Here the most common scapegoats were the Jews and the clergy, although beggars (and later religious radicals) ran them a close third. Fateful for the development of intolerance was above all the conjuncture of politics and religious fervour, as well as the emergence of forms of intolerant public discourse, something to which the modes of polemical discourse of the Reformation were to contribute mightily: the violence of the language often employed in theological and religious polemics was to construct an ideal situation for the deployment of actual violence, and to translate the vehemence of polemic into a fierce politics of intolerance. The age of the Reformation did not give rise to a 'persecuting society', but the virus of intolerance and persecution was always present and could become virulent when the conditions were right.

4   Heresy executions in Reformation Europe, 1520–1565

William Monter

To the best of my knowledge, no general synthesis of trials and executions for heresy in Reformation Europe has ever been attempted. We are all aware that executions for heresy occurred throughout western Europe after Luther's successful defiance of papal authority in December 1520. We hear vague reports of massive executions of Anabaptists in the aftermath of the German Peasants' War, and again after the collapse of the New Jerusalem at Münster. And the dreary tale of religious persecution continues. In Mediterranean Europe, a nascent Protestant movement was snuffed out by organised repression from the Roman and Spanish Inquisitions. In France and the Low Countries, we hear many reports about executions of Huguenots and about the vast havoc wrought by Alva's 'Council of Blood'. Englishmen remember the persecutions under Mary Tudor. But nobody has tried to measure overall religious persecution in Reformation Europe (not forgetting that early Protestant governments also put several people to death for heresy). Just how bad was it? Should Reformation Europe be considered as the zenith of R. I. Moore's 'Persecuting Society'?

The obstacles standing in the way of a provisional census of heresy executions in Reformation Europe are considerable; but enough evidence remains to permit some fairly precise estimates of both the timing and the geography of heresy prosecutions after Luther defied papal authority, and to offer at least one major provisional hypothesis about the institutional dynamics of these executions. An investigator of heresy executions in sixteenth-century Europe possesses the unusual advantage of having documentation available from the persecuted as well as from the persecutors. In general, it seems safer to begin with the judicial archives of the persecutors, which are usually more complete, although the easily-available compilations of the persecuted help fill in some gaps in documentation. Since religious persecution has never been much celebrated by Catholic scholars – least of all in the ecumenical climate of the past fifty years – not much work has been done on this subject recently. However, we possess enough reliable archivally-based work from various regions of western Christendom to make a global reconstruction of heresy executions possible for Reformation Europe.

Table 4.1 *Protestants executed for heresy in Reformation Europe*
(annual averages)

Region	1520–29	1530–54	1555–65	1566–99
German Empire	38	13	2	0.7
Switzerland	4	2	1	0.1
Low Countries[1]	1.2	20	40	(2.7)
France[2]	1	12	(20)	0.5
England + Scotland	2	1.6	30	0.1
Spain (Inquisition)	0	0.5	12	2.0
Italy (incl. Sicily)	0	0.6	3	2.2
Totals	46+	50	106	8.3

[1] Excludes years 1567–1574 which saw Alva's 'Council of Troubles', with 1,100 executions
for a poorly differentiated mixture of iconoclasm, rebellion, sedition, and occasional heresy.
[2] Excludes years 1560–1564, thereby omitting 200 deaths for 'rebellion' or 'sedition'
during first War of Religion in 3 parlementary capitals.

Possible, and desirable. Desirable because we cannot understand the history
of Reformation Europe by paying vastly disproportionate attention to the
scattered and feeble signs of religious toleration, most of them clustered in
the final third of the century. In Reformation Europe, particularly in its pre-
confessional age (for my purposes, until *c.* 1560–1565), responsible governments tried very hard to repress heresy, including frequent recourse to the
death penalty. Just how well and how thoroughly and how consistently, did
they do their job?

Let me put my provisional numbers up front. Heresy executions in Reformation Europe, from 1520 to *c.* 1565, accounted for approximately 3,000
legally sanctioned deaths across Latin Christendom. (I am persuaded that this
figure contains a margin of error no greater than 10 per cent.) About two-
thirds of those executed were Anabaptists, of whom perhaps 1,000 died in
present-day Germany and Switzerland, while almost as many perished in the
Low Countries. Perhaps 300 heretics of other varieties also perished before
1565 in the Low Countries, which was clearly the epicentre of heresy
executions even before the Duke of Alva added another thousand victims
with his 'Council of Blood' from 1567–1574. Nearly 500 perished in the
Kingdom of France, while Tudor England accounted for over 300. The Spanish Inquisition executed almost 150 so-called 'Lutherans' before 1567 and
another 70 thereafter, the last coming in Sicily in 1640. Least bloodthirsty
of all, the Roman Inquisition, founded in 1542 especially to combat Protestantism in Italy, had executed fewer than 50 Protestants before 1570.

Let me now put my main thesis up front. The relative scarcity of executions
for heresy by the lone truly clerically-run institution of this group, the Roman

Inquisition – under 2 per cent of these provisional totals – points towards the generalisation that heresy executions became a form of state-building in Reformation Europe. From the failure of the papal legate to arrest Luther at Augsburg in 1518 until the outbreak of the wars of religion, ecclesiastical justice proved utterly inadequate to punish accused heretics. Europe generally, and Germany in particular, lacked any continuous experience with trials and executions for heresy in Luther's lifetime.[1] If there is one constant motif running through the history of heresy executions in Reformation Europe, it is the complete failure of old-fashioned ecclesiastical institutions to frighten dissenters. Everywhere one looks, from Scotland to Portugal, episcopal courts and papal inquisitors (where they still existed) had the primary responsibility for controlling heresy, but lacked the means to do so effectively.

Sooner or later – usually, sooner – secular justice took control of heresy prosecutions. The rise of Anabaptism in Germany in the immediate aftermath of the great peasant rebellions of 1524–25 offered a pretext to many governments in the Holy Roman Empire, led by the Austrian Habsburgs, to condemn these religious radicals as seditious. The careful investigations of Claus-Peter Clasen have established the statistical and legal parameters of the persecution of Anabaptists: after May 1525, when the first execution of an Anabaptist was recorded in a Swiss Catholic canton, large numbers of these religious radicals suffered death by law within a few years. Of Clasen's 850 known executions, 80 per cent occurred between 1527 and 1533. The two worst years were 1528 and 1529; the regions most affected were Habsburg provinces, above all Tyrol in the aftermath of Gaismair's revolt, where 30 per cent of them perished. Ferdinand I's government issued an imperial mandate in January 1528 charging these radicals not only with heresy but also with sedition, justifying the death penalty on the basis of laws passed against the Donatists by the Christian Emperors of ancient Rome. A second imperial law of April 1529 ordered that Anabaptists be executed by fire or sword, *without prior ecclesiastical inquisition.*[2] In other words, Ferdinand I's officials took the first decisive step towards the full and complete secularization of heresy trials in the aftermath of the final great peasant rebellion of the 1520s in the Empire.

Similar processes occurred in many parts of the Low Countries, where other Habsburg officials first promulgated the famous placards against heresy in 1529. The transition from traditional methods for controlling heresy

---

[1] Bernd Moeller, 'Piety in Germany around 1500', in S. Ozment (ed.), *The Reformation in Medieval Perspective* (New York, 1971), 52 and notes 4–5 (last known Waldensian or Hussite heresy trials in the Empire held before Luther was born); Daniel Olivier, *The Trial of Luther* (1971; St. Louis, 1978), which details the various ineffective attempts to prosecute a notorious heretic through ecclesiastical court systems in an Empire whose humanists had savagely ridiculed papal inquisitors a short time before in the *Reuchlinstreit*.
[2] Claus-Peter Clasen, *Anabaptism: A Social History, 1525–1618* (Ithaca, 1972), 371, 375, 437.

through episcopal inquisitors seems particularly clear in the capital of the province of Hainaut, where the problem of Lutheranism first surfaced in the spring of 1525. Listen to a local diarist:

On Friday the 26th of May and the following Saturday, an act of justice was done in the city of Mons by officers of the Bishop of Cambrai [he names the bishop's Official and a protonotary], as judges of ten people accused of being Lutherans, eight men and two women. With them was a monk, Inquisitor of the Faith for the Diocese of Cambrai who, after their trials had been seen and judged, as such cases deserve, pronounced their condemnations at the market of Mons and at the churches of St. Germain and St. Waudru, publically according to their deserts. Namely, some of them got seven years, others four, others three or two, in prison on bread and water; then, their time having expired, they would carry some wax candles to their respective parish churches. Then some of them were publicly given yellow cloth crosses to wear on their right arms and others got yellow cloth caps with crosses of red cloth sewn on them, which they were to wear on their heads so that they could be recognized as people who had abused and lived contrary to the church of the Christian faith. Afterwards they were taken to the castle of Selles to perform the penances which had been enjoined on them by their definitive sentence, where the Great Bailiff of Hainaut was present. And the mysteries were certainly very handsome and great to make this condemnation, because it was done to give an example to others. May God in his grace see that they are well converted, because there was very little appearance that they would do so, judging by the attitude they displayed. Through their confession, they no longer believed that Our Lady was a virgin, nor that the body of Our Lord was in the Eucharist, that holy water and river water were one and the same thing, that there was no Purgatory and that as soon as a person dies he goes straight to heaven or hell, and other smaller errors they had held, all of which they renounced while asking mercy of God and the Bishop of Cambrai, accepting the sentence which had been given to them.[3]

The unusual pomp and circumstance, accompanied by the relatively discreet presence of the secular 'Great Bailiff', evoke images of a Spanish-style *auto de fe*. But would it work? The orthodox diarist was overtly sceptical. His next mention of Lutherans occurred eight years later, in strikingly different circumstances:

The Lord of Esmeriez arrested a servant of the previous Lord of Esmeriez who had been his barber, and charged him with being a Lutheran. He had him taken to Mons for his trial, which was done on Wednesday May 28, 1533, and on that same day was taken from the castle of Mons and led to Pons-sur-Sambre, to have him executed and burned the following Thursday, where the Lord of Esmeriez was present in person, because it was the first act of criminal justice he had done.

At the barber's trial and execution, no ecclasiastical officials of any sort intervened, whereas the local seigneur sat at the centre of the spectacle. The

---

[3] Antoine de Lusy, *Le journal d'un bourgeois de Mons 1505–1536*, ed. A. Louant (Brussels, 1969), 357–58 (#916).

diarist closed this entry with the laconic observation that 'at Nivelle someone had been similarly put to death for such reasons, and at Lille several who belonged to this Lutheranism'.[4]

For almost a decade after Luther faced Emperor Charles at the Diet of Worms, relatively few acknowledged Lutherans suffered martyrdom (as distinct from the Anabaptists, whom Luther so vehemently repudiated). Mons in 1525 seems fairly typical. Two Augustinians were burned at Brussels as followers of Luther in 1523, opening the series of heresy deaths in Reformation Europe. Here and there one finds a few 'Lutherans' put to death in the 1520s. But except for German Anabaptists, the totals are extremely low. Even in the Low Countries, there were only two known deaths during the 1520s in populous Flanders, where Charles V had installed a newly-revitalized Inquisition in 1522; only three in the province of Holland; in Brabant we find only one (in 1525) at cosmopolitan Antwerp, that commercial and publishing metropolis, and another at the court residence, Mechelen, in 1529; in the French-speaking regions, we find one death for Lutheranism at each of the episcopal centres, Tournai and Liége, both in 1528.[5] Another handful of Lutheran heretics died in free cities or prince-bishoprics along the western fringe of the Empire, a layman and a monk at Metz (1524–25), a monk at Nancy (1525), another at Besançon (1528).[6]

Outside the Empire, heresy executions seem extremely rare during the 1520s. In France, one finds a half-dozen interesting cases at Paris, ranging from a hermit burned in 1523 for claiming that Jesus was the son of Joseph (a chronicler claimed that 'this hermit had been induced in part to preach thus by the books of Luther') to a nobleman and translator of Erasmus, in 1529; elsewhere, one finds such heretics as Pierre de Bar, burned at Rouen in 1528, whose opinions about the virginity of Mary were probably influ-

---

[4] *Ibid.*, 316 (#781). Lusy's remark about Lille is confirmed by M.-P. Willems-Closset, 'Le protestantisme à Lille . . . (1525–1565)', *Revue du Nord*, 52 (1970), 215: six Lutherans were beheaded in spring and summer 1533, the first local victims.

[5] See the exhaustive compilations of F. Vander Haegen *et al.* (eds.), *Bibliographie des Martyrologues Protestants Néerlandais*, 2 vols. (The Hague, 1890), II, 639–814, which synthesizes the three major martyrologies of van Haemstede, Crespin, and van Braght. It should be supplemented by Jean Meyhoffer, *Le martyrologue protestant des Pays-Bas, 1523–1597* (Nessonvaux, 1907); A. L. E. Verheyden, *Le martyrologe protestant des Pays-bas du sud au XVIe siècle* (Brussels, 1960), 172 (Antwerp, 1525). More recently, see the exemplary study of the Flemish Inquisition by Johan Decavele, *De Dageraad van de Reformatie in Vlaanderen (1520–1565)*, 2 vols. (Brussels, 1975); on the important province of Holland, see James Tracy, *Holland under Habsburg Rule, 1506–1566* (Berkeley, 1990), 147–75. For the earliest executions in Walloon regions, see Gérard Moreau, *Histoire du Protestantisme à Tournai jusqu'à la veille de la Révolution des Pays-Bas* (Paris, 1962), 249–59, esp. 257; and Léon-E. Halkin, *Le cardinal de la Marck, Prince-Evêque de Liège (1505–1538)* (Liège-Paris, 1930), 162, 186–8.

[6] Jean Crespin, *Histoire des martyrs persecutez et mis à mort pour la verité de l'Evangile, depuis le temps des apostres jusques à présent*, ed. D. Benoît, 3 vols. (Toulouse, 1885–89), I, 244, 247ff, 252.

enced by his Spanish *conversa* mistress rather than Luther.[7] In the British Isles, Scottish authorities burned Patrick Hamilton as a Lutheran in 1528, but their English counterparts remained concerned during the 1520s with pursuing the remnants of Lollardy rather than with nascent heresies from the Continent. One can find traces of condemnations for Lutheran opinions in several corners of western Europe, in places as distant as Spanish Valencia, where an Augustinian monk was penanced for 'Lutheranism' at a public *auto de fe* in 1528,[8] but no recorded executions – yet. In Italy, one finds no confirmed executions of Protestants until the 1540s.

Gallican France, the largest monarchy of western Europe, imitated its Habsburg rivals by removing the prosecutions of 'Lutherans' from ecclesiastical officials and old-fashioned papal Inquisitors into the hands of royal judges during the 1530s. Although Francis I made no sudden bursts of legislation with immediate and bloody consequences, he was clearly travelling along a parallel path. In southern France – ancient stronghold of Cathars and Waldensians, and seedbed for the creation of Inquisitors by the medieval papacy – two unrelated episodes loosened these Inquisitors' grip on heretics just as the Reformation movement began to make headway. The Parlement of Aix condemned one Inquisitor for abuses in trials of Waldensians (who had begun to merge with the newest type of anti-Papal movement) in Provence in 1533; five years later, the Parliament of Toulouse ousted an Inquisitor and executed another (apparently for sodomy, possibly for heresy), thereby removing this institution from any effective role in prosecuting heretics.[9] In northern France, where papal Inquisitors wielded less power, the famous 'affair of the Placards' in 1534 goaded the king into using the Parlement of Paris to carry out exemplary punishment on these well-organised conspirators, who had even affixed one of their obnoxious heretical procla-

---

[7] See three independent eyewitness chroniclers of the 1520s who agree with and complement each other: Nicolas Versoris, 'Livre de Raison (1519–1530)', ed. G. Fagniez, in *Mémoires de la Société de l'Histoire de Paris et de l'Ile de France*, 12 (1885), 122–23, 127–8 (quote, 128), 182, 188, 206–8, 213; Pierre Driart, 'Chronique (1522–1534)', in *ibid.*, 22 (1895), 78–89, 104–5, 114–15, 120, 124, 138–9, 142; L. Lalanne (ed.), *Journal d'un bourgeois de Paris sous le règne de François Ier (1515–1536)* (Paris, 1854), 145–6, 250–1, 291–2, 317, 326–7, 375, 378–84, 403. For Pierre de Bar, see A. Heron (ed.), *Deux chroniques de Rouen* (Rouen, 1900), 132–3; compare Raymond A. Mentzer, *Heresy Proceedings in Languedoc 1500–1560* (Philadephia, 1984), 25–6, for even clearer examples of Spanish *converso* Judaizers tried by the Parlement of Toulouse.

[8] Jeroni Soria, *Dietari*, ed. F. Momblanch Gonzalez (Valencia, 1960), 124–5: the local Augustinian prior, Fr. Martí Sanchis, was banished for four years and prohibited from saying Mass at the *auto* of 26 May 1528 *perque creya en les coses del Lutero eretje questa en Alemanya*.

[9] See Gabriel Audisio, *L'Inquisiteur et le barbe* (Toulouse, 1979), for the Provence Parlement's attack on the Inquisitor Jean de Roma; Mentzer, *Languedoc* 28–32, for the unedifying problems at Toulouse, where one Inquisitor was arrested on heresy charges and subsequently deposed in 1534, while his assistant was executed in 1539 for either sodomy or heresy (the sources remain unclear).

mations to the door of a royal bedroom. In the wake of this episode, at least twenty people were executed for sedition and heresy by order of the Parlement in late 1534 and early 1535.[10] But it was not until 1539 – a decade after Ferdinand I's imperial edict or Charles V's placards in the Low Countries – that a French royal edict officially transferred primary jurisdiction over heresy cases to secular courts.

It is difficult to find any parallel evolution elsewhere in western Europe. The two major kingdoms which had never known medieval Inquisitors, England and Castile, followed enormously different religious–political trajectories during the 1530s, but neither executed more than a handful of Lutherans. Henry VIII, royal schismatic, foe of Luther and Pope alike, approved a few executions from either camp during the late 1530s, and burned Dutch Anabaptists as well.[11] In Castile the Spanish Inquisition pursued its traditional prey, the *Judeoconversos*, and added the Erasmian *alumbrados*, throughout the 1530s; but few people died for either offence and fewer still for 'Lutheranism' during this decade.[12] Apart from France, the only important innovation in the pursuit of Protestant heretics during the quarter-century after the 1529 Habsburg laws was the foundation of the Roman Inquisition in 1542.

However, none of these systems – certainly not the Roman Inquisition, let alone the ambidextrous Henrician prosecutions of Papalists and Protestants, or the still-unruffled Spanish Inquisition – accounted for very large numbers of Protestant victims between 1530 and 1554. The Anabaptists of Germany, Switzerland (Protestant Berne beheaded about thirty of them during this period), and the Low Countries provided by far the bulk of known victims.

[10] On the repression at Paris after the 'Affair of the Placards', see *Journal d'un bourgeois de Paris* 444–52; Driart 'chronique', 172–8, and by a contemporary manuscript in the municipal library of Soissons, published in *Bulletin de la Société pour l'histoire du protestantisme français*, 11 (1862), 253–8.

[11] English heresy executions are of course best approached through John Foxe, *Acts and Monuments*, ed. J. Pratt, 8 vols. (1563; London, 1877). In addition to executing Lollands until at least 1530, Henry VIII's government also executed about twenty Dutch Anabaptists between 1535 and 1540; a half-dozen native 'Lutherans' died between 1532 and 1540 (the most prominent early English Protestant martyr, William Tyndale, died at Brussels in 1534). As G. R. Elton pointed out in *Policy and Police* (Cambridge, 1972), 388, implementing royal supremacy over the church led to well over two hundred executions for *lèse-majesté* under Henry VIII. Obviously, no contemporary secular government approached Henry VIII's record for variety of heretics executed (there were no Catholic martyrs in Reformation Europe outside England), though some surpassed him in quantity.

[12] It is difficult to find a 'Lutheran' executed by the Spanish Holy Office before 1539, when a naturalized Englishman, born in Antwerp, died at San Sebastian: see William Monter, *Frontiers of Heresy: The Spanish Inquisition from the Basque Land to Sicily* (Cambridge, 1990), 37. Arguably, the first branch of the Spanish Inquisition to be seriously concerned with Protestantism was in Sicily, where a native *Luterano* was burned in 1542. Before the great anti-Protestant hunt began in 1559, three French *Luteranos* died at *autos* in northern Spain (at Saragossa, 1546; Barcelona, 1552; and Logroño, 1556), but they were outnumbered by the nine Italian *Luteranos* executed at Palermo before 1559.

Table 4.2 *Heresy executions in the low countries (1532–97)*
(total numbers, including Council of Blood)

Province(s)	1523–9	1530–54	1555–66	1567–74	1575–97
Holland	3	170	20	80	0
Flanders	2	101	161	300	26
Brabant	4	125	115	300	19
other Flemish	0	50	25	75	3
Liége	1	25	2	24	3
Tournaisis	1	23	26	180	1
other Walloon	0	30	30	200	1

Even though the famous episode of the Anabaptist New Jerusalem occurred on imperial soil, the various German states, as Clasen has shown, sharply *reduced* their recorded executions of Anabaptists after 1533. Meanwhile, during the regency of Mary of Hungary in the Low Countries, about five hundred executions can be verified. About one-fifth of them came from the Flemish Inquisition, and another fourth from the province of Holland, the epicentre of Anabaptist activity. The great city of Antwerp enforced the placards vigorously against Anabaptists, as did many lesser places. Heresy executions were ubiquitous throughout the seventeen provinces and the Prince-Bishopric of Liége. They spilled over even into the most remote Habsburg province governed from Brussels, Franche-Comté, where episcopal and papal inquisitors had been fully removed from heresy trials by 1534.[13]

The only statistically significant cluster of heresy executions before 1555 in a land without native Anabaptists occurred in France. Its two largest appellate courts, the Parlement of Paris and the Parlement of Toulouse, together accounted for more than two hundred known heresy executions from the early 1530s to the beginning of organized Protestant churches in France in the mid-1550s. The Parlement of Paris averaged over twenty death sentences a year for heresy between 1545 and 1549; at Toulouse, the peak came later, in 1554, with fifteen death sentences. Other French Parlements (Rouen, Bordeaux, Dijon, Grenoble) contributed smaller numbers of executed heretics,

[13] For Low Countries heresy executions 1530–1555, see sources cited in note 5 of this chapter for Liége and the Walloon areas: Léon-E. Halkin, *Histoire religieuse des règnes de Corneille de Berghes et Georges d'Autriche, Princes-Evêques de Liége (1538–1557)* (Liége, 1936); Marie-Sylvie Dupont-Bouchat, 'La répression de l'hérésie dans le Namurois au XVIe siécle,' *Annales de la Société archéologique de Namur*, 56 (1972), 179–230 (seven deaths 1537–1554, none of them recorded in martyrologies); Robert Muchembled, *Le temps des supplices* (Paris, 1992), 100, 152, on Artois. On the southernmost enclave of the Netherlands government, see Lucien Febvre, *Notes et documents sur la Réforme et l'Inquisition en Franche-Comté* (Paris, 1912), 34–41.

perhaps fifty in all, between 1530 and 1554.[14] The notorious 'crusade' against the Waldensians of Provence in 1545, when three thousand were massacred within a month by troops commanded by the First President of the Parlement of Aix, offered the unusual spectacle of an appellate court enforcing its arrest warrants with cavalry and artillery. Since only twenty-two arrest warrants had been issued, however, the incident generated a certain amount of scandal; the Parlement Président-cum-military commander was later imprisoned by royal order and tried by the Parlement of Paris.[15] For our purposes, therefore, these Waldensians cannot be counted as legally-executed Reformation-era heretics.

Executions for heresy in Reformation Europe probably peaked during the decade 1555–1564. Several significant episodes cluster between these dates. It seems deeply symbolic that Gian Pietro Carafa, a founder of the Roman Inquisition, he who boasted that he would bring faggots to burn his own mother if she were proved to be a heretic, became Pope Paul IV in 1555. His pontificate coincided with the Catholic restoration in England under Mary Tudor. It also coincided with the surprising discovery of Protestant groups in two major cities of Castile in 1557, a shock which moved the Spanish Inquisition into a feverish crusade against '*Luteranos*' during the following decade. Neither kingdom, England or Castile, had known any medieval papal Inquisitors, and neither had hitherto executed many native Protestants. When both places made concerted efforts to uproot the Protestant movement in the late 1550s, their results were diametrically opposite. Paul IV granted emergency powers to the Spanish Inquisition which enabled it to execute even repentant heretics who were first offenders; suitably armed, Spain's Holy Office proceeded to exterminate native Protestantism in Spain during the decade after 1557 through a vigorous campaign, at the price of well over a hundred public executions.[16] On the other hand, England – which had executed almost twice as many Protestants as Spain between 1555 and 1564 – acquired a Protestant sovereign and state church after 1560, which nourished

[14] See my unpublished research on the criminal arrêts of the Parlement of Paris, supplementing Nathaniel Weiss, *La chambre ardente* (Paris, 1889); Mentzer, *Heresy Proceedings*, on Toulouse; H. Patry, *Les débuts de la Réforme protestante en Guyenne, 1523–1559: Arrêts du Parlement de Bordeaux* (Bordeaux, 1912); Crespin, *Histoire des martyrs*, and my work on the Parliament of Rouen.

[15] See Gabriel Audisio, *Les Vaudois du Lubéron: une minorité en Provence* (Mérindol, 1984), 347–407, 531–3.

[16] The classical study remains Ernst Schäfer, *Beiträge zur Geschichte des spanischen Protestantismus und der Inquisition im 16. Jahrhundert*, 3 vols. (Gutersloh, 1902); the useful account of Henry Charles Lea, *A History of the Inquisition of Spain*, 4 vols. (New York, 1908), III, 429–55, relies on it. Extremely thorough on the Crown of Castile, Schäfer's work contains some lacunae on tribunals in the Crown of Aragon, which executed at least fifty *Luteranos* (only two of them native Spaniards) between 1557 and 1566. See my *Frontiers of Heresy*.

indelible memories of 'Bloody Mary' in order to promote anti-Catholic sentiment.[17]

In 1555, Philip II replaced his father as sovereign in the Low Countries, which had been the epicentre of heresy executions in Europe ever since the mid-1530s. During the first decade of his reign, before the virtual breakdown of persecution by 1565, annual averages of executions for heresy doubled over the averages of Mary's regency.[18] Meanwhile, in France, a well-organised Reformed church, whose members had infiltrated even the sovereign Parlements, increasingly frightened Henri II. Although our evidence is less complete here than for most other regions of western Europe, it seems probable that French executions for heresy reached their single-year statistical peak in 1559, symbolically capped by the execution of a judge of the Parlement of Paris that Christmas.[19] Only in the German Empire – the original home of the Reformation and of massive heresy executions – was there relative peace and quiet after the religious settlement following the Augsburg Diet in 1555. Even prosecution of Anabaptists fell off: Claus-Peter Clasen notes that only three Anabaptists were burned for heresy anywhere in the Empire (excluding the Low Countries) after 1550.[20]

Simultaneous with this great upsurge in heresy executions in the mid-1550s came the riposte from Protestant Europe. Reformation Europe saw the first significant general outbreak of religious persecution after the invention of the printing press. As the weight of heresy persecutions moved away from Anabaptist communities to the 'mainstream' Reformed and Anglican traditions, which controlled their own printing presses, a new genre of Protestant martyrologies soon emerged. Between 1554 and 1563 three of them appeared, printed in those same vernaculars in which Protestants usually read their Bibles. In 1554, in the Republic of Geneva (where Calvin had recently helped to arrange the execution of Servetus for heresy), Jean Crespin, a lawyer turned printer, published the first of many editions of his *History of Martyrs persecuted and put to death for the truth of the gospel, from the time of the*

---

[17] Major authorities such as A. G. Dickens, *The English Reformation* (London, 1964), 264–72, count slightly over 280 executions for heresy under Mary Tudor. This is almost exactly double the Spanish Inquisition's totals for *Luteranos* executed during the great persecutions of 1557–66, many of them (as Lea noted) being penitent first offenders.

[18] See authorities cited in notes 5 and 13 of this chapter. It is noteworthy that the city of Antwerp, which led the fight against introducing a Spanish-style Inquisition for the whole Low Countries in the mid-1560s, executed an average of over ten heretics per year after 1555 – the highest such average for any Netherlands jurisdiction up to that time. See F. E. Beemon, 'The Myth of the Spanish Inquisition and the Preconditions for the Dutch Revolt,' *Archive für Reformationsgeschichte* (1994).

[19] See my unpublished research. At the Parlements of Bordeaux and Aix, the total numbers of trials and executions for heresy peaked in 1559.

[20] Clasen, *Anabaptism*, 373. In the Low Countries, a dozen Anabaptists were burned between 1574 and 1588; the final martyr was buried alive in 1597.

apostles to the present, which linked the martyrs of the early church and those of late-medieval Europe with the cycle of people holding mainstream Protestant beliefs recently executed for heresy.[21] Five years later the more ecumenical Antwerp pastor Adrian van Haemstede published another martyrology, overlapping partially with Crespin, but giving fuller information on persecutions in the seventeen provinces of the Netherlands.[22] Four years later came the huge vernacular edition of John Foxe's *Acts and Monuments*, reaching back to pre-Reformation times like Crespin, but with its original research confined essentially to England.[23]

All three martyrologists had been religious refugees. Not surprisingly, the first two were natives of the Low Countries, where persecution had hit not only Anabaptists but also mainstream Protestants much harder than anywhere else. And not surprisingly, all three – but especially those by Crespin and Foxe – became best-sellers. All were repeatedly reprinted, often in updated editions which incorporated the most recent known martyrs; even Haemstede, who had fallen into disrepute with the Dutch Reformed church by the time of his death in 1562, continued to be reprinted in updated versions which omitted the original author's name. Only much later, in the seventeenth-century Dutch 'Golden Age' (which was also a 'Golden Age' of religious toleration), do we find printed martyrologies from the Mennonite branch of the Anabaptist tradition; one important strain of that tradition, the Hutterites, never printed its carefully-maintained chronicle of martyrdoms until the twentieth century.[24]

Each early martyrology was deliberately selective, commemorating only those who were executed for upholding its author's particular creed. Of course, they could and did copy extensively from one another, since they were all engaged in compiling a kind of Protestant calendar of saints, many of whom overlapped. But all of them (even Foxe, who worked under the uniquely favorable conditions of a Protestant government in his native land) had mostly random and scattered sources of information, so they necessarily

---

[21] See Jean-François Gilmont, *Jean Crespin: un éditeur réformé du XVIe siècle* (Geneva, 1981); for the fullest recent account, which does not entirely replace A. Piaget and G. Berthoud, *Notes sur le Livre des Martyrs de Jean Crespin* (Neuchatel, 1930). Neither work pays systematic attention to the problem of Crespin's sources of information.

[22] See Vander Haeghen, *Bibliographie*, 269–378, on Haemstede's *History and Death of Pious Martyrs who have Shed their Blood for the Truths of the Gospel from the Time of Christ until AD 1559.*

[23] See J. F. Mozley, *John Foxe and his Book* (London, 1940).

[24] See Vander Haeghen, *Bibliographie*, II, 23–37, on the various editions of Dutch Anabaptist martyrologies from Jacob Outerman (Haarlem, 1615), to the scholarly T. J. van Braght (Dordrecht, 1660). The Hutterite martyrs' list was first published by A. J. F. Zieglschmid, *Die älteste Chronik der Hutterischen Brüder* (Philadelphia, 1947); see also Josef Beck (ed.), *Die Geschichts-Bücher der Wiedertäufer in Österreich-Ungarn, 1526–1785*, 2nd edn (Nieuwkoop, 1967).

omitted many names of qualified martyrs of their own confessions. Furthermore, every Reformation-era martyrology excluded many people executed by Catholic authorities (and occasionally by Protestants) for certain types of heresy. None of them, for example, considered a mere iconoclast, executed for the crime of sacrilege, to be worthy of commemoration as a martyr (for instance, the six ultra-violent Battenberger Anabaptists executed at Amsterdam in 1540).[25] Nor would they commemorate those extremist anticlericals executed for gross blasphemy, *e.g.*, against the virginity of Mary. Nor anyone who recanted after conviction in order to procure an easier death for himself. Nor anyone who revealed the names of fellow-Protestants to his jailers, even though he was nevertheless executed for heresy and maintained his beliefs to the end. Many such people have fallen into my net, since I have gone fishing for them primarily in the records of secular Catholic authorities.

It is easy enough to see how such militant martyrologies as Crespin's fed into Protestant confessionalism and form part of the background of the Wars of Religion which erupted in 1562 in France and 1566 in the Low Countries. Curiously enough, in both cases the outbreak of hostilities was immediately preceded *not* by intensified rates of persecution, but rather by the virtual cessation of executions for heresy. In France, it was the Queen Mother Catherine de' Medici who persuaded her teenaged son to issue a general religious pardon in March 1560 which effectively decriminalized the Reformed church.[26] In the Low Countries, it was the pressure of local magnates on the regent Margaret of Parma which led to the virtual cessation of heresy executions in 1565.

Of course, this situation changed radically once warfare actually broke out. The legal systems of both countries were pushed to their limits in order to deal with the multitudes of French Huguenots captured after the rebellions of 1562; for example, more than 120 of them were executed by the Parlement of Toulouse after a failed coup in May 1562 – twice the total executions for heresy by the same institution during the preceding thirty years.[27] And in the Netherlands, once again the epicentre of the legal repression of heresy, the 'Council of Troubles' instituted by the Duke of Alva has an even sadder record, with more than 1,000 documented executions between 1567 and 1574.[28] The most savage repression fell on the rebellious Walloon cities of

---

[25] Tracy, *Holland under Habsburg Rule*, 170.

[26] This little-known but highly important royal edict, presented to the Parlement of Paris on 11 March 1560, can be read in the 'Journal' of Nicolas Brulart, in D.-F. Secousse, ed., *Mémoires de Condé*, 6 vols. (London, 1743–45), I, 9–11.

[27] See Joan Davies, 'Persecution and Protestantism: Toulouse 1562–1575, *The Historical Journal*, 22 (1979), 31–51, esp. 34.

[28] A. L. E. Verheyden, *Le Conseil des Troubles: Liste des condamnés (1567–1573)* (Brussels, 1961), for the fullest introduction. It is noteworthy how Alva followed Philip II's secret

Valenciennes and Tournai, each suffering even more executions than Toulouse.[29]

However, the most important point for us to keep in mind is that these executions were not simply deaths for heresy, carried out by secular authorities. There was now abundant justification for secular judges to hand down death sentences to members of a rival religious organisation (and in the age of confessionalism, the significant word is indeed 'organisation') for sedition, *lèse-majesté*, rebellion, and conspiracy. Even the Protestant ministers and schoolteachers executed in the later 1560s were officially condemned for non-religious charges, and were no longer burned at the stake but hanged.[30] The crime of heresy had become so fully secularised that it almost disappeared from legal vocabularies – except in the case of Netherlands Anabaptists, who stubbornly persisted in denying the legitimacy of all secular governments and continued to suffer death by ways now traditionally associated with punishing heretics.

By 1575 executions of Protestants for heresy had entered its final phase. In the Low Countries, once the 'Council of Troubles' ceased functioning, heresy executions ceased entirely in the rebellious and Protestant north and became relatively scarce even in the southern provinces which re-formed the Habsburg Netherlands: even the Mennonite martyrologies show a sharp decline across the final quarter of the sixteenth century, with the last such death occurring in 1597 at Brussels, where the whole sorry business had begun seventy-four years previously. In France, where the Holy League mobilized Counter-Reformation zealotry across much of the kingdom and often controlled court systems by the late 1580s, there were only a few token executions of Reformed Protestants for heresy: the Foucault sisters, condemned to death by the Parlement of Paris in 1588, suffered virtually the last of the old-style martyrdoms.[31] Elizabethan Britain was now clearly Prot-

---

instructions (508) that he create a special tribunal to judge heretics and rebels, but *por ningun caso se llame Inquisition, por ser nombre tan odioso a aquellas pueblos*.

[29] Valenciennes recorded 128 deaths between 1567 and 1570, including 57 in four days in January 1569: see the works of P. Beuzard, summarized in H. Platelle (ed.), *Histoire de Valenciennes* (Lille, 1982), 108–9. Tournai surpassed even this with 181 deaths recorded during the same four-year period: see Meyhoffer, *Martyrologue*, 158–9. Many executions of political leaders were carried out at the capital in Brussels, whose heresy totals reached almost 150 during the Alva years: Verheyden, *Martyrologe*, 228–38.

[30] The failure of the French state and its legal system to execute Huguenots for heresy after 1560, and particularly its failure to impose the traditional mutilations and burnings on those whom it did condemn, go a long way to explain the much-studied popular Catholic 'rites of violence' in France, which exploded between 1562 and 1572. Despite the famous studies by Natalie Davis, Jeanine Garrison-Estèbe, Denis Crouzet *et al.*, this problem has never been placed in its legal-chronological context.

[31] For final heresy executions by the Parliament of Paris, see Pierre de l'Estoile, *Mémoires-Journaux*, 12 vols. (Paris, 1875–96), III, 120–1, 166 (Foucault sisters), 286; corroborated by Archives de la Préfecture de Police, Paris, Ab 10, fols. 183v, 245v (Marie Vuade, June 1589)

estant, and burned nobody for heresy after 1575,[32] although it continued as in Henry VIII's day to create sizable numbers of Catholic martyrs, in Ireland as well as in England. The Holy Roman Empire and Switzerland cranked along, executing six known Anabaptists in the 1590s and five more before 1618.[33]

The only region of Europe in which heresy executions remained relatively frequent in the final quarter of the sixteenth century was in Fernand Braudel's Mediterranean world. Counter-Reformation Rome was the only place in Catholic Europe where almost twice as many heretics were executed during the final third of the sixteenth century as during its middle third – but their numbers are hardly huge: about 25 heretics died at Rome between 1546 and 1566, and about fifty between 1567 and 1600. Elsewhere in Italy, at such centres as Venice or Milan, the picture seems similar.[34] In Spain, Seville offered thirty such spectacles after 1570; when Philip II announced his intention to preside over an *auto de fe* at Toledo in 1591, an unrepentant Scot had to be imported from Seville in order to die in the royal presence. In northern Spain, the Navarrese Inquisition executed a dozen Frenchman in two years in the early 1590s. A Huguenot died at an *auto* in Saragossa in 1604, the last such instance in mainland Spain.[35] Even in Habsburg Spain, religious toleration loomed on the horizon around 1600.

Heresy executions began in Reformation Europe in 1523; they generally peaked around 1560 and became relatively rare after 1570, except in the

and by the interrogations in Archives Nationales, Paris, X2a 956 (27 and 28 June 1588, Foucault sisters; 6 May 1589, Marie Vuade; 12 May 1589, Marie de Flins). This brief Parisian revival of the old custom of burning the bodies of executed heretics was not followed at nearby Rouen, where the final execution for heresy in May 1588 simply hanged an offending schoolteacher, but burned the 'blasphemous' anti-Catholic manuscript found in his possession: Archives Départementales Seine-Maritime 1B3212 (Guillaume Reilley, 27 May 1588).

[32] Philip Hughes, *The Reformation in England*, 3 vols. (London, 1950–54), III, 411–13, prints the royal warrants for burning two Anabaptists at Smithfield in 1575.

[33] Clasen, *Anabaptism*, 437.

[34] For sixteenth century heresy executions at Rome, see Domenico Orano, *Liberi pensatori bruciati in Roma dal XVI al XVIII secolo* (1904; Livorno, 1971), 7–90, 118, slightly modified by Luigi Firpo, 'Esecuzioni capitali in Roma (1567–1671)', in *Eresia e Riforma nell'Italia del Cinquecento* (Florence, 1974), 307–42; Orano's list includes many non-heretics, such as the half-dozen Catholic sodomites burned on August 13, 1578 (55–61: compare my *Frontiers of Heresy*, 292 n. 34). For fourteen heresy drownings at Venice, see Paul F. Grendler, *The Roman Inquisition and the Venetian Press, 1540–1605* (Princeton, 1977), 57–60. Milan, like Venice, had a half-dozen deaths for heresy during the final third of the century: see Biblioteca Ambrogiana, Ms. Ambrosiana S.Q. ✠ 1.6. ('Esecuzioni capitali [1568–1630]'). After 1567, the busiest spot in Italy for executions of Protestants outside of Rome was probably the Spanish Inquisition's tribunal at Palermo (*Frontiers of Heresy*, 49, 168–9), which in 1542 had also recorded the first such execution in Italy.

[35] For the Spanish Inquisition's executions of *Luteranos* in Philip II's Spain after 1575, see Schäfer, II, 288–342 on Seville and my *Frontiers of Heresy*, 240–50; also Geoffrey Parker, *Philip II* (Boston, 1978), 99–100.

Catholic Mediterranean. They form an ominous statistical mountain on the legal landscape of late-Renaissance Christendom, beginning virtually *ex nihilo* (except in late-Lollard England or *converso*-ridden Spain). By the early 1550s they had become sufficiently commonplace for such Protestant literati as Crespin and Foxe to hit independently on the idea of connecting ancient with modern Christian martyrdoms. The Hutterites, who had an even clearer vision of the value of martyrdom as a form of apostolic Christian witness, kept fairly careful score of their sixteenth-century martyrs but felt no need to print it. The general phenomenon, like the 'price revolution' of the sixteenth century, can be studied through statistical and geographical tabulations. But obviously its significance does not end with such a tabulation. One must fit these statistics into many kinds of contexts.

Let me suggest one such context, occasionally hinted at but never, to my knowledge, clearly spelled out – perhaps because it connects two groups of historians who rarely read each other's works, namely historians of the Reformation and historians of witchcraft. If one seeks to illuminate not the history of the Protestant Reformation but the history of European witchcraft persecutions, then this statistical mountain encumbering the legal horizons of so many European regions between 1520 and 1565 assumes enormous significance. It goes a very long way to explain a very curious and very great gap in a chronologically incoherent story. If European witchcraft doctrine was quite well developed by the late fifteenth century, with an acceleration of recorded trials and deaths in several places and with the publication of the *Malleus Maleficarum* in 1486, why was this doctrine largely kept on the shelf until the final third of the sixteenth century? Why was the *Malleus* never reprinted between 1520 (a pregnant date!) and 1585? Why was the theoretical secularisation of most of the doctrines in the *Malleus* only completed after 1580 by such legally-trained demonologists as Jean Bodin? And, when witch-hunting revived across western Europe after 1560, why did it spread so far and accelerate so quickly? One crucial part of the answer is that so many governments had previously secularised heresy trials by the 1530s.

Let me try to make some simple chronological *rapprochements* between these two major aspects of Renaissance Europe as a persecuting society. In the Holy Roman Empire: religious peace of Augsburg 1555, first major witch-panic (over sixty deaths) in a small Lutheran city, 1562. In Tudor England: end of Marian persecutions 1558, first witchcraft statute stipulating the death penalty 1563, soon accompanied by a few executions. In the kingdom of France (which lacked a statute about witchcraft), this *rapprochement* seems incredibly close. Leafing through the criminal *arrêts* of the Parlement of Toulouse for summer 1562, one finds death sentences for two Huguenot traitors on one page and, literally on the next page, the first two death sentences from France's earliest known major witch-hunt, which eventually involved 35 imprisoned defendants from four neighbouring villages.[36] Instead of intervals of five or seven years, one began as the other was ending.

Since I have said so much about the Low Countries, let me offer a *rapprochement* which is more structural than chronological: if large numbers of executions for heresy followed Charles V's famous placards of 1529, it is equally true that large numbers of executions followed his son's placards of 1592 about witchcraft. The importance of both placards was to remove jurisdiction over a 'mixed' crime (one shared between spiritual and secular courts) from the gentler hands of ecclesiastical judges, enabling even seigneurial courts to pronounce – and implement – death sentences for this offence. What the new Lord of Esmeriez in Hainaut did to his father's barber in 1533, his successors did to unpopular old women across many parts of the Habsburg Netherlands sixty years later – now charged with a different type of *lèse-majesté* against God and humanity. In between had come the wars of religion, fought here with special savagery, perhaps delaying the start of effective witch-hunting far longer than in most neighbouring states.

If I have spoken of the 3,000 heresy executions of Reformation Europe as a statistical mountain, it resembles a foothill when compared to the witchcraft Alps of Europe's persecuting societies. The order of magnitude is approximately one to ten: 3,000 heresy deaths within a half-century after 1520 (excluding Alva's 'Council of Troubles'), but slightly more than 30,000 witchcraft deaths within the 'confessional century' after 1560.[37] In both instances, the epicenter of persecution was in the Holy Roman Empire, where the Dominican Inquisitors who wrote the *Malleus* had hunted witches during Luther's infancy. But if 2,000 Anabaptists had perished in the Empire and the Low Countries by 1575, over 20,000 witches followed them after 1580.

This *rapprochement* works in two other ways. First, there is the virtual absence of executions for witchcraft by the major Inquisitions of Braudel's Mediterranean world. As we have seen, this was the only European region where heresy executions either persisted (Spain) or actually increased slightly

---

[36] Archives Départementales Haute-Garonne, Toulouse, B3440, fols. 317–18 (1 July 1562).

[37] Although this seems a perversely low general estimate, there are weighty reasons to continue downsizing our overall totals of witchcraft executions in Europe from 1560 to 1730. For Germany, the centre of this phenomenon, Wolfgang Behringer has recently proposed a total of 22,500 deaths: see Robert Muchembled, *Le roi et la sorcière: L'Europe des bûchers, XVe–XVIIIe siècle* (Paris, 1993), 109–13, taken from Behringer's contribution to a recent anthology, Muchembled (ed.), *Magie et sorcellerie en Europe* (Paris, 1995). I would add another five thousand executions in the western borderlands theoretically included within the old Holy Roman Empire, today part of Belgium, France, and Switzerland; but I would add under a thousand for the old kingdom of France (a figure far below the most widely known but utterly unsubstantiated current estimates), plus 2,500 for all of northern and northwestern Europe (half of them in Scotland), where we possess very reliable evidence, plus a few hundred for Mediterranean Europe. The great unknown, apart from France, remains Poland.

(Rome) during the final third of the sixteenth century. It was also the only region where the major Inquisitions never abandoned their claims to jurisdiction over maleficent witchcraft, although in practice neither was ever able to enforce any monopoly over witch-trials. Wherever ecclesiastical justice was still willing and able to put stubborn heretics to death as late as 1600, it had little desire to see witches burned.[38] Second, there is a negative *rapprochement*, a counter-correlation. The major kingdoms of northern and eastern Europe (Sweden, Poland, Bohemia, Hungary) were spared heresy executions during the Reformation era. Lacking any recent experience with the secularisation of an ecclesiastical crime, they waited a very long time before stepping up the prosecution of witches by secular judges. The witch-craze reached these kingdoms a century later than western and west-central Europe.

Indeed, there are many ways to fit the history of heresy executions in Reformation Europe into place as the missing piece, providing both the precedent for and immediate prelude to the history of executions for witchcraft in confessional Europe. It is also possible, for example, that the widespread popular acceptance of the doctrine of the witches' Sabbath during the great persecutions of the confessional century – a relatively obscure concept among the laity at the time of the *Malleus Maleficarum* – owed more to fresh and vivid memories of clandestine conventicles uncovered by heresy-hunters during the preceding decades than to recycled tales about the orgies of medieval heretics. In fact, I can see only two great differences between the persecution of heretics during the Reformation and the persecution of witches under confessionalism. The first is in scope: witch-hunts were even more widespread than heresy hunts, and ten times more fatal. The second is that witches never published any martyrologies.

---

[38] The Spanish Inquisition's famous aberration in Navarre from 1609 to 1614 was exactly that, an aberration – and fewer than a dozen people died because of it: see the classic account by Gustav Henningsen, *The Witches' Advocate: Basque Witchcraft and the Spanish Inquisition* (Reno, 1980), and my *Frontiers of Heresy*, 270–5, 314–15.

5 *Un roi, une loi, deux fois*: parameters for the history of Catholic-Reformed co-existence in France, 1555–1685

Philip Benedict

At first glance, France's history in the sixteenth and seventeenth centuries seems to present a series of paradoxes for the historian of tolerance and intolerance. In 1562, the country became one of the first powerful monarchies of the Reformation era to grant freedom of worship to more than one Christian confession, yet over the following decade this pioneer in religious toleration witnessed the era's bloodiest and most horrifying episodes of popular religious intolerance, culminating in the Saint Bartholomew's Massacre. Over the subsequent decades, France moved more successfully toward establishing peaceful co-existence between Catholics and Protestants. Then, despite this success, Louis XIV earned himself an enduring place in the annals of intolerance by revoking the Edict of Nantes. This essay will suggest that the apparent paradoxes of this situation disappear when certain of the potential oversimplifications and pitfalls contained within that somewhat Whiggish construct, the 'history of toleration', are recognised, and when the effort is made to write a history of Catholic-Reformed co-existence in France adequate to the complexity of the phenomena. The essay will also try to outline the basic elements of such a history – not always an easy task, since many aspects of the subject remain poorly understood.

The 'history of toleration'

Toleration is a quality that most members of modern liberal societies prize – until they have to put up with something truly intolerable. Where they might draw the line is infinitely varied. Tolerance is not a polymorphously perverse attribute, capable of extension in any direction, possessed by certain individuals or societies and lacked by others. Instead, the toleration or prohibition of specific forms of thought or behaviour is intimately bound up with prevailing ideas about both the particular matter at stake and the larger nature of the political community, with practical considerations of power, and with the extent and character of the personal contacts between those who might do the persecuting and those who might be persecuted. There can be no unified history of toleration, except perhaps a history of the idea itself and of the

65

migrations of arguments for toleration from the contexts in which they originally developed to other ones deemed analogous. A history of the social practices normally denoted by the concept involves multiple, if sometimes interconnected, histories of the tolerance or intolerance of specific groups or forms of behaviour.

To keep the scope of this chapter within manageable proportions, the focus here will be entirely upon the largest religious minority to emerge in early modern France and the one whose existence within the realm posed the most disruptive and enduring questions of public order: the Reformed Protestants.[1] Between 1555, when the first churches were established in France along the lines urged by Calvin and the ministers he sent out from Geneva, and 1562, when the first of the Wars of Religion broke out, Reformed churches proliferated across France with extraordinary rapidity. A thousand or more Reformed churches may have been founded in these years. Many soon met in public, often seizing Catholic churches to do so. Some attracted the majority of the population of the community in which they were located. In a few towns, such as Castres, the ideas of the 'new religion' were so thoroughly dominant by late 1561 that the city magistrates had carried through the equivalent of a civic Reformation. Although the exact strength of the movement in this period may never be known, its adepts probably numbered at least a million and a half people by the time its growth had run its course. Over the next three centuries, its ranks would be thinned at several moments by the blows that would befall it, but until the end of the nineteenth century, the questions of what claims the Reformed could make upon the political nation, what rights the faith was to be accorded, and how its members interacted with their Catholic neighbours were the most pressing issues that religious, racial, or ethnic divisions posed for France.

The sudden emergence of so large a religious minority is the basic historical fact from which any history of Catholic-Reformed relations in France must start. How thoroughly did the transformation of the religious situation alter prevailing views about the wisdom of tolerating two faiths within the kingdom? How did the law grapple with the existence of a large religious minority and with the challenge to public order created by the sudden emergence of deeply antagonistic understandings of Christianity? How deep were the social fissures that opened up between the two faiths, and to what extent did the existence of these religious divisions trouble the social order? These are the fundamental historical questions posed by this transformation. The exploration of these questions for the period from 1555 to 1685 offers three

---

[1] Other histories of toleration could be written about the Lutherans, the Anabaptists, the Jews, those Catholic movements that with time came to be defined as heterodox such as the Jansenists, the treatment of 'atheists' and 'libertines', and the problems raised by the criminalisation of blasphemy and sodomy.

sets of parameters for understanding the apparent mixture of tolerance and intolerance that marked the history of Catholic-Reformed co-existence over these years.

Ideas about freedom of conscience and worship

It is useful to begin with the *Begriffsgeschichte* of the phrases 'toleration' and 'freedom of conscience'. As the detailed semantic analysis of William H. Huseman has shown, nobody in sixteenth-century France conceived of the former as a good thing. The verb *tolérer* was most often employed around 1560 by the partisans of a hard line against heresy to denote a distressing course of action that they opposed. Roughly synonymous with *souffrir* or *endurer*, the word denoted the unpleasant experience of being subjected to some evil.[2] The first edition of the dictionary of the Académie Française, published in 1694, put only a slightly more positive spin on the word, defining *tolérance* as 'condescension or indulgence for what one cannot prevent', as in the phrase 'it is not a right, but a tolerance.' Only in the eighteenth century did the word take on the range of positive connotations most famously expressed in the classic entry on the subject in the *Encyclopédie*, where tolerance is presented as the humane recognition of our species' incapacity for arriving at moral or intellectual certitude, and of the consequent unfairness of punishing anybody for their beliefs.[3]

As for the expression 'freedom of conscience,' Joseph Lecler has shown that its initial appearance in the Reformation era, in the writings of Luther, Melanchthon, and with slightly different phraseology, Calvin, denoted something quite different from the modern concept. The phrase initially referred not to the freedom that individuals might enjoy from having their deepest religious convictions subject to government constraint and punishment, but to the conscience's liberation through faith from the fear and doubt that were its fate for those still mired in the errors of Catholicism. It was in France between 1559 and 1561 that authors first began to speak of '*liberté de conscience*' in the sense in which the phrase is understood today. Typically, such liberty was simply proposed as a remedy for the problems facing the country rather than as a positive good in itself, but the phrase entered into the law codes in the Edict of Amboise of 1563 and was linked in the writings of certain authors with opposition to the forcing of consciences, depicted as a

---

[2] Huseman, 'The Expression of the Idea of Toleration in French During the Sixteenth Century', *Sixteenth Century Journal*, 15 (1984), 293–310.

[3] *Encyclopédie, ou Dictionnaire raisonné des arts et sciences*, 3rd edn (Geneva, 1777), XXXIII, 590; Jean Delumeau, 'La difficile émergence de la tolérance', in Roger Zuber and Laurent Theis (eds.), *La Révocation de l'Edit de Nantes et le protestantisme français en 1685* (Paris, 1986), 359–64; Elisabeth Labrousse, *'Une foi, une loi, un roi?' La Révocation de l'Edit de Nantes* (Geneva, 1985), 95.

form of oppression. The phrase thus had more positive semantic associations. But many contemporaries resisted this. Theodore Beza called '*liberté aux consciences*' 'a thoroughly diabolical dogma'.[4]

Just as the semantic associations of 'tolerance' were largely negative, so the strongest traditions that French political culture inherited from its medieval past were profoundly antithetical to the acceptance of religious division within the kingdom. The precocious development of French national identity in the later Middle Ages had highlighted the kingdom's special fervor for the defence of the church as one of the most evident marks of its status as God's chosen nation. The country was believed to have entered into a special covenant with the divinity at the time of Clovis that subsequently linked its continued existence to its enduring fidelity to the faith. 'I am famed for always having been Catholic, never having nourished heresy, and never will', spoke the figure of France in Georges Chastellain's fifteenth-century mystery play, *Le Concile de Basle*.[5] From 1215 onward, the coronation oath sworn by all new monarchs included a pledge to be diligent in expelling from their lands all heretics designated by the church.[6] Theological and legal circles were meanwhile dominated by the views of Saint Augustine, incorporated into both canon law and scholastic thought, that justified the civil punishment of heresy by Christian rulers on the grounds that (1) this protected society against pestilential doctrines that threatened to lead others astray; (2) advanced the glory of God by demonstrating abhorrence for doctrines contrary to his honour; and (3) contributed to the potential redemption of the heretics themselves by providing the sort of sanction that was often necessary to induce people to abandon erroneous views.[7]

Although these traditions would powerfully shape the response to heresy in the sixteenth century, European culture was sufficiently varied at the end of the Middle Ages to provide intellectual resources to defend as well as oppose the extension of rights of worship to more than one Christian church. Political theories presenting secular government as a purely human construction whose highest priority was maintaining civil order had been articulated by scholastic theorists. Erasmus combined an emphasis on the virtues of peace with scepticism about the possibility of arriving at certain knowledge. When the German evangelicals began organising their own forms of worship,

---

[4] Joseph Lecler, 'Liberté de conscience. Origines et sens divers de l'expression', *Recherches de Science Religieuse*, 54 (1966), 370–406.

[5] Colette Beaune, *Naissance de la nation France* (Paris, 1985), 207–16, esp. 213.

[6] Richard A. Jackson, *Vive le Roi! A History of the French Coronation from Charles V to Charles X* (Chapel Hill, 1984), 58.

[7] On the development of the ideas justifying the punishment of heresy within the medieval church, see Ernest W. Nelson, 'The Theory of Persecution', in *Persecution and Liberty: Essays in Honor of George Lincoln Burr* (New York, 1921), 3–20; Edward Peters, *Inquisition* (Berkeley, 1989), 11–67.

he suggested that allowing non-seditious sects to worship as they chose was a lesser evil than trying to suppress them and provoking war.[8] At least one French author of the early sixteenth century followed Erasmus in articulating certain of the premises that would subsequently undergird defences of freedom of conscience. Pierre du Chastel, a scholar who briefly lodged with Erasmus in Basle and subsequently became Francis I's royal librarian, Grand Almoner, and the bishop of Tulle, Mâcon, and Orléans, declared in 1547 that nobody should be executed for heresy, 'since no mortal man, whoever he may be, can through any human argument or reasoning judge with certainty what is true'.[9]

Du Chastel, however, was an isolated voice. Active debate about whether or not magistrates should punish heresy or permit more than one manner of worship really only began in France as the Reformed churches proliferated in the later 1550s. Then, pamphlets, political and legal assemblies, and handwritten memoranda took up with urgency the issue of how to repair the widening religious schism. One current of opinion advocated a policy of concord that sought to obtain the agreement of all parties to a moderate reform of the Gallican church that would be acceptable both to Rome and to those who had left the communion of the church, and would thereby bring about the reunion of both parties. Certain of the '*moyenneurs*' who championed this course advanced as one argument in its favour the impropriety or unworkability of any '*forcement de conscience*', although they were often far more reluctant to envisage granting freedom of worship, which they saw as threatening to social unity and stability.[10] Others were willing to defend granting the Reformed freedom of worship, especially once the failure of the Colloquy of Poissy dampened hope that a reunion of the churches might be possible. Those who argued in favour of this position, most notably the Chancellor Michel de L'Hôpital, a friend of du Chastel's, did so overwhelmingly on pragmatic grounds: the Reformed had simply grown too numerous and too strong to be denied rights of worship without irreparable harm to the kingdom. The example of both the Roman Empire – under those Christian emperors who had allowed the Arians churches of their own – and contemporary Switzerland (far more than Germany the great illustration of successful religious co-existence at this time) demonstrated that polities could house several Christian churches and still thrive. More principled arguments also appear briefly in a few of these tracts, specifically that forcing people to act contrary to the promptings of their conscience was an illegitimate form of

[8] Joseph Lecler, *Histoire de la tolérance au siècle de la Réforme* (Paris, 1955), I, 134–8.

[9] Malcolm C. Smith, 'Early French Advocates of Religious Freedom', *The Sixteenth Century Journal*, 25 (1994), 34.

[10] Mario Turchetti, *Concordia o tolleranza? François Bauduin (1520–1573) e i 'moyenneurs'* (Geneva, 1984); Smith, 'Early French Advocates', 38–40.

violence, and that the political order did not depend on Christianity, since excommunicates remained citizens.[11]

Against this view, hard-line Catholics defended the traditions of Catholic France, reiterated the Augustinian arguments for punishing heresy, and recalled the king's coronation oath. One even maintained in a Sorbonne debate that the Pope could excommunicate a king who favoured heretics and release his subjects from their obligations of obedience to him. The hard-line Catholics also charged that Calvinism was seditious by nature, a charge soon buttressed with references to the Huguenot efforts to advance their cause by force from the conspiracy of Amboise onward. By the later 1560s, certain Catholic polemicists had developed an account of the country's recent past that was little more than an extended chronicle of Huguenot efforts to destroy the country's churches and exterminate its royal family.[12]

Catherine de Medici – a foreigner to the kingdom's political traditions – had been receiving reports from the provinces throughout 1560 and 1561 illustrating the difficulties of maintaining order between members of the rival faiths. Eager for the support of the heavily Protestant Bourbon family, she accepted the arguments of the partisans of toleration. The Edict of Saint-Germain of January 1562 granted the Reformed freedom of worship 'until such time as God by his grace reunites [our subjects] in one sheepfold.' But the majority of the kingdom's Parlements protested vigorously, and the descent into civil war was swift. The bulk of the political nation, it appears, was unwilling as yet to accept such a policy.[13]

For their part, the kingdom's Protestants were also divided over the desirability of religious tolerance, with the most powerful voices again being hostile to it. Calvin and Beza, of course, were both strongly committed from the 1553 execution of Michael Servetus onward to the view that civil magistrates were obliged to use the power of the sword to defend the true faith against heretics. A 1561 synod of the churches of Guyenne and Haut-Languedoc similarly declared the suppression of heresy to be a magistrate's duty, while the majority of the petitions and appeals that the Reformed

---

[11] *Mémoires de Condé* (London, 1740), II, 732–42, 892–929; Lecler, *Histoire de la tolérance*, II, 36–62, 68–72; Smith, 'Early French Advocates', 37–8, 40–8.

[12] Barbara B. Diefendorf, 'Simon Vigor: A Radical Preacher in Sixteenth-Century Paris', *The Sixteenth Century Journal*, 18 (1987), 399–410; Diefendorf, *Under the Cross: Catholics and Huguenots in Sixteenth-Century Paris* (Oxford, 1991), 50–61; Philip Benedict, 'Of Marmites and Martyrs: Images and Polemics in the Wars of Religion', *The French Renaissance in Prints from the Bibliothèque Nationale de France* (exhibition catalogue, Los Angeles, 1994), 111–14, 121.

[13] A. Lublinskaja (ed.), *Documents pour servir à l'histoire des guerres civiles en France* (Moscow, 1962), docs. 1–13; André Stegmann (ed.), *Edits des guerres de religion* (Paris, 1979), 10; Lucien Romier, *Catholiques et huguenots à la cour de Charles IX* (Paris, 1924), 303ff; Diefendorf, *Under the Cross*, 62.

addressed to the crown between 1559 and 1561 sought to persuade the rulers not to allow two kinds of churches in the kingdom, but to embrace the one true church, and to stamp out popish idolatry as a most Christian king should.[14] Some within the new Reformed churches dissented. Pierre Viret opposed state punishment of heresy and was more willing than either Calvin or Beza to extend toleration to sectarians and to believe that people of different religions could live peacefully together. An early member of the church of Beaugency, Jean Bonneau, was called before the consistory for maintaining that it was wrong for the magistrates to punish heretics. Significantly, Bonneau was made to retract his views.[15] The Beza-Calvin position was the dominant one.

Active discussion of issues of freedom of conscience and worship continued throughout the subsequent century and a third. No comprehensive effort has yet been made to survey the entire discussion, but its contours appear to have been modified in three ways.

First, Catholic opinion about the practical wisdom of tolerating two faiths oscillated significantly as the Wars of Religion advanced. In the later 1570s, after more than a decade of bloodshed had taken a vast toll in lives without resulting in the elimination of heresy, certain of those who initially favoured defending unity of religion by force swung around to accept the most powerful prudential argument against this, namely that its human and political costs were simply too great to bear. At the Estates-General of 1576, a number of leading Catholic noblemen who had previously been ardent persecutors of the Huguenots were willing to advocate peace and toleration of Reformed worship 'until by means of a council, another meeting of the estates, or any other means ... God can bless us with only one religion'. A bare majority of the Third Estate voted in favour of renewed war and repeal of the generous conditions granted the Protestants under the Peace of Beaulieu, despite vigorous royal lobbying in this direction.[16] The pendulum swung in the other direc-

---

[14] Robert M. Kingdom, *Geneva and the Coming of the Wars of Religion in France, 1555–1563* (Geneva, 1956), 87; *Mémoires de Condé*, I, 341–96, 409–80; II, 481–530, 546–60, 578–84, 644–59, 743–5, 807–11, esp. 647.

[15] Robert Dean Linder, *The Political Ideas of Pierre Viret* (Geneva, 1964), ch. 8; Yves Gueneau, 'Protestants du Centre 1598–1685 (Ancienne province synodale d'Orléanais-Berry). Approches d'une minorité' (thèse de 3e cycle, Université François Rabelais de Tours, 1982), 33–4. See also G. Baum, E. Cunitz and E. Reuss (eds.), *Opera Calvini* (Brunswick, 1863–80), XV, 435–46.

[16] Lecler, *Histoire de la tolérance*, II, chs. 4–5. For the details on the Estates-General of 1576: Mark Greengrass, 'A Day in the Life of the Third Estate: Blois, 26th December 1576', in Adrianna E. Bakos (ed.), *Politics, Ideology and the Law in Early Modern Europe: Essays in Honor of J. H. M. Salmon* (Rochester, 1994), 73–90; Mack Holt, *The French Wars of Religion, 1562–1629* (Cambridge, 1995), 108–9 citing the particularly revealing speeches of Louis de Bourbon, duke of Montpensier, and Pierre Blanchefort. I would like to thank Prof. Holt for allowing me to see his work prior to publication. Montaigne's views similarly evolved over

tion after the duke of Alençon's death raised the spectre of a Protestant succession. No precedents existed of Protestant monarchs who had not sought to bring the religious establishment of their kingdoms into line with their own personal beliefs. Many Catholics consequently feared that their faith would be subjected to the sort of persecution then being meted out to their co-religionists in England unless Protestantism was quickly eradicated and Navarre's accession to the throne blocked. When the bishop of Le Mans tried to argue at the Estates-General of 1588 that good example, teaching, and prayers were the only proper weapons for combatting heresy, he was shouted down and censured. Opinion shifted once more after Henry IV converted in 1593, reducing the threat of a Protestant king. The especially intense devastation of the Wars of the League, combined with the fact that the Protestants again survived a period of proscription and emerged with their power intact, further reinforced the view that there was no practical alternative to toleration. By the early seventeenth century, even the Assemblies of the kingdom's Catholic clergy professed their willingness to tolerate Reformed worship until such time as it might be possible to reunite the country once again in the true faith. The arguments of those Catholic historians and political writers of the early seventeenth century who defended allowing Reformed worship rarely recognized a generalised right to freedom of conscience or worship, however. Both Jacques-Auguste de Thou and Jean Silhon, for instance, asserted that rulers could legitimately strive to maintain unity of religion. Once a heresy had grown strong, though, it was wisest to leave it in peace.[17]

Secondly, a number of Reformed thinkers came with time to articulate stronger and more generally applicable arguments for freedom of conscience and worship. In the tracts and memoranda written by Philippe du Plessis-Mornay between 1576 and 1597, this influential Huguenot statesman began to defend rights of worship for Catholic and Reformed alike, even embracing certain of Castellio's ideas on freedom of conscience after spending time in the circles around William of Orange in the Low Countries.[18] In the gener-

---

the early decades of the Wars of Religion towards the acceptance of two faiths within the kingdom. Malcolm C. Smith, *Montaigne and Religious Freedom: The Dawn of Pluralism* (Geneva, 1991).

[17] Bernard Dompnier, *Le venin de l'hérésie. Image du protestantisme et combat catholique au XVIIe siècle* (Paris, 1985), 116–18; Lecler, *Histoire de la tolérance*, II, 108; François Laplanche, *L'Ecriture, le sacré, et l'histoire. Erudits et politiques protestants devant la Bible en France au XVIIe siècle* (Amsterdam, 1986), 392; Etienne Thuau, *Raison d'état et pensée politique à l'époque de Richelieu* (Paris, 1966), 207, 274–5. As this last work makes clear, a few Catholic authors advocated freedom of conscience or worship as a broader value, on the grounds that only God controlled people's consciences.

[18] Du Plessis-Mornay's various writings on this subject may be found in his *Mémoires et Correspondances* (Paris, 1824). Lecler, *Histoire de la tolérance*, II, 90–1, 181–4; and Marie-Madeleine Fragonard, 'La liberté de conscience chez Du Plessis-Mornay (1576–1598)', in

ations following the Edict of Nantes, the broadest current within Huguenot opinion sought to solidify the rights of worship that the Edict granted the Reformed with the narrow legal argument that the decree was perpetual and irrevocable by virtue of its frequent confirmation and more akin to a treaty between the king and his subjects than an ordinary law. Since kings were obliged to respect the treaties they entered into, they could not annul it. But a few thinkers built upon the historicisation of Old Testament precedents by the humanists and theologians of the Academy of Saumur and the new emphasis on natural law arguments that Grotius and his successors deployed to meet the sceptical challenge of the late sixteenth century, in order to articulate general arguments for freedom of conscience. Moyse Amyraut's vast *Morale chrestienne* (1652–60) argued that God was the author of the laws of nature and good government as well as of religion. In affairs of state, the laws of nature and good government took priority, and dictated that constraint was of no value in matters of conscience, since only persuasion and good example could convince people of religious truth. The examples of ancient Israelite rulers who had destroyed idols were irrelevant to Christian practice, since all of the events of the Old Testament were purely figurative except for the proclamation of the Ten Commandments.[19] At the end of the century, Pierre Bayle defended freedom of conscience for all, even atheists, with a battery of arguments that turned the classic religious justifications for persecution inside out. Thus, he observed that while those who punished heretics claimed to be defending God's honour against those who affronted it, the majority of those guilty of heresy in fact acted from a sincere effort to honour God as they understood this was supposed to be done. In such a situation, the persecutors were themselves guilty of offending God by arrogating to themselves His function of judging each individual's faith. Bayle also drew upon natural law to argue that the functions of secular government were purely temporal, and he had no difficulty imagining a town in which the members of ten religions lived together in 'the same concord . . . as in a city where various kinds of artisans support one another' – so long as all embraced 'the tolerance I support' and did not try to harm the others through persecution.[20] Under pressure to defend the constantly challenged rights of

Hans R. Guggisberg, Frank Lestringant and Jean-Claude Margolin (eds.), *La liberté de conscience (XVIe–XVIIe siècles): Actes du Colloque de Mulhouse et Bâle (1989)* (Geneva, 1991), 135–52, provide important secondary treatments.

[19] For the development of Amyraut's views on toleration, see Laplanche, *L'Ecriture, le sacré, et l'Histoire*, 387–9, 484–9. More generally, this magisterial work demonstrates the importance of the new exegetical methods of the school of Saumur. Richard Tuck, 'The "modern" theory of natural law', in Anthony Pagden (ed.), *The Langauges of Political Theory in Early-Modern Europe* (Cambridge, 1987), 99–119; and Tuck, *Philosophy and Government 1572–1651* (Cambridge, 1993) are no less important in demonstrating the nature and advance of natural law thinking in the seventeenth century.

[20] Elisabeth Labrousse, *Pierre Bayle* (The Hague, 1964), II, 497–591.

worship granted their minority faith, a number of Huguenot theorists thus contributed significantly to the development of the far richer and more powerful set of arguments for toleration that had emerged within the European republic of letters by the end of the seventeenth century.[21]

Thirdly, another argument was added to the arsenal of toleration's defenders with the advance of modes of thinking that emphasised the needs of the state and its financial and military well-being. At the moment of the Revocation of the Edict of Nantes, the most forthright argument against the measure by a Catholic figure of influence came from the military engineer and army officer Sébastien le Prestre de Vauban, who stressed the costs to the state of driving abroad a group with the military and commercial skills of the Huguenots.[22]

The overall universe of discourse thus grew more favourable to arguments for freedom of conscience or worship by the end of the seventeenth century. Still, the great majority of political and legal theorists remained opposed to the principle of either freedom of conscience or worship. The professors at the kingdom's law schools continued to teach that obdurate heresy was quite properly a capital offence. The Paris faculty of theology censured an English Benedictine who declared in a book published in France in 1627: 'the prince is required by God's law to maintain each person in his kingdom in whatever religion he professes without molesting them for their consciences'.[23] The majority of the Reformed were scarcely better disposed to generalised freedom of conscience or worship. In 1690, a synod of the then Huguenot dominated Walloon churches in the Netherlands censured the propositions that reason and piety require the toleration of all heresies, that the magistrate has no right to use his power to abolish idolatry or stop the progress of heresy, and that all people may not just believe but also teach what they wish.[24] It is wrong to think that the Revocation was an anachronistic throwback to a bygone era of intolerance. Instead, it was the act of a monarchy that had grown considerably in strength since the sixteenth century, could imagine that the eradication of heresy was within its grasp with few of the costs that had been associated with pursuing the goal a century earlier, and was pleased to carry out a policy that the great majority of the Catholic majority continued to consider fitting for a Most Christian King.

---

[21] A development remarked upon by Bayle himself in his *Supplément* to his *Commentaire philosophique sur ces paroles de J. C. contrains-les d'entrer*. Labrousse, *Bayle*, 542n. Delumeau's contrary assertion that 'tout avait été dit dès le XVIe siècle' is unconvincing. Delumeau, 'Difficile émergence de la tolérance', 374.

[22] Geoffrey Adams, *The Huguenots and French Opinion 1685–1787: The Enlightenment Debate on Toleration* (Waterloo, Ontario, 1991), 19–30.

[23] L. W. B. Brockliss, *French Higher Education in the Seventeenth and Eighteenth Centuries: A Cultural History* (Oxford, 1987), 323–4.

[24] Frank Puaux, *Les précurseurs français de la tolérance au XVIIe siècle* (Paris, 1881), 122.

The law and its observance

Government policy thus evolved within a field of discourse dominated by the idea that the king ought to repress false belief, but which at the same time contained space for the conviction that political necessity might occasionally impel the toleration of two or more forms of worship within one realm. The law itself followed a complicated course. From 1562 to 1598, legal measures granted, revoked, and modified permission for Reformed worship in rapid succession, with the measures granting permission attempting at the same time to define terms on which the two confessions could peaceably coexist. During the period from 1598 to 1685, the fixed star of the Edict of Nantes lent considerably greater stability to the broad parameters of the law, but details continued to be modified. At every point from 1562 to 1685, a gap existed between the letter of the law and its implementation.

It is more difficult than might be imagined to establish just what the law decreed in the matter of religious toleration from 1560 to 1598. Eight different edicts, all but the first of them edicts of pacification bringing a civil war to a close, accorded the Reformed more or less generous freedom of worship.[25] The evolution of their provisions betrays an effort to define terms acceptable to both sides. The Edict of January 1562 allowed the Protestants to assemble wherever they chose outside the walls of the kingdom's cities; the following four edicts restricted Protestant worship to a limited number of localities; the more generous 1576 Peace of Beaulieu restored complete freedom of worship for the Reformed except in the vicinity of Paris or the royal court, but this provoked the formation of the first nationwide Catholic League; and the subsequent edicts of pacification, including the Edict of Nantes, again limited the Reformed to a specified set of localities. Three other royal decrees formally revoked all Reformed freedom of worship – in 1568, 1572, and 1585. The measure of 1585, occasioned by the spectre of a Protestant succession to the throne and the formation of the second Catholic League, was particularly severe. It suspended freedom of conscience as well as of worship for the Reformed, made the practice of Catholicism obligatory for all Frenchmen within six months, and gave all ministers a month to leave the country. From 1585 to 1591, and longer in those parts of the country controlled by the League, Reformed belief was once more punishable as heresy.

What must be stressed is that royal ordinances provided only a general framework for the law in early modern France. Decisions of special royal

---

[25] The laws are assembled in E. and E. Haag, *La France protestante* (Paris, 1858), vol. 10, pièces justificatives; Stegmann (ed.), *Edits des guerres de religion*; Diefendorf, *Under the Cross*, 72; Jourdan, Decrusy and Isambert, *Recueil général des anciennes lois françaises* (Paris, 1833).

commissions and *arrêts* of the country's Parlements could modify the law to fit local conditions. For instance, a commission sent in the fall of 1561 to pacify the Agenais, one of the corners of southern France most troubled by clashes between Huguenots who sought to take over Catholic houses of worship and Catholics determined to stop their assemblies, allowed the Protestants of this area a measure of toleration in October 1561, several months before the Edict of January granted them rights of worship throughout the kingdom.[26] Conversely, although kingdom-wide royal proscriptions of Protestant worship are known only for 1568, 1572, and 1585, the decisions of local authorities led to its prohibition in many regions upon the outbreak of other civil wars as well. During the First Civil War of 1562–3, the Parlement of Normandy, which had fled Huguenot-controlled Rouen and reassembled in Louviers, decreed that Protestant worship would be outlawed in all cities that returned to obedience to the king over the course of the conflict. In Tours in the same period, those Huguenots who were not massacred when the city was retaken by the royal and Catholic forces were required to make a confession of faith before representatives of the archbishop and to leave town if the views they expressed were deemed contrary to the Catholic religion.[27] The governor of Dieppe told the inhabitants of that city that the king willed that Reformed services cease after the outbreak of the Sixth Civil War in 1577. A few years previously, following the Saint Bartholomew's Massacre, Dieppe's Protestants had not simply been prohibited from assembling for their own services; they had also been required to participate in Catholic worship.[28]

In practice, the chronology of the civil wars and the local balance of power appear to have determined when the Reformed were actually able to assemble for worship in any given community. The rare surviving Protestant baptismal registers from this era provide the best evidence about when different churches were able to assemble for worship. The material relates primarily to fourteen churches.[29] The pattern varied from locality to locality. In such

---

[26] Estienne de la Boëtie, *Memoire sur la pacification des troubles*, ed. Malcolm Smith (Geneva, 1983), 9, 100–6; Smith, *Montaigne and Religious Freedom*, 56.

[27] Archives Départementales de la Seine-Maritime, B, Parlement, Arrêts, Arrêt of 26 August 1562; David Nicholls, 'Protestants, Catholics and Magistrates in Tours, 1562–1572: The Making of a Catholic City during the Religious Wars', *French History*, 8 (1994), 17.

[28] Guillaume and Jean Daval, *Histoire de la Reformation à Dieppe*, ed. Emile Lesens (Rouen, 1878), I, 119–20, 122.

[29] For the churches of Caen, Gien, La Rochelle, Loudun, Monoblet, Montpellier, Montauban, Nîmes, Anduze, Rouen, Ruffec, Saintes, Verteuil, Vitré, see A[rchives] C[ommunales] Loudun, GG 195; A. C. Montauban, 12 GG 1–8; A. C. Montpellier, GG 314–320; A[rchives] D[épartementales] Seine-Maritime, 4 E 3388; A. D. Calvados, C. 1565–70; A. D. Charente-Maritime, I 1–18, 146–7; A. D. Gard, 5 E 10/10–11, 5 E 169/2, UU 92–93; A.D. Ille-et-Vilaine, 3 E Vitré; Archives Nationales, TT 244 (15), 250 (1), 264 (159–60), 275 (10–15); Bibliothèque de la Société de l'Histoire du Protestantisme Français, MS 1082 (1).

Protestant strongholds as La Rochelle, Montauban, Nîmes, and the Cévennes (Anduze, Monoblet), the Reformed assembled for worship throughout the period in sovereign disregard of the legislation that intermittently prohibited this. In cities that remained under effective royal control for most of the period, Reformed services were recurrently, although not absolutely consistently, interrupted by each civil war except the brief, localized Seventh Civil War of 1580. In localities where the military balance swung back and forth between the two faiths, such as Montpellier and Verteuil (Angoumois), the royal legislation was respected at certain moments but defied at others. During Henry IV's long battle against the Catholic League, Reformed worship resumed in many predominantly Catholic but none the less royalist towns (e.g. Caen, Gien, Vitré) even before the Edict of Mantes of July 1591 formally annulled the 1585 prohibition of the faith – evidence of the early implementation of a regime of tolerance in these towns that has not previously been noted.[30] (League-controlled cities, of course, continued to prohibit Reformed worship until they recognized Henry IV's authority.) In at least a few places and times, we know from other sources, Protestant congregations met secretly for worship even when outlawed, as for instance in Paris after 1563, or in heavily Protestant Dieppe during the First, Second, Fifth, and Sixth Civil Wars.[31] A number of French cities thus housed the equivalent of the Dutch 'churches under the cross' at certain moments in the Religious Wars. Such assemblies were decidedly dangerous, for individuals were executed for heresy or for participating in prohibited worship at several moments during the Religious Wars when such gatherings were outlawed. Executions for one or the other offence took place in Paris in 1562, 1569, and 1588–9.[32]

For their part, the Protestants did not hesitate to forbid Catholic worship in those localities which they dominated politically and numerically during the initial years of the Wars of Religion. Castres and Montpellier were two towns where a combination of anti-clerical violence and civic legislation

---

[30] Further evidence of the same pattern comes from Dieppe and Houdan. In the former city, Protestant worship resumed in September 1589, after the royalist governor invited back to the city the many Protestants who had fled across the Channel to Rye, in order to reinforce the city against the threat of attack by partisans of the Catholic League in the region. Houdan's elders were able to re-establish their church by May 1591 (two months before the Edict of Mantes), whereupon they wrote to Geneva's Company of Pastors to request a minister. Daval and Daval, *Histoire de la Reformation à Dieppe*, I, 141–2; Sabine Citron and Marie-Claude Junod (eds.), *Registres de la Compagnie des Pasteurs de Genève, Tome VI 1589–1594* (Geneva, 1980), 201.

[31] Diefendorf, *Beneath the Cross*, 123; Daval and Daval, *Histoire de la Reformation à Dieppe*, I, 35, 41–2, 94, 120, 123.

[32] William Monter, 'Les executés pour hérésie par arrêt du Parlement de Paris (1523–1560)', *Bulletin de la Société de l'Histoire du Protestantisme Français* (forthcoming). I would like to thank Prof. Monter for providing me with a copy of this article prior to publication.

forced Catholic worship to cease in the fall and winter of 1561–2, even before the outbreak of the First Civil War. In both, the toleration granted the Reformed throughout the kingdom by the Edict of January did not beget similar toleration for Catholics in response. Roman worship did not resume in either town until the Peace of Amboise in 1563. When the Huguenots secured control of Orléans and Rouen at the outset of the First Civil War, Catholic services were initially allowed to continue there, but within less than a month they were forced to cease: in Orléans by decree of the city fathers following the massacre of Protestants in Sens; in Rouen following a local wave of iconoclasm, the seizure of arms from the city's Catholics, and the flight of the Parlement and much of the clergy. In Lyons, Catholic worship was forbidden as soon as the Protestants took control of the city, while Montpellier's Huguenot authorities went further yet in October 1562, making attendance at the *prêche* mandatory.[33] After the First Civil War, however, the initial Protestant impulse to uproot the abominations of the mass was tempered by the recognition that respecting the terms of successive edicts of pacification was beneficial for the cause as a whole. In La Rochelle, the great Huguenot stronghold from 1568 until 1628, Catholic worship was permitted in each period of peace between those dates, although outlawed during each period of civil war.[34]

Some localities tried to follow an independent course of establishing a stable regime of religious co-existence even amid the periods of open civil war. The inhabitants of two communities in Dauphiné, Nyons and Saint-Laurent-des-Arbres, took formal vows in the 1560s to 'live in peace, friendship, and confederation' with one another despite 'the diversity of religion that is among them,' and to defend their communities against attack by the troops of either religious party. A decade later, the duke of Montmorency-Damville sought to promote the toleration of both faiths over a broader area as the leader of the '*Protestants et Catholiques unis*' in Languedoc. Such efforts succeeded intermittently in Montpellier, where both faiths worshipped side by side between 1574 and 1577 and again after 1582, although a regime of Protestant exclusivity prevailed between 1577 and 1582. They likewise

---

[33] Jean Faurin, 'Journal sur les guerres de Castres', in M. de la Pijardière (ed.), *Pièces fugitives pour servir à l'histoire de France*, XV (Montpellier, 1878), 13; Charles d'Aigrefeuille, *Histoire de la ville de Montpellier* (Montpellier 1877; repr. Marseille, 1976), I, 438; Philip Benedict, *Rouen during the Wars of Religion* (Cambridge, 1981), 97–8; Bernard de Lacombe, *Les débuts des guerres de religion (Orléans 1559–1564): Catherine de Médicis entre Guise et Condé* (Paris, 1899), 170–96, 328; Richard Gascon, *Grand commerce et vie urbaine au XVIe siècle: Lyon et ses marchands* (Paris, 1971), 482, 492.

[34] Etienne Trocmé, 'L'Eglise réformée de la Rochelle jusqu'en 1628', *Bulletin de la Société de l'Histoire du Protestantisme Français*, 99 (1952), 138. Catholic worship likewise ceased during the period of the League in the Protestant bastions of Die, Montélimar, Loriol, Livron, and Nyons in Dauphiné. Elisabeth Rabut, *Le roi, l'église et le temple. L'Exécution de l'Edit de Nantes en Dauphiné* (Grenoble [?], 1987), 73, 89, 100, 108, 168.

succeeded in the little town of Saillans in Dauphiné, where the commissioners sent to oversee the implementation of the Edict of Nantes in 1599 found that both churches had exercised their religion 'in full liberty for a long time'. Elsewhere, however, they broke down, as in Nyons, which by 1576 was a Huguenot *place de sûreté* where Catholic worship was forbidden in times of war.[35] Overall, the successful establishment of such regimes was probably rare. More often, the problem was enforcing the restoration of toleration decreed by the successive edicts of pacification. Particularly in the first decade of the civil wars, each new edict met with official foot-dragging and violent popular opposition in many cities, Catholic and Protestant alike. It often took the dispatch of special royal commissioners and a period of months or even years before those of the minority faith who had fled town dared to return home.

A far more stable and enduring regime of co-existence followed Henry IV's triumph over the Catholic League. The Bourbon accession brought into the kingdom the little principality of Béarn, where Reformed Protestantism had been established as the religion of state and Catholicism outlawed under Jeanne d'Albret. Henry IV's Edict of Fontainebleau of 1599 allowed the limited reestablishment of Catholicism as a *quid pro quo* for the privileges granted France's Protestants under the Edict of Nantes, but local resistance initially stalled the implementation of this edict. The effective restoration of Catholic worship only came after Louis XIII led a small army into Béarn in 1620.[36] During the renewed civil wars of the 1620s, the rights of the Protestants to gather for worship remained undisturbed in both principle and general practice, although following the troubles these rights were revoked in certain localities to punish the inhabitants of the 'R.P.R.' for their participation in the rebellion.[37] Catholic worship fared less well in many cities that took up the standard of revolt in these years, as the exaltation of a militant and triumphalist Protestantism gripped the population for a final time. In Montpellier, many of the scenes of the early 1560s were replayed: the churches were systematically purged of their idols; Catholics were driven to the *prêche* with sticks jocularly baptised 'the consistory's dusting rods'; and

[35] Marc Venard, *Réforme protestante, Réforme catholique dans la province d'Avignon au XVIe siècle* (Paris, 1993), 935; Stegmann, *Edits des guerres de religion*, 117; Rabut, *Le roi, l'église et le temple*, 78, 168; Gérard Cholvy et al., *Histoire de Montpellier* (Toulouse, 1984), 152; Archives Communales de Montpellier, GG 3–4 (demonstrating the resumption of Catholic worship after 1582).

[36] Pierre Tucoo-Chala and Christian Desplat, *La Principauté de Béarn* (Pau, 1980), 277–87, 311–14; Philip Benedict, *The Huguenot Population of France, 1600–1685: The Demographic Fate and Customs of a Religious Minority* (Philadelphia, 1991), 71.

[37] The national synod of 1637 listed 38 localities where churches had been closed since the civil wars of the 1620s. Jean Aymon, *Tous les Synodes Nationales des Eglises Reformées de France* (The Hague, 1710), II, 597. For evidence demonstrating the temporary closure of other churches: Benedict, *Huguenot Population*, 132–4.

the mass ceased, as it also did in La Rochelle.[38] With the exception of these incidents, however, the general principle that both faiths had the legal right to gather for worship was not challenged until the Revocation. Instead, contestation over rights of worship by the militants on both sides shifted to arguments and legal battles over whether or not the Reformed had the right to assemble in specific localities under the complicated terms of the Edict of Nantes.

Establishing the legal parameters for the peaceful co-existence of two religious faiths in France involved more than simply decreeing that each one had the right to assemble for worship. From the start, every edict that granted the Reformed freedom of worship also contained provisions designed to mitigate the possibility of violence between the members of each faith and to specify the rights and obligations of the Reformed minority. The number of such provisions tended to increase with each successive edict, as new sources of resentment and potential conflict were constantly revealed.

To minimise friction, each edict from 1562 onward specified that butchers' shops were to remain closed on all *jours maigres* and that the Protestants were to respect Catholic feast days. The burial of deceased Protestants soon proved to be a particularly nettlesome issue, as the interment of heretics in hallowed ground proved so offensive to Catholic sensibilities that incidents recurred in which Huguenot corpses were disinterred or dragged to the local refuse heap. From 1570 onward, successive edicts obliged the Protestants to obtain their own burial grounds, forbade Catholic attempts to interfere with their doing so, and sought to spell out procedures whereby Huguenot corpses might be taken to these burial grounds without creating 'scandal' or 'tumult'. Beginning with the 1570 Peace of Saint-Germain, each edict also guaranteed the Protestants access to educational and caritative institutions and to royal and municipal offices, creating an equality of civil rights that contrasts markedly with the situation of the dissenters in post-1688 England. The Peace of Saint-Germain was also the first to grant the Protestants control over a certain number of fortified towns as places of refuge in the event of further civil wars.

The Saint Bartholomew's Massacre of 1572, in the wake of which thousands of panicked Protestants abjured their faith and thousands of others fled abroad, opened new wounds. As the crown sought to close these, it decreed that past abjurations were not binding on those who chose to resume their prior faith and that the children of French subjects born abroad were French *regnicoles* if they chose to return to the country. Catholics were forbidden to continue holding processions to commemorate the events of Saint Barthol-

---

[38] André Delort, *Mémoires inédits sur la ville de Montpellier au XVIIe siècle (1621–1693)* (Montpellier 1876–78; repr. Marseille, 1980), 7–9; D'Aigrefeuille, *Histoire de la ville de Montpellier*, II, 48; Trocmé, 'Eglise de la Rochelle', 138.

omew's Eve, and reparations were even granted the widows and children of
the massacre victims in the form of six-year tax exemptions. Once again,
these royal decrees of nationwide scope must be recognised as providing
only the broad framework for the co-existence of the two faiths. Additional
measures might be decreed locally. One particularly important tactic to which
royal governors began to have recourse from early on in the Wars of Religion
was that of dividing the seats in certain city councils between members of
the two faiths in numbers roughly proportional to their strength within the
community, creating a French equivalent to the regimes of parity of certain
German free imperial cities.[39]

From 1598 to 1685, a string of edicts, *arrêts*, and declarations emanating
from the Conseil du Roi and the Parlements modified details of the civil
situation of the Reformed in ways that became considerably more restrictive
once Louis XIV began to rule on his own. Henry IV attempted a deliberate
balancing act, alternately gratifying one party and then the other when faced
with petitions alleging violations of the terms of the religious peace or
requesting modifications of these terms. With the increasing influence of the
dévot party at court and the death or disgrace of many of Henry IV's old
councillors, royal policy grew more hostile to the Reformed by the later
1610s. Louis XIII and Richelieu sought particularly to erode Protestant political power, as illustrated by the 1629 repeal of the military concessions
granted the Huguenots by the secret articles of the Edict of Nantes and by
numerous decisions tilting the balance in *consulats mi-partis* in favour of the
Catholics. An edict of 1634 prohibited Protestant ministers from preaching
in the 'annex' churches attached to certain congregations, while three years
later members of the faith were forbidden from gathering in their temples
for prayer meetings or other acts of worship without a minister present. After
the death of Louis XIII and Richelieu, the loyalty that the Protestants showed
to the crown during the Fronde and the need to rally as much support as
possible for the war against Spain led Mazarin to demonstrate more generosity toward the Huguenots on occasion – especially in 1654–5, when
Cromwell, whose support he sought, made a diplomatic issue of their situation. In these years, the Protestants regained lost rights of worship or rep-
resentation in city government in a number of localities. With the onset of
Louis XIV's personal rule in 1661, however, the aggressively pro-Catholic
policy that would culminate in the Revocation of the Edict of Nantes began
in earnest. Teams of royal commissioners were dispatched to the provinces
in 1662 to verify the titles of each local church and to close down those
found to be in violation of the strict terms of the Edict of Nantes. Measures

[39] The city councils of Lyon, Montpellier and Orléans were all divided in this fashion following
the Peace of Amboise.

limited the size of the parties that could accompany Reformed funeral convoys, banned the singing of psalms in the street, and required members of the faith to respect the Catholic *temps clos* for marriages of Lent and Advent. Old guarantees of impartial justice were eliminated by first cutting back the jurisdiction of the bi-partisan Chambres de l'Edit and then, between 1669 and 1679, dissolving them. Still other measures removed the equal access to civil employment that the Reformed had previously enjoyed by imposing quotas on them in many guilds and professions and excluding them entirely from some. Particularly bitterly resented were the measures that restricted parental authority over their children by decreeing that all children of a Catholic father and Protestant mother must be raised as Catholics, and that parents must respect the wishes of children as young as seven who expressed a desire to convert to the Roman church. In 1680, Catholic conversion to Protestantism was entirely forbidden, as was intermarriage with a member of the faith.[40]

The events that greased the final slide to the Revocation have often been narrated, and need only be quickly recapitulated. The growing piety of the king; the discovery and ruthless exploitation by several iron-fisted administrators of the capacities of royal dragoons billeted in Huguenot houses to generate conversions; exaggerated reports of the numbers of conversions thus obtained the virtual extinction of the Protestant cause; and finally the pressures on the king to restore his lustre as a defender of the faith after his failure to respond to the call for a crusade to drive the Turks back from Vienna and his conflict with the Pope over the issue of the *Régale* – all these contributed their part. As recent historians have stressed, however, a deeper logic was also at work. The enduring hostility to religious pluralism on the part of the successive Bourbon kings, the Catholic church, and so much of the political nation created a larger ideological context that encouraged the Revocation. If so many Protestants were now returning to the true faith and the crown's strength had increased to the point where it could no longer be argued that the revocation of tolerance for the Huguenots would produce an unacceptable level of internal warfare, what was the point of retaining a regime of toleration

---

[40] Daniel Ligou, *Le Protestantisme en France de 1598 à 1715* (Paris, 1968), chs. 3–5; Dompnier, *Venin de l'hérésie*, ch. 9; G. Bonet-Maury, *La liberté de conscience en France depuis l'Edit de Nantes jusqu'à la séparation (1598–1905)* (Paris, 1909), 26–30; Janine Garrison, *L'Edit de Nantes et sa révocation. Histoire d'une intolérance* (Paris, 1985); Ruth Kleinman, 'Changing Interpretations of the Edict of Nantes: The Administrative Aspect, 1643–1661,' *French Historical Studies*, 10 (1978), 541–71; *Edits déclarations et arrests concernans la réligion p. réformée 1662–1751* (Paris, 1885); Paul Gachon, *Quelques préliminaires de la Révocation de l'Edit de Nantes en Languedoc (1661–1685)* (Toulouse, 1899); A. T. van Deursen, *Professions et métiers interdits. Un aspect de l'histoire de la Révocation de l'Edit de Nantes* (Groningen, 1960).

that had always been viewed as a necessary evil, especially when there was important symbolic capital to be obtained by doing away with it?[41]

The history of how the law was modified to adjust to the presence of France's Reformed minority can thus be envisaged as a movement in two parts. Over the course of the Wars of Religion, the crown groped along a twisting path to define a set of terms to govern the toleration of two faiths that was neither so generous as to provoke massive Catholic resistance, nor so restrictive as to prompt the same from the Reformed. In the formula that finally proved successful, Catholicism's position as the established faith of the kingdom was reaffirmed by a variety of measures that required the Protestants to respect Catholic practices and that restricted Reformed worship to a defined set of localities. At the same time, the Protestants were accorded impressive guarantees of equal civil rights and special arrangements to ensure their security and their access to impartial justice. All of the edicts of pacification, however, included wording to the effect that their provisions were only a temporary necessity until such time as the entire kingdom might be reunited in the true faith, always the fondest hope of royal policy. Once a stable regime of toleration was established, successive rulers whittled away at the various rights and privileges granted the Reformed, until at last they were entirely revoked.

How effectively enforced were the laws that defined the civil rights of the Reformed and the character of their obligations toward Catholic customs or rituals? A set of remonstrances that the Reformed presented to Henry IV in 1596 and published in the following year detailed more than fifty recent violations of the provisions of the Peace of Bergerac, which then governed affairs in those areas that recognised the prince of Navarre as king. Four sorts of violations were particularly frequently alleged: (1) fines or threats of legal action made against the Reformed for failing to attend processions, drape their houses on feast days, or otherwise participate in or show due respect for Catholic ceremonies, even though the law did not require them to do this; (2) attempts to block them from municipal offices; (3) attempts to stop them from worshipping in places where they believed that the terms of the Peace of Bergerac allowed them to do so; and (4) 'scandals' arising out of Catholic attacks on their funeral processions or the desecration of burial sites.[42] Where they could, the Protestants, too, disregarded aspects of the law that they did

---

[41] Ernest Lavisse, *Histoire de France*, vol. 7, part 2, (Paris, 1906), 39–80; Jean Orcibal, *Louis XIV et les Protestants* (Paris, 1951); Garrisson, *Edit de Nantes et sa révocation*, 9–27, 184–262; Labrousse, *'Une foi, une loi, un roi?'*, 25–6, 167–95; Pierre Chaunu, 'La décision royale (?): un système de la Révocation' in Zuber and Theis (eds.), *Révocation de l'Edit de Nantes*, 13–28.

[42] *Plaintes des Eglises réformées de France, sur les violences et injustices qui leur sont faites en plusieurs endrois du Royaume* (n.p., 1597), reprinted in [Simon Goulart], *Mémoires de la Ligue* (Amsterdam, 1758), VI, 428–86.

not like. Reports of foreign travellers make it clear that meat was openly sold on *jours maigres* in many Huguenot dominated communities in southern France in the seventeenth century. The habit of working on feast days became so deeply entrenched in such places that even Catholic artisans followed suit.[43] The royal edict of 1662 requiring the Reformed to respect the prohibitions against celebrating marriages during certain periods was followed by a sharp drop in the number of Protestant weddings in Lent in a few parts of the country where the authorities were particularly vigilant in their surveillance of Huguenot behaviour, especially Poitou and Saintonge, but it was flouted in Languedoc, Provence, and even parts of northern France.[44] A gap always existed between the letter of the law on these issues and actual behavior across the length and breadth of the realm, although we are still far from being able to indicate the full contours of the gap or the extent to which it narrowed or widened over time.

Co-existence in practice: cooperation and conflict

Discussion of the extent to which the laws governing Catholic-Reformed co-existence were actually observed leads us from the legal history of toleration to the social history of inter-group interaction. Several outstanding recent studies have greatly enhanced our understanding of the aspect of that history that is at once most immediately visible in the sources of the period and most troubling to modern sensibilities: the numerous incidents of popular violence, often accompanied by appalling acts of ritual humiliation and dismemberment, that punctuated the era. Other recent historians, moved by an understandable desire to combat the impression that violence is a necessary consequence of religious diversity, have highlighted the many forms of peaceful interaction that marked much of the day-to-day co-existence of the two groups. A full picture of Protestant–Catholic relations needs to make room at once for the evidence of frequent, cordial interaction between members of the two faiths and for the recognition that a continuing sense of difference set them apart – differences that could, in certain situations, spark violence or panic.

If the years between 1560 and 1598 burned themselves into the memory of subsequent generations as the '*temps des troubles de religion*', this was not simply because of the eight formally declared civil wars, but also because

---

[43] Elie Benoist, *Histoire de l'Edit de Nantes* (Delft, 1693–95), III, 23–4, 40; Hans Bots, 'Voyages faits par de jeunes hollandais en France. Deux voyages types: Gysbert de With et Nicolas Heinsius', in *La découverte de la France au XVIIe siècle* (Paris, 1980), 475; Gregory Hanlon, *Confession and Community in Seventeenth-Century France: Catholic and Protestant Coexistence in Aquitaine* (Philadephia, 1993), 22.

[44] Benedict, *Huguenot Population*, 83–6.

of the numerous incidents of religious rioting that troubled even putative periods of peace. Natalie Zemon Davis and Denis Crouzet have offered particularly fruitful models for understanding this violence.[45] In community after community, Protestant crowd actions began with mockery of the processions, eucharistic rituals, and other rites of the Catholic church, and with iconoclastic attacks on the statuary and altarpieces that decorated France's churches and streets. Initially scattered, such incidents became a vast wave between 1560 and 1562, as the churches now being organised across the country grew in strength and daring. Efforts to rescue imprisoned coreligionists and physical violence against the clergy soon followed, as, on rarer occasions, did attacks on Catholic laymen. Catholic crowd actions most commonly took the form of violent reactions to a Protestant provocation perceived as an act of sacrilege, of attacks on Huguenots gathered for or returning from worship, and of efforts to prevent their burial in hallowed ground. Often, they grew into larger bloodlettings in which dozens or even hundreds of heretics were hunted down, dismembered, and hurled into nearby bodies of water. In each case, the violence expressed powerful and widely shared attitudes that were fundamental to each group's religious outlook. On the Protestant side, the violence was part of the fundamental drive of the Reformation to purify society of the false forms of worship that had infected divine service, to proclaim a new understanding of the Gospel and to insist upon the rights of those who embraced it to assemble for worship, and to do away with an overgrown and unnecessary clerical establishment. On the Catholic side, it expressed the view that heretics were a dangerous threat to the moral and political order who properly deserved punishment and even eradication, overlain in many instances with fears that they threatened the natural order as well, for an angry God might scourge the kingdom with plagues and earthquakes if the blot of heresy were not removed. In other words, most of the crowd actions were the expression through extra-legal means of the principles that in other circumstances justified the legal proscription of one faith or the other.

After reaching its paroxysm in the Saint Bartholomew's Massacre, the spontaneous religious violence that was so common between 1560 and 1572 diminished in frequency. Crouzet has explored the psychology of this decline:

---

[45] Davis, 'The Rites of Violence: Religious Riot in Sixteenth Century France', *Past and Present*, 59 (1973), 51–91, reprinted in Davis, *Society and Culture in Early Modern France* (Stanford, 1975); Crouzet, *Les guerriers de Dieu. La violence au temps des troubles de religion, vers 1525–vers 1610* (Seyssel, 1990). Also extremely commendable on Huguenot iconoclasm is Olivier Christin, *Une révolution symbolique. L'iconoclasme huguenot et la reconstruction catholique* (Paris, 1991), and see further the pioneering Janine Estèbe, *Tocsin pour un massacre. La saison des Saint-Barthélemy* (Paris, 1968); Benedict, *Rouen*; Diefendorf, *Beneath the Cross*; Mark Greengrass, 'The Anatomy of a Religious Riot in Toulouse in May 1562', *Journal of Ecclesiastical History*, 34 (1983), 367–91.

as the Huguenots rallied from the demoralisation and shock of the event to mount a successful defence of their key strongholds from La Rochelle to Montauban, the initial Catholic euphoria at the apparently mortal blow delivered to their enemies gave way to guilt at the sheer horror of the event itself, and a shift toward enterprises of penance and personal reform.[46] My own research has highlighted the local political causes of the decline: within most communities, the balance of power between the two faiths, often uneasy between 1562 and 1572, had tipped clearly in favour of one party or the other after 1572. In most localities in northern France and parts of the South, the ranks of the Reformed underwent massive attrition through flight, massacre, and abjuration, making them a far smaller and less politically threatening minority. In certain of the communities in which the Reformed were in the majority, they established their firm political control by the early 1570s. In either event, tension ebbed and intra-community violence declined, even if warfare continued between strongholds committed to each side.[47]

Religious violence in the years after 1572 has been little studied, but it would be wrong to think that it ever entirely disappeared. A preliminary inventory of religious riots from 1600 to 1685 reveals the irregular recurrence of violent episodes across these years.[48] Incidents were particularly frequent in the decade of renewed religious warfare in the 1620s and in the period immediately preceding the Revocation, but no decade was spared. Many of the flashpoints for trouble were the same as in the early years of the Wars of Religion, but a few new ones also appeared. Thus, with the construction of more permanent Reformed temples, attacks upon the physical structure of the temple itself became a favoured method for Catholics to demonstrate their hostility to the presence of Reformed worship in their community.[49] As aggressively missionising Catholic religious orders established themselves under the umbrella of royal protection in towns that had previously been Protestant strongholds, they became a focus of Huguenot anger. These incidents of religious violence were generally minor, but fears of a recurrence of

---

[46] Crouzet, *Guerriers de Dieu*, II, 112ff; Crouzet, 'Le règne de Henri III et la violence collective', in Robert Sauzet (ed.), *Henri III et son temps* (Paris, 1992), 211–25.

[47] Benedict, *Rouen*, 95–163, 240–2.

[48] My inventory of such incidents is based primarily on the numerous episodes of violence mentioned in Benoist, *Histoire de l'Edit de Nantes*. Other incidents are revealed by Dompnier, *Venin de l'hérésie*, 166–8; Alain Croix, *La Bretagne aux 16e et 17e siècles: La vie, la mort, la foi* (Paris, 1981), 94; René Favier, *Les villes du Dauphiné aux XVIIe et XVIIIe siècles* (Grenoble, 1993), 88; Henry Ronot, 'Une famille de peintres protestants à Langres au début du XVIIe siècle: les Michelin', *Bulletin de la Société de l'Histoire du Protestantisme Français*, 96 (1949), 71–2; Alfred Leroux, 'L'Eglise Réformée de Bordeaux de 1660 à 1670', *Bulletin de la Société de l'Histoire du Protestantisme Français*, 69 (1920), 178; Frank Puaux, 'Ephémérides de l'année de la révocation de l'édit de Nantes', *Bulletin de la Société de l'Histoire du Protestantisme Français*, 34 (1885), 87.

[49] On this phenomenon, see Solange Deyon, 'La destruction des temples', in Zuber and Theis (eds.), *Révocation de l'Edit de Nantes*, 239–58.

events comparable to the worst episodes of the sixteenth century continued to haunt both sides. In 1645, a rumour swept through the Parisian congregation at Charenton that bands of Catholics had gathered in the nearby woods to slaughter all present. Shrieks of terror and a scramble to secure the temple door ensued.[50] In 1690, comparable rumours that the Huguenots were about to burn their way across two predominantly Catholic regions in the Midi led the authorities of these areas, Bigorre and the Agenais, to put the militia on full alert.[51] The establishment of a measure of peace between the two confessions had clearly not eliminated the memory of past horrors and the suspicion of the other faith that this endangered.

As has already been suggested, the history of popular violence forms just one part of the story of Catholic-Reformed relations. In the initial years of the Reformed churches' growth, the decision to embrace or reject the new faith often cut right through individual families. While those who drafted the edicts of pacification felt compelled to prohibit parents from disinheriting their children strictly 'from hatred of their religion', relations between family members who chose different faiths frequently remained cooperative and cordial.[52] Local studies of religious life in the seventeenth century have revealed numerous instances of amicable relations between members of the two faiths, even between their spiritual leaders. In Besse (Dauphiné), an episcopal visitation found in 1672 that the parish *curé* 'plays boules with the Huguenots, often eats with them, and had close contacts and friendship with the minister'. In Pontacq (Béarn), the two faiths shared the same church building and even, despite an episcopal prohibition, the same church bells.[53] Detailed community studies have shown that Catholics and Protestants did business with one another, served as godparents for one another's children, placed their children as apprentices or servants in the households of members of the other faith, and even intermarried – the acid test of the strength of social barriers between different groups within a community. Of 482 marriages celebrated in the Catholic churches of Nîmes between 1609 and 1621, 117 involved one part-

[50] 'Charenton en 1645. Récit d'un voyageur alsacien', *Bulletin de la Société de l'Histoire du Protestantisme Français*, 67 (1921), 155, cited in Dompnier, *Venin de l'hérésie*, 164. For another Protestant panic, this one in 1621, see Daval and Daval, *Histoire de la Reformation à Dieppe*, I, 214–17; Ferdinand de Schickler, *Les Eglises du Refuge en Angleterre* (Paris, 1892), I, 390–1.

[51] Jean-François Soulet, *Traditions et réformes religieuses dans les Pyrénées centrales au XVIIe siècle (le diocèse de Tarbes de 1602 à 1716)* (Pau, 1974), 299; Hanlon, *Confession and Community*, 255.

[52] Barbara B. Diefendorf, 'Les divisions religieuses dans les familles parisiennes avant la Saint-Barthélemy', *Histoire, Economie et Société*, 7 (1988), 55–77.

[53] Dompnier, *Venin de l'hérésie*, 140; Soulet, *Traditions et réformes*, 300. Similar reports from other regions in Robert Sauzet, *Les visites pastorales dans le diocèse de Chartres pendant la première moitié du XVIIe siècle* (Rome, 1975), 226–7; 'Les Paroissiens de Sainte-Cathérine de Honfleur: Leur curé et le pasteur en 1659', *Bulletin de la Société de l'Histoire du Protestantisme Français*, 46 (1897), 90–3.

ner (typically, the woman) who had recently converted to the faith to allow the marriage to be celebrated.[54]

Although the character of everyday Catholic-Reformed social interaction in the localities has begun to be illuminated, again much remains to be done. To begin with, it must be observed that work to date has been content to underscore the fact of Catholic–Protestant cooperation, rather than trying to measure its precise frequency. The 24 per cent of Catholic marriages in Nîmes that involved a partner who had until recently been of the opposite faith takes on different significance when it is realized that the city was approximately 80 per cent Protestant at the time. Had no tendency existed toward religious endogamy within the city's population, fully four fifths of all Catholic marriages would have been mixed marriages. The considerable interaction that marked everyday social relations between Catholics and Protestants should not obscure the strong tendency toward group endogamy.

The most interesting question that historians have just begun to address concerns possible changes over time. It might be expected that with the achievement of a relatively stable political equilibrium in different local communities, everyday interaction between the members of the two faiths would gradually eradicate the mistrust between them and produce a lowering of social barriers. At the same time, however, elements within both churches worked through the seventeenth century to limit or eliminate certain social practices that blurred the boundaries between the two groups. Reformed consistories reprimanded church members who sent their children to Jesuit schools or attended Roman ceremonies. The Catholic hierarchy, and occasionally even lay churchwardens, admonished parish priests who socialised too convivially with Huguenots. By the fourth decade of the century, the authorities of both churches no longer permitted members of the other faith to act as godparents. Meanwhile, champions of the two faiths engaged one another in numerous public debates, whose result was rarely to win converts for either side, but which did have the effect of reinforcing the pre-existing convictions of those attending and deepening their awareness of the points of doctrine that separated them from their neighbours.[55] Even while ongoing

---

[54] Robert Sauzet, *Contre-Réforme et Réforme catholique en Bas-Languedoc: Le diocèse de Nîmes au XVIIe siècle* (Louvain, 1979), 166. The extent of good relations between most members of the two confessions in religiously divided communities has been highlighted particularly effectively by the detailed community studies of Gregory Hanlon on Layrac (Hanlon, *Confession and Community*) and Elisabeth Labrousse on Mauvezin. Labrousse indicates some of her findings in her '*Une foi, une loi, un roi?*', 81–9. For further evidence of ties of godparentage and domestic service across the confessional divide, see Miriam U. Chrisman, 'Family and Religion in Two Noble Families,' *Journal of Family History*, 8 (1983), 205; G. E. de Falguerolles, 'Les paroissiens de l'Eglise Réformée à Puylaurens (1630–1650),' *Bulletin de la Société de l'Histoire du Protestantisme Français*, 111 (1965), 100.

[55] Dompnier, *Venin de l'hérésie*, chs. 7–8; Falguerolles, 'Paroissiens de l'Eglise Réformée à Puylaurens,' 100; Sauzet, *Contre-Réforme et Réforme catholique*, 173–8.

social and commercial interactions may have knitted members of the two faiths more tightly together, a powerful cultural dynamic thus worked to heighten awareness of confessional differences.

Research that I am currently doing on seventeenth-century Montpellier suggests that, of these two processes, the latter may well have been the more powerful. My evidence is of four kinds. First, three samples of marriage contracts at evenly spaced periods from 1605–9 to 1665–9 reveal that where a small but not totally insignificant number of contracts from the initial period made explicit provisions for the parties to the marriage to continue to practice different faiths after they were married – 10 of 535 contracts, to be exact – this form of family religious organization all but disappeared by the third period in question, when just 1 contract in 600 made such provisions. Secondly, although the contracts themselves do not reveal those more numerous other kinds of mixed marriages where one party converted prior to the wedding, some clues about the frequency of such marriages can be obtained by linking together contracts involving members of the same family. Of seven cases where two siblings married in different churches, suggesting a probable conversion for matrimony's sake, four came in the first period, one in the second, and two in the third. (Studies of other regions have also suggested that intermarriage between members of the two faiths declined as the century advanced.[56]) Thirdly, although by the fourth decade of the century Protestants could no longer act as godparents for babies baptised in the Catholic church, Montpellier's Catholic baptismal registers note a number of cases where a Catholic stood in for a 'heretic' at the baptismal font. One finds 18 such cases among 533 baptisms in 1648, but just 2 among 153 cases in 1667.[57] Fourthly, where the religion of the notaries who recorded the marriage contracts is known, it appears that Protestant couples increasingly chose to do business with Protestant notaries and Catholics with Catholics.[58] All of these observations involve relatively small samples, and evidence for a single com-

---

[56] Gueneau, 'Protestants du Centre', 312; Hanlon, *Confession and Community*, 109 (although the evidence of this graph is not entirely conclusive).

[57] Archives Communales de Montpellier, GG 11, GG 202. Between these two dates, the city's Catholics were divided among three parishes. The figure for the second period concerns only one of these parishes, Ste Anne.

[58] For the periods 1605–9 and 1635–9, the only two so far for which I have identified the religion of a significant number of the more active notaries, I have calculated a crude integration/segregation index to observe how the members of the different faiths distributed their business. For each period in question, I first inferred from the overall breakdown of the city's population by religion the distribution of contracts among the notaries of different faiths that would have been expected had people displayed absolutely no tendency to select a notary of their own faith (hypothesis of perfect integration = 0) and had they always chosen a notary who shared their religion (hypothesis of perfect segregation = 1). I then calculated the actual distribution of contracts among the notaries of different religions as a percentage of the difference between these two values. For the first period, the integration/segregation index was 0.32; for the second 0.67.

munity clearly needs additional confirmation before it can support confident generalisations. Still, it would appear that the two confessions may have become increasingly sharply separated and self-enclosed communities as the century advanced, just as was the case in religiously divided cities in Germany at the same time.[59]

Time also softened but little the fundamentally hostile images that intellectuals of each party maintained of the other. Such late seventeenth-century Catholic historians as Bossuet, Maimbourg and Meurisse no longer suggested that Luther and Calvin were fathered by the devil or likened their followers to apes in the manner of certain anti-Protestant polemics of the later sixteenth century, but their depiction of the reformers as headstrong individuals who bucked at legitimate authority and of Protestantism as the religion of republicanism repeated with only modest variation the charges of sedition and immorality most commonly levelled against the faith in the early years of the Wars of Religion.[60] The mocking satire of clerical fraud and popular superstition found in much sixteenth-century Reformed propaganda disappeared from Huguenot publications by the mid seventeenth century, but this is largely attributable to changing tastes and to governmental repression, for Protestant pastors faced expulsion from the kingdom if they expressed opinions that royal administrators deemed slanderous of the Roman church. When, on the eve of the Revocation, Huguenot ministers began to publish outspoken defences of their cause from the safety of exile, they drew amply on the stock bogey-men of seventeenth-century European anti-Catholicism: the Inquisition, the mistreatment of the Indians, and the claim that Catholics could never be loyal subjects since they always owed a share of their political fealty to the Pope in Rome.[61] Faced with increasingly intense Catholic proselytisation, the Reformed also revised their catechisms to spell out more clearly the reasons why theirs was the true faith and the Roman church was in error.[62]

---

[59] Etienne François, 'De l'uniformité à la tolérance. Confession et société urbaine en Allemagne, 1650–1800', *Annales: Economies, Sociétés, Civilisations*, 37 (1982), 788; François, *Protestants et catholiques en Allemagne. Identités et pluralisme. Augsbourg, 1648–1806* (Paris, 1993).

[60] Dompnier, *Le venin de l'hérésie*, chs. 2–4, provides an excellent account of the image of Protestantism in the militant Catholic literature of the seventeenth century. This may be usefully compared with G. Wylie Sypher, ' "Faisant ce qu'il leur vient à plaisir": The Image of Protestantism in French Catholic Polemics on the Eve of the Religious Wars', *The Sixteenth Century Journal*, 11 (1980), 59–84; Benedict, 'Of Marmites and Martyrs'.

[61] [Claude Brousson], *Estat des Reformez en France* (Cologne, 1684); Jacques Solé, *Le débat entre protestants et catholiques français de 1598 à 1685* (Paris, 1985), 175–94, 1364–5; Guy Howard Dodge, *The Political Theory of the Huguenots of the Dispersion, With Special Reference to the Thought and Influence of Pierre Jurieu* (New York, 1947; repr. New York, 1972), 14.

[62] Kathleen L. M. Faust, 'A Beleaguered Society: Protestant Families in La Rochelle, 1628–1685' (PhD. dissertation, Northwestern University, 1980), 353.

The extent to which such views were shared by the less well educated or more broad minded members of each faith may well be questioned.[63] When, in the wake of the Revocation, a Protestant from the Cévenol market town of Saint-Hippolyte-du-Fort set out an '*abrégé très sincère*' of his beliefs so that his children would remember the faith into which they were baptised, the document was anything but prolix in its explanation of the points of difference with the church of Rome. The author, Pierre Lézan, listed only three items: (1) 'we' worship one God in three persons and address our prayers to God with the sole intercession of Christ, while the Roman church believes that one should also pray to the saints; (2) 'we' say our prayers in a language understood by all, while the Roman church uses a language people cannot understand to keep them ignorant; and (3) 'our' communion service conforms to the model of the Bible and the practice of the church until the Council of Constance, while the Roman church's does not. Still, the very fact that Lézan sought in this manner to keep alive within his family a sense of his ancestral faith's differences from Rome is a telling sign of the importance he placed upon remaining true to that faith, as is his claim that the conversion of one of his sons to Catholicism 'nearly killed' him and his wife.[64] With the growth over time of literacy and the efforts of the opinion makers of both confessions to underscore the flaws of the other, it seems probable that the strength of confessional identity was stronger in 1685 than in 1600.

Despite the fact that the intense inter-confessional violence of the years 1560 to 1572 gave way to generally more peaceful, although by no means entirely untroubled, Catholic-Reformed interaction over the subsequent century, the two confessions thus remained divided by mutually hostile visions of one another and a strong tendency toward group endogamy. Indeed, both the strength of group identity and the degree to which social networks were segregated along confessional lines may have been greater in 1685 than they had been in the early years of the Wars of Religion. In such a situation, the failure of the Revocation of the Edict of Nantes to reunite all Frenchmen in a single church becomes anything but surprising. Rather than remain within the Roman church in the wake of the forced abjurations of 1685, the majority of Nouveaux Catholiques preferred to flee the country or to abstain from worship. Soon, they would begin to organise the clandestine assemblies of the 'Desert', bringing the history of Reformed worship full circle to the situation of the years between 1555 and the Edict of January 1562.

With the chief parameters for the history of Catholic-Reformed co-existence between 1555 and 1685 now sketched, it can be seen that it was anything

---

[63] Elisabeth Labrousse, 'Conversions dans les deux sens', in *La conversion au XVIIe siècle* (Marseille, 1983), 161–72, does just this.

[64] 'Pierre Lézan, secrétaire du consistoire de Saint-Hippolyte 1663–1700: Extraits de ses mémoires', in Clément Ribard, *Notes d'histoire cévenole* (Cazillac, 1898), 57–61.

but paradoxical that France should have been in the 1560s at once one of the first countries in Western Europe to grant rights of worship to a Protestant minority and the site of the bloodiest interconfessional violence of the era. Both were part of the difficult adjustment to the sudden emergence of a situation of religious pluralism for which little in the country's traditions prepared it. Catholic intolerance was encouraged by France's most deeply rooted political myths, which linked the nation's existence to its historic success in combatting heresy; Reformed intolerance was encouraged by Calvin's insistence that Christian magistrates were obliged to uphold the true faith, and by the hopes that took root amid the surge of Protestant sentiment around 1560 that the established church might soon be swept away. Since the advance of the Reformed was accompanied by provocative gestures of rupture with the established church order, violence between the two groups soon followed. While the dominant outlook on both sides of the religious divide was hostile to the toleration of more than one faith, the country's cultural traditions none the less contained intellectual resources that could be deployed to justify a policy of toleration, especially as a temporary concession to urgent political necessity. The very strength of the Reformed movement's growth created such a necessity – or at least so it seemed to a ruling queen regent who was a stranger to the country's political traditions. But toleration initially proved impossible to implement. Recurring civil wars and violence led to constant alterations in the royal legislation governing the rights and privileges granted the Reformed, while in nearly all religiously divided localities, the adherents of whichever faith was politically the weaker were forced to interrupt public worship and then to struggle to resume it time and again.

After the great bloodbath of Saint Bartholomew, spontaneous interconfessional violence declined significantly. By 1598, the elements of an enduring legal regime to govern the co-existence of the two faiths had been defined, and the succession crisis that troubled the country after 1584 had been resolved. Even the worst periods of confessional tension had never eliminated all neighbourly relations between members of the two groups. Now, the retreat of confessional violence and the establishment of a successful legal framework for their mutual co-existence allowed their generally peaceful character to come to the fore.

Yet again it is no paradox that the achievement of more peaceful co-existence between the two religions was followed three generations later by the revocation of the rights of worship granted the Reformed. Peaceful co-existence does not appear to have engendered more frequent economic interaction or intermarriage. Instead, continuing inter-confessional competition for souls and the efforts of rigorists on both sides to combat certain practices that linked people together across the religious divide fuelled an ongoing process of boundary demarcation and group reinforcement. Mutual suspicion, continued skirmishing over the precise extent of the legal privileges granted the Reformed, and intermittent violence continued to mark relations between the groups. Once the realisation set in among the Huguenots that their original dream of the complete transformation of the Gallican church along Reformed lines would never be realised, the ever-present threat of the repeal of their legal privileges moved certain of their theorists to articulate broad arguments in favour of the principle of freedom of conscience. The majority of their spokesmen defended their rights of worship on far narrower grounds, however, while the impetus that pushed the 95 per cent of the population that remained Catholic to embrace the general principle of toleration was far weaker yet. For the vast majority of the population, the granting of rights of worship to heretics remained, as it had been at the outset, a political concession to a group whose eradication, although perhaps desirable, carried too high a cost in lives to be practicable. In an era of growing state power, that was a weak foundation for enduring rights of worship, for as the power of the monarchy grew, the political calculus changed. In the absence of a widely shared belief in the principles of freedom of conscience or freedom of worship for all, a regime of toleration extracted essentially as a political concession to some always remained vulnerable to repeal by royal fiat. At the same time, the reinforcement of group identity among both confessions over the course of the seventeenth century guaranteed that, when royal fiat undid the regime of co-existence worked out at so much bloodshed between 1562 and 1598, the religious division of the kingdom would prove beyond repeal.

6 Confession, conscience and honour: the limits of magisterial tolerance in sixteenth-century Strassburg

Lorna Jane Abray

Proponents of dozens of conflicting visions of reformed Christianity coexisted uneasily in sixteenth-century Strassburg, forcing debate on the permissible limits of religious diversity.[1] Thanks to the astonishing variety of opinion in Strassburg, to its magistrates' reluctance to punish people for their beliefs (and also perhaps to the loss of most of its judicial records), Strassburg regularly appears in general histories of the sixteenth century as a model of religious tolerance towards individuals, or even toleration of faiths, an exceptional polity in an age that is often thought rarely to have hesitated before killing dissenters.[2] While the rarity of executions for religious crimes does point to a relatively tolerant policy, Strassburg's Reformation history encompasses a well-documented array of other forms of intolerance: official and familial bullying of nuns in the 1520s and again in the 1590s, the pursuit and harassment of suspected Anabaptists that peaked between the mid-1520s and the early 1540s, the demonstrations against Catholic services and priests in the 1540s and 1550s, and anti-Calvinist displays of the 1580s and 1590s.[3]

---

[1] See, for example, Marc Lienhard (ed.), *Croyants et sceptiques au XVIᵉ siècle: Le dossier des 'Epicuriens,'* Société savante d'Alsace et des régions de l'Est (hereafter SSARE), Collection Recherches et Documents, vol. 30 (Strasbourg, 1981). *Täuferakten Elsass.* Manfred Krebs and Hans Georg Rott (eds.), *Elsass I. Teil, Stadt Strassburg, 1522–1532* and *II. Teil, Stadt Strassburg, 1533–1535* (Gütersloh, 1959–60) and Marc Lienhard, Stephen F. Nelson, and Hans Georg Rott (eds.), *Elsass III. Teil, Stadt Strassburg, 1536–42* and *IV. Teil, Stadt Strassburg, 1543–52* (Gütersloh, 1986 and 1988) (hereafter TAE), indices in vols. 2 and 4, 'Duldung,' 'Gewissensfreiheit.' For the general context, Hans R. Guggisberg, 'The Defence of Religious Toleration and Religious Liberty in Early Modern Europe: Arguments, Pressures, and some Consequences', *History of European Ideas*, 4 (1983), 35–50, and Bob Scribner in Chapter 3.

[2] To cite a recent survey text, 'Strasbourg remained an island of toleration in a sea of persecution and oppression', De Lamar Jensen, *Reformation Europe: Age of Reformation and Revolution*, 2nd edn (Lexington, MA, 1992), 138.

[3] François Joseph Fuchs, 'Les catholiques strasbourgeois de 1529 à 1681', *Archives de l'église d'Alsace*, n.s. 22 (1975), 142–69 and Joseph Fridolin Vierling, *Das Ringen um die letzten dem Katholizismus treuen Klöster Strassburgs* (Strasbourg, 1914). TAE for texts on the treatment of Anabaptists. Erdmann Weyrauch, *Konfessionelle Krise und soziale Stabilität: Das Interim in Strassburg, 1548–1562* (Stuttgart, 1978). Lorna Jane Abray, *The People's Reformation: Magistrates, Clergy and Commons in Strasbourg, 1500–1598* (Ithaca and Oxford, 1985), 88–90, 122, 161.

Coercion was everywhere part of the sixteenth-century's religious politics, and recognition of this has moved historians of Strassburg to become increasingly attentive to discord and repression in the city.[4] For the city's secular rulers, arbiters of repression or tolerance, diversity of religious opinion constituted a complex political problem that threatened to bring their new duties to defend the city's evangelical confessions into conflict with more traditional measures of their honour as magistrates.

Officially Catholic until 1529, Strassburg's magistrates thereafter maintained a collective identity as evangelicals[5]. Their original confession, the *Tetrapolitana* of 1530, drafted by the local clergy but presented to the Emperor at Augsburg in the name of the regime, defined the city as evangelical in the Swiss and South German mode. In 1536 the city's theologians reached a concorde with their Saxon counterparts, making the 1530 Augsburg Confession Strassburg's second definition of the true faith. Biconfessionalism encouraged multiple disputes about where the city stood, making its Lutheran status ambiguous until 1577, when the city's preachers signed the Bergen Book, or even 1598, when the magistrates finally accepted what by then had become the Formula of Concord. None of these declarations of faith created uniformity of belief, or even practice. Catholic observances were outlawed in 1529, but Catholicism survived and recovered a legal status

---

[4] Nikolaus Paulus' arguments against the dominant liberal Protestant presentation of Strassburg's history at the turn of the century ('La liberté de conscience et les professeurs du séminaire protestant de Strasbourg au 16ᵉ siècle', *Revue catholique d'Alsace*, 9 (1890), 108–21, 158–61, 200–12; *Protestantismus und Toleranz im 16. Jahrhundert* (Freiburg im Breisgau, 1911) had little influence. At mid-century Philippe Dollinger still accepted much of the convention of Strassburg's tolerant reformation, but substituted 'moderation' for 'toleration', 'La tolérance à Strasbourg au XVIᵉ siècle', in *Hommages à Lucien Febvre*, vol. 2 (Paris, 1953), 241–49. Miriam Usher Chrisman, *Strasbourg and the Reform* (New Haven and London, 1967), chapters 6 and 11, presented the leaders of the local reformation, both clerical and lay, as mediating men, working to tamp down ideologically driven controversy, at the same time that she recognized patterns of religious discrimination in the city. Recent studies continue the work of defining and accounting for the local balance between persecution and indulgence: Thomas A. Brady, 'Architect of Persecution: Jacob Sturm and the Fall of the Sects at Strasbourg', *Archiv für Reformationsgeschichte*, 79 (1988), 262–81 and 'The Earth is the Lord's and our Homeland as well: Martin Bucer and the Politics of Strasbourg', in Christian Krieger and Marc Lienhard (eds.) *Martin Bucer and Sixteenth Century Europe. Actes du colloque de Strasbourg (28–31 août 1991)*, 2 vols. (Leiden, 1993), I, 129–49; Marijn de Kroon, 'Martin Bucer and the Problem of Tolerance', *Sixteenth Century Journal*, 19 (1988), 157–68; Marc Lienhard, *Religiöse Toleranz in Strasburg im 16. Jahrhundert*; John S. Oyer, 'Bucer Opposes the Anabaptists', and R. Emmet McLaughlin, 'The Politics of Dissent: Martin Bucer, Caspar Schwenkfeld and the Schwenkfelders of Strasbourg', both in *Mennonite Quarterly Review*, 68 (1994), 24–50 and 39–78; Peter Matheson, 'Martin Bucer and the Old Church', and Martin Greschat, 'The Relation between Church and Civil Community in Martin Bucer's Reforming Work', both in D. F. Wright (ed.), *Martin Bucer: Reforming Church and Community* (Cambridge, 1994), 5–16 and 17–31.

[5] Johann Adam, *Evangelische Kirchengeschichte der Stadt Strassburg bis zur französische Revolution* (Strasbourg, 1922) remains the best survey of the city's sixteenth-century confessional history.

at mid-century. While the great wave of sectarian activity that so frightened magistrates and preachers from the mid-1520s to the mid-1530s ebbed thereafter, Anabaptists and spiritualists never disappeared from the sixteenth century city, and meanwhile, the influx of French-speaking Protestant refugees from the 1560s on kept the city's 'sacramentarian' past part of its Lutheran present throughout much of the latter half of the century.

The magistrates, responsible for order, feared that variety in religion threatened civic peace. From time to time they tolerated public services by both evangelicals and Catholics or by Calvinists as well as Lutherans (in the 1520s, the 1550s, and the 1560s), but these were difficult decades, when the magistrates had to bow to foreign pressures, and offended local sensibilities by so doing.[6] The exercise of toleration in Reformation Strassburg was always unstable because of its emotional colouration by fears of disorder. Unlike conformity or indifference, toleration in the sixteenth century could not coexist with ease of mind and in Strassburg it was never the policy of choice, but always one undertaken to stave off a larger disaster. As the city council said to the evangelical clergy, in uneasy recognition of their legal obligation to permit Catholic services in the aftermath of the Schmalkaldic War, 'there is a great difference between the meaning of the little word "tolerate" and the idea of taking something for right.'[7]

Strassburg's magistrates did not recoil from what they understood to be legitimate violence in defence of right religion. They drowned, burned, banished, flogged, and fined violators of their religious order. For crimes against Christian norms of doctrine and morality they:

> drowned Thomas Buhl in 1518 for blasphemy;[8]
>
> executed a man, perhaps Meister Georg, the executioner, for blasphemy, in 1520[9]
>
> put Thomas Saltzmann to death in 1527 for blasphemy;[10]
>
> drowned Hans Heinrich Schoen in 1533 for bigamy;[11]

---

[6] Abray, *The People's Reformation*, chapters 4 and 5.

[7] Archives de Saint Thomas, housed in the Archives municipales de Strasbourg, 87/47 (1554), f. 8v.

[8] Rodolphe Reuss, *La justice criminelle et la police des moeurs à Strasbourg au XVIe et au XVIIe siècle* (Strasbourg, 1885), 255.

[9] Léon Dacheux (ed.), 'Annales de Sébastien Brant', *Bulletin de la Société pour la conservation des monuments historiques d'Alsace* (hereafter *BSCMHA*), n.s 19 (1899), 45, #4402, note, and Reuss, *La justice*, 255–6.

[10] TAE I, #110, 133–4, #113, 135–6, #114, 136–7 and IV, addendum to #114, 397–8. Léon Dacheux (ed.), 'Les chroniques de Jacob Trausch et de Jean Wencker', *BSCMHA*, n.s. 15 (1892), #2677, 37. Léon Dacheux (ed.), 'La chronique strasbourgeoise de Sébald Büheler', *BSCMHA*, n.s. 13 (1888), #232 and 233, 76. See below 104.

[11] TAE II, 321, n. 1. Rodolphe Reuss (ed.), 'Les éphémerides de Jacques de Gottesheim, docteur en droit, prébendier du grand-choeur de la cathédrale (1524–1543)', *BSCMHA*, n.s. 19 (1899), 276. He was a priest who also passed himself off as a nobleman, 'von Schoenberg'.

drowned Claus Frey in 1534, for bigamy;[12]
burned two now-nameless sodomites in 1539;[13]
burned a now-anonymous woman for witchcraft in 1564;[14]
decapitated Georg Koch for blasphemy in 1569;[15]
beheaded Casper Meyenlauer and drowned his mother-in-law, for incest, in 1574;[16]
burned a now-nameless woman in 1579 for witchcraft, [17]

and sent no one knows how many others away to fates unknown, and flogged or fined still more, their stories likewise now unknown.

For all their antipathy to toleration, and for all the misery they inflicted, Strassburg's rulers avoided falling into routinised religious persecutions. To understand how they regulated repression, it is important to move beyond arguments about relative degrees of tolerance and intolerance, or distinctions between tolerance of individuals and toleration of faiths. Instead, we need to focus on the clash between the confessional impulse towards conformity (with its attendant risk of persecution) and the gubernatorial impulse towards the preservation of civic peace by expedient avoidance of conflict (with its attendant risk of perpetuating potentially explosive religious differences).[18] Success in keeping the peace was an old measure of magisterial honour; the creation of religious concord was a new, and difficult standard. In Strassburg rulers resolved tensions between confession and honour, and thus tensions between the desirable goal of religious concord (to be achieved, if necessary, by force) and the regrettable expedient of toleration of faiths (always, in practice, achieved by force) in conservative ways driven by their commitment to freedom of conscience and to long-standing local judicial practice. Three categories of documents demonstrate that the controlling ideas at play in the council chambers of sixteenth-century Strassburg were not so much tolerance and intolerance, but confession, conscience, and honour. The first set consists of magisterial endorsements for clerical confessions of faith. Next come a series of statements, sometimes public, sometimes official but not widely publicized, and sometimes private, showing the oligarchs' consistent concern

---

[12] TAE II, #366, 16, #456, 208–9, #504, 275, n. 30, and #564, 321–42, which reprints much of Wolfgang Capito's *Ein wunderbar geschicht* (Strasbourg, 1534). See below 106–7.

[13] 'La chronique strasbourgeoise de Sébald Büheler', #275, 83.

[14] 'La chronique strasbourgeoise de Sébald Büheler', #415, 113. According to Büheler, this was the first such execution in a long time.

[15] Ratsprotokolle, minutes of Rat und XXI (hereafter RP), housed in the Archives municipales de Strasbourg (hereafter AMS) 1569, ff. 286v-287v, 305v-308v, 319v-320v, 327v-328v. See below 104–5.

[16] 'La chronique strasbourgeoise de Sébald Büheler', #500, 129.

[17] Aloys Meister and Aloys Ruppel (eds.), 'Die strassburger Chronik des Johann Georg Saladins', *BSCMHA*, n.s. 23, #2504, 342.

[18] Compare Mario Turchetti, 'Religious Concord and Political Tolerance in Sixteenth- and Seventeenth-Century France', *Sixteenth Century Journal*, 22 (1991), 15–26.

to protect freedom of conscience. Third are the mandates and ordinances regulating religious practice. A fourth set of fragmentary records allow us to test how well, in practice, the magistrates managed to do their duty to protect the true faith without violating their own, or anyone else's conscience.

The documents that develop Strassburg's evolving sense of orthodoxy through the ratification of formal confessions of faith also establish the force of the magistrates' commitment to what they accepted as God's word. Not only did the original Reformation magistrates choose to risk imperial wrath by opting for evangelical theology, their successors too maintained commitments to their confessional principles in the face of real threats to their sovereignty, from both the Emperor and the French. As their lawyers reminded them, a decade or so after they had effectively ripped up the clauses in the Religious Peace of Augsburg most obnoxious to their majority, what they had done was utterly illegal and 'their graces [could] thank God almighty they had gotten away with it', instead of provoking invasion or other punishments of their burghers by the Catholic powers.[19] Strassburg's rulers were sensitive to any criticism that they were not true to the evangelical faith, particularly if it came from the clergy, and proclamation after proclamation on religion strove to impress on their subjects the strength of their evangelical allegiance. One example, from 1597, shows the late Reformation magistrates summing up their inheritance and intentions. Warning their subjects not to attend Calvinist services outside the city, the oligarchs remind them of the 'loyal and fatherly way our dear forefathers worked and occupied themselves to hold themselves and their subjects to the recognized truth of the holy Evangel, the unaltered Augsburg Confession', and how they themselves 'are no less inclined, but equally zealous . . . to see the word of God purely and clearly taught in the schools and from the pulpits'.[20]

With equal conviction, three generations of Strassburg magistrates insisted that their zeal for the word of God did not authorise them to force anyone's conscience; forcing consciences, in their view, was the worst tyranny imaginable.[21] As they said to themselves and their clergy during the 1533 synodal proceedings – activities albeit largely directed at encouraging conformity– 'the council does not want to force anyone's conscience'.[22] In 1535 the oligarchs altered the wording of an oath not to launch public attacks on the Strassburg church's doctrines, recently drafted to restrain Anabaptist criticism, because some were misreading the intent of the original wording, and

---

[19] AST 87/61c, ff. 4v-5r, composed in 1574. For the city's relations with the Empire and with France, see Abray, *People's Reformation*, chapter 4.

[20] Archives de Saint Thomas (hereafter AST), housed in the Archives municipales de Strasbourg 84/112, f. 703r.

[21] RP 1580, ff. 259v-260r.

[22] TAE I, #441, 178.

putting it about that the magistrates made them 'swear to believe what the preachers teach'. Since that was not the regime's intention, the Senate and Privy Council (XXI) changed the wording of the article.[23] In 1581 the magistrates reminded their subjects that all burghers swore annually not to taunt or molest each other over religion.[24] They were careful to protect their own rights, too. As Barthel Keller explained his refusal to ratify the Formula of Concord in 1577, 'This is over my head and I am reluctant to bind my conscience to it.'[25] Suspicion of the clergy played a part here, as it had more transparently in 1534 when Carl Mieg had balked at the Tetrapolitan Confession, saying that as a layman, he feared being trapped into something he did not understand and then forced to confess and believe it.[26] Perhaps the most striking statements of their devotion to freedom of conscience are those that are imbedded in laws limiting freedom of practice, like the 1597 mandate against Calvinist services: 'We do not wish to afflict anyone's conscience in religious matters, or to force anyone into our church, which is founded on God's word, because we well know that Almighty God wants a voluntary and unforced worship service'.[27]

As for magisterial honour, it was rooted in very old ideas about a presumed divine commission to rulers. Strassburg's Protestant clergy, like their Catholic predecessors, regularly expounded on Romans 13 and both individually and collectively the magistrates considered themselves to be appointed by God to protect the good and punish the wicked. Hans Hammerer, for example, saw the hand of God in his election as Ammeister, the city's senior office for commoners.[28] Another layman, not a magistrate but the humanist, satirist and religious propagandist Johann Fischart, summed up the commonplaces of the sixteenth century in a gloss on St. Paul published in Strassburg in 1588. Secular rulers exist 'to legislate wholesome laws and customs, to appoint good men to the councils, the church, and the schools; to reconcile citizens who quarrel with each other; to administer justice; to protect the dutiful and the pious; to punish miscreants; to watch over the poor, widows and orphans . . . in short, to foster the common tranquility, security, calm, and peace'.[29]

---

[23] TAE II, #647, 439. Compare the 1538 mandate, TAE III, #816, 139–42, and the revised *Täuferartikel* of that same year, #817, 142–3.

[24] AST 84/48a, #94.

[25] RP 1577, ff. 725v–732v.

[26] TAE II, #523.

[27] AST 84/112, ff. 703r–704r.

[28] RP 1565, f. 1v. This was not a boast, but part of his personal prayer for divine guidance in the execution of his duties.

[29] *Ordenliche Beschreibung*, sig. Aii recto-Aiii verso. See also Hans-Christoph Rublack, 'Political and Social Norms in Urban Communities in the Holy Roman Empire', in Kasper von Greyerz (ed.), *Religion, Politics and Social Protest* (London, 1984), 24–60, and R. W. Scribner, 'Police and the Territorial State in Sixteenth Century Württemberg', in E. I. Kouri

Constitutionally Strassburg's rulers derived their authority from their relationship to the Emperor, and had done so without a rival within their walls after exiling their Bishop in 1262.[30] It was their right and duty to legislate for their subjects on civil and criminal matters. The sixteenth-century magistrates had inherited *Stadtrechte* from the twelfth and thirteenth centuries, as well as a body of legislation built up but not codified in the fourteenth and fifteenth centuries. In the course of the sixteenth century local law took a slight tint from the imperial *Constitutio Criminalis Carolina*, ratified at the Regensburg Diet in 1532, a deeper one (particularly with respect to marriage law) from the city's conversion to Protestantism, and a still stronger coloration through the slow acculturation of Roman law. The effects of the *Carolina* were attenuated because the Regensburg Diet had ratified it only after the edition of the so-called 'Salvatorische Clausel,' protecting the precedence of local laws; Strassburg took advantage of that saving clause, for example in formulating religious legislation against the Anabaptists, where it was unwilling to accept the imperial demand for summary execution.[31] The city had earlier begun what was to prove a very lengthy process of creating a local codification of its statutes; a considerable body of morals legislation had already been brought together in a single text, the *Constitution und Satzung* of 1529, when the *Carolina* was passed, a larger (but still partial) compendium finally appeared in two parts early in the seventeenth-century, with the publication of the *Reformierte Ordnung* of 1620 and the *Polizeiordnung* of 1628.[32] In all this mass of legislation the crucial text is already present at least as early as 1471: 'It isn't right to pass judgement without hearing out the accused, we shouldn't do it.'[33]

The duty to legislate produced five sets of laws bearing on the policing of religion, and thus on the limits of tolerance:

---

and Tom Scott (eds.), *Politics and Society in Reformation Europe: Essays for Sir Geoffrey Elton on his sixty-fifth Birthday* (London, 1987), 103–20, in particular 104–5, on humanist and evangelical influences.

[30] Wilhelm Weigand (ed.), *Urkunden und Stadtrechte bis zum 1294. Urkundenbuch der Stadt Strassburg* (Strassburg, 1879), 467. Karl Theodor von Eheberg, *Verfassungs-, Verwaltungs- und Wirtschaftsgeschichte der Stadt Strassburg bis 1681* (Strassburg, 1899), and Ulrich Crämer, *Die Verfassung und Verwaltung Strassburgs von der Reformationszeit bis zum Fall der Reichstadt, 1521–1681* (Frankfurt, 1931).

[31] Horst Schraepler, *Die rechtliche Behandlung der Täufer in der deutschen Schweiz, Südwestdeutschland, und Hessen, 1525–1618* (Tübingen, 1957), 21–2, on the imperial legislation; in Strassburg no one was ever executed, let alone without a trial, for Anbaptism. TAE III, #816, (1538), 138–9.

[32] Reuss, *La justice*, 31–3. Roland Ganghoffer, 'Droit savant et droit pénal à l'époque de Charles Quint', in *Charles Quint, le Rhin et La France* (Strasbourg, 1973), 115 and 123

[33] Archives départementales du Bas-Rhin, G370A, f. 10v; the same caution is repeated in G371, f. 17r, the Jura municipalia of 1563/64.

mandates intended to stifle religious argument, both oral and written;
mandates intended to keep subjects out of religious services run by
   the established clergy's confessional rivals, whether Catholic, sectarian, or Calvinist;
mandates and orders forcing religious instruction on children,
   apprentices, and nuns;
a mandate obliging fathers to have their children baptized within six
   weeks of birth;
mandates on blasphemy.

In the eyes of the magistrates, none of these laws constituted a violation
of freedom of conscience. The mandates against debate were intended to
inhibit freedom of expression in order to preserve the peace, and not to coerce
anyone's beliefs.[34] Likewise, barring attendance at rival services was distinguished from the kind of legislation that *would* constrain consciences, by
creating obligations to attend the services of the established church.[35] This
compulsion they explicitly rejected for independent adults of both sexes.[36]
The patriarchal framework of thought used by the Strassburg magistrates
removed the taint of violating conscience from the next two sets of legislation: children, apprentices, and nuns were all dependent persons over whom
the magistrates could claim to exercise the paternal duty of instruction;[37] the
obligation to baptise was likewise not seen by its authors as a coercion of
Anabaptists' consciences, but as the city fathers protecting vulnerable infants
from the misguided actions of lesser fathers who would deprive them of
religious instruction by separating them from the true church.[38] In
Strassburg's blasphemy legislation, magisterial honour and the honour of God
entwined, with fatal consequences for some, although the magistrates again
did not regard this legislation as incompatible with freedom of conscience.
Blasphemy, after all, was an overt, public act, not a private mental state.
Criminal law covering blasphemy predated the Reformation and underwent
no fundamental change because of it.[39] On no occasion did the magistrates

---

[34] Abray, *The People's Reformation*, 48–9.
[35] *Ibid.*, chapter 5.
[36] For example, RP 1544, f. 523r. If the records of Anabaptist interrogations are representative,
   they did not consistently credit husbands with responsibility for their wives' religious conformity – or the capacity to enforce it.
[37] Obligation of heads of households to send dependents to church, Disciplinary Ordinance, in
   Roehrich, *Mittheilungen*, 1: 252–4. For attempts to convert the nuns, Fuchs, 'Les catholiques'
   and Vierling, *Das Ringen*.
[38] TAE provides abundant documentation for the first half of the century. Brady, 'Architect of
   Persecution', on the introduction of compulsory baptism. TAE III, #816 (1538), 141–2 on
   the insistence that legislation against the sects was not coercing consciences.
[39] The 1628 codification of municipal criminal law refers to acts of 1510, 1516, 1522, 1526,
   1529, 1533, 1549, 1552, 1566, 1568, and 1603; *Der Statt Strassburg Policeij Ordnung*

confound the accusations of blasphemy made by the local clergy against their theological rivals with legal charges of blasphemy. Under the local blasphemy statute, words had to be said 'irreverently' to come under the law, and blasphemy legislation was never invoked to prosecute Catholic, Calvinist, or sectarian theologies.

Strassburg's rulers were convinced that they had made good laws. Another, no less important standard by which magisterial honour could be measured, was the fair enforcement of their laws. To make good on their promise that no one should be judged without a hearing, the magistrates ran an elaborate court system. Minor offences punishable only by fines were dealt with by a junior body, the *Siebnergericht*; in theory any offence carrying the threat of corporal or capital punishment went to the Senate (*Rat*), sitting as a court of law, although in practice particularly serious cases received the attention not just of the Senate but of the Senate and Privy Councils (Rat und XXI) together.[40] Some business also went in the first instance to new courts set up as part of the local reformation: a Marriage Court, created in 1529, the *Wiedertaüferherren* who investigated – 'talked with' might be more accurate – Anabaptists from 1530 until 1590, and a Morals Court set up in 1548.[41] The marriage court and the *Wiedertaüferherren* both aimed at reconciliation, a hearkening back to a fifteenth-century emphasis on making things right between two parties, rather than the forward-looking sixteenth-century emphasis on individual correction that animated proponents of the Morals Court.[42]

Besides the marriage court, the lords investigating Anabaptism and the Morals Court, Strassburg had another, non-judicial, mechanism for dealing with religious dissent. In 1533 the synod recommended the creation of a

---

(Bibliothèque nationale et universitaire de Strasbourg, M40.765), 8. AST 84/48, 1, i, undated, may be the 1510, 1516, or 1522 text. The Disciplinary Ordinance of 1535 includes the Constitution und Satzung ... wie das Gotslestern, Fluchen, Spielen ... gestrafft werden soll, from 1529, and the renewed mandate of 1533; see Timotheus Wilhelm Roehrich, *Mittheilungen aus der Geschichte der evangelischen Kirche des Elsasses*, 1 (Strassburg, 1855), 265 and 281–2. In 1568 the regime published a new 'Constitution' against blasphemy and swearing (Bibliothèque nationale et universitaire de Strasbourg, R22 (12) and RP 22 September 1568, ff. 400r-402v. Its preamble cites the Ten Commandments and 'other' texts of divine and human law (of which only the Imperial *Policey und Halsgerichto* ordinance is named) to underline the absolute duty of civil authorities rigorously and zealously to pursue and punish those who insult the honour of God.

[40] Reuss, *La justice*, 10–14 and Crämer, *Die Verfassung*, 55–80.

[41] The records of the marriage court are lost, but see François Wendel, *Le Mariage à Strasbourg à l'époque de la réforme, 1520–1692* (Strasbourg, 1928). Relatively full records of the Wiedertäuferherren are extant only from 1556–1573 (AMS 1/14) but a great deal of fragmentary surviving evidence has been gathered in the TAE. The records of the morals court have disappeared.

[42] On the distinction between mediation and punishment, see Pieter Spierenburg, *The Spectacle of Suffering: Executions and the Evolution of Repression from a Preindustrial Metropolis to the European Experience* (Cambridge, 1984), 7–11.

body to continue its work of hearing out those who were troubled about the doctrine taught in Strassburg. Unlike the courts, this was a mixed body: two magistrates, two church wardens, and two preachers were delegated to make themselves available to anyone who wanted their services, and to bring people's concerns forward to the Senate and XXI. If the commissioners refused to bring someone's concerns to the Senate and XXI, that person was free to approach the council directly.[43] Created expressly to prevent complaint that the regime was forcing consciences, the commission seems to have had little business.

The court system, however, had considerable business with religious cases. The loss of the bulk of the city's judicial records in 1870 makes it difficult to reconstruct case law and impossible to be sure about very much of what happened as Strassburg's rulers arrested, tried, sentenced, and punished. What follows must, of necessity be tentative, even on central points, but enough information survives to give an outline of how repression operated, and thus the limits of tolerance.

Strassburg's record books for arrests are lost. What evidence remains points to a serious effort in principal to identify religious dissidents, not necessarily for 'trial', but to talk to them. (One of the operating conditions of a system of belief that does not want to 'make rules for the Holy Spirit' is the obligation to listen to holy fools, and the magistrates' motives for hauling people in for questioning may not have been straightforwardly punitive, given how much time they spent with dissidents engaging in what was psychologically close to begging, asking over and over, 'Why can't you agree with us?'[44]) People with doubts about the righteousness of the clergy's teachings were invited to come forward. Denunciations were invited – without much success.[45] Sometimes people were identified on the basis of warrants issued elsewhere; Veit Barthel, a sectarian who eventually died still waiting to be extradited to Electoral Saxony for trial, wrote a signed letter to the magistrates, not long after the Saxons asked for any news of him.[46]

Veit Barthel complained because he did not receive a formal hearing. He did not want mercy, he said, just his rights; Strassburg's rulers were liars

---

[43] TAE II, #433, 135–6.

[44] See, for example, the records of interrogations in AMS 1/14.

[45] Legislation governing the repression of Anabaptism obliged burghers to identify suspicious people, AMS R4, f. 139r (1537). Legislation against blasphemy likewise called for denunciation of offenders, but on at least one occasion the magistrates commented on the lack of compliance, Ratsprotokolle, minutes of Rat und XXI, housed in the Archives municipales de Strasbourg 1555, f. 172v #3 and 173v.

[46] Barthel's arrest, TAE III, #928, 345–7, and IV, #686a, 545. Hans-Christoph Rublack's commentary on the operation of the hue and cry in fifteenth-century Strassburg ('Political and Social Norms', 29) applies better to the recognition of an individual as 'foreign' – e.g. by dress or speech – than to the recognition of individuals by personal identities.

and without honour to hold him without a hearing.[47] The loss of the city's trial records makes it impossible to know what 'being heard' actually meant in the Strassburg courts. The *Wiedertaüferherren*, who were all magistrates, were models of patience, but whether they modelled their conduct in that capacity on their behaviour on other benches, is impossible to say. That they had no criminal jurisdiction as investigators of Anabaptism may have made a considerable difference in the way they treated their suspects.

Like the arrest records, books recording criminal sentences have also been lost, but evidence does remain of cases where the laws, particularly in capital cases, were not applied as first pronounced, or even applied at all. For example in the mid-1520s Juncker Wolff Haffner von Wasselnheim was sentenced to have his tongue torn out and then to be put to death for blasphemy; the sentence was commuted to life imprisonment, then changed to a combination of a recurring annual fine of four pounds to charity and a form of neighbourhood-arrest designed to keep him outside the city centre. Released from imprisonment, he fled – which is probably exactly what the magistrates expected.[48] An Anabaptist named Michael Meckel certainly did not receive the execution the law prescribed for his repeated violations of orders of exile.[49] Haffner's and Meckel's cases point to a pattern of using the lesser rather than the greater penalties the law provided in cases where sentence of death could be pronounced, a pattern confirmed by two further cases of blasphemy. Thomas Saltzmann was brought to trial in 1527 as an anti-Trinitarian blasphemer, for saying that the Old and New Testaments contradict each other, that Christ was a false prophet who deserved his death, and that there was only one God, who had appeared to Moses in the burning bush. Saltzmann stood by the idea that Christ was not God, but claimed witnesses exaggerated the outrageousness of his language. By the end of his trial he was full of repentance, and his judges commuted their original sentence of burning to decapitation.[50] Twenty-two years later Georg Koch, a mercenary from Fulda, came to trial for saying the Romans would not have killed Christ if he hadn't done something to deserve it. Koch was sentenced to have his tongue ripped out and be burned; the sentence was then commuted so that the executioner was ordered to begin by decapitating him, and then to mutilate and burn his corpse.[51] The magistrates could invoke grace and equity, part of the norms of sixteenth century law enforcement, to mitigate punishment for non-capital

[47] TAE III, #839, 240–1 (1538).
[48] TAE I, #114, n. 1, 136 and addendum, TAE II, 589–90. Specklin #2250 and #3987; Fragments, 13; Brady, *Ruling Class*, 365 and 436.
[49] Lorna Jane Abray, 'La vie d'un anabaptiste strasbourgeois au 16e siècle: Michael Meckel', *Revue d'histoire et de philosophie religieuses* 57 (1977), 195–207.
[50] See note 10. Perhaps not coincidentally, Saltzmann had been the only member of his guild not to side with the magistrates against the peasants in 1525.
[51] See note 15.

sentences as well, because while laws were expected to be severe, law enforcement was expected to be variable. Status, submissiveness to one's judges, the rarity or frequency of the offence, and the current sense of how threatening the offence was to good order all came into play in selecting penalties for the guilty.[52] Indeed, as Richard van Dülmen points out, there was an expected stage in early modern German trials where the judges heard arguments for clemency and took into account how different sentences might affect the interests of the criminal's kin or guild.[53] This stage is clearly documented in Georg Koch's case: evidence of mental debility was brought forward, attributed both to congenital weakness and to a battlefield blow on the head from a Turk, and officers from his regiment intervened to beg for mercy.[54]

Just as the right to legislate is an attribute of sovereignty, so too was the right to bend or suspend one's own laws in the interests of equity: limiting legitimate punishment was a display of power. Moreover 'mild' penalties encouraged people to see the magistrates as 'fatherly' and honourable in their comportment; the beneficiaries were as often as not the family or workmates of the accused, or even the magistrates, rather than the criminals themselves. Thus, after hearing petitions from his friends and kin, the Senate and XXI intervened to lighten the Rat's sentence on Georg Silberrad, a convicted blasphemer. The infamy attached to corporal punishment tainted kin and workmates, as well as the convict, and as a gesture to them, Silberrad, who had been sentenced to be pilloried and whipped, instead had his sentence commuted to a private rather than a public punishment, perhaps the month in prison on bread and water recommended by those who petitioned on his behalf.[55] Exile is milder than execution, and was not necessarily dishonouring; one could go into exile without ever being touched by the hangman, and thus one's associates were spared shame.[56] Still, exile might well be a death sentence in itself, as it was for the Anabaptist Michel Sattler, convicted and killed in Horb after being forced out of Strassburg. The beneficiaries in this case were the magistrates, who avoided carrying out the imperial mandate on him.[57] Finally, the exercise of clemency moved the

---

[52] Richard van Dülmen, *Theatre of Horror: Crime and Punishment in Early Modern Germany*, trans. Elisabeth Neu, (Cambridge, 1990), 24–5.

[53] van Dülmen, *Theatre of Horror*, 28–9.

[54] See note 15. The case is complicated by the mixing of civil and military jurisdictions.

[55] RP 1540, f. 53 r-v. Sebastian Franck made Strassburg's tendency to commute penalities proverbial ('Wo man anderswo henkt, da steicht man zu Strassburg mit Ruten aus', *Germaniae Chronicon* (1538), quoted by Klaus Depperman, 'Sebastian Franks Strassburger Aufenthalt', *Mennonitische Geschichtsblätter*, 46 (1989), 146), but it should be remembered that the substitution of whipping for execution still defamed its victim, and if coupled with exile, could make the hope of finding asylum elsewhere slender.

[56] van Dülmen, 22, 44–5, 49. Pieter Spierenburg, *The Spectacle of Suffering*, 19, 21, 59.

[57] Horst Schraepler, *Die rechtliche Behandlung*, 38–42.

magistrates' judicial work from the dishonourable side of justice, represented by the hangman, to the honourable side of practising Christian mercy. Not for nothing did sixteenth-century rulers use 'the sword' rather than 'the noose' as their symbol of office.

One last feature of Strassburg's criminal jurisprudence might, or might not, work to the advantage of religious dissidents: the refusal to set up a court with criminal jurisdiction over heresy.[58] Strassburg's rulers wanted nothing to do with an inquisition; they did not have the theological competence to run one themselves and they were quite unwilling to recreate any sort of clerical court. The Württemberg theologians were thus only half right in their explanation of why the Strassburgers never tried and executed their notorious sectarian prisoner, Melchior Hoffmann: they 'have been holding him in prison so that he may not do any more harm to others, preserving him, no doubt, above all because they do not think he errs deliberately, but rather that he has fallen into error out of a foolish zeal, deluded by the Devil and evil persons'.[59] But there was something else going on besides suspicion that Hoffmann was a victim of an evil spirit: Hoffmann was quite obviously a pious man, sincere in his beliefs, and able to argue his position with considerable effectiveness; the magistrates were unwilling to set up a mechanism to try his *Geist* in a criminal court to see if it were holy, because to do so would be to set themselves against him in unwinnable theological combat. Instead, they kept him prisoner, trying to break him by holding him in terrible conditions, year after year after year. If he had recognised his beliefs to be wrong, the magistrates might have released him, or been able to move on to try him for the civil offence of sedition without worrying about being accused of tyrannising over his conscience, but as long as he held to his beliefs, they were paralysed.

For Claus Frey, on the other hand, the lack of procedure for heresy trials was more immediately fatal.[60] Frey, who had fled Rothenburg an der Tauber when his Anabaptist beliefs got him into trouble, was drowned in Strassburg in 1534 for bigamy with Elisabeth Pfersfelder. Frey cast his desertion of his first wife and his relationship with Pfersfelder in religious terms. Held in captivity in the hope of his conversion for nearly a year – a treatment he considered neither gracious or merciful – Frey continued to reject the sacraments and to denounce marriage. According to pastor Wolfgang Capito, who wrote a pamphlet intended to destroy Frey's claim to Christian inspiration,

---

[58] The body set up to carry on the work of the 1533 synod had no power to punish; the magistrates continued to reject any thought of a local inquisition in the second half of the century: RP 1567, f. 453v and 1577, ff. 96r-99r.

[59] TAE III, #712a (1536), 29–30.

[60] See note 12. Klaus Deppermann, *Melchior Hoffman: Social Unrest and Apocalyptic Visions in the Age of Reformation*, trans. Malcolm Wren, ed. Benjamin Drewery (Edinburgh, 1987), 291–3, 350–1.

the magistrates would have pardoned him had he agreed to go back to his first wife. He went to his death defiantly, cursing and striking the pastor detailed to attend him at his execution, and denouncing the Strassburg church. There is no reason to doubt the sincerity of Frey's conviction that his relationship with Pfersfelder was theologically sound, but unlike Melchior Hoffmann, Frey had broken a widely recognised law and flaunted its violation during his time at liberty in Strassburg. Unlike Hoffman, he had no one to intervene and request mercy on him, for by the time of his arrest he had alienated the local sectarian communities by his behaviour with Pfersfelder.

Frey's execution, despite his conviction that he had scriptural grounds for his behaviour, was unusual; so was Melchior Hoffmann's long imprisonment. What stands out in the case law is how the magistrates' statutes allowed them to try cases of religious dissent within the parameters of secular criminal law, where the ordinary judicial mechanisms of grace and pardon could be exercised to the benefit of dissenters without – at least in the magistrates' view – compromising their dedication to religious unity. Thus they generally kept matters of belief out of their criminal courts, preferring to tell critics of the local church to leave town, rather than to imprison or to execute dissidents; in policing religious practice, they drew on traditional magisterial attributes of *Gnade* and *Billigkeit*, grace and equity, to temper their pursuit of confessional unity. They believed that their inherited judicial system was praiseworthy, and while, after the mid-1520s, they showed no particular reluctance to legislate on doctrine and morality, their defence of evangelical beliefs and practices was carried out through a criminal court system that claimed no jurisdiction in cases of conscience, and that had traditional and expedient habits of avoiding the most severe penalties the laws allowed. Legitimate judicial authority exercised in conventional ways defined the honour of Strassburg magistrates, and that honour was the wellspring of the city's reputation for tempering punishment by charity. Honourable magistrates, the members of Strassburg's Senate and XXI generally attempted to respect both confession and conscience.

7 One Reformation or many? Protestant identities in the later Reformation in Germany

Euan Cameron

The later German Reformation between the Peace of Augsburg and the Thirty Years' War offers some of the least promising ground in which to explore the history of tolerance. In this period the non-Catholic established churches of Germany fragmented amid mutual acrimony, for reasons as much political as theological. Following his defeat of the Schmalkaldic League in 1547, Charles V transferred the electoral dignity of Saxony to his Lutheran ally Duke Moritz. With it came the city and university of Wittenberg. The theologians of anti-imperial Jena and Magdeburg soon accused Philip Melanchthon's faculty of temporizing with the Emperor over the Interim, and of diluting the heritage of Martin Luther's Reformation. The ensuing controversies took much of their bitterness from the theologians who felt deprived of the one leader whose stature had held them together, then betrayed by their colleagues in the face of military defeat.[1] Until Counter-Reformation Catholicism began to threaten the Lutheran churches from its Bavarian base, Protestants could afford the luxury of always stressing what divided them from other Protestants rather from Catholics.[2] While Lutheranism remained divided, no one could agree on how to interpret the clause of the Peace of Augsburg which gave only 'those who subscribed to the Augsburg Confession' legal rights. The Reformed tradition, the 'second Reformation' or, if one prefers, German Calvinism, exploited that ambiguity to grow and spread, while rival theologians fulminated ineffectually against each other.[3] The Formula of Concord, which partly re-united the Lutheran churches in 1577, accentuated the strife between Lutheran and by now well-established

---

[1] On the politics of this period see F. Lau and E. Bizer, *A History of the Reformation in Germany to 1555*, trans. B. A. Hardy (London, 1969), 201–7; E. Iserloh, J. Glazik, and H. Jedin, *Reformation and Counter Reformation*, trans A. Biggs and P. W. Becker (London, 1980), 284–8; on the theology, see e.g. R. Kolb, 'Dynamics of Party Conflict in the Saxon Late Reformation: Gnesio Lutherans vs. Philippists', *Journal of Modern History*, 49 (1977), 1289–1305; R. Kolb, *Nikolaus von Amsdorf (1483–1565): Popular Polemics in the Preservation of Luther's Legacy* (Nieuwkoop, 1978).

[2] As remarked by B. Nischan, *Prince, People and Confession: The Second Reformation in Brandenburg* (Philadelphia PA, 1994), 55.

[3] See Jill Raitt, *The Colloquy of Montbéliard: Religion and Politics in the Sixteenth Century* (New York and Oxford, 1993), 51–2, 57.

Reformed churches in Germany. Such strife not only divided states against each other: in the Palatinate under Ludwig VI between 1576 and 1583, in Saxony under Christian I between 1586 and 1591, and in Johann Sigismund's Brandenburg after 1613, it provoked damaging splits within the hierarchies of church and state in individual principalities.[4]

The intensity of the intolerance generated by these conflicts was crudely portrayed in a number of broadsheets, such as the *Geistlicher Rauffhandel*, or 'spiritual brawl' of *c.* 1619, where Luther, Calvin, and the Pope were depicted swinging books and pulling each other's ears and beards.[5] Memorable epigrams were coined in the heat of controversy: Theodore Beza commented that Johann Pappus (the Tübingen Lutheran who taught in Strassburg's *Gymnasium* in the 1580s) differed no more from *Papa* than *lupus* from *lupa*; hard-line Lutheran clergy in Brandenburg reputedly prayed that God might fill them with hatred of Calvinism; at Heidelberg a distich circulated which exhorted Casimir to expel the servants of Luther, or kill them with sword, wheel, water, rope, and fire.[6] As Émile Léonard put it, 'in early seventeenth-century wars it was as a Catholic, Lutheran or Calvinist that one killed or was killed'.[7]

The theological issues at stake in this period were serious enough. Calvinists and Lutherans taught double and single predestination respectively, with a partisanship unknown to first-generation reformers. Lutherans urged against Calvinists and 'Zwinglians' that baptism was essential to salvation, and that private or emergency baptism was therefore necessary and legitimate. They insisted that Christ's risen body was physically present in the consecrated Eucharist; that even the unworthy who received the elements also received Christ's body; and that Christ's risen body could be present anywhere in creation at any one time (the so-called doctrine of 'ubiquity').[8] As the

---

[4] For the Palatinate see V. Press, *Calvinismus und Territorialstaat: Regierung und Zentralbehörden der Kurpfalz, 1559–1616* (Stuttgart, 1970), 267ff; V. Press, 'Die "Zweite Reformation" in der Kurpfalz', in Heinz Schilling (ed.), *Die reformierte Konfessionalisierung in Deutschland – Das Problem der »Zweiten Reformation«: Wissenschaftliches Symposion des Vereins für Reformationsgeschichte 1985* (Gütersloh, 1986), 111ff; on Saxony see K. H. Blaschke, 'Religion und Politik in Kursachsen 1586–1591', in Schilling (ed.), *Konfessionalisierung*, 79–97; on Brandenburg see most recently Nischan, *Prince, People and Confession*, 81ff.

[5] See the reproductions in Ruth Kastner, *Geistlicher Rauffhandel: Illustrierte Flugblätter zum Reformationsjubiläum 1617* (Frankfurt, 1982), 5; also Nischan, *Prince, People and Confession*, 136.

[6] E. G. Léonard, *A History of Protestantism*, ed. H. H. Rowley, trans. J. M. H. Reid and R. M. Bethall (London, 1965–7), II, 35; G. A. Benrath, 'Irenik und Zweite Reformation', in Schilling (ed.), *Konfessionalisierung*, 356: 'O Casimire potens, servos expelle Lutheri: Ense, rota, ponto, funibus, igne neca!'

[7] Léonard, *Protestantism*, II, 213.

[8] See the summaries in Nischan, *Prince, People and Confession*, 137ff; Raitt, *Montbéliard*, 73ff, 137ff.

Reformed tradition sought to sweep away all the language and apparatus of worship which was not manifestly based on Scripture, so the Lutherans insisted even harder on retaining religious pictures, vestments, church music and hymns.[9] Above all, the 'second Reformation' signified the change in eucharistic belief by the practical gesture of breaking ordinary bread before the congregation, rather than consecrating and distributing an unleavened wafer.[10]

These differences and disputes raised a crucial question of identity: did Protestant believers 'belong' first or foremost to their state church, to their confession, or to a greater Protestant communion across Europe? The early Reformers had taught that a church should only be as large as the lay community of its members: no extra-national unity was necessary. The criterion of a 'true church' was simply that it possess the 'marks of the Church', essentially the Gospel and the two true sacraments. This standard was elastic, and open to various interpretations: how different from each other could two 'true churches' be? How defective, in particular, could 'sacraments' be while remaining 'true'? Such uncertainties provoked the search for 'confessional' standards.[11] It is usual to date this quest for 'confessional' solidarity and coherence from the second or third generation of reform, between approximately 1560 and 1620. By then, the founding fathers of the Protestant churches, Luther especially, had become icons; loyalty to their legacy was an end in itself.[12] However, some recent scholars have claimed that the Reformation comprised two fundamentally different streams of thought: that Lutheranism arose out of the late scholastic theology of salvation, especially among nominalist Augustinians; while the Zwinglian and broader reformed tradition grew from the ethical Christian humanism of the northern Renaissance.[13] One historian speaks of a 'humanist Reformation' distinct from and antagonistic to the Lutheran one.[14]

If the differences between Lutheran and Reformed prove fundamental and unbridgeable, then the intolerance of later sixteenth-century Germany must

---

[9] Raitt, *Montbéliard*, 136–7; Nischan, *Prince, People and Confession*, 132ff, 147ff.

[10] Nischan, *Prince, People and Confession*, 138 and refs.

[11] A basic discussion of early reformed ecclesiology may be found in E. Cameron, *The European Reformation* (Oxford, 1991), 147, 192 and refs.

[12] For celebration of the images of reformers, see Theodore Beza, *Icones, id est, Verae Imagines* ... (n. p., 1580); for later Lutheran reverence for the image of Martin Luther, see R. W. Scribner, 'Incombustible Luther: the Image of the Reformer in Early Modern Germany', in *Popular Culture and Popular Movements in Reformation Germany* (London, 1987), 323–53; Kastner, *Geistlicher Rauffhandel*, 167–225; numerous Luther-worshipping pamphlets, e.g. *Memoria Thaumasiandri Lutheri Renovata* (n.p., n.d., but early seventeenth century); on confessionalism in general see Nischan, *Prince, People and Confession*, 1–2 and refs.

[13] See the arguments of A. E. McGrath, *The Intellectual Origins of the European Reformation* (Oxford, 1987), and McGrath, *Reformation Thought: An Introduction* (Oxford, 1988), esp. 6–11, 41–2.

[14] On the 'humanist Reformation' see esp. Léonard, *Protestantism*, I, ch. 4.

reflect more than just the stresses and strains of contemporary church politics; it must derive from the essence of the Reformation. However, if Protestants writing after *c.* 1555 showed any *residual* awareness that the various Reformed churches taught the same basic message, and shared more with each other than with their enemies, then historians must set the many expressions of *odium theologicum*, from clergy and laity alike, in context. This chapter will explore several areas where such residual awareness of a common Protestant identity might be shown. First, on several occasions Protestant churches interceded with each other, and in joint missions to Catholic powers, on behalf of Reformed congregations in trouble. To the extent that Lutherans (for example) were prepared to back up Calvinists in distress, to that degree at least they showed some sense of common cause. Secondly, many educational centres of Protestant Europe drew students, and used materials, from beyond their own narrow confessional spectrum. Finally, sixteenth and early seventeenth-century Protestant controversial theologians defined – and sometimes betrayed – their sense of identity in the histories of the Reformation which they wrote themselves.

Those reformers who spoke up on behalf of fellow Protestants demonstrated their religious solidarity in a very public way. In the early decades such solidarity was expressed through leagues and alliances like the League of Schmalkalden, which of course combined Lutheran princes and both Lutheran and Reformed cities.[15] Apart from the state churches, most Protestants wished no good at all to the sectarians and Anabaptists. Gradually, however, there arose significant groups of orthodox Protestants who lived as minority groups in their countries. These 'persecuted brethren' posed a problem for prospective intercessors, who needed reassurance that they were indeed 'true' Protestants. Catholic régimes sometimes played upon such doubts or disagreements, in the hope of dividing their enemies. Francis I of France, when faced with a protest from Strassburg about the massacre of the Waldenses in the Luberon in 1545, alleged that these were not 'pious people', but seditious rebels and extremist heretics whom the Protestants should disown.[16]

Just such an effort to obtain cross-confessional support for persecuted Protestants, made in the spring of 1557, amply demonstrated the risks and the possibilities. The Company of Pastors of Geneva had from 1555 begun to

[15] Literature on the League of Schmalkalden is discussed in Cameron, *European Reformation*, 270–1 and notes 11–17.
[16] François I's letter is printed in C. Schmidt, 'Aktenstücke besonders zur Geschichte der Waldenser', *Zeitschrift für die historische Theologie*, 22 (1852), 258–9; note also the reaction to it in *Joannis Calvini Opera quae supersunt Omnia*, ed. G. Baum, E. Cunitz, and E. Reuss, (Braunschweig, Berlin, 1853–1900) (hereafter *CO*), XII, cols. 133–6; see E. Cameron, *The Reformation of the Heretics: the Waldenses of the Alps 1480–1580* (Oxford, 1984), 190.

plant settled churches in the 'Waldensian' valleys of the Cottian Alps between Grenoble and Turin, at the time wholly under French rule. The regional *parlements* had threatened these churches; Geneva was therefore anxious to secure the support not only of the Swiss Confederation, but of the German Protestant princes. By their intercession it was hoped to shame Henri II into avoiding a repetition of the Luberon massacre, recently made notorious by Jean Crespin's pamphlet.[17] Guillaume Farel and Theodore Beza were sent in an embassy to solicit support. Initially, they tried to reassure potential intercessors in general terms that the Waldenses were 'good Christians' who had long since opposed Roman errors, and in particular to reassure the princes that they had never been rebellious against their secular overlords. Some fairly bland confessions of faith were passed around to support these claims.[18] For many this might have been sufficient; but not for certain hardline Lutherans, who were highly touchy on the issue of eucharistic doctrine, and alarmed at the thought of their churches supporting 'sacramentaries'. Farel and Beza sought to allay such fears by an equivocation. At Göppingen on 14 May 1557 they presented to the Duke of Württemberg a confession entitled 'thus it is believed and taught concerning the Lord's Supper in the churches of Switzerland and Savoy'.[19]

The result was nearly a disaster. Jakob Andreae of Tübingen, and also Johann Pappus, to whom the confession was later shown, were no doubt surprised and relieved to learn that the Swiss churches believed that 'the substance of the same Son of Man ... in which he was born and suffered for us ... and that the true blood which he poured out for us ... is truly and really presented and offered [in the supper]'. They may, however, have found the confession's rejection of 'a local conjunction, or a diffusion of the human nature of Christ, or a material and natural commingling of Christ's substance with ours, or a crass transubstantiation' bewildering. The problem arose not with the Germans but with fellow-Swiss. Heinrich Bullinger criticised the confession in a host of detailed notes and letters, objecting both to its tortuous language and to the whole principle of fudging over theological dispute with ingenious words.[20] The ensuing correspondence lasted most of

---

[17] For the Luberon massacre, see G. Audisio, *Les Vaudois du Luberon: une minorité en Provence (1460–1560)* (Mérindol, 1984), esp 347ff; Cameron, *Reformation of the Heretics*, 147ff and refs.; [J. Crespin], *Histoire mémorable de la persécution et saccagement du peuple de Mérindol et Cabrières et autres circonvoisins, appelez Vaudois* (n. p., 1556); for interest among other protestants, see H. Aubert *et al.* (eds.), *Correspondance de Théodore de Bèze* (Geneva, 1960–), (hereafter Beza, *Corresp.*) II, 238, 240.

[18] For the start of the embassy see Beza, *Corresp.* II, 62ff; *CO* XVI, cols. 459ff.; for the 'eirenic confessions' see Cameron, *Reformation of the Heretics*, 211 notes 45–6.

[19] The text of confession is found in *CO* XVI, cols. 469–72.

[20] *CO* XVI, col. 479: 'Possunt quidem verba artificiose concinnari, et spes quaedam componi consensionis, remanente interim in re ipsa dissidio'.

the summer.[21] Moreover, this encounter began a sequence of such rows between Calvinists and Lutherans over the Eucharist. These were to culminate in the Colloquy of Montbéliard of 1586, where the suspicions and disagreements were revealed in all their glaring relief.[22]

The theological bitterness of the Göppingen episode can, however, obscure its lessons for the history of inter-Protestant intercessions. The quarrel broke out *not* between Lutheran and Reformed, but rather between two groups of Swiss Reformed Protestants, in response to Farel and Beza's over-enthusiasm to accommodate Lutheran sensitivities for the sake of the alpine Waldenses. Moreover, the diplomatic enterprise survived the theologians' row over the eucharistic issue. The Elector Palatine and the Duke of Württemberg, in a letter of 28 May 1557, felt able to recommend the Waldenses to the city council of Strassburg as 'the poor persecuted Christians in Piedmont, called Waldenses'.[23] By October Farel and Beza were able to report that their protégés were living in peace and quiet and without persecution.[24] Whether he was deterred by the wave of international attention, or just weary of trying to hold down a difficult position in Piedmont, Henri II decided not to repeat in the alpine valleys his father's infamous massacre of twelve years earlier. The Waldensian problem was left for Duke Emanuele Filiberto of Savoy to try to tackle after his restoration in 1559.[25]

The 1557 episode showed that it was not, after all, necessary to resolve intractable theological issues before one group of Protestants could care about the fate of another. Even as the theologians were pursuing their ever more acrimonious debates, German, Swiss, French and in due course Netherlands Protestants showed themselves willing to make at least some limited measure of common cause. At Naumburg in 1561, the German princes identified themselves with the faith of the Elizabethan Church of England, which was not Lutheran, whatever else it was; they also interceded with Charles IX of France on behalf of his Protestant subjects and extended olive branches to

[21] The ensuing correspondence may be followed in *CO* XVI, cols. 538–41, 545f, 567f, 571, 590–6, 609–17, and Beza, *Corresp.* II, 73–5, 82f, 86–94, 238–42, 251; see also T. Balma, 'La Ville de Strasbourg et les Vaudois', *Bollettino della società di Studi Valdesi*, 67 (1937), 63–95; A. Hollaender, 'Eine schweizer Gesandtschaftsreise an den französischen Hof im Jahre 1557' *Historische Zeitschrift*, n.s. 33 (1892), 385–410; A. Pascal, 'Le Ambascerie dei cantoni e dei principi protestanti di Svizzera e Germania al Re di Francia in favore dei Valdesi durante il periodo della dominazione francese in Piemonte (1535–1559); contributi ad una storia diplomatica dei Valdesi di Piemonte', *Bollettino Storico-Bibliografico Subalpino*, 18 (1913), nos. 1–3, 91–119, nos. 5–6, 314–36, and 19 (1914) nos. 1–3, 27–38.
[22] Raitt, *Montbéliard*, 51ff; also Robert D. Linder, 'The Early Calvinists and Martin Luther: A Study in Evangelical Solidarity', in Jerome Friedman (ed.), *Regnum, Religio et Ratio: Essays Presented to Robert M. Kingdon* (Kirksville, MO, 1987), 103–16.
[23] *CO* XVI, cols. 499–500.
[24] Beza, *Corresp.* II, 119.
[25] For the 1561 campaign see Cameron, *Reformation of the Heretics*, 162–3 and notes.

the Scots, as well as the Danish and Swedish Protestants.[26] The indefatigable Beza was able to report to Bullinger, on 19 June 1566, that the Duke of Savoy had so offended the princes gathered at the Reichstag at Augsburg that they were willing to send ambassadors to reproach him for his conduct towards his Calvinist subjects.[27] The German prince most associated with this move was, unsurprisingly, the Calvinist-inclined Elector Palatine; however, he seems to have carried the others with him despite their reluctance to accept his confessional position.[28] As the religious wars in France and the Netherlands grew ever more savage in the 1580s and 1590s, churchmen and lay people in still thoroughly Lutheran Brandenburg spoke out for 'our brothers and sisters in the Palatinate, Hesse, . . . France, the Netherlands, and wherever else', and even went to fight for them. Joachim Friedrich von Hohenzollern, administrator of Magdeburg and son of Elector Johann Georg, denounced Catholic attacks on foreign Protestants as a threat to the Reformation as a whole, and urged international collective action.[29] Even more paradoxical was the reaction of Count Frederick of Montbéliard, as Jill Raitt has recently noted. He had rejected the requests of the Calvinists at the colloquy of 1586 to be treated on the same footing as the Lutherans. Yet he became increasingly active on the side of the French Huguenots who had been driven into his lands following the 1585 Treaty of Nemours. When Montbéliard was devastated by Guisard troops in reprisal, it was largely the Swiss who gave generously to help the Count's theoretically Lutheran subjects. Here it was dramatically demonstrated how even the bitterest confessional divisions were no barrier to inter-Protestant solidarity against a common political enemy.[30] It may be objected that such support demonstrated not inter-confessional solidarity, but merely a prudent desire to keep the enemies of one's own confession occupied elsewhere: however, sectaries such as the Anabaptists never benefited from such intercession; Waldensian heretics, whose Protestantism had been suspect in the past, were protected only *because* they had embraced magisterial Protestantism.

Few features of a church can define it so completely as the way in which it educates its future ministers. The Reformation, moreover, had given the train-

[26] Raitt, *Montbéliard*, 53f; however, relations between Elizabeth I and the Lutheran princes were at times soured by confessional suspicions: see E. I. Kouri, 'For True Faith or National Interest? Queen Elizabeth I and the Protestant Powers', in E. I. Kouri and T. Scott (eds.), *Politics and Society in Reformation Europe: Essays for Sir Geoffrey Elton on his Sixty-Fifth Birthday* (London, 1987), 411–36 and esp. 421–7.

[27] Beza, *Corresp.*, VII, 141–6.

[28] See discussion in Raitt, *Montbéliard*, 57.

[29] Nischan, *Prince, People and Confession*, 61–3; B. Nischan, 'Confessionalism and absolutism: the case of Brandenburg', in A. Pettegree, A. Duke, and G. Lewis (eds.), *Calvinism in Europe, 1540–1620* (Cambridge, 1994), 190ff.

[30] Raitt, *Montbéliard*, 187ff.

ing of future ministers added importance. Ministers had to preach true doctrine as well as administer true sacraments; in practice they usually spent much more time doing the former than the latter. The doctrine which they imbibed would largely determine the message which they preached. In the light of this, one might have expected that the training of Lutheran and Reformed clergy in the later sixteenth century would have taken place in watertight compartments; that absolute 'confessional' purity would have been required from teachers and students alike. Ministers and academic theologians were undoubtedly required to submit to the twists and turns of confessional religious politics.[31] Some Lutheran churches, for instance in early seventeenth-century Denmark, did attempt to ensure that only Lutheran universities were attended by their students. However, surprisingly often the training and recruitment of students was much less confessionally programmed. Bullinger's Zurich sent most of its gifted sons to receive their education outside the city, rather than competing to recruit expensive professors for its own *lectorium*. Many of these students received bursaries to study in German universities, and not just Reformed ones. While Basle was the most popular destination, it was closely followed by Wittenberg, Heidelberg, and Marburg, before Geneva, Lausanne, and Strassburg. Although the Wittenberg matriculations were concentrated in its Philippist period before the mid-1570s, and the Heidelberg matriculations dwindled markedly during the reign of the Lutheran Duke Ludwig, in neither case did Zurich students cease attending an institution altogether when its confessional colour changed.[32] In the Rhine Palatinate, universities were likewise selected by prospective ministers with a striking catholicity of taste. Besides the home university of Heidelberg, ministers studied at Wittenberg (again mostly before the 1570s), Tübingen, Marburg, and the Strassburg *Gymnasium*; and in lesser numbers at Bremen, Rostock, Erfurt, or even Jena.[33] During the tolerant but still officially Lutheran electorate of Joachim Friedrich of Brandenburg in the early 1600s, close links were established between the universities of Frankfurt-on-the-Oder and Leiden. Leiden's humanists, Justus Lipsius especially, proved attractive to Brandenburger students as to those from other parts of Germany.[34]

It is also striking that in the Rhineland's 'Second Reformation' the great school-book of Lutheran theology, Melanchthon's *Common Places*, remained

---

[31] For the ways in which Lutheran clergy were required to submit to the official line on contested issues of dogma, see G. Strauss, 'The Mental World of a Saxon Pastor', in P. N. Brooks (ed.), *Reformation Principle and Practice: Essays in Honour of Arthur Geoffrey Dickens* (London, 1980), 165–7; note also the purge of the Wittenberg faculty of theology in 1574, or the similar episodes at Heidelberg in 1576 and 1583.

[32] This point derives from a paper presented by Dr Karin Maag to the Reformation Studies Colloquium at Cambridge, April 1994.

[33] B. Vogler, *Le Clergé protestant rhénan au siècle de la réforme* (Paris, 1976), 58ff.

[34] Nischan, *Prince, People and Confession*, 70–1.

the standard text under a 'Calvinist' dispensation. No doubt much of the most popular theological instruction was biblical and literary rather than credal and systematic; and some of the student mobility described took place in subjects other than theology.[35] Yet it would be naïve to suppose that late sixteenth-century students, so many of whom did become clergy or at least held conscious theological opinions, would have studied in cities of differing Protestant characters without imbibing a sense of what one might call Reformed cosmopolitanism. Students could move between different parts of the Protestant world, in a way that they certainly could not move between the Protestant and Catholic worlds. The Scots scholars John Johnston and Robert Howie, who travelled from Lutheran Rostock and Helmstedt to Calvinist Herborn and Heidelberg in the mid-1580s, clearly saw nothing strange about studying under famous scholars of diverse views.[36]

The remainder of this chapter will consider the histories of the Reformation produced in the confessional era. Nowhere can a church's own sense of its identity be more clearly revealed, than in its own historiography. Within a very few decades the reformers established a framework of traditions and conventions within which Reformation history was written.[37] It is therefore significant that the theory of Protestant church history was first conceived within a quite homogeneous group of scholars and churchmen. Melanchthon's pupil Viktorin Strigel (1524–69) set out, in a short work published in 1554, one of the earliest Protestant views of church history. He wrote that church history stood in relation to secular history as the soul did to the body; it thus had its own sources, especially the Bible and the Fathers, and its own priorities.[38] Theologians showed increasing awareness of the didactic value of church history as the later sixteenth century progressed. David Chytraeus of Rostock (1531–1600) in his *De lectione historiarum* of 1563, defined 'church' history in the broadest possible sense, as that of the invisible, univer-

---

[35] H. Meylan, 'Le Recrutement et la formation des pasteurs dans les églises réformées du xvie siècle', in Meylan, *D'Érasme a Théodore de Beze* (Geneva, 1976), 247; Vogler, *Clergé protestant rhénan*, 54ff.

[36] J. K. Cameron (ed.), *Letters of John Johnston c. 1565–1611 and Robert Howie c. 1565–c. 1645* (Edinburgh, 1963), xviiiff.

[37] On early reformed historiography, see for example A. G. Dickens and J. M. Tonkin with K. Powell, *The Reformation in Historical Thought* (Cambridge MA, 1985); H. Scheible, 'Die Anfänge des Reformatorischen Geschichtsschreibung', in *Texte zur Kirchen- und Theologiegeschichte* (Gütersloh, 1966).

[38] V. Strigel, *De ratione legendi historias*, printed in *Selectarum declamationum professorum academiae Ienensis*, vol. 1 (Strasbourg, 1554), 506–20, as discussed in Emil Clemens Scherer, *Geschichte und Kirchengeschichte an den deutschen Universitäten: ihre Anfänge im Zeitalter des Humanismus und ihre Ausbildung zu selbständigen Disziplinen* (Freiburg im Breisgau, Herder, 1927), 49–51.

sal church.[39] Christoph Pezel (d. 1604) of Wittenberg, in a speech delivered in 1568 on the purpose and value of history, praised the certainty, age, continuity, and divine origin of church history; he also pointed out how useful it was for theologians to learn how human error had corrupted true doctrine in the past. He divided Christian history into four periods of roughly five centuries each, the last being that of the Reformation.[40] Within a few decades the theological value of church history had become a truism, found in textbooks such as David Chytraeus's *De studio theologiae* (1572) and Petrus Piscator of Jena's *De studiis theologicis* (1610).[41] The theory of church history, then, originated with a small group of followers and pupils of Philipp Melanchthon; that is, moderate, eirenic Lutherans.

If the origins of the theory of Reformation church history were Philippist, the same was only partly true of the earliest examples of historical writing itself. The *Chronicon* of the astronomer Johannes Carion (1499–1537), originally published in German in 1532, may be regarded as the prototype of Lutheran world history. However, the humanist Latin revision made by Philipp Melanchthon in 1558–60 had the widest influence.[42] Additions made up to 1565 by the Wittenberg physician and crypto-Calvinist Kaspar Peucer (1525–1602) brought 'Carion's' work up to the accession of Charles V, and therefore included a brief discussion of the rise of Luther and the indulgence dispute, but little more. Peucer's disgrace and imprisonment forestalled further additions.[43] The first full-scale history of the Reformation proper by a German was the *Commentaries on the State of Religion and the Commonwealth* of Johann Sleidan (1507–1566).[44] Many historians have remarked on the frustratingly non-committal quality of Sleidan's *Commentaries*. Fueter lamented the lack of any discussion of the late medieval church, or of the

[39] Scherer, *Geschichte und Kirchengeschichte*, 106–7; D. Chytraeus, *De Lectione Historiarum recte Instituenda* (Rostock, 1563). On Chytraeus, see *Theologische Realenzyklopädie* (Berlin and New York, 1977–), vol. 8, 88–90.
[40] Scherer, *Geschichte und Kirchengeschichte*, 107; Christoph Pezel's *Oratio de argumento historiarum et fructo petendo ex earum lectione* is found in P. Melanchthon, *Opera*, vol. 5 (Wittenberg, 1580), sigs. bir-viv.
[41] Scherer, *Geschichte und Kirchengeschichte*, 121, with reference to D. Chytraeus, *De studio theologiae recte inchoando . . . commonefactiones* (Rostock, 1572) and P. Piscator, *De studiis theologiis rite formandis et instituendis oratio* (Jena, 1610).
[42] J. Carion, *Chronica durch Magistrum Johan Carion fleisig zusamen gezogen, menigklich nützlich zu lesen* (Wittenberg, [1532]); the Melanchthon recension appeared as *Chronicon Carionis, latine expositum et auctum multis et veteribus et recentibus historiis* (Wittenberg, 1558; second part, *ibid.*, 1560); see also *Philippi Melanthonis Opera quae supersunt omnia*, ed. C. G. Bretschneider (Halle, 1834–60), XII, cols. 712–1094; E. Fueter, *Geschichte des neueren Historiographie* (Munich and Berlin, 1911), 186ff.
[43] For Peucer's text see Melanchthon, *Opera*, vol. 5, esp. 703–6; Scherer, *Geschichte und Kirchengeschichte*, 54–5.
[44] J. Sleidan, *De statu religionis et reipublicae Carolo Quinto caesare commentarii* (Strassburg, 1555).

evolution of Reformed doctrine, or of the characters of the leaders of the movement.[45] Ingeborg Berlin Vogelstein has expressed surprise that Sleidan could ignore completely the appearance of some of Luther's most important works. [46] One must therefore classify Sleidan's confessional position and his legacy with some caution.

Sleidan worked in the Strassburg milieu just before and just after the Schmalkaldic War. His city's church was 'Zwinglian' under Bucer before 1549, and technically Lutheran under Marbach afterwards (though with many of the same personnel as before).[47] He might therefore have been expected to look on the various types of 'magisterial' reformer with some impartiality, and to regard them as about very similar things. Although Sleidan's avowed intention was to avoid value judgements at all costs and weave his narrative out of summaries of the sources, there is enough in the text to confirm that such was indeed his view.[48] He began with a fairly full coverage of Luther's campaign against indulgences and the widening rift with the Church hierarchy. However, while Luther occupied centre stage for the first few years, references to Zwingli and other Swiss preachers were inserted where appropriate. He described Zwingli's opposition to indulgence-selling at Zurich, his objection to mercenary service, the quarrel with the Bishop of Constance over married priests and the abortive January 1523 disputation.[49] Sleidan narrated the removal of images from the Zurich churches with none of the misgivings which coloured the story of the Wittenberg iconoclasm of 1521–2, because all was done 'without tumult' and by consent of the magistrates.[50] His discussion of the eucharistic debate was eirenic almost to a fault: Zwingli 'who almost in all other things agreed with Luther, dissented from him about the Lord's Supper ... but all agree on this opinion, that the body and blood of Christ are taken spiritually, not corporally; with the heart, not the mouth.'[51]

However, this inclusive, comprehensive attitude towards the magisterial reformers most emphatically did not extend to sectaries or rebels. The Zwickau prophets 'talked of conferences they had with God, who had commanded them to destroy the wicked ... Thomas Muncer was one of this

[45] Fueter, *Historiographie*, 201ff.

[46] Ingeborg Berlin Vogelstein, *Johann Sleidan's Commentaries: Vantage Point of a Second Generation Lutheran* (Lanham and New York, 1986), 64ff, 69ff.

[47] Fueter, *Historiographie*, 201; Berlin Vogelstein, *Johann Sleidan's Commentaries*, 15–22; on this period in Strassburg's history see L. J. Abray, *The People's Reformation: Magistrates, Clergy and Commons in Strasbourg, 1500–1598* (Oxford, 1985).

[48] Sleidan, *Commentarii* (1555 edn.), preface.

[49] *Ibid.*, fos. 18r , 36v, 39r, 44r-v; see also E. Bohun (trans.), *The General History of the Reformation of the Church, written in Latin by John Sleidan, L.L.D., faithfully Englished* (London, 1689), 22, 48, 51, 57.

[50] Sleidan, *General History of Reformation*, trans. Bohun, 72ff; cf. 52.

[51] *Ibid.*, 97ff; cf. 141 for later coverage of the eucharistic debate.

herd, who afterwards raised a popular insurrection.'[52] The 1525 Peasant War
was 'in great measure occasioned by busie and pragmatical preachers, of
whom Thomas Muncer . . . was the Ring-Leader, who at length leaving off
the preaching of the Gospel, broached an odd and new kind of doctrine . . .'
Pfeiffer was 'a bold and desperate fellow, who bragged much of dreams and
nocturnal visions'. Of the Anabaptists, Sleidan commented that Luther and
Zwingli both wrote against them, and told the story of one at St Gallen who
beheaded his brother in sight of his parents, claiming a divine command to
do so.[53] Sleidan's outlook was, therefore, that of a common sense non-
theological observer. He felt that he could tell the difference between a
clergyman working patiently for change within the structures of an urban
church, and a fanatical visionary breathing fire and sword. Instinctively,
he wished to keep doctrinal disputes in what he perceived as their proper
place.

Before leaving the mid-century, a little must be said about the other great
tour de force of early Protestant historiography, the *Magdeburg Centuries*.
The compilers of this monumental collection could hardly be more different
from Melanchthon or Sleidan. Not just the chief editor, Matthias Flacius
Illyricus (1520–75), but several of his contributors such as Johannes Wigand
(1523–87) and Matthäus Judex (d. 1564), were militant arch-Lutheran polemicists at the most critical stage of the intra-Lutheran feuds of the 1540s and
1550s.[54] The detailed thematic matrix for each century volume incorporated a
highly programmatic discussion of the origins of true (i.e. Lutheran) doctrine
in the past history of the church.[55] Yet a number of factors conspired to
prevent the *Magdeburg Centuries* from generating a narrowly Lutheran tradition of Reformation history. In the first place, they never reached the sixteenth century; the volume on the thirteenth was the last to appear, in 1574.
Secondly, the resulting preoccupation with 'forerunners' of the Reformation
forced Flacius and his team to look for rather general resemblances between
medieval opponents of the post-Hildebrandine Church and their own school;
proto-Protestants, rather than proto-Lutherans. This same tendency appeared
in Flacius's other major historical work, the *Catalogue of Witnesses to the
Truth* of 1556.[56] In the early seventeenth century it took only a modest

[52] *Ibid.*, 52.

[53] *Ibid.*, 83ff, 110.

[54] M. Flacius *et al.*, *Ecclesiastica historia, integram ecclesiae Christi ideam . . . secundum sing-
ulas centurias perspicuo ordine complectens*, 13 vols. (Basel, 1559–74); for the editors, see
Fueter, *Historiographie*, 249ff; for some polemical works by Wigand and Judex and their
impact, see G. Strauss, 'The Mental World of a Saxon Pastor' 166.

[55] Fueter, *Historiographie*, 251ff; see also the table at the beginning of each volume of the
Centuries.

[56] M. Flacius Illyricus, *Catalogus Testium Veritatis qui ante nostram aetatem reclamarunt papae*
(Basle, 1556); on the *Catalogus* see E. Cameron, 'Medieval Heretics as Protestant Martyrs',
in D. Wood (ed.), *Martyrs and Martyrologies: Papers read at the 1992 summer meeting and*

amount of revision to make both these basic works of Lutheran historiography suitable for a Calvinist readership: the *Catalogus* was edited by Simon Goulart and first published in this form at Lyons in 1597, and the *Centuries* by Ludwig Lucius for the Basle edition of 1624–5.[57] In any case, it seems that little use was made of the *Centuries* in the historical syllabi of sixteenth-century German universities, where the Philippist texts still dominated instruction.[58]

By accident or by design, therefore, the first major texts of Reformation historiography did not promote two clearly distinct schools of church history, one Lutheran and the other Calvinist. The most influential works were written by Philippists, or by those who like Sleidan straddled the two confessions. As 'confessionalisation' grew more rigid and acrimonious, however, one would expect to see church history become more controversial.

Having begun with the school of Philipp Melanchthon, one ought to consider its contribution to later sixteenth-century historiography first, then that of the Gnesio-Lutherans, and finally the Calvinists. Further minor works of historical education were produced in the mid-century by pupils of Melanchthon, such as Georg Major's *Lives of the Fathers* and *Catalogue of Doctors of the Church*, or Chunemann Flinsbach's *Ecclesiastical Chronology*.[59] However, some of the most interesting contributions were made by the great Rostock scholar David Chytraeus, who remained a moderate despite his conversion from Philippist to Gnesio-Lutheran beliefs. His enlarged *Chronology* appeared in 1569; in 1578 he published a massive collection of documents and commentaries entitled the *History of the Confession of Augsburg*.[60] The *Confession of Augsburg* deserves closer scrutiny. Much more than Sleidan, Chytraeus presented his narrative as a *catena* of original documents linked by fairly brief editorial narratives. One of the most interesting of such passages was the introduction to the chapter on the eucharistic controversy. This section was entitled 'treaties of agreement with the Zwinglians, who dis-

the 1993 winter meeting of the Ecclesiastical History Society (Oxford, 1993) 185–207, esp. 198ff, 207.

[57] See 'S. G. S.' [= S. Goulart, ed.], *Catalogus Testium Veritatis, qui ante nostram aetatem Pontifici Romano atque Papismi erroribus reclamarunt* (Lyon, 1597); later edition (Geneva, 1608); L. Lucius (ed.), *Historiae Ecclesiasticae volumen I/II/III*, 3 vols. (Basle, 1624–5).

[58] Scherer, *Geschichte und Kirchengeschichte*, 127ff.

[59] G. Major, *Vitae patrum in usum ministrorum verbi* . . . (Wittenberg, 1544); later edns, e.g. (Wittenberg, 1578); G. Major, *Catalogus doctorum ecclesiae Dei a mundi initio ad nostra tempora* (Wittenberg and Basle, 1550); C. Flinsbach, *Chronologia ecclesiastica ab orbe condito* . . . (Wittenberg and Strassburg, 1552); see Scherer, *Geschichte und Kirchengeschichte*, 51ff.

[60] D. Chytraeus, *Chronologia* . . . *recognita et addita* (Rostock, 1569); D. Chytraeus, *Historia Augustanae confessionis* (Frankfurt, 1578), here cited in the French edition, *Histoire de la confession d'Auxpourg* (Antwerp, 1582). For Chytraeus's Gnesiolutheranism see P. F. Barton in *TRE* vol. 8, 88.

agreed with Luther on the point of the Lord's Supper'. The prefatory remarks insisted that these documents were included for the sake of completeness 'and not to renew old bitternesses'. Philipp of Hesse, it was pointed out, had wished the parties at Marburg to recognise each other as 'brothers, members of the same church, and companions in the same faith and confession against the Roman Catholics'.[61] Chytraeus chiefly blamed Johannes Brenz for the failure to include the Swiss in the Augsburg Confession, and closed the section with editions of the *Tetrapolitana* and the Wittenberg Accord.[62] The Lutheran congregation of Antwerp had this collection of documents translated into French in 1582, and published it in an effort to reassure their French-speaking Calvinist neighbours ('our Christian friends and brothers') that the Lutherans were *not* only 'half-reformed', even though they used such popish-sounding terms as 'sacrament of the altar'.[63]

A very different impression is conveyed in the church histories written from the hard-line Lutheran standpoint, and particularly in the works of two authors to be considered here, Johann Pappus and Lucas Osiander. Johann Pappus, the conservator of Lutheran orthodoxy in the Strassburg *Gymnasium* in the 1580s, published his *Epitome of Church History* out of his lecture-notes, at his students' request, in 1584.[64] Like the *Magdeburg Centuries*, however, Pappus' *Epitome* focused chiefly on the early church. The book was divided into three major sections, dealing in turn with the calling of the peoples to Christianity, the early persecutions and martyrs, and the heresies and councils called to deal with them. References were made to sixteenth-century controversies, but only obliquely. The *Epitome* accused un-named 'modern heretics' of reviving the errors of the Manichaeans on original sin; it blamed scholastics for repeating Pelagian errors; it defended the Lutherans, at some length, from the charge that their 'ubiquity' revived the Eutychian Christological heresy. Finally, it made some swipes against iconoclasts, and accused sacramentarians of following Berengar of Tours.[65] There was thus no sustained historical discussion of the Reformation issues: the one promised from Pappus's hand at the end of the *Epitome* never appeared. A strictly Lutheran version of Reformation history was only incorporated in the much later recension of the work by Eusebius Bohemus (1626) and in Heinrich Kipping's *Supplement* to the *Epitome* of 1661.[66]

---

[61] Chytraeus, *Confession d'Auxpourg*, 457ff.
[62] *Ibid.*, 467–98.
[63] *Ibid.*, sigs. *3v–4r.
[64] J. Pappus, *Historiae Ecclesiasticae de conversionibus gentium, persecutionibus ecclesiae, haeresibus et conciliis oecumenicis Epitome* (Strasbourg, 1584); Scherer, *Geschichte und Kirchengeschichte*, 123f.
[65] Pappus, *Epitome*, 262f, 303, 349–61, 368–9.
[66] *Ibid.*, 370; later enlarged edns. by E. Bohemus (Wittenberg, 1626) and H. Kipping (Bremen, 1661); see Scherer, *Geschichte und Kirchengeschichte*, 123–4.

Meanwhile the Tübingen theologian Lucas Osiander the elder (1534–1604) had produced his virulently Lutheran *Centuries of Church History*, which first appeared in eight volumes at Tübingen between 1592 and 1604.[67] Osiander spent nearly all his career in Württemberg, latterly as general superintendent. He took notes for Jakob Andreae at the Colloquy of Montbéliard, on which Andreae's polemical *Acta*, published soon after the event, were based.[68] His two-part volume on the sixteenth century was written out of sequence and published early, in 1602–3, before the immediately preceding centuries. In his preface he explained that at sixty-eight years old he feared he might not live to finish the work, and wished at least to see his coverage of the Reformation in print. This sixteenth-century volume's predictably abusive anti-Calvinist preface was dated, with a lack of taste or tact, on St Bartholomew's Day 1602. The Saxon monk Martin Luther, bereft of earthly authority, by divine inspiration, had dared to challenge the Goliath of the papacy; but his work had been impaired first by Karlstadt's 'Berengarian' error on the eucharist and his iconoclasm and then by Zwingli's 'heresy'. The Marburg colloquy was futile, because the Zwinglians would not yield to the truth on the supper, and their agreement on other issues proved (he said) to be insincere. 'To convert heresiarchs may be numbered among things impossible'. The refusal of the Zwinglians to sign the Confession of Augsburg in 1530 should, Osiander claimed, disprove the claims of contemporary German Calvinists that they actually adhered to it now. The Wittenberg Accord he dismissed as a pretence at surrender by Martin Bucer.[69] He resisted Catholic allegations that Luther was to blame for all the heresies and divisions in the Church: Luther could not be held responsible for the ways in which 'perverse men who falsely claimed to be Evangelicals had corrupted Gospel doctrine with their fanatical opinions'. Finally, he rejected the argument of those who alleged that it would be better to refrain from attacking the Calvinists, so as to form a stronger alliance against the popish enemy. God had enough strength to repel the papists: 'one must not do evil in order that good may come'.[70]

The preface was vitriolic enough; in the text itself, however, Osiander did not really sustain the programmatically Lutheran stance throughout the structure of the book. Rather, he inserted his anti-Calvinist polemic in the form of asides and glosses on the point which the narrative had reached. Zwingli, for example, opposed indulgence-selling in Zurich just as Luther did in

[67] L. Osiander, *Epitomes historiae ecclesiasticae centuriae* . . ., 8 vols. (Tübingen, 1592–1604); several subsequent editions by 1623.

[68] Raitt, *Montbéliard*, 160–1; on Lucas Osiander and his family see also Léonard, *Protestantism*, II, 216 n.8.

[69] L. Osiander, *Epitomes historiae ecclesiasticae, centuriae decimae sextae pars prima/secunda* (cited in the edn. of Tübingen, 1608–10; earliest edn of this vol. 1602/3), sigs.):(2^r–3^r.

[70] *Ibid.*, sigs.):(3^v–4^v.

Saxony: 'would that this man, who was somewhat learned, intelligent, and energetic, had only attacked papal impostures, and had not soon afterwards corrupted teaching on the Lord's Supper and other articles'. In so far as Zwingli did attack papal errors, he was 'undoubtedly instructed by Luther's writings'.[71] His verdict on Zwingli was, ultimately, less damning than it might have been: 'Zwinglian religion [was] partly Evangelical, partly corrupted by human and philosophical opinions'; his gloss on the Berne disputation referred to 'Zwingli's false teaching mixed with the truth'.[72] The polemical intent which was undoubtedly present in Osiander's work rather resembles a superficial varnish on a more neutral narrative: hence, for example, he interpolated an attack on Calvin into his discussion of the start of the sacramentarian debate in 1524: Calvin 'seemed' to reject the opinions of Zwingli and Oecolampadius, but was only presenting the same ideas 'in other smoother words and phrases, such that he seduced many even of the good and learned'.[73] The Zurich reformers took the blame for the rise of Anabaptism there; the Zwinglians and south German cities he held solely at fault for not having signed the *Augustana* in 1530.[74]

The reason for this curious disparity between the intent and the structure of Osiander's Reformation history was simple: for all his zeal, Osiander was not writing an original narrative. He acknowledged his dependence on certain sources identified by marginal notes. For events up to the middle of the sixteenth century he relied heavily, while not exclusively, on Johann Sleidan's *Commentaries*. For the later sixteenth century he used an even more improbable source: the *General Historien*, a continuation of Sleidan first published in German at Basle in 1577, under the name of 'Adam Henricpetri'.[75] This work showed a remarkable interest in French and Low Countries affairs, which in due course transmitted itself to Osiander. That interest may be explained by the fact that 'Adam Henricpetri' is believed to be a pseudonym of Philippe de Marnix van St-Aldegonde, the Netherlands Calvinist and author of the fervently anti-Catholic *Tableau des differens de la religion*.[76] Two examples of the resulting pan-Protestant approach may be cited: Osiander described the introduction of the Reformation in England under Elizabeth I from 1558 onwards in entirely positive terms (though Elizabeth's diplomatic dealings with the Lutherans *may* have influenced him here); secondly, he prefaced a sympathetic account of the Waldenses' defensive

---

[71] *Ibid.*, 68–9, 85.
[72] *Ibid.*, 89, 123.
[73] *Ibid.*, 98.
[74] *Ibid.*, 118–21, 144ff, 184f.
[75] 'A. Henricpetri', *General Historien: Der aller namhafftigsten ... Geschichten, Thaten und Handlungen ...* (Basle, 1577); the same pseudonym was used in a contemporary history of the Dutch revolt. NUC questions the attribution to P. de Marnix.
[76] See P. de Marnix, *Tableau des differens de la religion*, 2 vols. (Leiden, 1603–5).

war against the Duke of Savoy in 1560–1 by saying 'the Waldenses have a slightly purer religion than other Calvinists'.[77] Despite Osiander's intention, no doubt, an awareness of wider Protestant concerns and sympathies leaked through into his history from the sources which he used.

One may now turn, finally, to see how the historical writing produced in the Germanic Reformed or 'Calvinist' tradition of the later sixteenth century depicted the identity of the Reformation movement. Heinrich Bullinger's Reformation history may be left on one side, since Bullinger presented his account as a narrative of events in Switzerland from 1519 to 1532; he minimised the wider European context and thereby avoided discussing the thorny question of Zwingli's dependence, if any, on the ideas of Luther.[78] In Heidelberg, the centre of German reformed thought, historical studies developed relatively slowly. Viktorin Strigel taught there briefly; some notes were appended to Sleidan's works by his successor Wilhelm Xylander. J. J. Grynaeus taught some history there in the 1580s. In 1614 Janus Gruterus published pseudonymously a *Chronicle of Ecclesiastical and Political Chronicles*.[79] However, the most significant Heidelberg contribution to Reformation history before the Thirty Years' War must be the *Annals of the Renewal of the Gospel throughout Europe* published by the court preacher and theologian Abraham Scultetus (1566–1624) in 1618–20. This two-volume account contained a detailed year-by-year survey of the Reformation over the first twenty years between 1516 and 1535.[80] Just as Lucas Osiander had reasons for his hostility to Calvinists, so Scultetus had motives in his past career to express anti-Lutheran spleen in his historical writing. Between April and October 1614 he had been seconded to help Elector Johann Sigismund of Brandenburg to introduce the Second Reformation in Berlin and the Electorate. There he experienced virulent Lutheran hatred of Calvinism at first hand.[81] However, the normal rhetoric of German Calvinists did not allow for the exclusive approach adopted in Lutheran polemics. Luther was portrayed by the Calvinists as the great initiator of reform; as one of the first of a series of great figures who had step by step rolled back the errors of medieval Catholicism. The Second Reformation came, as it were, not to abolish Luther's work but to complete it. In this light, for instance, Scultetus felt able celebrate the

---

[77] Osiander, *Centuriae decimae sextae*, 674–5, 693; for Elizabeth's diplomatic initiatives with the Lutherans, see above, n. 26.

[78] J. J. Hottinger and H. H. Vögeli (eds.), *Heinrich Bullingers Reformationsgeschichte*, 4 vols. (Zürich, 1838–1813); Fueter, *Historiographie*, 260–3.

[79] Scherer, *Geschichte und Kirchengeschichte*, 72–5, with ref. to 'Johannes Gualterius' [= Janus Gruterus], *Chronicon chronicorum ecclesiastico-politicorum* (Frankfurt, 1614).

[80] A. Scultetus, *Annalium evangelii passim per Europam ... renovati decades duae*, 2 vols. (Heidelberg, 1618–20); for Scultetus, see G. A. Benrath (ed.), *Die Selbstbiographie des Heidelberger Theologen und Hofpredigers Abraham Scultetus (1566–1624)* (Karlsruhe, 1966); further references in Nischan, *Prince, People and Confession*, 291 n. 18.

[81] Nischan, *Prince, People and Confession*, 115–16.

Reformation centenary of 1617 in his own distinctive way with his jubilee sermon.[82]

The *Annals* resembled the work of Sleidan more closely than that of Osiander. Scultetus was a meticulous collector of documents, and deployed the printed editions of the Reformers' works to good effect, citing chapter and verse for each part of his story. He narrated the advent of the Reformation in terms of several parallel movements, above all those of Luther and Zwingli: 'As did Luther in Saxony, so Zwingli in Switzerland pressed on prudently the business of Christ'.[83] He denied Luther the heroic, unique stature accorded him by the Luther-worshippers, and portrayed him as one of many who 'recognized the deceits of the Roman court', along with Zwingli, Capito, Oecolampadius, and even some of the 'forerunners', including the Strassburg preacher Johann Creutzer, John of Wesel, even Hus, Wyclif, and the Waldenses.[84] When considering the city reformations, Scultetus gave distinct and separate coverage to each in turn; this treatment makes his view of the progress and spread of the Reformation through reforming preachers in the self-governing cities look strikingly modern.[85] He clearly regarded the 'renewal of the Gospel'; as a series of parallel enterprises, led by a range of figures with diverse gifts and characters.

Scultetus did allow himself some criticisms of Luther and the Lutherans; but his attitude to Luther himself was intermittently disrespectful rather than hostile, and the more caustic remarks were saved for Luther's followers. He remarked early on how inferior Luther was to Wyclif in his eucharistic doctrine: how Luther had even said that he would sooner accept transubstantiation than deny Christ's bodily presence.[86] In the year 1525, he opined, there were three serious impediments to the Gospel: the Anabaptists, the Schwenckfeldians, and Luther's tastelessly ill-timed wedding.[87] He discussed the origin of the doctrine of 'ubiquity' with withering sarcasm, describing it as an invention of late French scholasticism, popularised by Brenz and Jakob Swidelin.[88] Luther's party was blamed, directly or indirectly, for a range of misfortunes, from the rise of the sects to the sacramentarian dispute and the failure to include Strassburg in the Augsburg Confession.[89] He noted rather gleefully that the Strassburg Lutherans Marbach and Pappus held opposing

---

[82] For Scultetus's rhetoric see *ibid.*, 116–17; for his attitude to the Luther centenary see Nischan, 'Confessionalism and absolutism', 187–8, based on Scultetus, *Historischer Bericht wie die Kirchenreformation in Teutschlandt vor hundert Jahren Angefangen . . . hiebey sind zufinden . . . Sculteti Newjahrs und Jubelfest Predigten im Jahr 1617 gehalten* (Heidelberg, 1618).
[83] Scultetus, *Annalium . . . Decades*, I, 115.
[84] *Ibid.*, I, 8–11.
[85] *Ibid.*, I, 80ff, 118ff.
[86] *Ibid.*, I, 12–13.
[87] *Ibid.*, I, 239, 273ff.
[88] *Ibid.*, I, 226–7.
[89] *Ibid.*, I, 76, 227; II, 291.

views as to whether or not the *Tetrapolitana* was a Zwinglian confession.[90] In all of this, however, there was never any doubt that the Lutherans were infinitely closer to the Gospel than either the Catholics on the one hand or the sectaries on the other. It was, therefore, never a part of German Calvinist historiography to suggest that the Lutheran Reformation was so defective as hardly to be a Reformation at all; nor to claim that the Reformed tradition was wholly independent of the Lutheran. There were limits to 'confessional' narrow-mindedness, even among Calvinist theologians who agonized over Lutheran 'ubiquity' as though it would inexorably entail the restoration of the mass and the papacy itself.[91]

There is a curious asymmetry between Lutheran and Calvinist views of the Reformation in the confessional period. Put simply, most Lutherans were exclusive; most Calvinists were inclusive. Lutheran hardliners felt that they were the only true heirs of the Reformation, while the rest were 'heretics', 'fanatics', or 'sacramentaries'. So-called Calvinist 'eirenic' writings, such as those of Franciscus Junius, Bartholomaeus Pitiscus, and above all David Pareus, criticised just this Lutheran exclusivism, and pressed Lutherans to recognise themselves as sharers in a common enterprise with the Reformed.[92] The most probable explanation for this asymmetry seems to be that Lutheranism was after 1555 an introverted creed, no longer expanding and at peace with the Empire. Calvinism in contrast was insecure in German law, seeking allies abroad, and expanding aggressively both within and beyond the Reich. It was therefore in the Lutherans' interest to keep Calvinists at arm's length; and in the Calvinists' interest to broaden their base of support.[93]

'Confessionalism' is still an essential concept for understanding late sixteenth-century German protestant attitudes. Nevertheless, if 'Confessional' barriers are regarded as absolute, it becomes hard to explain the rise of the Protestant leagues in Germany in the first decades of the seventeenth century, or the success of the Leipzig Colloquy of 1631.[94] Lutheran anti-Calvinism should be seen as relative rather than absolute: hatred of Calvinism diminished as fear of Catholicism increased. The evidence surveyed here suggests that its extreme manifestations should not be taken absolutely at face value. When Conrad Schluesselburg (1543–1619) published his *Three books on the*

---

[90] *Ibid.*, II, 292.

[91] See Nischan, 'Confessionalism and absolutism', 195–7.

[92] For example in D. Pareus, *Irenicum, sive de unione et synodo evangelicorum liber votivus* (Heidelberg, 1614, 1651); on this see G. A. Benrath, 'Irenik und Zweite Reformation', in Schilling (ed.), *Konfessionalisierung*, 349–58; Léonard, *Protestantism*, II, 230ff.

[93] For analysis of this question see Benrath, 'Irenik und Zweite Reformation', 356–8; Raitt, *Montbéliard*, 58–9, Nischan, 'Confessionalism and absolutism', 200–1.

[94] For Johann Bergius and the Leipzig Colloquy of 1631, see Nischan, *Prince, People and Confession*, 240ff; Nischan, 'Confessionalism and absolutism', 202–3.

Theology of the Calvinists, in which ... it is shown that they think rightly on almost none of the articles of Christian Teaching, or when an opponent of Pareus named Leyser claimed that Lutherans had more in common with Catholics than Calvinists,[95] they were making a debating point; they were not offering a balanced verdict on the real relationship between the two main Protestant creeds. Common sense – not a quality always found in controversial theologians – led to a slightly different verdict from that prompted by an obsession with eucharistic doctrine, Christology, or predestination. Common sense led later sixteenth-century Protestants to care about each other's sufferings, to study at each other's universities and *gymnasia*, and to read and re-edit histories of each other's early Reformation movements. *Explicit* eirenicism may have been confined to slightly unusual, not to say eccentric figures such as David Pareus or his Lutheran counterpart Georg Calixtus (1586–1656). There was also, however, a more widespread, residual sense of a wider Protestant identity. It was nearly always betrayed, or implied, rather than proclaimed; nevertheless, even the steadily hardening confessionalism could not wholly obliterate it. It was a long way short of toleration, but at least it kept the extremes of intolerance in some sort of proportion.

[95] C. Schluesselburg, *Theologiae Calvinistarum libri iii ... in quibus demonstratur, eos de nulla fere doctrinae Christianae articulo recte sentire* (Frankfurt, 1592, 1594); Léonard, *Protestantism*, II, 231.

8   Toleration in the early Swiss Reformation: the art and politics of Niklaus Manuel of Berne

Bruce Gordon

Preaching on the fraternal hatred of Joab and Abner, Calvin gave sombre council to his Genevan audience:

> Thus we see that in Christendom people are tearing one another apart; let us realise that this is being taken into account by God, and even if men harden themselves, God does not change his mind. We have already seen battles for such a long time. There is no end to them. And even apart from battles, we have seen how many people have been killed by wars. This has not been the case merely in one place and in a single army, but has gone on among princes who claim to be Christians and Catholics – and yet they are killing an infinite number of people. And then the war has swept through one country like a storm. One sees poor people dead among the bushes, and others who are left have to endure hunger and thirst, and heat and cold, and many deprivations – to such a degree that if you cut their throat, you would do them a favour. For they are suffering and will die ten times, so to speak, before death strikes the final blow.[1]

II Samuel is a book about war, deceit and murder: it is the book of Saul and Abner, Samuel and Jonathan, David and Bathsheba; and Calvin preached on the book between 1562 and 1563 as the Wars of Religion had begun to engulf his native France.[2] Again and again, Calvin's principal message rings through: war of any sort is wrong, leading to the destruction of God's image in humanity, and claiming as its victims the poor, children, widows and the destitute.[3]

Without doubt, it was France which was foremost in the mind of the ailing reformer. Yet, in his denunciation of wars between Christians, Calvin raised the spectre which haunted his Swiss neighbours throughout the sixteenth century: the fear of war. Although one religious war had brought a peace and

---

[1] J. Calvin, *Sermons on 2 Samuel. Chapters 1–13*, trans. D. Kelly (Edinburgh, 1992), 85.

[2] See M. Holt, *The French Wars of Religion, 1562–1629* (Cambridge, 1995), 50–75.

[3] Calvin's attitude towards war was complex. He conceived of the Christian life in terms of a 'battle' in which the faithful were to accept the commands of God. This, as Bouwsma suggests, led Calvin to argue that disease, destitution and death itself are 'disciplines' of duty. As for war itself, Calvin argued that decisive wars for God's honour are justifiable, whilst he deplored the reality that most wars are initiated by greed and ambition. W. J. Bouwsma, *John Calvin: A Sixteenth Century Portrait* (1988), 56, 183–5.

stability of sorts in 1531, there was hardly a moment from the advent of Zwingli's reform preaching until the end of the Thirty Years' War, when the Swiss did not believe themselves to be on the precipice of a conflict which would tear their vulnerable Confederation asunder.[4]

The centrality of war to the mental world of the Swiss Reformation should not surprise us, for in essence the medieval patchwork of the Confederation was woven together by a series of military alliances.[5] The sixteenth-century Swiss historical consciousness was shaped by a bittersweet conjunction of patriotism, fuelled by memories of the great deeds of Swiss soldiers against Imperial and Burgundian foes, and a deep despair stirred by agonising defeats on the fields of Italy. This equivocal history, where liberty and freedom mixed with servitude and moral decay, moulded the religious and political thoughts of the first generation of Swiss reformers. The use of force and coercion occupied a central place in the plans of most reformers and although the demise of Zwingli's bellicose religious politics at Kappel neutralised Zurich as a force, the sword soon passed to Berne and the resurgent Catholic states, both of whom were prepared to use war to obtain their territorial and confessional goals.[6] War remained a threat to early modern Swiss society as long as the central dilemma of its reformation remained unanswered: the relationship between confession and politics. For the first generation of reformers, this problem emerged in a precise form: was the Confederation to be sacrificed for the sake of the Gospel?[7]

The inability of early Swiss reformers to provide an adequate answer to this question reflects what Irene Backus has called the 'fluidity of theology' of evangelical thought in the Confederation.[8] The motor of the Swiss Reformation was driven by the extraordinary pace of events which threatened at every moment to overtake the reformers. Zwingli and his colleagues were

---

[4] The centrality of mercenary service and war to the mentality of the Swiss reformation needs to be studied. On the emergence of the Swiss as a military force, see *Die Murtenschlacht. Ein Schweizer Ereignis in Europas Geschichte zwischen Mittelalter und Neuzeit, 1476–1976,* Kolloquiumsakten (Freiburg and Berne, 1976), and N. Stein's excellent monograph, *Burgund und die Eidgenossenschaft zur Zeit Karls des Kühnen* (Frankfurt and Berne, 1978). For the Reformation, the most important work remains H. Meyer, *Der Zweite Kappeler Krieg. Die Krise der Schweizerischen Reformation* (Zurich, 1976). For the relations between the Swiss and the French during the Wars of Religion, A. P. von Segesser. *Ludwig Pfyffer und seine Zeit. Ein Stück französischer und schweizerischer Geschichte im sechzehnten Jahrhundert,* 4 vols. (Berne, 1881–82).

[5] B. Gordon, 'Switzerland', in A. D. M. Pettegree (ed.), *The Early Reformation in Europe* (Cambridge, 1992), 70–93.

[6] On the Counter Reformation in Swiss lands, see P. Stadler, 'Das Zeitalter der Gegenreformation', *Handbuch der Schweizer Geschichte,* 1, (Zurich, 1980), 573–670.

[7] G. W. Locher, 'Zwingli's Political Activity: Its Motives and Objectives', in *Zwingli's Thought. New Perspectives* (Leiden, 1981), 267–76.

[8] I. Backus, 'The Disputations of Baden, 1526 and Berne, 1528: Neutralising the Early Church', *Studies in Reformed Theology and History,* 1 (1993), 121.

forced to formulate and defend theological concepts and ecclesiastical practices in haste, and contradictions are often evident. As it became clear that
the Reformation was not going to sweep all before it, Zwingli moved towards
a military resolution to break Catholic Swiss recalcitrancy. This, however,
remained a minority view, and if we are to understand the Swiss Reformation
we must move beyond a purely Zwingli-centred perspective to examine other
influential currents. For there was another powerful voice which declared
against religious wars, arguing that the Swiss Confederation could withstand
the apparent contradiction of two confessions. This was the voice of Niklaus
Manuel, the artist, dramatist, politician and reformer of Berne.[9] A man whose
fundamentally different understanding of reformation clashed with Zwingli's
perspective, creating a critical rift in the early Swiss evangelical movement.
It was the more moderate position held by Manuel, however, which ultimately proved more influential in the preservation of the Confederation.

It is tempting to compare the careers and thought of Zwingli and Manuel.
Born in the year of 1484, their youths were passed in those formative decades
when the Swiss emerged from Habsburg hegemony and proclaimed their
independence, only to be slaughtered on the fields of Italy in the service of
foreign masters. The unresolved emotions stirred by these events shaped the
dispositions of these two men: both were to witness battles in which Swiss
butchered Swiss, and later find expression for their horror in poetry. Manuel
served as soldier in order to support his family, whilst Zwingli spent ten
years as a parish priest in Glarus, among a people well accustomed to fighting.[10] Their utter revulsion at the moral turpitude of mercenary service, with
its destructive tendencies for Swiss communities, filled them with zeal for
reform.

They were both artists. Zwingli was a musician of some talent, whilst
Manuel, as we shall see, was one of the greatest poets of his day.[11] There were
also, naturally, great differences. Zwingli, the humanist and priest, studied in
Vienna and Basle, and was an intimate of the circle of humanists around
Erasmus. Manuel was trained as a painter in an Italian workshop; his gifts
found articulation not in the turning of a Latin phrase but in capturing the

---

[9] There is no modern biography of Manuel which treats both his political and artistic activities.
J. P. Tardent, *Niklaus Manuel als Staatsmann* (Berne, 1979), is primarily a study of Manuel's
involvement in Bernese politics. Karl von Grüneisen, *Niclaus Manuel. Leben und Werk eines
Malers und Dichters, Kriegers, Staatsmannes und Reformators im sechzehnten Jahrhundert*
(Stuttgart and Tübingen, 1837); C. Menz and H. Wagner (eds.), *Niklaus Manuel – Maler,
Dichter, Staatsmann. Exhibition catalogue* (Berne, 1979); H. A. Michel, *et al.* (eds.), *450
Jahre Berner Reformation. Beiträge zur Geschichte der Berner Reformation und zu Niklaus
Manuel* (Berne, 1980–81); Derek van Abbé, 'Niklaus Manuel of Berne and his interest in
the Reformation', *Journal of Modern History*, 24 (1952), 287–300.
[10] G. Potter, *Zwingli* (Cambridge, 1976), 24.
[11] There is no modern critical edition of Manuel's works. The essential work remains J. Bächtold, *Niklaus Manuel* (Frauenfeld, 1878). All citations from Manuel's works are from this
edition.

spiritual world of the common people who populate the pages of his dramas, speaking in dialect. While Zwingli was to find his ideal of the Christian society in the gathering around the Lord's Table, for Manuel it was in the brusque, bawdy existence of everyday life. For Manuel, the true Christian life manifested itself in the discourse of the streets, in the revelry of a festival and in family life. He had no interest in the moralising of church discipline.

Indeed, no life could be more remarkable than Manuel's own. The illegitimate son of an apothecary, Manuel acquired his training as a painter in his native Italy before moving north to Berne. He possessed little formal education, and could be described neither as a humanist nor a scholastic, thus setting Manuel outside the usual environment for reformers. In Berne, he supplemented his training by learning the art of glass blowing, and he supported his family on commissions received from local patrons.[12] Although clearly influenced by Dürer and the Italians, it is remarkably difficult to identify Manuel's teachers, and art historians are united in their judgement that ultimately Manuel created an eclectic style of his own.[13] The altar panels which he painted for the Dominican church are a useful example. The figures are a curious mixture of late Gothic and Renaissance styles, suggesting the transition taking place in Berne. Facing one another are a Gothic Madonna and the Apostle Luke, dressed in the fashionable attire of a Renaissance artist. Hugo Wagner is not alone in his opinion that the artist depicted on the panel is Manuel himself, full of pride and expressing the new-found confidence of the craft guilds which were wresting power from the patriciate in Berne.[14]

In his works of devotional art, Manuel continued to contrast medieval motifs with Renaissance innovations. Thus we see traditional medieval figures transported into a Bernese landscape of Renaissance provenance. Equally varied was Manuel's choice of subject matters: when not working for a church, he favoured landscapes, such as in his *Pyramus and Thisbe* or his *Judgement of Paris*.[15] At every turn, Manuel betrays neither slavish adherence to any one school of painting or an especial stylistic consistency; art historians can identify a wide range of possible influences.

In the midst of his artistic work, and in order to support his family, Manuel, like many of his compatriots, entered mercenary service and headed south in the pay of Francis I.[16] The year was 1516 and Manuel and twelve thousand Swiss were sent to Milan, where they were to await the expected attack by

[12] H. Wagner, 'Niklaus Manuel – Leben und Künstlerisches Werk', in *Niklaus Manuel Deutsch. Maler, Dichter, Staatsmann* (Berne, 1979), 19.

[13] *Ibid.*, 18.

[14] *Ibid.*, 24.

[15] *Ibid.*, 26.

[16] There were 8.000 Swiss in the French garrison. When Maximilian drew back from confrontation, Francis I was able to conclude the perpetual peace of Fribourg with the Swiss. The Swiss received 300,000 écus for the Milan expedition, R. J. Knecht, *Francis I* (Cambridge, 1982), 67–8.

Maximilian I, who in turn was leading an army with 20,000 Swiss soldiers.[17] When the attack failed to materialise, the disgruntled Bernese soldiers turned for home, and little is known of Manuel's first entry into soldiering. What is known is that when he reached Berne he began work on his most famous creation, a mural painted on the wall of the Dominican church; a study of life and death visible to all the citizens of the city known as the *Totentanz*.[18]

The *Totentanz* offers us the first significant insight into Manuel's religious and social views. The painting, completed between 1517 and 1519, shows a long line of people from all classes of life: the pope, princes, priests, peasants, Jews and Turks. In the freedom which death has given them, they are able to reflect upon their final hour. In death they are equal, for no one escapes its grasp, but, as Jean-Paul Tardent has pointed out, Manuel's statement is not pitched on a social revolutionary level.[19] Although each has succumbed to death, the privileges which they enjoyed in this world and the hierarchies of power which they occupied are not questioned.[20] Manuel conceived of the world along conventional lines as a pyramid in which each person had their appointed place and role.[21] The biting satire of the text is not aimed at the order itself, but rather at its abuse and perversion by men and women.

There is no mistaking Manuel's political message in the *Totentanz*. He is a convinced republican, and his views on the rule of the state flow from the mouths of the mayor, the magistrates and the citizens rather than the princes and dukes, who, for Manuel, represent a form of oppressive authority, where the land and its inhabitants are held as a personal possession.[22] True political order, however, is found in the constitution of the city, where the guilds are the guarantors of liberty and social care.

In addition to his republicanism, two more spiritual themes are prominent in Manuel's *Totentanz*. Contrary to what we might expect, the spirit of the *Totentanz* is neither dismal nor sombre, for as each of the characters comes forward we meet robust, often witty individuals who offer candid reflections on their lives. Some are refined and aloof, others burly and coarse, but never

---

[17] H. Weisflecker, *Maximilian I. Die Fundamente des habsburgischen Weltreiches* (Munich, 1991), 180–4.

[18] P. Zinsli (ed.), *Der Berner Totentanz des Niklaus Manuel* (Berne, 1979).

[19] J. P. Tardent, *Niklaus Manuel als Staatsmann* (Diss. Berne, 1968), 65.

[20] *Ibid.*, 65.

[21] Beerli writes: La Danse macabre su cimetière des Innocents présentait alternativement des clercs et des laïcs, en parcourant, du haut en bas, toute l'échelle sociale. Le 'Totentanz' de Berne sépare nettement l'ordre spirituel de l'ordre temporel, et introduit de nouveaux personnages dans la ronde. A cette différence près, il illustre la même conception médiévale d'une société statique et fortement hiérarchisée. Nous comparerons la Danse de Nicolas Manuel à celle de ses devanciers: l'analyse des coïncidences et des divergences nous fera voir la part de la tradition et l'apport des temps nouveaux. C. A. Beerli, *Le Peintre poète Nicolas Manuel et L'évolution sociale de son temps* (Geneva, 1953), 117.

[22] Tardent, *Niklaus Manuel*, 66.

are they mere stilted representatives of particular virtues or vices. The most fascinating and daring aspect of Manuel's work is how he brought the people of Berne into his depiction of cosmic reality by painting real people into his picture. Where we cannot make an exact identification he has left unmistakable clues, such as family crests.[23] Manuel held a mirror to the society in Berne making the point that the most significant spiritual moments take place in the midst of the everyday commerce of life.[24] The men and women in Manuel's *Totentanz* embody his belief in an unreflective, non-contemplative Christianity in which each person lives by acting and doing, a *Freude am Dasein*. Death is omnipresent, engaging each of the characters in an exchange of wisdom, and it is death which sets the boundaries to this life, though, indeed, in the end it is powerless to destroy it. Life is found in a true existence in the limited time granted to each person. The nature of this true existence emerges later in Manuel's work.

A second distinguishing theme is Manuel's obvious sympathy for the common people and the outsiders of society. This affinity finds expression in his *Fastnacht* plays and the later evangelical literature, where Manuel makes use of various literary devices to express his belief that the most profound truths are found in the mouths of artisans, beggars, children and widows. The widespread appeal of Manuel's writings attests to his striking ability to place the reader in the predicament of the speaker. Manuel's interest in giving a voice to the common people is an element of his early work which would become a cornerstone of both his literary and political activities in the service of the Reformation.

Manuel's evolving interest in the political life of Berne is further seen in his painting for the high altar of the Dominican church in 1518.[25] On one altar panel we see the pope dreaming of St Dominic, the order's founder, supporting the troubled Church. On the other panel, St Thomas sits at table with Francis I, a timely reminder of Berne's recent renewal of its alliance with France in 1515.[26] This commitment to the continued alliance with France was integral to Manuel's Reformation politics and proved a serious stumbling block in his relationship to Zwingli.

Between 1518 and 1520 Manuel received a series of commissions for altar paintings and murals, most of which have not survived. In examining the

---

[23] Wagner, 'Niklaus Manuel', 30.

[24] Beerli points out that forty of the panels have identifiable crests: two from members of the clergy, fifteen from noble families of Berne or her allies, one from a solicitor in Fribourg, sixteen from influential burgher families in Berne and six from artisan families. Beerli, *Le Peintre Poète Nicolas Manuel*, 112.

[25] Wagner, 'Niklaus Manuel', 28.

[26] The Bernese chronicler Anselm tells how this agreement enabled the French king to advertise in each Swiss territory for soldiers, offering a yearly pension of 2,000 francs. Historischer Verein des Kantons Bern (ed.), *Die Berner Chronik des Valerius Anselm* (Berne, 1884–1901), vol. 4, 134–5.

extant work, we search in vain for clear indications that Manuel had moved towards 'Lutheran' teachings. References to contemporary social and political issues abound, most quite specific to Berne, but those which speak to religious problems are generally commonplaces of the anticlerical genre evident throughout northern Europe. The turning point for Manuel was not to come until the winter of 1522. In that year Manuel again took up military service, as a clerk for Albrecht von Stein, the Bernese commander in the French service.[27] What Manuel saw during that winter campaign changed his life. In Novara, the Swiss troops, whom Manuel had praised in his *Totentanz*, plundered and marauded the city, raped the women and murdered children. The Bernese chronicler Anselm, whose account was written with the assistance of Manuel, describes how churches were despoiled and nuns violated.[28] Although it is not clear whether Manuel took part in these acts of violence, his later accounts contain no attempt to exonerate himself.

The response to the barbarity of the Swiss troops was outrage, and Manuel himself was shattered by the experience. The soldier in the *Totentanz* is described as a *redlich* man, but Manuel had seen how quickly his beloved Confederates had devolved into animals, driven by greed and lust. Manuel was slightly wounded in the engagement and forced to give up military service; for the Swiss, however, things became worse. The French and Swiss army suffered a tremendous beating at Bicocca: the legendary Swiss soldiers proved no match for the German *Landesknechte*.[29]

The psychological impact of what happened in Italy destroyed Manuel's belief in the glory of Swiss military prowess. War was a horror which reduced men to beasts and destroyed the possibility of community. The sight of Swiss fighting against Swiss led Manuel to despair and fear for the future of the Confederation. It was at this moment, the slight evidence suggests, that he underwent a conversion to the evangelical cause.[30]

If we look at Manuel's next piece of literature, his *Traum*, we find some indications of what this conversion meant.[31] His point of departure is a rejection of his previously cherished ideal of the community as the highest good. The optimistic republicanism of the *Totentanz* has given way to the psychological insight that communities are not inherently good, but are, rather,

---

[27] Tardent, *Niklaus Manuel*, 74–5.

[28] Anselm, *Die Berner Chronik*, vol. 4, 514.

[29] K. Brandi, *The Emperor Charles V. The Growth and Destiny of a Man and of a World-Empire*, (1965), 202.

[30] On Manuel's conversion, see G. W. Locher, 'Niklaus Manuel Deutsch als Reformator', in H. A. Michel (ed.), *450 Jahre Berner Reformation* 385–7. Also, Tardent, *Niklaus Manuel*, 74–7.

[31] There is some discussion about the provenance of this work, see P. Zinsli, 'Der "seltsame wunderschöne Traum" – ein Werk Niklaus Manuel's?', in H. A. Michel (ed.), *450 Jahre Berner Reformation* , 350–79.

divided into those people who seek self-satisfaction and those who are devoted to its higher goals.[32] The evangelical impulse, given the situation in Berne, came not from Zwingli but Luther, whose writings give shape to Manuel's central dilemma. After the Italian campaign, Manuel was confounded by the question of how man could be reduced to a bestial state in which all cultural developments and refinements were so easily abandoned. This was not Zwingli's question, but rather the conundrum faced by a Renaissance man in crisis. From Luther Manuel received the answer that all human worth and authority exists only insofar as it is received from God. This troubled relationship between human nature and human authority which so haunted Manuel in the early 1520s looms large in his next stage as an artist and proponent of the Reformation, his *Fastnacht Spiele*.

Peter Pfrunder's excellent book on *Fastnacht* culture in Swiss lands has demonstrated the many dimensions and multi-layered character of these events, and how the plays were open to a wide spectrum of interpretation by different social groups.[33] The patrician class, the guilds, the beggars and the rural peasantry had widely varying expectations and interests in these spectacles.[34] Nevertheless, these divergent interests constituted a well-established *Fastnacht* culture in Berne into which Manuel's two plays, *Vom Papst und seiner Priesterschaft (Totenfresser)* and *Ablasskrämer*, fitted. These plays were performed alongside short dramaticals, processions, dances and games.[35]

The satire of Manuel's plays is uncompromising. In the *Totenfresser*, the plot centres on the burial of a wealthy peasant with a clear sub-text in which the author provides an unambiguous denunciation of the corruption of the papal church and the avarice of the clergy, who abuse the sacred occasions of life for profit. Closely allied to the greedy clergy are those who profited most from the mercenary service, the noble families of Berne. The central conflict of the play is between the pope, supported by his bloodthirsty soldiers and insatiable clergy, and the truth of the Gospel, represented in the figure of Dr Lupolt Schuchnit, whom many assume to be Martin Luther.[36] In the middle stand the peasants, who represent the audience for whose souls the two sides battle. They are, however, no passive participants, for we note a further development of Manuel's interest in how common people are able to receive and articulate the Christian message. It is the peasant Amman von

---

[32] Tardent, *Niklaus Manuel*, 78.
[33] P. Pfrunder, *Pfaffen, Ketzer, Totenfresser. Fastnachtkultur der Reformationszeit- Die Berner Spiele von Niklaus Manuel* (Zurich, 1988).
[34] *Ibid.*, 126.
[35] *Ibid.*, 143.
[36] G. W. Locher, 'Die deutsche Reformation aus schweizer Sicht', *Zeitschrift für Kirchengeschichte* (1978), 31–5.

Maraschwil, for example, who argues that the corruption of the clergy does not undermine the authority of civil government.

> Should one permit the current clergy that
> which they devise in their proud, stupid noodles.
> They would peel our skins over our ears.
> But worldly government, that must one have.
> Christ demonstrated this in numerous places (in Scripture),
> worldly government comes from God,
> As Christ answers Pilate:
> 'You would have no power over my life,
> unless it has been given to you from above'
> So also did he permit taxes and duties,
> this I understand well from the Gospel.
> . . .
> I can, however, from no one understand
> that he has given money to the priests[37]

Manuel's religious thought is centred on his belief that the old church was an institution of exploitation and, thereby, the primary source of injustice in society. In the *Fastnacht* plays, as in his *Traum*,[38] Manuel articulates a position he was later, in light of the Peasants' Revolt, to modify, but not abandon. He argues that the ecclesiastical orders, from the simplest monk to the pope, would never abandon the system which sustained their profligate, indolent lives, even if they knew themselves to be in error. The laity, on the other hand, once they came to see how they had been exploited as victims of the church, would quickly be won to the Gospel.[39] It would suffice that they should be made aware of the Gospel, and events would follow their own course. Manuel held out little hope for the reform of the clergy; there could be only one remedy: the forceful destruction of the clerical order.[40]

In 1523 Manuel emerged from his roles as social critic and religious agitator to become a politician.[41] He was appointed *Landvogt* of Erlach, near the Bielersee, an office he was to hold for five years. This was a clear step on the ladder of political preferment in Berne and Manuel's brief was clear: he was to strengthen the presence of the Berne magistrates among the traditionally unruly peasantry.[42]

---

[37] *Totenfresser*, 1317–27, 1334–5, Bächtold, 81.
[38] F. Vetter, 'Ein Traum. Gesicht vom Welkrieg und von Papst und Kardinal', *Blätter für bernische Geschichte, Kunst und Altertumskunde, 12 (1916), 295ff.*
[39] Tardent, *Niklaus Manuel*, 82.
[40] *Ibid.*
[41] *Ibid.*, 87–95.
[42] On the relations between the peasants and the magistrates before the reformation in Berne, see P. Bierbrauer, *Freiheit und Gemeinde im Berner Oberland 1300–1700* (Berne, 1991), esp. 244–250.

Manuel's maturing as a religious thinker, combined with his new position of authority, was the provenance for an ideal of reform which in its embryonic form was already of a different orientation from the work of his contemporary Zwingli. For Manuel, the social-revolutionary potential of the Reformation was to be directed towards the hierarchical church, not the whole of society. Thus, in contrast to Zwingli's vision of a reformation of the whole society, his *corpus christianum*, Manuel began to argue for a reformation limited to the clergy. Social issues come to the fore only in the context of his polemic against clerical abuse. Political power is brought into question only when the Pope's claims to territorial authority are ridiculed, otherwise Manuel was an obedient servant of the state. His primary interest was the curtailing of ecclesiastical influence in civil affairs, not to challenge the political and social structures of Berne. Indeed, in his early works, Manuel demonstrated a clear disinterest in discussing the wider political and religious events rocking the Swiss Confederation. It was the extent of power exercised by the Bernese council which absorbed him, not the larger question of the crisis facing the Swiss. Manuel anticipated Zwingli's later position that the spiritual renewal of the people could be attained without change to existing social and political structures.[43]

Manuel's measured response to church reform grew from his relations with the peasants of his *Landvogtei*. He was certain of the eventual triumph of the Reformation in the city, but as to what would happen in the rural areas he was less certain. In the *Fastnacht* plays, as we have noted, the peasants are portrayed as those who perceive the truth and unmask the mendacity of the clergy, but in reality Manuel was to experience something quite different. The peasants were extremely suspicious of the urban rulers and demonstrated little enthusiasm for evangelical teaching. Manuel, however, remained sanguine, believing that the peasants were the ideal audience for the Gospel. They were resourceful people of the land, who with their hard work eked out a meagre living and, thereby, stood close to the heart of the saviour.[44]

The events of the Bernese Reformation did not bear out this optimism.[45] The evangelical preaching made extremely modest gains in the rural lands, and Manuel was confronted by the disinclination of the peasants to accept

[43] Heiko Oberman has shown how the decisive events of the early reformation in Zurich were controlled by the council, which pursued a policy of 'peaceable order'. Zwingli introduced reform by giving a theological interpretation to a local civic event (the disputation of 1523) held under the auspices of the magistrates. H. A. Oberman, 'Zwingli's Reformation Between Success and Failure', in *The Reformation: Roots and Ramifications* (Edinburgh, 1994), 189–94.

[44] Tardent, *Niklaus Manuel*, 87.

[45] T. de Quervain, *Kirchliche und soziale Zustände in Bern unmittelbar nach der Einführung der Reformation (1528–1536)* (Bern, 1906).

religious teachings which carried the threat of increased urban hegemony.[46] His *Fastnacht* plays, which had been such an important vehicle for the Reformation in the city of Berne, found little echo in the countryside.

His service as *Landvogt* provided Manuel with an acute understanding of the peasant mentality, and he realised that his conception of reform from below was misconstrued, a conclusion brought into sharp relief by the events of 1525. Despite his flirtation with a violent overthrow of the clergy, Manuel always believed that the first fruits of religious reform would be peace.[47] The fact that peasant unrest in Erlach had little to do with acceptance of the evangelical faith was not lost on the *Vogt*, and he was quick to appreciate the reluctance of the peasants to take up arms for the Gospel.

The reform movement in Berne was quickly absorbed into a process of increased urban control over the rural territories. As an official of the civic magistrates, and in response to his experiences in governing a resentful peasantry, Manuel inevitably became an advocate of centralised rule. The peasants' revolt had polarised the reform movement in most Swiss territories, leaving two choices: magisterial reform or sectarianism. Having jettisoned his earlier vague and rather dreamy conceptions of reform, Manuel set himself to serving his Bernese lords, working to reduce rural autonomy. A good deal of his time was spent sorting out jurisdictional conflicts between rural territories and the city. Manuel made it clear that he had no place for the old *Gewohnheitsrecht*, so often used to justify rights preserved by the rural *Gemeinde*.

Manuel believed that proper order and peace could only be established when the confusion of overlapping authority was resolved.[48] Nevertheless, according to Manuel, the power of the central government was not without limitations. Under no circumstances could the secular authority interfere with the faith of the individual. In particular, Manuel could not accept that the majority of the Bernese council could enforce a decision of faith on the people. When in 1526 the council voted to retain the Catholic faith, Manuel stormed out of the chamber claiming that this was a burdening of the conscience. Following his outburst of anger, Manuel turned to express his rage in more satirical form: he sent a case of Erlach wine to the council

---

[46] Commenting on the refusal of the Bernese Oberland to accept the reform mandates of the city council, Bierbrauer writes: Die reformatorische Bewegung, die einen zentralen Bereich des sozialen Lebens umgestalten wollte, deren Neuerungsabsichten unabsehbare Folgen mit sich bringen konnten und die in ihrer Eigendynamik schwer kalkulierbar schien, war für die Bauern zweifellos eine Bedrohung in diesem Sinn, und ihre ablehnende Haltung resultierte – diese Feststellung sei zunächst als Hypothese formuliert – aus der Sorge um eine mögliche Destabilisierung des politisch-sozialen Ordnungsgefüges. *Freiheit und Gemeinde*, 250.

[47] Tardent, *Niklaus Manuel*, 99.

[48] Manuel's letter to the Berne council of 21 August, 1525. Printed in R. Wustmann, 'Briefe Niklaus Manuels', *Zeitschrift für Kulturgeschichte*, 4 (1905), 152–3. Manuel declares that he is a servant of the council and prepared to do what the council commands him.

accompanied by a brilliant letter in which he parodied the Catholic understanding of the passion of Christ and the Eucharist.[49]

This spirit of parody is found again in Manuel's *Barbali*, written in the
same year of 1526 and marking a return to serious literary work.[50] The story
is simple. A young girl, Barbali, is told by her mother that she must enter a
nunnery. When the girl refuses, the mother invites a series of clerics to persuade her of the rightness of the vocation. In a feisty defence, Barbali
espouses fairly conventional evangelical teachings: the monastic life is contrary to the Gospel; the principle of Christian life is love of neighbour; the
true manifestation of Christ is internal, appearing to those who despair of
salvation. At the centre of the text, however, is Manuel's discussion of
coercion in religion. Again, the central theme is obedience to legitimate
authority.

The various clerics argue from authority; there is no way, they charge,
that a young girl can discern the message of the Gospel. The spirit of truth,
Barbali retorts, is in those who confess Christ, enabling them to recognise
and respond to the truth. Thus, when she is told to attend church, Barbali
asks what the fables and legends taken from Aesop, which are the stuff of
the priests' sermons, have to do with her.[51] She hears only nonsense from
the pulpit and therefore stays at home. What the priests take for the truth is
against the natural order, for they have forbidden her from having children,
a gift sanctioned by Scripture.

When pressed to submit to the obedience of the religious life, Barbali
responds with reference to Paul's admonition on food and drink.[52] Indeed,
Manuel reaffirms his belief in the Christian magistracy, but rejects the idea
that worldly powers can use the sword to force people to 'correct' faith.[53]

Barbali is not the most gripping of Manuel's dramatic works, but it
remains deserving of greater attention. It argues for the possibility of a lay
theology; it is centred on the New Testament (no Old Testament references),
particularly Paul; and it virtually denies any mediating role to the clergy.
Although Manuel had abandoned his idealised vision of the Christian life,

---

[49] Bächtold, xxxii–xxxiii.
[50] For an excellent discussion of the text, see Beerli, *Le Peintre Poète*, 257–66.
[51] 'Was gond mich seine fablen an,/ Die er findt im Esopo stan?/ Die schmirbt er denn mit
heidenmist,/ so er an siner kanzlen ist,/ von legenden, märlin und dem ban,/ ouch henkt er
ein sentner ablass dran.' Bächtold, 954–99.
[52] Beerli writes: 'L'argument essentiel de cette championne de l'Evangile reste naturellement
la maxime de saint Paul: "Qui ne travaille pas ne doit pas manger". A l'idéal de la vie
cloîtrée – "chanter, jeûner, porter d'humbles vêtements, prier. lire . . ." – Manuel et ses
contemporains opposent l'idéal de la vie laborieuse.' *Le Peintre Poète*, 261.
[53] 'Ich ker mich nüts an der väter leben/ Min gott hat inen sin gsatz ouch g'geben./ Hand sie
gloubt und ton, was er büt,/ wol inen, wo nit, hilft's alles gar nüt!/ Sie habind ioch ton, was
man tut, / so ist der gloub das obrest guot./ Das rich gottes kumpt nit mit usserlichen berden,/
man wirti nit hie oder da zeigen werden.' Bächtold, 1693–1700.

he retains a place for some old themes: the practical nature of the Christian life which is this-worldly and manifested in human relationships. Clericalism, towards which Zwingli was increasingly moving, is rejected out of hand.[54] In addition, *Barbali* marks a clear shift in Manuel's thinking; he offers his first coherent rejection of coercion in matters of faith.

Following the heady events of 1528 when Berne finally turned to Reformation, Niklaus Manuel emerged as the major political leader.[55] In his ascent from local to Confederate politics the jumble of religious and political ideals which characterised his early years began to assume a more articulate form. Manuel's political and religious activities between 1528 and 1530 did much to shape the future of the Swiss Confederation. He was elected to the small council in Berne in 1528 and served his city in two crucial roles: as diplomat and eventually as *Venner*, traditionally in Berne a military post which had evolved into a senior political office in the state.[56]

Manuel's diplomatic activities were concentrated in areas of dangerous religious tensions within the Confederation: Basle, Solothurn, Glarus and the *Gemeine Herrschaften*. From 1528 until his death in 1530 Manuel was Berne's pre-eminent diplomat and the most prominent Swiss advocate for a peaceful resolution to the increasing number of confessional skirmishes. This was a role for which he was uniquely well qualified. Elegant and refined, Manuel was a persuasive orator and skilful negotiator who, in Tardent's words, was a 'born diplomat'.[57] Manuel was present in Basle during the tense period of December/January 1528–29 when the city was in danger of being consumed by popular movements. He had been sent by the Berne council to help negotiate the growing crisis in the city.[58] Manuel's attitude towards Reformation emerged quite clearly; he wanted to help the implementation of the Reformation, but not at any price.[59] One sees how determinative was his fear of war and anarchy. Manuel was alarmed by the volatile situation in Basle, where the reform was being pushed by local communities, and he refused to support a Reformation which threatened either the authority of the ruling council or the peace and order of the state. Manuel threw himself into the negotiations between the Council and the two confessional parties, believing that the only solution lay in a religious debate. He reassured his Catholic

---

[54] Barbali's fiercest attack is upon those clerics who hold that the message of the Gospel is hidden to the laity: 'Schend, wi üch gschrift antwurt gibt/ Ich red von mir selb die wort nit./ Sagend nit, dass das evangeli finster si!/ Der Einvaltig man dächt sust darbi, / Ir wärind verloren, drumb wär es üch verdeckt./ Mich wunder, dass üch das wort Pauli nit erschreckt'. Bächtold, 1361–1366.

[55] J. P. Tardent, 'Niklaus Manuel als Politiker', in Hans A. Michel *et al.* (eds.), *450 Jahre Berner Reformation*, 421ff.

[56] Tardent, *Niklaus Manuel*, 14–15.

[57] Ibid., 169.

[58] *Ibid.*, 135–6.

[59] *Ibid.*, 191–3.

colleagues that the Reformation would not be imposed by coercion and to his own party he insisted that the maintenance of order in the community and the authority of the council were more important than the rash introduction of reform.[60]

This was precisely the point which Manuel had articulated in his role as mediator in Glarus.[61] There was a large evangelical majority and a small, but active Catholic minority which resisted attempts to have the mass outlawed. Manuel agreed with the Zurich colleagues that this was a matter not merely of establishing the Reformation, but a question of the authority of the ruling council.

The most serious conflict, however, was in the Mandated Territories.[62] It was here that a serious inconsistency of the Reformed party emerged. Having argued against allowing the Catholic minority to exercise its rights to determine its form of worship in Glarus, both Zwingli and Manuel pressed the case for the evangelical minorities in the Mandated Territories. This general agreement masked a more serious division which emerged among the Reformed states. Manuel, while sharing with Zwingli the goal of turning the Mandated Territories to the Reformation, sharply opposed the strategy favoured by Zurich. Above all else, he condemned Zwingli's practice of sending missionaries into the communities who preached evangelical doctrines and advocated opposition to the Catholic authorities.[63] Manuel saw this as an affront to established authority which could lead to rebellion and violence.

The conflict between Catholics and Reformed started to broaden in the spring of 1529 when the five Cantons (*die fünf Orte*) concluded an alliance with Ferdinand of Austria. Zwingli was convinced that Ferdinand and Charles planned an attack on the Reformed Cantons and he formulated a plan to defeat the Catholic Cantons militarily before they received assistance from the Habsburgs.[64] He argued that the Catholic Cantons had to be forced to give up the Habsburg alliance and to allow the free preaching of the Gospel in their territories. The Bernese councillors warned the Zurichers against war; their grounds were pragmatic. Berne would come to Zurich's defence, but never engage in any pre-emptive strike. Manuel went to Zurich in early June to represent this view and on 3 June he spoke to the assembled Zurich council.[65]

Manuel comes straight to the point. No war should be undertaken without the knowledge and consent of the rural people, and in light of its recent

---

[60] *Ibid.*, 193.
[61] *Ibid.*, 132.
[62] *Ibid.*, 174–81.
[63] On Zwingli's activities, see M. Haas, *Huldrich Zwingli und seine Zeit* (Zurich, 1969), 216–18.
[64] On the foreign policy of the Swiss Cantons during 1529, see R. Hauswirth, *Landgraf Philipp von Hessen und Zwingli* (Basle, 1968).
[65] Text of the speech is printed in Bächtold, xliii–xlv.

difficulties in the Oberland, Berne is not prepared to begin a religious war.[66] He defends Berne's politics from the Gospel, which, he argues, has as its fundamental message peace and unity. The Zurichers, he tells his audience, were indeed the first among the Confederates to receive the Gospel and they have done much good; but there have also been errors.[67] It has only been Berne's mediation which has prevented civil war. In a direct attack on Zwingli, Manuel points to the Zurich reformer's fundamental error in believing that the common people of *Schwyz* were desperate to hear the evangelical faith and would gladly have accepted it if true preaching were allowed. Although it is true, Manuel admits, that there was much French gold behind the opposition of the Catholic Cantons, the refusal to accept the Reformation is not merely a question of money. The simple people believe in the mass and this belief cannot be changed by violence or coercion.[68] Decisions of faith can only be made by individuals.

In a remarkable confession, Manuel admits that he too once believed that it was simply a matter of exposing the people to the Gospel.[69] Yet now he had seen that Catholics, even when they had heard the Gospel, remained unconverted. Nevertheless, he adds, one can negotiate and argue with them.

In the second part of the speech, Manuel exhorts the Zurichers to abandon their militarist policies. Concessions to Catholics, he continues, would not deprive the Reformed of ultimate victory, that was in God's hands, but rash military action would bring down both the Reformation and Confederation. Patience, on the other hand, would bring further gains. Here he probably had in mind Schaffhausen and Solothurn.[70]

Manuel's words had a great effect on the Zurich council and for a few days Zwingli saw his support fall away. After Manuel had left for Berne, however, Zwingli was able to regain the support of those magistrates who had previously supported his call to military action.[71]

One week after Manuel's speech, Zurich declared war on the Catholic Cantons, citing the burning of Jakob Kaiser as its cause. Manuel was caught

---

[66] 'Dann unsere herren schulthess und rät sind nit willens, einichen kreig anzefachen, sunders zuovor ire gemeinden aller schmach und schand, inen zuogefüegt, genzlichen berichten, darmit, so man in ein feld kom, kein schmach and schand ingelegt werdi: dann man sye gar kriegsch, so es schön wette si und die sunn schin, wenn es aber ützit ein wenig regnoti, so wurd ein grosser unwill under dem volk.' *Ibid.*, xliii.

[67] 'Ir, unser trüw lieb Eidgnossen und christenlich mitburger von Zürich, die da ersten und anfenger sind gsin, habent mit der güetigkeit und ze wegen bracht; so habent unsere herren von Bern domalen fast gescheiden, es wär sunst langest krieg worden.' *Ibid.*, xliv.

[68] 'Nu ist wol müglich und ze glouben, dass man gelt und penzion geb und nin richlich; dann man in gar vil mindren und kleinfüegeren sachen, dann dise ist, gelt geben hat; aber es ist vil einfaltigs shlechts volk, das us rechter fromkeit daruf verharren wil.' *Ibid.*, xliv.

[69] *Ibid.*

[70] Tardent, *Niklaus Manuel*, 249.

[71] Haas, *Huldrich Zwingli*, 231.

between the Zurichers and the Catholics; throughout June he worked frantically to get the Zurich troops out of Catholic lands. In order to do so he was forced to make serious concessions.

The First Peace (*Landfriede*) of Kappel was really the work of Niklaus Manuel. He was the person who had prevented the war and he wrote the terms of the treaty. The central issues involved war reparations demanded by Zurich and the free preaching of the Gospel in Catholic lands.[72] The five Cantons were ordered by a tribunal to pay 2,500 crowns, and when they refused the Reformed Cantons imposed a blockade.[73] Manuel was reluctant to agree to this, fearing that it would lead to a civil war, but the Catholics finally agreed to pay. In the matter of faith, Manuel refused to demand freedom of conscience for the evangelicals in Catholic territories, for this he saw as coercion of faith. Nor was he prepared to demand the free preaching of the Gospel in Catholic lands, though this brought him into direct conflict with Zwingli.[74] Manuel held to the principle that each Canton was free to establish its faith. It was this principle which was to underpin the whole Swiss Reformation, and Manuel was its author.

Manuel did not accept Zwingli's argument that Scripture could be an adequate foundation for the political life of the Confederation. The contrast between Manuel and Zwingli is not that the former was the slippery politician, sacrificing ideals to expediency, whilst the latter stood by his biblical principles. Manuel believed passionately in the ultimate triumph of the Gospel, and that the present structures of the Confederation, based on negotiation and mediation, would facilitate that final victory. Manuel grounded the Reformation in a more radical manner than Zwingli, who ultimately believed that war and the destruction of opposing institutions could bring about the Reformation. For Manuel, the coexistence of Catholics and Reformed was a temporary, but endurable situation. While that situation continued it was incumbent upon both parties to maintain the integrity of the Confederation.

The complexity of the beliefs of a man such as Niklaus Manuel are reflective of a period of the Reformation when those in positions of authority had little time to disentangle religious and political issues. For Manuel, the prospect of confessional war among the Swiss would only strengthen the hand of the hated Habsburgs. This fear drove his search for peace. The establishment of the Reformation in Swiss lands was, in his mind, inexorably tied to the preservation of peace, a goal which embraced an alliance with the French monarchy in order to keep Charles V out of the Confederation. As Tardent

[72] On the first Peace of Kappel, see Haas, *Huldrich Zwingli*, 238–44.
[73] J. Strickler (ed.), *Eidgenössischen Abschiede*, vol. 4, (Zurich, 1876), 146a.
[74] M. Haas, *Zwingli und der Erste Kappelerkrieg* (Zurich, 1965), 182, Also, Tardent, *Niklaus Manuel*, 279.

argues, this conviction marked Manuel's conception of Reformation as fundamentally different from that of Huldrych Zwingli.[75]

Niklaus Manuel died shortly after the First Kappel War without having to witness the destructive religious war he so feared. His influence, however, on the Swiss Reformation was considerable. He was an artist, laymen and politician, not a theologian, and his religious ideas were neither entirely consistent nor clear-cut. Yet in his artistic work and then later in politics we see a man struggling to understand human freedom and divine righteousness. Although he shared much with Zwingli, Manuel's distinctive background led him to very different conclusions about religion and society. Zwingli's reform movement was achieved at the cost of the alienation of the rural and lay populations, who saw his goals as essentially clerical. Manuel moved from an idealised concept of reform to a *modus vivendi* based on a shrewd assessment of both Confederate politics and the disposition of the common people. He understood the limitations of the evangelical movement, given the political realities facing the Swiss. Unlike Zwingli, he sought to ground the reform movement in those institutions which held together the loose Confederation.

Manuel was the architect of Confederation with two religions. In this we find a certain degree of toleration. He believed that if the Confederation were to survive then religion had to remain a matter of individual choice, with the 'individual' understood as the legitimate government of the state. Toleration, therefore, was integral to the preservation of existing structures, a theme first encountered in the *Totentanz*. But Manuel was more than a dry constitutional theoretician. Through his art and political service he came to be a passionate opponent of coercion of faith, and after his death his arguments found wide currency among Manuel's supporters in Berne and Geneva. It is not surprising that Niklaus Zurkunden, who followed Manuel into public service in Berne, engaged Calvin in a long and amicable correspondence on this issue.[76]

Above all, Manuel's sense of toleration was derived from his fear of religious wars. The Second Kappel War was precisely what Manuel had feared. The war resolved nothing; it only proved the point which Manuel had put to the Zurich council. In a chastened Zurich, Heinrich Bullinger emerged as an eloquent opponent of religious wars in the second generation of the Swiss Reformation, rejecting foreign alliances and the employment of mercenaries.[77] In this manner, like so many others after Kappel, Bullinger wore the mantle of Niklaus Manuel, not Huldrych Zwingli.

---

[75] Tardent, *Niklaus Manuel*, 283.

[76] E. Bähler, *Nikolaus Zurkinden von Bern 1506–1588. Vertreter der Toleranz im Jahrhunder der Reformation* (Berne, 1912), 28–58.

[77] B. Gordon, 'Calvin and the Swiss Reformed Churches', in A. Pettegree, A. Duke and G. Lewis (eds.), *Calvinism in Europe 1540–1620* (Cambridge, 1994), 64–81.

9   Tolerance and intolerance in sixteenth-century Basle

Hans R. Guggisberg

The topic of this chapter has been widely discussed in recent historical litera-ture. I may not have much to add, but I do not intend to offer just a summary of already published results. Instead I should like to focus on a few specific manifestations of tolerance and intolerance in sixteenth-century Basle which I have studied with particular interest and insistence for a number of years.

In the first part of this chapter I should like to say something about how the behavioral attitudes which we define as tolerance or intolerance appeared during the Reformation period. The second part shall be devoted to the his-tory of Basle from around 1540 to the end of the sixteenth century. There I shall draw from my research on Sebastian Castellio.

In Basle like everywhere else the Reformation was a fundamentally intolerant movement of religious renewal which struggled against an equally intolerant establishment of ecclesiastical tradition. This establishment was particularly strong here because Basle was an episcopal seat with a bishop, a chapter, and a complete administrative and spiritual infrastructure. That the last bishop residing in Basle was an admirer of humanism and a man of conciliatory inclinations did not change the situation fundamentally. The Reformation was carried through by a group of reform-minded parish priests and monks who were actively supported mainly by members of the craft guilds. Victory was reached in early February 1529, after an outburst of iconoclasm and a short-lived political rebellion. Very soon, however, reaction set in, the oligarchic régime of the merchants' guilds was restored, and a Reformed church order was worked out which – at least on paper created a system of rigorous disci-pline, unity and control. Oecolampadius, the scholarly theologian and former collaborator of Erasmus, had done much to spread the new faith as a teacher and preacher since 1523. During the crisis of 1528/29 he kept rather in the background, but when it was over he became the organizer and the first 'Antistes' of the new Reformed church. Like the other Reformation leaders of his time, he was convinced to be an *'instrumentum divinae voluntatis'*. He was undoubtedly a man of the highest moral standards, a pious man and a devoted (if not a charismatic) leader of his church. He did, however, not oppose the persecution of the Anabaptists which was particularly cruel in and around Basle. Tolerance, let alone religious liberty, was not a relevant issue to him.[1]

There is thus no doubt that the Reformation was an intolerant movement in Basle. We can say this without risking to be accused of undue simplification. But still: by saying this not everything is said.

Let us look briefly at some documents of the 1520s, and then at some facts and figures of the same dramatic years before the breakthrough of the Reformation. Four times during this period, the city government (*Bürgermeister und Rat*) tried to mediate in the religious conflict. This happened through official decrees of religion which aimed at appeasing the general unrest and at restoring peace and order. They were issued in the late spring of 1523, on 23 September and 21 October 1527, and on 29 February 1528. The first decree ordered the preachers to base their sermons on the Bible alone and not on the writings of 'Luther and other doctors'.[2] Several disputations followed, but none of them produced decisive results. Between the first decree on religion and the three others a number of important things came to pass, most of them in 1525. During that year the peasants of the '*Landschaft*' rose against the city, there was an attempt at political revolt within its walls, Oecolampadius replaced the mass by an evangelical communion service, and the secularisation of the monasteries was started.[3] In spite of the general advance of the Reformed party, however, conservative resistance remained strong. The city council again and again postponed crucial decisions. Its decree of 23 September 1527 concerned the mass. It was not officially abolished, but the council proclaimed that henceforth nobody in the city republic should be forced to hear it.[4] On 21 October the council went one remarkable step further: It decided that everyone should be free to follow his or her own conscience.[5] The decree of 29 February 1528 corroborated this statement and generalised it considerably: It pointed out that because faith is God's gift to man, it is unfair that a citizen should hate his neighbour on its account. It further stated that men should tolerate ('*dulden*') each other, pray for each other, live in peace with each other and that everyone should be free to believe what he or she hoped would bring salvation.[6]

---

[1] Hans R. Guggisberg, *Basel in the Sixteenth Century: Aspects of the City Republic before, during, and after the Reformation* (St. Louis, MO, 1982), 19ff; Hanspeter Jecker, 'Die Basler Täufer: Studien zur Vor- und Frühgeschichte', *Basler Zeitschrift für Geschichte und Altertumskunde*, 80 (1980), 6–131, esp. 104ff.

[2] *Aktensammlung zur Geschichte der Basler Reformation in den Jahren 1519 bis Anfang 1534*, ed. E. Dürr and P. Roth, 6 vols. (Basle, 1921–50) (hereafter ABR) 1, 67.

[3] Guggisberg, *Basel in the Sixteenth Century*, 27f.

[4] ABR 2, 715.

[5] ABR 2, 720f.

[6] ABR 3, 50.

It can hardly be denied that these statements sound rather progressive. They seem to emanate from a fundamental attitude of toleration. Rudolf Wackernagel has not hesitated to link them to the local humanist tradition.[7] There are elements in these texts which indeed would seem to concur with what can be called the humanist argument for tolerance, namely the warning against theological controversy, the implication that man is not only free but capable to take decisions in religious matters, and finally the expectation that consensus will eventually be restored. It seems to me, however, that one should not idealise these documents. The members of the Basle council ('*Kleiner Rat*') were not humanists but politicians representing material interests. They wanted to restore peace and order and to maintain the prosperity of the commercial town. Their decision to establish something like general liberty of conscience did not have to be motivated by a well thought-out concept of religious tolerance but rather by the desperate hope that the conflict could still be calmed down and would eventually go away. The four decrees can be interpreted as results of humanist wisdom, but also – and I am inclined to believe that this would be more correct – as consequences of indecision, helplessness, and fear. They were, in any case, not successful. No one really wanted religious co-existence. The council itself was divided. Among the citizenry the aim of both parties was the same, namely total victory and the elimination of the opposing opinion. Irenic admonitions from Erasmus of Rotterdam, Conrad Pellican, Bonifacius Amerbach, and others were of no avail.[8] The struggle went on until it reached its climax on 8/9 February, 1529.

During these years of turmoil there occurred another conflict in the city republic of Basle which showed that intolerance also prevailed outside the strictly religious sphere. I am referring to the Paracelsus episode of 1527/28. Recommended by Oecolampadius and by the circle of friends around Johannes Froben, Theophrastrus von Hohenheim was elected city physician and lecturer in the medical faculty of the university in the spring of 1527. Right from the beginning, the behaviour, activities, and opinions of the nonconformist natural scientist and medical practitioner were vehemently rejected by the professors of medicine and the other physicians, by the apothecaries, by many students and by the public authorities. The partisans of religious renewal resented Paracelsus's indifference to their cause. Froben's death in November 1527 deprived him of his main support. The small group of friends whom he had gathered around himself – one of them was young Johannes Oporinus, the later bookprinter – could not do anything to alleviate his situation. Disagreement on an honorarium for medical service in one specific case lead Paracelsus to burst out into insulting invectives against the

---

[6] ABR 3, 50.

[7] Rudolf Wackernagel, *Geschichte der Stadt Basle*, vol. 3 (Basle, 1924), 490.

[8] Alfred Berchtold, *Bâle et l'Europe, une histoire culturelle* (Lausanne, 1990), 308, 358, 420.

city government. Out of fear that he might get arrested, he fled from Basle in February 1528. Nobody tried to hold him back or to protect him, not even Bonifacius Amerbach. Basle was unable and unwilling to keep a difficult man whose originality was not recognized. His sojourn of about ten months is not a page of glory in the city's history.[9] The episode is well-known and does not have to be treated more comprehensively here. We shall, however, come back to Paracelsus later.

Everybody knows that the violent breakthrough of the Reformation in February 1529 put an end to the first flowering period of humanism in Basle, i.e. to the first period during which the city republic had become an international meeting point of new scholarship and of bookprinting. This fact is symbolised by Erasmus's departure to Freiburg. Many other scholars left with him or had already left before him. Also Hans Holbein the Younger, who had worked in Basle on and off from 1515 through 1526 and then again since 1528, left the city for good in 1532.[10] Amerbach stayed on, although he, too, like Erasmus, disapproved of the way the Reformation had been brought about. But he was a native and a man who took decisions with difficulty.

The Reformed church order of 1529 imposed a strict religious regime on the people of Basle. The new political constitution which had been drafted at the same time, was essentially characterised by the restoration of the oligarchic system. Ecclesiastical discipline was, however, not always rigorously enforced. Thus it was possible for Bonifacius Amerbach to keep his distance from the Reformed church for four years after its establishment without losing his posts as legal counsel to the city government and professor of jurisprudence. When Erasmus returned from Freiburg in 1535 he was enthusiastically welcomed, and no pressure was put on him to become a church member. When he died about a year later he was buried in the cathedral, and a monument was erected in his honour which still attracts historically interested visitors today. Small Catholic circles continued to exist, notably in the Kleinbasel quarter. The Carthusian monastery, although officially dissolved, was allowed to continue celebrating mass as long as there were still monks living in it. The bishop, now residing in Porrentruy, remained chancellor of the university which meant that its degrees continued to be acknowledged throughout the Empire. When Michel de Montaigne visited Basle in 1580 he noticed that among the scholars with whom he had conferred, there were still some who showed sympathy for the Catholic religion.[11]

---

[9] Robert-Henri Blaser, *Paracelsus in Basel: Sieben Studien über Werk, Wirkung und Nachwirkung des Paracelsus in Basel* (Muttenz and Basle, 1979).

[10] Alfred Berchtold, *Bâle et l'Europe*, 312ff, 326ff.

[11] Guggisberg, *Basel in the Sixteenth Century*, 38f; Michel de Montaigne, 'Journal de voyage en Italie', in *Oeuvres complètes* (Paris, 1962), 1108, 1288ff.

After the persecution of the Anabaptists had abated, it became possible for adherents of radical Protestant views to live in Basle without being molested as long as they did not openly articulate their dissent. In the 1540s the second flowering period of humanism and bookprinting began. At the same time the number of foreign religious refugees increased very sharply. Not all of them were scholars. Merchants and artisans, however, had to convince the government that they would not hurt local trade. New branches of textile manufacturing such as lace-making and velvet and silk weaving were introduced.[12] Because the bookprinting industry was not controlled by the guild system, it could profit from the skills of foreigners more easily. But on the whole the official policy concerning immigrants was shamefully timid and reluctant. In conferring citizenship on foreign refugees Geneva was much more liberal than Basle. In the city on the Rhine there was always fear of economic competition as well as of religious doctrines which might not be compatible with the Basle confession. Very reluctantly permission was granted to the French exiles to hold their own services after the Massacre of St. Bartholomew. The Italian, Dutch, and British, let alone the Spanish refugees never formed their own specific congregations. Tolerance was always restricted by economic and political, and in some cases also by religious considerations.[13]

Since I have discussed these problems elsewhere, I shall not go into them any further here.[14] Instead I would now like to concentrate on the case of Castellio. In doing this I shall not speak about his writings but about his personal situation. In other words I shall not deal with how he argued for tolerance but how he experienced tolerance or intolerance as a nonconformist foreigner in Basle.

After his breach with Calvin he had left Geneva and settled in the city on the Rhine in the spring of 1545. Here he found employment with the bookprinter Johannes Oporinus. With his growing family he lived in extreme poverty, because Oporinus's wages were low. This did not, however, keep him from working at his Bible translations into Latin and French. In 1553 he was appointed professor of Greek at the university. His material situation improved somewhat, but his life was not be a quiet one. Deeply irritated and upset by the execution of Servetus in Geneva (27 October 1553), he prepared his famous anthology of ancient and contemporary texts rejecting capital punishment in religious matters: *De haereticis an sint persequendi*. The book

---

[12] Traugott Geering, *Handel und Industrie der Stadt Basel: Zunftwesen und Wirtschaftsgeschichte bis zum Ende des 17. Jahrhunderts* (Basle, 1886), 461ff, 480ff.

[13] Andreas Staehelin, 'Die Refugiantenfamilien und die Entwicklung der baslerischen Wirtschaft' in *Der Schweizer Familienforscher*, 29 (1962), 85–95; Franz Gschwind, *Bevölkerungsentwicklung und Wirtschaftsstruktur der Landschaft Basel im 18. Jahrhundert* (Liestal, 1977), 167f, 140).

[14] Guggisberg, *Basel in the Sixteenth Century*, 39ff.

was printed by Oporinus. It came out in March 1554 and unleashed the well-known debate on the question whether alleged heretics should or should not be put to death.[15] Castellio's main adversaries were Calvin and Theodore Beza. By them and some of their followers he was attacked as a heretic himself and subsequently suffered considerable harassment also in Basle. Before looking at this problem, something must be said about his and his family's everyday life and about the social environment in which they lived.[16]

Castellio was the son of a Savoyard farmer and the descendant of a large but very lowly family. He lived in Basle from 1545 until his death in 1563, i.e. for almost eighteen years. He was married twice. His first wife, Huguine Paquelon, was the daughter of a tailor from Dauphiné who had become a citizen of Geneva in 1521. We do not know the date of the marriage, but it must have taken place when '*Maistre Bastian*' was still teaching school in Geneva. Huguine moved to Basle with her husband in 1545 and died there in childbed four years later. In 1549 Castellio had two daughters and a son. Only the first daughter had been born in Geneva. It would therefore be incorrect to say that he had come to Basle with a large family. Huguine's death was followed by a deep domestic crisis. All three children became dangerously ill. One daughter died, the other daughter and the son survived. In the summer of 1549 Castellio remarried. His second wife's name was Maria. We know practically nothing about her except that she, like Sebastian, was francophone and had relatives in Lyon. From 1551 until 1562 she gave birth to six more children, three daughters and three sons. In 1558 a niece who had been left an orphan, was taken into the family. Thus nine children had to be fed, clothed, and sometimes to be supervised in their studies. In addition, accommodation was often provided to foreign students and other visitors. Castellio was rarely away from Basle; therefore no letters were exchanged between himself and the members of his family. The children began to leave the house only after his death. When he died, his oldest daughter was just nineteen years old and his youngest son was a baby of barely one year. He had always been much concerned about the education of his children. In his will of 1560 he expressed his wish that all of them should learn German as well as a craft so that they might be able to support themselves with manual labour.

The Castellio family lived in two different Basle houses. In the 1550s they occupied a house on the southern bank of the Rhine near the former monastery of St Alban, in the neighbourhood of paper mills and not far from where

---

[15] Cf. Réproduction en fac-similé de l'édition de 1554, avec une introduction de Sape van der Woude (Geneva, 1954).

[16] For the following cf. Hans R. Guggisberg, 'Sebastian Castellio and His Family', in Phillip N. Bebb and Sherrin Marshall (eds.), *The Process of Change in Early Modern Europe: Essays in Honor of Miriam Usher Chrisman* (Athens, OH, 1988), 97–115.

the river Birs flows into the Rhine. It was a modest section of the town, inhabited mainly by artisans and employees of manufacturing establishments. The exact location of the house cannot be identified. Castellio had probably rented it, and it is possible that he shared it with other refugees. In 1559 he was able to purchase a house in the Steinenvorstadt where he was to live until his death. This house no longer exists, but its location is clearly established. The Steinenvorstadt was not one of Basle's more fashionable sections either. It was the street in which the weavers had their shops, and it belonged to the parish of St Leonhard. Its inhabitants generally were not wealthy. They were known to tend toward unrest and opposition against the authorities.

In Basle, Castellio always remained a foreigner. He never obtained citizenship, and he never seems to have acquired more than a fragmentary command of the German language.[17] If he wanted his children to be better integrated in the German-speaking urban community, he was also concerned that they should enjoy the protection of influential people. This he sought to ensure by providing them with adequate godfathers and godmothers. Among them we find the printer Jerome Froben, the schoolmaster Thomas Platter, the theologians Simon Sulzer and Martin Borrhaus, and the eminent Bonifacius Amerbach himself. Among the women who consented to act as godmothers were Barbara Froben, Jerome's wife, and Agnes, the daughter of Celio Secondo Curione.[18]

Bonifacius Amerbach had been Castellio's benefactor all along. He had supported him financially on several occasions, and, shortly after his arrival in Basle, had hired him as tutor of his son Basilius. In his will of 1560 Castellio designated Jean Bauhin and Johannes Brandmüller as guardians of his wife and children. The physician Jean Bauhin (1511–88) was probably the best and most reliable friend the Castellio family had in Basle. He was a francophone refugee like the Savoyard scholar, a neighbour or co-tenant in the house on the bank of the Rhine and as such always extremely helpful. He came from Amiens, had settled in Basle already in 1541, practised medicine, worked for bookprinters and was generally well-connected among nonconforming circles. Historians of medicine mainly remember him as the father of the two more eminent scholars Jean II and Caspar Bauhin. Johannes Brandmüller (1533–96) was considerably younger than Castellio. He was of Swabian origin and had come to Basle as a student of theology. In the 1550s he was a parish preacher; eventually he became a professor of Old Testament. Both Bauhin and Brandmüller seem to have shared Castellio's theological opinions. The same can be assumed of Basilius Amerbach (1543–91), Bonifacius's son, Castellio's former pupil and later a professor of jurisprudence like

---

[17] Hans R. Guggisberg, 'Sebastian Castellio and the German Reformation', in ARG, Sonderband Washington (1993), 325–343, esp. 340f.
[18] Guggisberg, 'Sebastian Castellio and His Family', 104ff.

his father. Basilius had always remained close to the Castellio family, and although not mentioned in Sebastian's will of 1560, was to become its most active guardian after 1563.

Quite obviously, the Basle circle of Castellio's friends and acquaintances was much wider than that of the more or less official protectors just mentioned. It consisted of foreign students and scholars, but also of academic and non-academic townspeople. Many of these can be identified; most of them openly agreed with his views and particularly with his criticism of doctrinal hairsplitting, dogmatic authority and intolerance. In addition to those already mentioned the list would have to be completed with the names of scholars such as Curione, Felix Platter, and Theodor Zwinger as well as with those of the bookprinters Oporinus and Pietro Perna. Perna had come to Basle from Italy in 1542. After Oporinus's death (1568) he became the main publisher of Castellio's works. It cannot be denied that the Savoyard scholar had many friends in Basle. Most of them were of his own generation, but some belonged to the generation born after 1530: Brandmüller, Basilius Amerbach, Felix Platter, Theodor Zwinger. In spite of his connections with prominent townspeople, however, Castellio himself was not prominent, neither professionally nor socially. He taught at the modest faculty of arts and, unlike most of his colleagues, never moved up to one of the higher faculties. With his family he lived on the margin of urban society, in modest, if not scanty domestic circumstances.

If Castellio had friends in Basle, he also had enemies. He was by no means liked by everyone. This brings us to the question as to how he personally experienced tolerance and intolerance in this city.

De haereticis an sint persequendi was not the only work of criticism against the killing of heretics written in Basle during the year 1554 and exported from there into other territories. David Joris at the same time wrote and published a *Christian Warning to all Regents and Governments . . . that nobody must be . . . persecuted, let alone be killed because of his faith.*[19] Moreover, several manuscript pamphlets defending Servetus were circulated in the city. They came from the Grisons, from Italy, and from Germany. Among their authors were Guillaume Postel and Matteo Gribaldi. Some of these pamphlets must have been copied in Basle and sent out again. None of them was printed in the sixteenth century. In the same year 1554, Curione tried to publish his *De amplitudine beati regni Dei* in Basle. The book was rejected, but he soon found a willing printer in Poschiavo (Valtellina) who brought it out without delay.[20] It has been rightly stated that in 1554 Basle

---

[19] *Christelijcke Waerschouwinghe aen allen Regenten unde Ouvericheden . . . Datmen niemant om sijn Gheloof en behoort te . . . vervolghen, veele min te dooden* (n.p., 1554).

[20] Uwe Plath, *Calvin und Basel in den Jahren 1552–1556* (Basle and Stuttgart, 1974), 154ff, 164ff.

witnessed a great campaign for religious tolerance.[21] In this campaign Calvin was criticised not only for having condoned the execution of Servetus, but also for his doctrine of predestination.

It is not surprising that the reactions from Geneva and Lausanne did not take long to come. On several occasions in 1554 and 1555 Calvin and Beza expressed themselves indignantly on the Basle 'Academicians', who '. . . as true followers of Socrates' were out to destroy religion.[22] Calvin and Beza were right in assuming that their former collaborator Castellio stood behind the anti-Geneva upsurge in Basle and quite particularly behind *De haereticis an sint persequendi*. It seems possible that an investigation against the Savoyard scholar was undertaken in Basle well before the first direct complaints from Geneva arrived there. Direct evidence of such a move of the Basle government is lacking, however. Castellio was neither officially rebuked nor was the propagation of *De haereticis* hindered.[23] But this situation was soon to change.

On account of a letter from Calvin to Antistes Simon Sulzer, the Basle censorship authorities in the summer of 1554 suppressed the Commentary on Romans 9 which Castellio had wanted to include in the second edition of his Latin Bible. Calvin had requested that this measure be taken because Castellio's text contained critical remarks concerning the doctrine of predestination.[24] How Calvin had got hold of Castellio's commentary remains unknown. Shortly before his complaint arrived in Basle, Sulzer had received a letter from Heinrich Bullinger which contained a general admonition to watch the activities of the dissident foreigners within Basle's walls more carefully.[25] The result of these entreaties was the suppression of Castellio's Commentary on Romans 9. Oporinus had to take it out of the already printed copies of Castellio's Bible. Among the people responsible for the whole scheme was Martin Borrhaus, the professor of theology and one-time friend of the Savoyard scholar. He had obviously been recruited for this task by the censorship committee of the city council.[26] But the Basle government could not prevent Castellio's text from being

---

[21] Carlos Gilly, *Spanien und der Basler Buchdruck bis 1600* (Basle and Frankfurt a.M., 1985), 295.

[22] Joannis Calvini Opera quae supersunt omnia, ed. G. Baum *et al.*, 59 vols. (= CR 29–87, Braunschweig, Berlin, 1863–1900) (herafter CO), 15, 200.

[23] Cf. Castellio's own allusion in *De haereticis a civili magistratu non puniendis*, 19 (below, note 31).

[24] Plath, *Calvin and Basel*, 168f. Cf. CO 15, 189.

[25] Cf. CO 15, 168f.

[26] On censorship in sixteenth century Basle, cf. Carl Roth, 'Die Bücherzensur im alten Basel', *Zentralblatt für Bibliothekswesen*, 31 (1914), 50–68; Rudolf Thommen, 'Zensur und Universität in Basel bis 1799), *Basler Iahrbuch (1944), 49–82*. By decree of February 23, 1558, responsibility for censorship was transmitted to the rector and the four deans of the university.

circulated widely in manuscript. It was to be printed separately on many later occasions.[27]

Among other things the affair had brought about a certain rapprochement between Calvin and Sulzer. This was, however, not to last very long because at this same time the Basle Antistes very decidedly began to set the Basle church on a Lutheranising course and to lead it away from the other Swiss Protestant churches.[28]

Castellio's next tract against the killing of heretics was the *Contra libellum Calvini*. It was written in the summer and fall of 1554 as an answer to Calvin's *Defensio orthodoxae fidei* in which the Genevan reformer had tried to explain why he had not opposed the execution of Servetus and why he thought that capital punishment for heretics was justified. As everyone knows, the *Contra libellum Calvini* was never printed during Castellio's lifetime. Its first edition came out in Holland in 1612. It then served the Dutch Remonstrants as a weapon in their struggle against Calvinist orthodoxy.[29] There is no evidence that the publication of *Contra libellum Calvini* had been suppressed in Basle. One may just as well assume that Castellio himself never tried to have the *Contra libellum Calvini* printed in Basle. While he had been working on it, his Commentary on Romans 9 had been suppressed and Curione's *De amplitudine* had been rejected by the censorship committee. Thus Castellio could not have expected to be successful with his own new work. Although criticism of Calvin was still widespread in Basle, the city government seemed to become more and more reluctant to let it articulate itself too openly and too loudly. Sulzer himself who certainly was not a friend of Calvin, must have felt irritated when he received letters both from Geneva and from Zurich which implied that he did not pay enough attention to what was going on in his own church.

The pamphlet war continued. Already in September 1554 Theodore Beza published his famous *Anti-Bellius* under the title *De haereticis a civili magistratu puniendis, adversus Martini Bellii farraginem et novorum Academicorum sectam*.[30] Castellio hit back with the particularly lengthy and autobiographically revealing treatise *De haereticis a civili magistratu non*

---

[27] Ferdinand Buisson, *Sébastien Castellion, sa vie et son oeuvre*, 2 vols. (Paris, 1892), vol. 2, 58, 373ff.

[28] Hans R. Guggisberg, 'Das lutheranisierende Basel – Ein Diskussionsbeitrag', in Hans-Christoph Rublack (ed.), *Die lutherische Konfessionalisierung in Deutschland* (Gütersloh, 1992), 199–201.

[29] *Contra libellum Calvini, in quo ostendere conatur haereticos jure gladii coercendos esse* (n.p. 1612). There is no modern edition of this tract. Calvin's *Defensio orthodoxae fidei* is reprinted in CO 8, 453–644. On the use of *Contra libellum Calvini* in the Dutch debates preceding the Synod of Dordrecht, see Hans R. Guggisberg, *Sebastian Castellio im Urteil seiner Nachwelt vom Späthumanismus bis zur Aufklärung* (Basle, 1956), 79ff.

[30] Reprinted in *Theodore Bezae Vexelii volumen Tractationum Theologicarum* (Geneva, 1570), 85–169.

puniendis. This work was not finished until the spring of 1557. It remained unpublished, too (until 1971), and contemporary readers hardly took notice of it.[31] New attacks from Geneva began toward the end of 1556. The debate still centred around the question of how to deal with heretics, but other issues like the doctrine of predestination and Castellio's Bible translations increasingly dominated it. Both translations were condemned as heretical works, the Latin translation because it contained many words from classical antiquity, the French translation because its language and style were considered too vulgar. The objections against Castellio's Latin Bible were summarized by Beza in the preface of his own Latin Translation of the New Testament (1556).[32] Because the critiques from Geneva also contained personal invectives, Castellio wanted to defend himself again and to explain his pedagogical and philological intentions. At this point, the conflict took a new turn. While the attacks initially came from Geneva and Lausanne once more, they were now openly supported also in Basle. Without being prompted by Calvin, the Basle censorship authorities in the spring of 1557 prohibited the publication of Castellio's *Defensio suarum translationum Bibliorum.*[33] The specific reasons for this measure are not quite clear, but they seem to have been dictated not only by theological but also by political considerations. Together with Zurich and Schaffhausen, the Basle government at that time was engaged in a mediation effort between Berne and Geneva which was to lead to the renewal of the *Combourgeoisie* between the two republics in 1558. Moreover, anti-Genevan theological opposition was flaring up in Berne and in the Bernese territories of the *Pays de Vaud.* It is possible that the Basle government did not want to kindle the fire at this moment.[34]

Whenever they detected any opposition to the doctrine of predestination, the Geneva church leaders suspected Castellio's authorship or at least his inspiration. In spite of their fundamental disagreement with him, they very obviously took the Savoyard critic seriously and considered him a real danger to their cause. They were afraid that he and his friends could still destroy their great achievement of religious renewal. It is therefore understandable that they sought to win allies in Basle who would actively support them. One of these was Martin Borrhaus who has already been mentioned in connection with the suppression of Castellio's Commentary on Romans 9 in 1554. When in the fall of 1557 Beza and Farel stopped in Basle on their

---

[31] *De l'impunité des hérétiques – De haereticis non puniendis.* Texte latin inedit publié par Bruno Becker, texte français inédit publié par M. Valkhoff (Geneva, 1971).

[32] *Novum D.N. Jesu Christi Testamentum, Latine ... nunc denuo a Theodoro Beza versum* (Geneva, 1556): 'Theodorus Beza Christianis lectoribus saltutem et pacem in Domino', see final paragraph.

[33] Buisson, *Sébastien Castellion*, vol. 2, 103ff.

[34] Lucien Cramer, 'La politique extérieure, la diplomatie et la guerre, 1536–1603', in *Histoire de Genève des origines à 1798* (Geneva, 1951), 286ff.

way to the Colloquy of Worms, they very probably conferred with Borrhaus and gave him directions.[35] The results of these contacts soon became visible. Borrhaus organised a meeting of all the professors of theology and preachers before which Castellio was summoned. He was requested to state his views on predestination. He did not say much, but what he said was enough to cause an official accusation of blasphemy before the city council. The bill of indictment specified that he not only denied predestination but also the godly inspiration of the letters of St Paul.[36] He had to appear before the rector of the university and a group of 'the most eminent professors' in order to defend himself against these charges. His defence was written down in German and transmitted to the council. In this document Castellio declared that he acknowledged the godly inspiration of the Pauline writings, but he admitted to have problems with the predestination doctrine. At the end he formally asked for tolerance:

As far as eternal damnation is concerned to which the godless are said to be pre-destined, I confess that I cannot believe it. I ask that my dissent on this point be tolerated. If somebody believes otherwise, I shall not condemn him. Moreover, I do not intend to spread confusion in the church. I want to live in it as a loyal member and to be at peace with everybody else as it becomes a true Christian. I also wish to do everything I can to further the well-being of the church of Christ and of the honest city of Basle.[37]

The hearing before the rector and the professors unexpectedly ended with Castellio's complete acquittal. He had admitted his doubts concerning pre-destination, but he had not, as Beza had hoped, been publicly condemned in Basle – at least not yet.[38]

In the course of the same year 1557 Castellio must have corresponded with Melanchthon. From this correspondence only one letter written by the *praeceptor Germaniae* has been preserved. Without referring to specific events Melanchthon here bestowed high praise upon Castellio both as a phil-ologist and as an advocate of religious peace. He offered the Savoyard his friendship and expressed his desire to meet him personally some day.[39] The contents of this epistle were made known to Calvin by François Hotman in

---

[35] Buisson, *Sébastien Castellion*, vol. 2, 109ff.
[36] Cf. Castellio's own account: 'De Praedestinatione Scriptum Sebastiani Castellionis ad D. Mart.Borrhaum' [1562], in *Sebastiani Castellionis Dialogi IIII* (Aresdorfij, per Theophil. Phil-adelph. [= Basel, Pietro Perna], 1578), 332ff.
[37] *Sebastiani Castalionis antwurt uff ettliche articul so im von den hochgelerten und erwürdigen Rectore und den anderen furnemsten herren der hohen schul zu Basell sindt fürgehalten worden.* Copy in Bonifacius Amerbach's handwriting, dated on 16 November 1557. Universit-ätsbibliothek Basel (hereafter UBB) Ms. O II 46, 14.
[38] [Sebastian Castellio], *De Praedestinatione ad M.Borrhaum.* UBB Ms. Jorislade XVI.
[39] *Philippi Melanthonis Opera quae supersunt omnia*, t.9 (= CR9), 359–60.

the spring of 1558. They caused immediate and most vehement indignation with the church leader of Geneva, because not more than three years ago Melanchthon had still expressed cautious agreement with Calvin on the execution of Servetus.[40]

More savage attacks on Castellio ensued in 1558. Calvin published his *Calumniae nebulonis cuiusdam de occulta Dei providentia responsio* in which he reacted on an anonymous tract attributed to Castellio.[41] The Savoyard replied with a *Harpago sive defensio* which was not printed until 1578.[42] Then Beza came out again with *Ad sycophantarum quorundam calumnias . . . responsio*. Here Castellio was again depicted as a traitor of the Reformation. Beza's accusations culminated in entreating the city of Basle and its university to get rid of him altogether and without delay. With this the aims of the Genevan attacks became very clear: the troublesome and dangerous critic should disappear and the Basle authorities should help to bring this about.[43]

But Castellio did not disappear. He did not write a new defence but added an appendix to the *Harpago* in which, after stating his views with much sharpness once more, he again pleaded for tolerance in his own name and in his personal case:

I ask you by the blood of Christ, leave me in peace and cease persecuting me. Grant me the liberty of my faith and the liberty to confess it, just as you wish that I grant you your own liberty. Do not always condemn those as apostates and blasphemers who do not agree with you. On the main points of religion I do not differ from you. I want courageously to serve the same religion you are serving. I disagree with you only on a few issues of interpretation, and many pious people share this disagreement with me. All of us are erring . . . Let us nevertheless treat each other kindly. We all know (or we should know) the tasks of Christian charity. Let us accomplish these tasks and by doing so reduce our common enemies to silence.[44]

These sentences remind the reader of Erasmus's theology of reduction, but they also contain a new element, namely the idea that tolerance consists in accepting *discordia*, i.e. in renouncing *concordia* or consensus. To my knowledge, this idea has never been expressed in Castellio's earlier writings.

---

[40] Mario Turchetti, *Concordia o Tolleranza? Francois Bauduin (1520–1573) ei 'Moyenneurs'* (Geneva, 1984), 176; cf. CO 15, 534; 17, 133, 341.

[41] CO 9, 273–318.

[42] This tract was included in *Sebastiani Castellionis Dialogi IIII* with separate pagination. The title was slightly revised: 'Defensio ad authorem libri cui titulus est Calumniae nebulonis'. See Hans R. Guggisberg, 'Pietro Perna, Fausto Sozzini und die Dialogi quatuor Sebastian Castellios', in *Studia bibliographica in honorem Herman de la Fontaine Verwey* (Amsterdam, 1968), 171–201, esp. 187.

[43] *Ad sycophantarum quorundam calumnias . . . responsio* (Geneva, 1558), 146.

[44] '[Harpago sive] Defensio', 55f.

It appears here for the first time, and it stands for a distinctive expansion and diversification of his original humanist concept of tolerance.[45]

The next charge from Geneva came in 1560. It was aimed at Castellio's Bible translations once more, and again the humanist was also personally attacked. In the introduction to their French translation of the New Testament Calvin and Beza called him an *instrument choisi de Satan* whose devilish mission it was to confuse the faithful and to give pleasure to all other blasphemers.[46] He was hardly ever condemned more savagely, not even in the Roman and Spanish indices of the late sixteenth century which usually contained his Bible translations.[47] At this point the Basle authorities allowed him to publish the *Defensio suarum translationum Bibliorum* which they had suppressed three years earlier. It came out in 1562, i.e. after another delay of two years, and even now a number of crucial passages were censured.[48] Again Borrhaus had been at work.[49] Moreover, the *Defensio* was no longer up to date, partly because it reacted on criticism uttered by Beza in context with his own Latin translation of the New Testament which had been published in 1557. But even so it aroused the indignation of the Geneva theologians as never before. Castellio's sister, her husband, and her son who lived near Geneva were repeatedly summoned before the *Consistoire* and accused as propagators of Sebastian's works.[50] Once more Beza wrote an anti-Castellio tract, this time under the title *Responsio ad defensiones S. Castellionis* (1563), and once more the city republic of Basle was directly addressed. The tract did not contain any new reproaches or arguments. It was, however, officially dedicated to the Reformed Basle clergy.[51] The aim was the same as that of earlier pamphlets: Beza wanted to make it possible for the Basle authorities, both ecclesiastical and secular, to proceed against the Savoyard. The new tract was devised to serve as a basis for a formal charge of heresy. The *instrument choisi de Satan*, the anti-reformer, the seducer of youth should be silenced once and for all. He should be removed from his university post and be expelled from the city.

The church leaders of Geneva never forgave the Basle authorities for

---

[45] Cf. Winfried Schulze, 'Concordia, Discordia, Tolerantia: Deutsche Politik im konfessionellen Zeitalter', in *Zeitschrift für Historische Forschung*, (1987), 43–79.

[46] Quoted by Buisson, *Sébastien Castellion*, vol. 2, 251.

[47] Hans R. Guggisberg, 'Castellio auf dem Index (1551–1596)', in ARG 83 (1992), 112–29.

[48] The *Defensio* was published by Oporinus. See Sape van der Woude, 'Censured Passages from Castellio's 'Defensio suarum translationum', in B. Becker (ed.), *Autour de Michel Servet et de Sébastien Castellion* (Haarlem, 1953), 259–79.

[49] S. van der Woude, 'Censured Passages', 261.

[50] Archives d'Etat de Genève (hereafter AEG), Régistres du Consistoire: 1561: March 27, April 1; 1562: November 26, December 10; 1563: January 7, 14, March 4, 18, May 27, June 3, August 26.

[51] Reprinted in *Theodori Bezae volumen primum Tractationum Theologicarum* (Geneva, 1582), 425–506.

having allowed the publication of Castellio's *Defensio suarum translationum*. Still, Beza's *Responsio* of 1563 again failed to bring about immediate success. One more move was necessary to set the Basle government in motion, and this move had to come from inside the Basle Reformed community. It was indeed to come about and to unleash what in the general context of Castellio's biography I would like to call the crisis of 1563.

In November of that year, Adam von Bodenstein – son of Karlstadt, physician and citizen of Basle, and adherent of Paracelsus – wrote a letter to the Basle council from Strassburg where he resided temporarily at that time. This letter contained numerous quotations from Beza *Responsio* and lengthy statements of Bodenstein himself which summarised and confirmed the charges of the Geneva theologians and gave them the local support they had always needed. The charges of heresy and seduction of youth were based on the following additional indications: 1. Castellio had translated Bernardino Ochino's *Dialogi triginta* which, in addition to many other heretical opinions condoned polygamy. 2. With the publication of this scandalous book (it had been printed by Perna), the Savoyard had most seriously damaged Basle's reputation in all other Protestant cities and countries.[52]

Now the wheels of prosecution started to turn. No meeting of theologians was convoked. Theological discussion was no longer wanted. Castellio received a copy of Bodenstein's letter to the council in the original German version. He was ordered to answer to the charges. This he did in a written Latin apology, dated on 24 November. Here he summarised again his theological and moral opinions and systematically refuted the charges brought against him. In regard of the translation of Ochino's *Dialogi* he pointed to the fact that the Basle authorities had not prohibited their publication.[53]

The consequences which Bodenstein's accusations had for Castellio remain unknown. We do not know if and when the trial started and how it was carried through. We know, on the other hand, that Bodenstein's initiative had direct or indirect consequences in Zurich: when the publication of the *Dialogi triginta* became known there, Ochino was immediately removed from his post as pastor of the Italian refugee community. Bullinger saw to it that the former vicar general of the Capuchin order who was seventy-six years old at that time could not find asylum anywhere else in Protestant Switzerland. So he went to Poland and later to Moravia where he died in 1564.[54] During the 'crisis of 1563' Castellio seems to have contemplated immigration to Poland,

---

[52] Staatsarchiv Basel (StAB), Kirchenakten A3, fols. 210ff., cf. Buisson, *Sébastien Castellion*, vol. 2, 483–93; see also *ibid.*, 368.
[53] Reprinted in *Contra libellum Calvini* (1612), fols. P ij ro ff.
[54] George Hunston Williams, *The Radical Reformation*, 3rd edn (Kirksville, MO, 1992), 1154.

too. But before he could realise this plan, his troubled life came to an end. He died in Basle on 29 December 1563.

So we remain ignorant about what might have happened to him, whether he would have been condemned for heresy or not, whether he would have been forced into emigration like Ochino in Zurich or whether the Basle authorities would have exonerated him once more. In other words we do not know how far tolerance or intolerance would eventually have gone in Castellio's case.

There remains the question as to why Bodenstein's accusations had been brought forward at all. Much remains unknown here, too, but some answers have become possible on the basis of very recent research done by Carlos Gilly. I shall summarise his findings in a few sentences.[55] They show that there were connections between Castellio's activities in Basle as an advocate of tolerance and the afterlife of Paracelsus in the same city. The man who personified these connections was Pietro Perna. He was, as I have already mentioned, a close friend of the Savoyard humanist and the main Basle publisher of his works after Oporinus's death (1568). His publishing programme was unusually many-sided. It contained theological, philosophical, and literary works as well as numerous books on natural science, magic, alchemy, witchcraft and Hermetism. In addition to this he was the promoter of what can be called the late sixteenth century Basle Paracelsus revival. What does this have to do with Bodenstein's intrigue against Castellio?

We are relying on an account of Theodor Zwinger, Castellio's former student who eventually became a professor of theoretical medicine and one of the most versatile exponents of late humanism in Basle. In a letter to a German colleague which he wrote in 1564, Zwinger stated that two years earlier Adam von Bodenstein had presented a short manuscript of Paracelsus to the Collegium Medicum of Basle and asked for permission to publish it. In order not to be suspected of envy and narrow mindedness, the physicians consented, but they remained sceptical and expressed their hope that future works of Paracelsus to be published would be less difficult to understand. Thus Bodenstein edited a number of other books of Paracelsus without specific approbation. But when it became obvious that all the writings of this author were of the same kind, the Collegium strictly forbade Bodenstein to publish more of them, neither in Basle nor elsewhere. Bodenstein seems to have tried to elude this verdict, because, as Zwinger goes on to report, on 27 January 1564 he was formally relegated from the university and from the medical faculty to which he had belonged as a *consiliarius*. Gilly has shown that the real reason for this relegation was not Bodenstein's Paracelsism but

[55] For the following see Carlos Gilly, 'Basel rehabilitiert Paracelsus', in *Basler Stadtbuch 1993* (Basle, 1994), 35–42.

the fact that three months earlier he had let himself be recruited by Calvin and Beza to denounce Castellio before the Basle government.

Consequently, no more Paracelsian books were printed in Basle for at least three years. Bodenstein tried to publish some in nearby Mulhouse but without much success. He also fell out with Perna who had made the first publications possible. This lasted until 1567 when Perna took Bodenstein back as an editor and resumed his Paracelsus programme. In his advertisement poster of 1578 he announced fifty-six titles of *Paracelsica*, and he also stated his plan to publish two complete editions, one in Latin and the other in German. This was the programme of the Basle Paracelus revival. It was to be carried out to a large extent. Theodor Zwinger himself became one of its most ardent supporters. Originally a critic of Paracelsian medicine, he became if not an adherent at least a respectful sympathiser who clearly saw and acknowledged its merits and was able to integrate it into general medicine.

Death prevented both Perna and Zwinger from seeing the Paracelsus publishing programme completed. They died in 1582 and 1588 respectively. It was Konrad Waldkirch, Perna's successor, who in 1589 and 1590 brought out the ten volumes of the first complete edition of Paracelsus's medical and philosophical writings in the German language.[56] With this edition, Paracelsus who had had such a difficult time in Basle himself, was rehabilitated by the town which had done him great injustice. As far as we can see, the Paracelsus revival was not disturbed by the Basle censorship authorities. But with Waldkirch's edition it had reached its end. No more books by Paracelsus were printed in Basle until 1965 when a slightly modernised five volume edition was published by the house of Benno Schwabe.

In this chapter I have discussed only a very small number of events and incidents which throw some light on the seesaw policy of tolerance and intolerance in sixteenth-century Basle. We have seen that, like everywhere else, political and economic considerations played a decisive part in the shaping of this policy. That the humanist tradition at times influenced the practice of tolerance can hardly be denied, but this fact should certainly not be idealised. When the city republic of Basle had become a member of the Helvetic League in 1501, the treaty had stated that it must always be ready and willing to mediate in conflicts between other Swiss cantons.[57] This task had often been accomplished, and Basle politicians of the sixteenth century had much experience as mediators. This experience they obviously also tried to use when it became necessary to deal with conflicts of parties within the city republic. When in the course of the Reformation troubles the council ordered tolerance, this emanated from the endeavour to maintain peace and order in

---

[56] Theophrastus Paracelsus, *Bücher und Schriften* (repr. Hildesheim, 1971–7).
[57] Hans Nabholz, Paul Kläui (eds.), *Quellenbuch zur Verfassungsgeschichte der Schweizerischen Eidgenossenschaft und der Kantone* (Aarau, 1947), 75ff.

a town which was already then an important crossing point of international commerce. Its prosperity was not to be jeopardised. That the decrees on religion of 1523, 1527, and 1528 were increasingly unrealistic, does not make the concern of the magistrate appear any less serious.

The bookprinters were often molested, it is true. But just as often they enjoyed a surprising amount of freedom. Guillaume Farel was certainly right when, in 1557, he wrote to Bullinger: 'What you did not allow to be published in Zurich, has been published in Basle without any difficulty.'[58] One must not forget that printing, in addition to being an important cultural activity, also was a business which obeyed the laws of international supply and demand. To curb it too much could entail the danger that some internationally well-connected entrepreneurs might want to move elsewhere. Foreign refugees could be a burden, but some of them could enhance the prosperity of the city by introducing new economic activities.

Why did many foreign religious non-conformists enjoy more tolerance in Basle than elsewhere? I have pointed out that most of them were critics of Calvin and his Reformation in Geneva. The Lutheranising Antistes Simon Sulzer who led the Basle church from 1553 through 1585 was a critic of Calvin, too, although his criticism came from another point of view. He certainly had his reservations concerning the radicals, but he never tried systematically to persecute them because as critics of Calvin they were his allies. This state of affairs, it seems to me, was of fundamental importance for the long-term second flowering period of humanism and evangelical radicalism in Basle. The decline of this second flowering period approached when Sulzer's 'Antistium' reached its end. Johann Jacob Grynaeus, Sulzer's successor, led the church of Basle back to Reformed orthodoxy. In the 1580s the *Basilea reformata* gradually ceased to be a heaven to humanist scholars and religious non-conformists. Waldkirch's edition of Paracelsus's works appears like a tail light of a vanishing era.

Let me take one last look at Castellio. He could live in Basle relatively unmolested from 1545 through the autumn of 1563. The most vehement attacks on him came from Geneva, and for a considerable time he was protected by his Basle friends and even by the authorities. Genevan propaganda and the attempts to mobilise resistance against him in Basle became more and more insistent during the 1550s. The publication of some of his writings was suppressed, but in 1557 the Genevan intrigues against him suffered another defeat. Calvin and Beza did not give up, however, and Castellio did not surrender either. From 1554 he was under increasing pressure, but I would venture to say that only in 1563 did the situation become really dangerous for him. The turning point had arrived when the church leaders of Geneva

[58] CO 16, 549.

had found a person in Basle willing to prefer an official charge against him. Very important was the fact that Bodenstein could base his heresy charge upon Castellio's translation Ochino's Dialogues. But we do not know the end of the story, and therefore we cannot pronounce a final verdict on the attitude of the Basle authorities toward Castellio in his 'crisis of 1563'.

It cannot be denied that the sixteenth-century city republic of Basle generally was a more tolerant place that other centres of the Reformation. But it did not have a law granting tolerance comparable to the Warsaw Confederation or the tolerance laws of Transsylvania. People like Castellio could find asylum in Basle, but they were never really safe. They were never really and truly free of pressure, discrimination and suspicion. The danger that persecution could suddenly flare up was never absent. Tolerance in sixteenth-century Basle was never unlimited, and you could never be sure that the limits had not been transgressed.

Ole Peter Grell

Exile is an experience very much constitutive of the 'Second Reformation', starting with Calvin's own flight from France to Basle in 1536 and ending with the exodus of Calvinists from the German Palatinate during the Thirty Years' War. Furthermore, between these events we have the mass emigration to Germany, England and the United Provinces of members of the Reformed communities in Southern Netherlands and France. Undoubtedly this shared social experience of displacement and diaspora became a central element of European Calvinism.[1]

The connection between tolerance and the exiles of the 'Second Reformation', however, is more tenuous. Obviously, the Reformed refugees had good, and perfectly understandable, reasons for their hatred of the Catholic Church, their main persecutor. But Calvin's fear of heterodoxy and his involvement in the execution of Michael Servetus in Geneva would indicate that persecution and exile did not necessarily breed tolerance among Reformed refugees, not even towards other Protestants, in the late sixteenth and early seventeenth centuries.

Thus two related questions spring to mind in the context of exile and tolerance. Firstly, what kind of tolerance did the Reformed exiles expect to be granted by the foreign, Protestant communities among whom they sought refuge, not to mention the tolerance they hoped to be accorded by the governments and Protestant churches under whom they sought shelter? In other words, did the exiles expect to be warmly welcomed in their new countries, and did the host governments consider them a valuable addition to the native populations to whom some form of toleration should be granted?

Secondly, how did these Reformed exiles react towards other Protestants, fellow-travellers who had experienced similar tribulations and who often differed from them on only minor doctrinal and ecclesiastical points? By today's standards we would expect them to have extended a helping hand to such fellow-refugees, born out of particular sympathy for those who had shared

---

[1] The significance for Calvinism of the social experience of exile is discussed in O. P. Grell, 'Merchants and Ministers: the Foundation of International Calvinism', in A. Pettegree *et al.* (eds.), *Calvinism in Europe 1540–1620* (Cambridge, 1994), 254–73.

their experiences. However, in the sixteenth and early seventeenth century such a 'liberal' reaction would have been the exception rather than the rule. Thus, for example the most inflexible and least compromising face of Calvinism in the United Provinces was that presented by the refugees from the Southern Netherlands who dominated the pro-war, anti-Spanish lobby in the Republic and constituted the backbone of the hardline Calvinist faction of the Reformed church, later known as the Counter-Remonstrants.

An excellent example of how these issues worked in practice can be found in the events surrounding the Dutch and Walloon, Reformed community in London from its renewed exodus, in 1553, until its re-establishment in the English capital during the reign of Elizabeth. The accession of the Catholic Queen Mary meant that the Dutch Reformed community in London was forced to leave their new home only three years after they had been permitted to establish their own church and obliged to seek a new place of refuge. It proved a difficult task at a time of confessional hardening within European Protestantism. Driven not only from country to country, but from city to city, the London refugees became heavily implicated in the Second Sacramentarian Controversy, which led to the decisive split between an emerging Calvinism and an already established Lutheranism.[2] The treatment of the exiled London Dutch community engaged many of the leading Protestant figures of the day, including Calvin and Bullinger. To the Reformed camp the refugees represented poor, godly wanderers, whereas to orthodox Lutherans they were 'the devil's martyr.'[3]

In what follows I shall concentrate on how the London Dutch refugees were received in Denmark by government and church officials. Likewise, I shall indicate why the Dutch community chose Denmark as its preferred destination and what their expectations might have been. This might prove

---

[2] See A. Pettegree, 'The London Community and the Second Sacramentarian Controversy, 1553–1560', *ARG*, 78 (1987), 223–52.

[3] Cited in Pettegree, 'Sacramentarian Controversy', 224. Considering the wide interest and the debate the matter caused, it is hardly surprising that, in 1560, a description of these peregrinations were published in Basle written by one of the leading members of the London Dutch community, the elder Jan Utenhove. See J. Utenhove, *Simples et fidelis narratio de instituta ac demum dissipata Belgarum, aliorumque peregrinorum in Anglia Ecclesia* (Basle, 1560). The early seventeenth century brought renewed interest in this case and Utenhove's book was translated into German by the minister in the town of Dillenburg, in Hesse-Marburg, Bartholomeus Roding, *Kurtzer, einfältiger und waarhafter historischer Bericht . . .* (Herborn in Nassau, 1608). In the eighteenth century an account from a Lutheran perspective of the events involving the refugees' stay in Denmark was provided by Bishop Ludvig Harboe in an introduction to D. G. Zwergius, *Det Siellandske Cleresie* (Copenhagen, 1754), 1–108. The controversial nature of this event is still in evidence in Oskar Bartel's biography of Johannes à Lasco from 1964, where the author refers to the behaviour of the Danish King, Christian III, as inhuman. See O. Bartel, *Jan Laski. Leben und Werk des polnischen Reformators* (Berlin, 1964), 165. Cited in M. Schwarz Lausten, *Biskop Peder Palladius og Kirken 1537– 1560* (Copenhagen, 1987), 207.

valuable, not least, because the Danish episode offers splendid material for an analysis of the reactions of the government of a confessional, Lutheran state towards religious exiles.

I shall then move on to the interest shown by the Swedish government of Gustav Vasa and his son, Erik XIV, in the London Dutch community during its peregrinations and re-settlement in London. The Swedish government's policies and initiatives provide a fascinating example of how an Erastian, Protestant state approached such matters.

Finally, I shall look briefly at the London community's attitude towards other Protestant denominations, especially the Anabaptists, who shared their experience of exile.

The Charter of July 1550, in which Edward VI granted the Dutch community in London the right to establish their own church, in effect permitted the strangers to establish a fully Reformed community in the midst of an English Church which by then was at most in Protestant terms a half-way house. The near total independence in doctrinal as well as ecclesiastical terms which the strangers were granted, surprised even the leaders of the foreign community. It is, however, noteworthy that the English government had a double purpose in granting the Dutch community their own church. By permitting the creation of a separate Dutch Reformed church the government intended to establish a model Protestant church while simultaneously creating a bulwark against the sects, in particular the Anabaptists.[4]

It was, in other words, a very confident and to some extent pampered community which at the accession of Mary decided to seek a new place of refuge abroad under the leadership of Johannes à Lasco, Jan Utenhove and Marten Micron. Utenhove explains their choice of Denmark as their destination in near providential terms. After the leaders of the community had decided to leave London they were fortunate enough to find that two empty Danish ships were anchored in the Thames, waiting only for favourable wind for Denmark. That the choice might not have been dictated by divine providence alone is, however, indicated by Utenhove's statement that the refugees had already heard from all their contacts that the Danish king was 'a particularly pious and godly king.'[5] They were not alone in considering Denmark a particularly promising area for extending Reformed influence in these years. In 1552 Calvin dedicated the first part of his commentary on the *Acts of the Apostles* to the Danish king, Christian III, followed two years later, at a time when he had yet to hear about the tribulations of the exiled Dutch community

---

[4] See A. Pettegree, *Foreign Protestant Communities in Sixteenth-Century London* (Oxford, 1986), 23–45.

[5] J. Utenhove, *Kurtzer, einfältiger Bericht*, 26.

in Denmark, by the dedication of the second part to Crown Prince Frederik.[6]

Furthermore, it was not as if the Dutch community had a wide choice of possible destinations in the confessional climate of the 1550s. Denmark, in spite of its geographical position, may well have seemed the best option available. If we are to believe the magistracy of Copenhagen, then the leaders of the Dutch community may have spent both money and time to convince the captains of the two Danish ships to bring them to Denmark, since the captains were under instructions from Copenhagen to sail to France to take on board a cargo of salt.[7]

The kingdom of Denmark and Norway, where around 170 members of the London Dutch community arrived in October 1553, had been ruled since 1536 by King Christian III, who personally was not only a committed Lutheran, but also a close friend of Johannes Bugenhagen, one of the leading Wittenberg reformers, and a regular correspondent of Luther.[8] In 1537 Denmark and Norway had received a Lutheran church order which had been written under Bugenhagen's supervision. Referring to the recent civil war (1534–36), which had preceded Christian III's accession to the throne, the preface to the new church order emphasised, that it had been drawn up, 'because of the recent unfortunate discord and dispute in the Kingdom. Consequently, the king and council had decided to introduce 'a Christian Ordinance in religion' in order to ensure 'that the Kingdom should remain settled in Religion and other matters.'[9] A decade earlier Christian III had already demonstrated his hostility to non-Lutheran Protestantism. The Haderslev Church Ordinance of 1528, introduced while Christian III was Duke of Schleswig and Holstein, incorporated an oath to be taken by all clergy which repudiated the teachings of the Sacramentarians (then the codeword for Zwinglians) and Anabaptists. Furthermore, the following year Christian III demonstrated his willingness to act when in the presence of Johannes Bugenhagen among others, he had Melchior Hoffmann, who had by then adopted a Sacramentarian interpretation of the Eucharist, condemned and expelled from his duchies.[10]

---

[6] See S. Kjöllerström, *Striden kring kalvinismen i Sverige under Erik XIV* (Lund, 1935), 24. See also M. Schwarz Lausten, *Christian den 3. og kirken 1535–1559* (Copenhagen, 1987), 207.

[7] For this letter, dated 3 November 1554, see Zwergius, *Cleresie*, 28–9. The explanation of the ships' original destination is included in an additional note, 29. See also Lausten, *Peder Palladius*, 208.

[8] See M. Schwarz Lausten, 'The Early Reformation in Denmark and Norway 1520–1559', in O. P. Grell (ed.), *The Scandinavian Reformation. From Evangelical Movement to Institutionalisation of Reform* (Cambridge, 1995), 29–41.

[9] H. F. Rørdam (ed.), *Danske Kirkelove*, 1 (Copenhagen, 1881), 47.

[10] See O. P. Grell, 'Scandinavia', in A. Pettegree (ed.), *The Early Reformation in Europe* (Cambridge, 1992), 102–3.

Even if no similar oath was included in the Danish Church Order, it very appropriately specified that on the feast of John the Baptist (24 June) ministers were expected to preach against the Anabaptists.[11] This time, however, Christian III and his advisors felt no need to include the Sacramentarians. Evidently by 1539 the Zwinglians or Sacramentarians were no longer considered a danger!

By late October 1553 most of the refugees, including, Johannes à Lasco, Utenhove and Micron had arrived in Elsinore. When the three leaders learnt that Christian III was then resident at Kolding, they immediately left for southern Jutland. Meanwhile most of the refugees continued their journey to Copenhagen. They had hardly arrived before the royal administrator and Lord Lieutenant of Copenhagen castle wrote to the magistracy in the city. Having been informed that more than 150 people had arrived he blamed the magistracy for allowing 'such a multitude of alien, foreign and unknown people into the kingdom especially here in the capital without prior information and without his Royal Majesty's knowledge or permission'. Before the magistracy allowed these people into Copenhagen they were instructed to make a list of their names and occupations, and to inquire about the reason for their arrival. Furthermore, the strangers should be obliged to swear an oath promising to obey the laws of the land. Finally, the magistracy was instructed to keep the exiles under observation to make sure that nothing untoward was going on, and 'that they were, what they pretended to be.'[12]

Considering that the population of Copenhagen at the time of the arrival of the London Dutch exiles would have been significantly below 10,000, the number of strangers alone would have been enough to have caused alarm.[13] The city authorities, however, treated the refugees well, making accommodation available for them and allowing them to ply their trades. This permission was much appreciated by the Dutch community. However, the magistracy was not prepared to show a similar flexibility in the religious domain. The oath they demanded from the exiles not only involved a promise to obey civil authority, but also included an assurance that the exiles rejected Anabaptism. Clearly, the magistracy had no wish to be caught out once more, having already been indirectly responsible for the arrival of the refugees on ships chartered by some of the burgomasters. A further confessional precaution can be seen in their refusal to allow the schoolmaster and elder of the Dutch community, Hermes Backerel, to continue his instruc-

---

[11] Rørdam, *Kirkelove*, 1, 65.
[12] The letter from the Lord Lieutenant of Copenhagen Castle, Peder Godske, dated 1 November 1553, is printed in Zwergius, *Cleresie*, 23–5 (my translation).
[13] See Lausten, *Peder Palladius*, 223–4.

tion of the community's children until further orders had been received from the king.[14]

Meanwhile à Lasco, Micron and Utenhove had arrived in Kolding, hoping to expedite matters for the exiles. The exiles clearly expected to be granted permission by Christian III to remain in Denmark and to be allowed their own church on a par with what they had enjoyed in London. If that was refused them, they, at least, expected to be allowed to demonstrate that their doctrines and rites were in accordance with Scripture.[15] This political innocence and incredible self-confidence had undoubtedly been fostered by the privileged treatment the Dutch community had received from the English government during the reign of Edward VI. This had not been limited to the above mentioned Charter, but had also included the tolerance of Johannes à Lasco's interference in English church affairs, as illustrated in his intemperate involvement in the vestments controversy surrounding John Hooper.[16]

Furthermore, by the 1550s Johannes à Lasco was a prominent Reformed theologian whose interpretation of the Eucharist was widely known. In 1552 he had published a series of sermons which sharply attacked Luther's eucharistic doctrine.[17] Accordingly, à Lasco immediately became a target for the orthodox Lutheran minister in Hamburg, Joachim Westphal, whose *Farrago*, constituted a broad attack on Reformed, eucharistic doctrine.[18] Thus, à Lasco's views would most likely have been known at the Danish court with its considerable interest in theological affairs within the Protestant camp and close contacts to Wittenberg. This is confirmed by one of Christian III's two Wittenberg educated court preachers, Paulus Noviomagus, who in a conversation with à Lasco in Kolding stated that:

The King has a very low opinion of your Church, because the Sacrament of the Altar has been contemptuously handled by you in London, and because there are supposed to be differences of opinion and sects among you. Accordingly the King and Council had already decided what answer to give you before your arrival.[19]

---

[14] See Utenhove, *Kurtzer einfältiger Bericht*, 109–10. It is noteworthy that the Bishop of Zealand, Peder Palladius, had specifically attacked the danger of Anabaptism to civil authority, while referring to recent disturbances in some towns on Zealand, in a pamphlet, entitled *An Instruction in Mildness and Meekness*, published in 1553. see L. Jacobsen (ed.), *Peder Palladius' Danske Skrifter*, 2 (Copenhagen, 1914–15), 373, 383.

[15] Utenhove, *Kurtzer einfältiger Bericht*, 26. See also the petition, which à Lasco, Utenhove and Micron delivered to Christian III. Here they stated that they wanted the same privileges they had enjoyed in London. They also emphasized the economic benefit their arrival might prove to the kingdom, 39.

[16] See Pettegree, *Foreign Protestant Communities*, 40–2.

[17] J. à Lasco, *Brevis et delucida de Sacramentis ecclesiae Christi tractatio* (London, 1552).

[18] J. Westphal, *Farrago confusanearum et inter se dissidentium Opinionum de coena Domeni* (Hamburg, 1552).

[19] Cited in Zwergius, *Cleresie*, 63.

Thus, the result of the exiles' petition for refuge and freedom of worship may well have been a foregone conclusion. The protracted religious negotiations which their leaders conducted in Kolding with the King's two German court preachers, Paulus Noviomagus and Henrik Buscoducensis and his German Chancellor, Andreas von Barby, never stood much chance of success. Denmark was, after all, a country which had recently seen the creation of a Lutheran, territorial church and whose ruler maintained close contacts with most of the leading Wittenberg theologians.

Both sides considered that they held a monopoly on 'true religion'. That the refugees from their position of weakness should have insisted on nothing less than freedom of worship cannot but strike the modern reader as admirable, but from a contemporary perspective it must have appeared an inflexible and unrealistic position. Had Christian III not been firmly committed to Lutheranism, political considerations alone would have militated against granting the London Dutch community freedom of worship, within what had by 1537 become a confessional Lutheran state.

Apart from believing that they alone were the only true Christians, a belief they shared with most denominations in this period, the exiles undoubtedly suffered from their highly polemical approach. Such aggressiveness had characterised the community from its foundation in London and it continued to hamper the refugees on their peregrination through Germany until their arrival in Emden.[20]

When Christian III responded to the London exiles' petition a week after their arrival in Kolding, he informed them that they were permitted to stay if they adhered to the Danish Church Order. Under no circumstances did the King want to put the religious equilibrium in Denmark at risk. However, he offered to help them find a more suitable place of refuge in Germany.[21] The exiles responded in typically aggressive style by attacking the Danish Church Order, pointing out that the country fell well short of a proper Protestant country, that some monastic orders were allowed to continue, and that these orders were still widely honoured in Denmark. This approach only served to precipitate their expulsion from the kingdom. On 17 November they were served with an extradition order. They were not allowed to join up with their followers in Copenhagen, but ordered to leave via Schleswig and Holstein. Christian III, however, paid the expenses they had incurred during their stay in Denmark and gave them 100 thalers towards the cost of their further

---

[20] For the peregrination, see Pettegree, 'Sacramentarian Controversy', 223–52. Even in Emden the arrival of the London exiles hardened the confessional approach, see A. Pettegree, *Emden and the Dutch Revolt* (Oxford, 1992), 38.

[21] The king's response is preserved in the Royal Archives, Copenhagen (Rigsarkivet), TKIA B. Different ecclesiastical matters 1531–1742, folder 5. See also Lausten, *Peder Palladius*, 212–13.

journey. The King's permission for à Lasco's children and their tutor, Godfrey van Winghen, to stay until the following spring was another minor royal concession.[22]

Having dealt with the exiles' leadership Christian III immediately turned his attention to the 150-odd exiles still waiting in Copenhagen. He instructed the bishop of Zealand, Peder Palladius, and the magistracy of Copenhagen to expel the refugees. First, however, the bishop should examine them and enquire whether any of them would accept the Danish Church Order in which case they would be permitted to stay. In their leaders' absence, negotiations on behalf of the refugees were conducted by the elder and schoolmaster, Hermes Backerel, and a Scottish minister, David Simpson, who had worked as a preacher in England. The examinations, which took place in early December, appear to have been conducted in a sympathetic atmosphere witnessed by the magistracy and other representatives of civil and ecclesiastical authority. Apart from a tailor and his wife, however, no converts could be found. Still, Palladius promised the Dutch that he would do his best to convince the King to allow them to stay in Copenhagen during the winter. However, the refugees were expelled on 12 December and Palladius only managed to obtain the King's permission to let five pregnant women and seven children stay on until spring. Evidently Christian III was deeply worried that the exiles might convert 'some simple people to their faith' and wanted them to leave the kingdom as quickly as possible.[23]

If the king, as already mentioned, was not negatively inclined towards the Dutch Reformed exiles from London before their arrival, he had not taken long to reach this decision. On 11 November, only three days after à Lasco and his colleagues had arrived in Kolding, he issued a placard against Anabaptists and Sacramentarians, forbidding them to settle in his realms. The placard did not directly refer to the refugees from London. It only mentioned the 'many Anabaptists, Sacramentarians and other sects, primarily craftsmen, who are now congregating in neighbouring countries' and who might immigrate to Denmark. Here they might initially practise their crafts quietly, but by the time a considerable number had gathered, they were likely to announce their 'evil intentions, and through their false actions and opinions cause rebellion and convert many simple people from the Holy Christian faith and God's Word and Gospel, which has already been done by such Anabaptists and Sacramentarians in other countries.'[24]

---

[22] *Ibid.*, 213–17. For the insistence that Utenhove, Micron and à Lasco did not return to Copenhagen, but left the kingdom via Schleswig and Holstein, see Utenhove, *Kurtzer einfältiger Bericht*, 106–7.

[23] For the king's letters to Copenhagen, see Zwergius, *Cleresie*, 40–6 (my translation). See also Lausten, *Peder Palladius*, 220–1.

[24] For this placard, see Rørdam, *Danske Kirkelove*, 1, 362–3 (my translation).

The placard specified that foreigners were not to be allowed to settle in the country before they had passed an examination by both the lay and ecclesiastical authorities, explaining their reasons for immigration and in particular the fundamentals of their faith. That the king and council should choose this moment to emphasise that only orthodox Lutheran immigrants were allowed to settle in the country, was evidently dictated by the arrival of the London Dutch community. The timing alone would confirm that. Thus, the placard was issued only the day after Johannes à Lasco, Utenhove and Micron presented their petition to Christian III. Furthermore, the wording of the placard corresponds closely with some of the instructions Christian III forwarded to Bishop Palladius and the magistracy in Copenhagen on 17 November concerning the refugees from London.[25]

Despite the expulsion of the Dutch refugees, the placard of 1553 does not appear to have been as effective as the government had hoped in preventing heterodox foreigners from settling in Denmark. Two years later another placard was issued, pointing out that Anabaptist and Sacramentarian refugee craftsmen, especially tapestry-makers and goldsmiths, had been allowed to take up residence in the country because of their skills and abilities, contrary to the previous placard. The king admitted that he recognised the value of such people for the economy, but considering the danger they represented to civil authority as well as to Lutheran uniformity, they were to be banished immediately. The tone of this placard was much sharper than the previous one, and it threatened with capital punishment not only the heterodox immigrants who stayed on, but also those who harboured them.[26]

Later in 1569, the arrival of a growing number of heterodox Protestant refugees from the Netherlands, fleeing the persecution initiated by the Duke of Alva, caused the government of Frederik II, Christian III's son and successor, to issue the so-called Strangers' Articles. They stated that all strangers who had settled in the king's realms within the last two years were obliged to agree to the 25 Strangers' Articles if they wished to remain. This was necessary because it had come to Frederik II's attention that a significant number of these recent immigrants differed in doctrine and ceremonies from the king and his subjects. In order to avoid strife and disagreement which

[25] Compare Rørdam, *Danske Kirkelove*, 1, 362–3 with letters printed in Zwergius, *Cleresie*, 41–6. There has been a peculiar hesitation within early modern Danish scholarship to consider the placard of 11 November 1553 to be connected with the arrival of the London Dutch refugees, see Zwergius, *Cleresie*, 66 and K. E. Jordt Jørgensen,' Jan Laskis Besøg i Danmark i Vinteren 1553', *Telogisk Tidsskrift*, 5th series, 6 (1935), 93–100, esp. 100. Jordt Jørgensen's argument that it would have taken more than two days to print the placard and that accordingly it cannot have been connected with the arrival of the London Dutch community, does not make sense. We only know that the placard was issued on 11 November 1553, not when it was printed!

[26] The placard of 1555 is printed in Rørdam, *Danske Kirkelove*, 485–8.

might cause rebellion and endanger the true religion which had been introduced by the king's father, Christian III, all recent immigrants had to accept the Strangers' Articles or leave the country. Those who remained, if caught, but only pretended to be orthodox, would be executed. Furthermore, town-councils were told not to grant citizenship to any foreigner who could not present an attestation, proving his orthodoxy from his local minister or superintendent.[27]

Evidently a confessional Lutheran state like Denmark was not prepared to grant asylum to Reformed refugees in this period. For most of the 1550s the Danish government appears to have considered the Reformed or Sacramentarians, as they labelled them, to be as dangerous to civil authority as the Anabaptists. Despite recognising the economic value of such immigrants the king and council remained opposed to allowing Reformed refugees settling in the realm. The repressiveness and intolerance of Lutheran confessionalism was, however, less stringent in Denmark and Norway than was the case in most territorial states in Germany. Johannes à Lasco and his followers were expelled, but they received economic assistance and help with their onwards journey. This was a fairly humane gesture by sixteenth-century standards, especially considering the aggressive and polemical stance of the refugees themselves, which cannot but have angered those who dealt with them.

Confessional preoccupations continued to play a considerable part in the Danish government's deliberations until the mid seventeenth century. However, the mercantilist policies which characterized the first years of Christian IV's reign caused the government temporarily to consider granting some form of toleration to Calvinist immigrants. In 1607 the diplomat Jonas Charisius was dispatched to the United Provinces in order to recruit Reformed craftsmen and merchants who were willing to settle in Denmark and Norway. Unusually, Charisius was allowed to promise these prospective immigrants freedom of worship. Ten years later this prospect of toleration evaporated when the Strangers' Articles of 1569 were re-issued as part of a series of laws the government enacted from 1617 onwards in order to enhance uniformity in state and church. Thus, in 1620 no similar promises were offered when new attempts were made to encourage Dutch craftsmen and merchants to settle in Denmark and Norway.[28]

While Denmark had witnessed a full Reformation by 1537, receiving its Lutheran Church Order, the Swedish Reformation had been a tortuous affair. The dismantling of the Catholic Church in Sweden began in the late 1520s more or less simultaneously with similar developments in Denmark, but Prot-

---

[27] For the Strangers' Articles, see *ibid.*, 2 (Copenhagen, 1886), 126–34, especially 126–8. See also T. Lyby & O. P. Grell, 'The Consolidation of Lutheranism in Denmark and Norway', in Grell, *Scandinavian Reformation*, 114–43.

[28] See O. P. Grell, 'Introduction', in Grell, *Scandinavian Reformation*, 9–10.

estantism in Sweden remained relatively weak, dependent on a few leading theologians and royal backing, and lacking significant popular support. Thus, the Swedish Reformation remained doctrinally vague, even after the country had received its first Protestant Church Order in 1571. It was not until the Uppsala Assembly of 1593 that Lutheranism was officially acknowledged as the doctrinal foundation of the Swedish church. Throughout the second half of the sixteenth century Sweden remained remarkably indecisive in religion, dithering between Lutheranism, Calvinism and Catholicism. This was undoubtedly a bequest from the reign of the Swedish Reformation king, Gustav Vasa (1521–1560).

During the last twenty years of his reign, Gustav Vasa had been firmly in control of all ecclesiastical matters in his realm, but he had deliberately refrained from taking any final decisions about ecclesiastical organisation and doctrinal issues. His personal disregard for confessional uniformity can be seen in his choice of two Reformed tutors for his sons, Dionysius Beurreus and Jan van Herboville. The result was that the Swedish church did not, either legally or practically, become part of the state. Later this would lead to occasional confessional conflicts between the crown and a semi-independent Swedish church which continued to be lead by the archbishop of Uppsala, as can be seen in the reigns of Gustav Vasa's three sons, Erik XIV (1560–68), Johan III (1568–92) and Karl IX (1599–1611).[29] Obviously, the lack of a confessionally binding church order had its disadvantages, but it also offered political opportunities. It meant that the Swedish government was able to pursue a flexible Erastian church policy, subordinating the interests of the church to the needs of the state!

Initially, during the early 1550s, Gustav Vasa and the Swedish government were as worried about the possible negative effects of the more extreme forms of Protestantism as most European governments. The activities of Melchior Hoffmann in Stockholm in the mid-1520s had already demonstrated to Gustav Vasa the dangers of such people.[30] In December 1550 a placard was issued forbidding foreign 'Spiritualists and heretical, false teachers' visiting Sweden. This order was evidently considered a necessary measure to prevent the resurgent Spiritualism and Anabaptism in the Netherlands and southern Germany from spilling over into Sweden.[31] Similar worries caused Gustav Vasa, when informed about the expulsion of the London Dutch refugees from

---

[29] For Sweden, see O. P. Grell, 'Scandinavia', in B. Scribner *et al.* (eds.), *The Reformation in National Context* (Cambridge, 1994), 123–7, O. P. Grell, 'Scandinavia', in Pettegree, *The Early Reformation*, 112–18.

[30] See Grell, 'Scandinavia', 114.

[31] For those developments in the Netherlands and Germany, see G. H. Williams, *The Radical Reformation* (Philadelphia, 1975), 453–504. For the Swedish placard of 1550, see Kjöllerstöm, *Striden kring kalvinismen*, 10.

Denmark in December 1553, to order the bishop of Växjö to assure that such people did not settle in his diocese.[32]

Shortly afterwards, however, Gustav Vasa changed his attitude to the Dutch exiles from London, not least because he realized the possible economic advantages they might offer to the country if he managed to encourage a fair number of these highly skilled craftsmen to settle in Sweden. According to Johannes à Lasco, Gustav Vasa promised the exiles not only freedom of worship but also generous salaries for their ministers.[33] However, apart from encouraging the odd Dutch craftsman to settle in Sweden this approach had little effect. The refugees clearly preferred the Emden they knew to the faraway Sweden about which they only had vague ideas. This royal initiative, however, seems to have been part of a wider plan by the king to encourage heterodox Protestants, preferably craftsmen, to settle in Sweden. His 1556 invitation to persecuted Bohemian Brethren to seek refuge in Sweden should probably be seen as part of these mercantilist policies, even if it may have been encouraged as a compassionate gesture by the royal physician, Dr Johannes Copp, who himself belonged to the Brethren.[34]

A number of the Reformed craftsmen who had found shelter in Emden made the move to Sweden during the late 1550s. Considering Emden's significance for the early Reformed diaspora and the close contacts between Sweden and East Friesland from, at least, 1556 which led to a trade agreement between the two countries in 1557 and the marriage between Gustav Vasa's eldest daughter and Count Edzard II of East Friesland in 1559, this is not surprising. The most significant Reformed recruit from Emden, however, was not a craftsman, but a scholar, Jan van Herboville, who became one of the leading Calvinist figures in Sweden in the 1560s. He arrived in Sweden in March 1558, having been recruited by another member of the Reformed faith, Dionysius Beurreus. The two men had met during Beurreus's two months stay in Emden on his way to London as Swedish ambassador. By then, Beurreus had resided in Sweden for nearly fifteen years initially employed as royal mathematician and physician, later taking over the role of tutor to Crown Prince Erik.[35]

Shortly after his arrival Herboville became involved in Gustav Vasa's plans for encouraging foreign craftsmen to immigrate to Sweden. On 3 May 1558 he was given authority by the king to recruit craftsmen in Emden and significantly to promise prospective immigrants freedom of worship, the right to employ their own minister and administer the sacraments 'as required by

---

[32] Kjöllerström, *Striden kring kalvinismen*, 10.

[33] This information can be found in a letter Johannes à Lasco wrote in May 1555, see J. à Lasco, *Opera*, ed. A. Kuyper, 2 vols. (Amsterdam, 1866), 709.

[34] O. Walde, 'Johann Copps bibliotek', *Nordisk tidsskrift för biblioteksväsen*, 1934, 51.

[35] Kjöllerström, *Striden kring kalvinismen*, 19.

true and pious Christians'. But even Herboville with his excellent contacts in Emden appears to have been unable to encourage any significant number to leave for Sweden.

Furthermore, it was probably on the request of Herboville, that Calvin dedicated his commentary on the minor prophets, published in February 1559, to Gustav Vasa and his son Erik, whom Calvin mentioned with particular approval in his dedication.[36]

In the summer of 1559 Gustav Vasa once more sought to reinvigorate his pro-immigration policies. He contacted his ambassador in London, Dionysius Beurreus, requesting him to find some skilled craftsmen who would settle in Sweden. At the same time his son, Duke Erik, contacted his representative in the Netherlands, Arnold Rosenberg, ordering him to do the same. Rosenberg informed Erik that without guarantees of their own church and freedom of worship, similar to those they enjoyed in Emden, it would prove difficult to recruit many craftsmen. He added that most of these people were Calvinists. According to Rosenberg they differed from the Lutheran churches only in their interpretation of the Eucharist, but more importantly there were several influential and wealthy people among them who would improve the financial basis of the kingdom by several thousand Guilders. Having emphasised the wealth of these potential immigrants while minimising the differences in religion Rosenberg pointed out that he needed a royal charter guaranteeing prospective immigrants such freedoms in order for matters to proceed.[37]

Eventually it was not Rosenberg in the Netherlands, but Beurreus in London who, in March 1561, received a royal charter from Erik XIV, who had succeeded his father to the Swedish throne. Beurreus appears to have developed close contacts with the recently re-established stranger churches in London upon his arrival in the city. Some months prior to the charter he had recruited a new royal physician for Erik XIV from the Dutch community in London.[38] Undoubtedly the main target for the charter were the Dutch and Walloon exile communities in London. Accordingly, Beurreus personally appeared before the consistory of the Dutch church in Austin Friars in May in order to promote the cause.[39]

The charter of 5 March stated that Erik XIV had been informed that many of those who had been exiled 'for the sake of devotion and truth' were willing to emigrate to Sweden if they could

---

[36] *Ibid.*, 20–5.
[37] See *Handlingar rörande Skandinaviens historia*, 26 (Stockholm, 1845), 6ff.
[38] See O. P. Grell, 'Huguenot and Walloon Contributions to Sweden's Emergence as a European Power, 1560–1648', *Proceedings of the Huguenot Society*, 24, 4 (1992), 380–1.
[39] A. A. van Schelven, *Kerkeraads-Protocollen der Nederduitsche Vluchtelingen-kerk te London 1560–1563* (Amsterdam, 1921), 189–90.

be permitted to live in peace according to the Gospel and the true religion of God. Moved by compassion for them, we grant all persons, of whatever condition and quality they may be, who desire to live peaceably and religiously, free ingress into, and residence in, our kingdom. And we undertake to defend and protect them, and to allow them to use and enjoy the same privileges and rights as our own subjects and vassals, provided that they not be exiles on account of crimes and misdeeds, that they submit to the laws of our realm, conduct themselves as pious Christians, and swear and preserve fealty to Us and our kingdom.[40]

In order to avoid misunderstandings Erik XIV added eight clauses to his charter, three of which dealt exclusively with the religious issues. The first clause simply stated that the immigrants should adhere to evangelical Christian doctrines in accordance with the Bible. The second forbade them to 'plant any sects or heresies in the religion from which both king and country benefited'. Furthermore, in cases of doctrinal conflict the Swedish bishops were to have the last word. Finally, the last clause forbade the immigrants to introduce new doctrines among the Swedes which were 'against the Word of God, or encouraged religious sedition and disturbances'.

There cannot have been much in either the letter itself or the added clauses to stop prospective Reformed emigrants from going to Sweden. Furthermore, the restrictive clauses may never have been intended for external consumption by the Swedish government. They do not appear to have been known to the leaders of the Dutch community in London. They were never discussed by the consistory nor do they appear to have been attached to the copy of the charter they received in London.[41] The vague non-confessional and evangelical character of the charter would have suited members of the foreign Reformed communities in London excellently, while the loose episcopal supervision suggested in clause two seems no more intrusive than what they were already experiencing in Elizabethan England.

Prospective Reformed immigrants were in effect granted full toleration by Erik XIV. The theological vagueness of the charter served the Erastian and mercantilist policies of a crypto-Calvinist king excellently. It made it possible for him to offer the widest possible religious tolerance for members of the Reformed faith, while simultaneously making it difficult for the leadership of the evangelical church in Sweden to accuse him of encouraging heterodoxy. This was, of course, greatly facilitated by the Swedish church's lack of doctrinal foundation, having been granted no church order.[42]

---

[40] See J. H. Hessels (ed.), *Ecclesiae Londino-Batavae Archivum*, 2 (Cambridge, 1892), no. 48.
[41] Only the letter, not the eight clauses attached to it, seems to have reached the London Dutch consistory, see Guildhall MS 7428/1, f. 15. For the added clauses, see Kjöllerström, *Striden kring kalvinismen*, 268–9.
[42] There has been a strong tendency among Swedish scholars of this period's history to interpret the charter as offering little or no religious toleration to the prospective immigrants. See

The charter of 1561 cannot be said to have worked wonders for the Swedish government. It undoubtedly encouraged a few Reformed refugees to settle in the country, but it never led to the mass immigration hoped for by Erik XIV. With hindsight the timing of the charter may have been unfortunate, being issues shortly after the reestablishment of the stranger churches in London, and preceding by more than six years the persecutions of the Duke of Alva which led to a mass exodus from the Netherlands. However, emigration to Sweden may, of course, simply have been perceived as a rather untempting proposition by most of the Reformed exiles in mid-sixteenth century metropolitan London.

Even if Reformed immigrants only arrived in limited numbers their effect on Swedish church affairs proved significant in the early 1560s. After his return from London Dionysius Beurreus quickly became involved in a public theological debate with the Swedish archbishop, Laurentius Petri, an ardent Lutheran, on a variety of subjects ranging from the doctrine of the Eucharist to whether images in churches should be allowed. The immigrants were clearly trying to move the Swedish church towards the Reformed position. Erik XIV may personally have sympathised with their position in 1564 when the immigrants produced their own confession which was nearly identical with the French Confession – *Confessio Gallicana* of 1559 – but political considerations alone would have prevented him from showing it. The outbreak of the Seven Years War with Denmark ensured that the king had to intervene on the side of the leading Lutheran theologians of the Swedish church in order to keep the country united. The immigrants were forbidden to proselytise, Calvinist teachings were declared false, the Reformed immigrants, however, were allowed freedom of conscience.[43] Clearly, a mercantilist pro-emigration policy held its dangers even within an Erastian state like Sweden. The result was that the attempt to entice foreign Reformed emigration to Sweden was put on ice for a generation. This development was, of course, further enhanced by the accession to the throne in 1568 of the crypto-Catholic King Johan III.

These tolerant, mercantilist initiatives were eventually resurrected by Duke Karl, the youngest of Gustav Vasa's three sons, in the mid-1590s, a few years before he succeeded to the throne as King Karl IX. It is probably no coincidence that Karl, like his brother Erik XIV, had benefited from a Calvinist tutor, in his case Jan van Herboville. Karl's attempts to recruit foreign Reformed craftsmen to come to Sweden proved highly successful. Among the many immigrants were Willem de Bessche who transformed Swedish

---

Kjöllerström, *Striden kring kalvinismen*, 35; Kilbom, *Vallonerne. Vallonindvandringen, Stormaktsvældet och den svenska Järnhanteringen* (Stockholm, 1958), 221; and G. Annell, *Erik XIV:s Etiska Förestillinger och deras Inflytande paå Hans Politik* (Uppsala, 1945), 181.
[43] Grell, 'Huguenot and Walloon', 379–80.

iron production and the manufacture of weapons. This mercantilist policy was continued by his son Gustavus Adolphus, who in 1627 convinced the Reformed merchant and entrepreneur, Louis de Geer, to settle in Sweden. It was thanks to De Geer that the military-industrial complex was established which made it possible to supply the Swedish armies during the Thirty Years' War. At his accession in 1611 Gustavus Adolphus had already managed to secure some measure of toleration for the Reformed, even if they were excluded from government jobs and forbidden their own church. In practice, however, the toleration granted the Reformed immigrants was considerably greater and the government connived at the existence of Reformed congregations and services in Stockholm and Gothenburg.[44]

Thus, by the early seventeenth century the Swedish government was finally able to reap the rewards of an Erastian and economically dictated toleration of Reformed immigrants in an otherwise Lutheran country. This policy, which in the 1560s had appeared to confirm the view expressed in confessional Lutheran states such as Denmark that Protestant heterodoxy constituted a serious danger to the religious, political and social stability of the state, had finally come good by the early seventeenth century. It could be argued that without the Erastian church policy pursued by Karl IX and Gustavus Adolphus the necessary economic and political conditions for Sweden's emergence as a European power in the early seventeenth century would never have been in place. At the same time Sweden's main rival in the Baltic, Denmark, would have had good reason to regret the confessionally dictated immigration policies the country had pursued since the arrival of Johannes à Lasco and his followers in 1553.

Another striking aspect of the contrasting policies pursued by the governments of Denmark and Sweden in this period is the opposing views of the two kingdoms' leading theologians, on whether some measure of toleration should be granted the Reformed immigrants. Theologically, little or nothing divided the leaders of the Swedish church from their Danish colleagues, both were Lutheran, but whereas the Danish church leaders argued for clemency and some measure of tolerance for the refugees who had arrived in the country in 1553, it was precisely their Swedish colleagues who wanted to restrict the freedom granted to immigrants in Sweden. Thus, in this instance the policy of Lutheran uniformity was promoted primarily by the Danish king and his lay advisers a policy they shared with the leading, Lutheran clergy in Sweden, not the Swedish government. One wonders if it was the religious stability guaranteed the Danish church by the Church Order of 1537 which made it possible for its Lutheran leaders to show a measure of tolerance which their Swedish counterparts could ill afford lacking similar security.

---

[44] See Grell, 'Introduction', in Grell, *Scandinavian Reformation*, 9–10.

Finally, if the London Dutch exiles had reason to complain about the lack of compassion shown by the Lutheran authorities in Denmark and Germany during their peregrination in 1553, it is relevant to ask how they themselves fared on the issue of toleration. Especially with regard to their treatment of Anabaptists, who more often than not shared their exile. In this connection it is worth remembering that when the refugees arrived in Wismar after their expulsion from Denmark, it was the Anabaptist leader, Menno Simons and his followers who welcomed the exhausted travellers into their own homes.[45] A Christian gesture for which the London exiles showed little gratitude neither then nor later.

Furthermore, while staying in Emden in the 1550s the London refugees appear to have been instrumental in hardening the attitude of the Emden church towards Anabaptists.[46] Hardly had the community been re-established in London before its attitude to Anabaptists was tested once more. In 1560–61 a group of liberal humanist members of the Dutch Reformed community led by the minister Adrian van Haemstede argued for a tolerant approach to local Anabaptists, describing them as 'erring brethren in Christ'. This politically and ecclesiastically sensitive question led to the excommunication of Haemstede and a group of his most influential supporters within the London community, such as the merchant and historian Emanuel van Meteren, and the Italian scholar and engineer, Jacob Acontius.[47] Considering Acontius's deep concern for the freedom of conscience, which resulted in his famous work on toleration, *Satan's strategy (Satanae Stratagemata)*, published in Basle in 1565, it is more than likely that his role in the whole affair was as central as that attributed to him by the minister to the London French community, Nicholas des Gallars, who informed Calvin, that Acontius was Haemstede's 'subtle and acute patron.'[48]

However, in spite of this hardline approach by the leaders of the community the Anabaptists continued to trouble the Dutch church. The problem was amplified in 1575 when the English authorities rounded up a group of Dutch Anabaptists in London. The Dutch ministers assisted the Bishop of London, Edwin Sandys, in their examination. When five of the Anabaptists were condemned to death and two of the most stubborn executed the London Dutch community came to be seen by contemporaries as deeply implicated in the affair, even if the church had made a half-hearted plea for mercy for the condemned. As had been the case in the Haemstede affair in 1561 this incident came to be seen as evidence, by more liberal Reformed communities

---

[45] See Pettegree, 'Sacramentarian Controversy', 227.
[46] Pettegree, *Emden and the Dutch Revolt*, 236–7.
[47] See P. Collinson, *Archbishop Grindal 1519–1583* (London, 1979), 134–40 and Pettegree, *Foreign Protestant Communities*, 169–81.
[48] Cited in Collinson, *Grindal*, 137.

on the continent, of an unnecessarily harsh attitude by the Dutch Reformed church in London.[49]

Evidently, the presence of Dutch Anabaptists in London presented the Dutch Reformed community in the city with two problems. Firstly, to be seen to tolerate such people could emperil the church's position *vis-à-vis* the English authorities and add substance to the popular belief that the community was a breeding-ground for heterodoxy. Secondly, the London community was clearly losing members to the Anabaptists on a regular basis, as can be seen from the consistory books. Out of a total of eleven excommunications between 1568–1585, five were on grounds of Anabaptism.[50]

In 1572 the community's fear of the growing effects of Anabaptism had become so serious that it was decided to send a minister and an elder to Bishop Edwin Sandys and the Archbishop of Canterbury, Matthew Parker, requesting them to take immediate action against the Anabaptists within and without the community.[51] However, the leaders of the community may well have drawn some consequences from its involvement in the examination and conviction of the five Dutch Anabaptists in 1575. Nine years later they refused direct assistance to the Lord Mayor of London in tracking down 'foreign rebels, Anabaptists and Papists' in the city in order that they could be expelled, because as they explained, they knew of no such people.[52]

Self-preservation in a foreign and often hostile environment may to some extent explain the London community's lack of compassion and tolerance of their Anabaptist co-refugees. More fundamentally, however, their hostility and lack of tolerance towards the Anabaptists were basically of the same kind as that which they themselves had encountered from the Lutherans among whom they sought refuge in 1553. Where the Lutherans perceived the Reformed to be as dangerous to their Reformation as the Anabaptists, the Reformed were only faced with the Anabaptist challenge to their particular Reformation. Having recovered what both Calvinists and Lutherans considered the true Apostolic faith, the vast majority of both Lutherans and Reformed were prepared to take all necessary measures to defend it. Those Protestants who considered tolerance and persuasion the only way forward, such as Haemstede and Acontius, remained an insignificant minority in the sixteenth century, often marginalised and victimised by their own co-religionists.

[49] See Hessels, *Ecclesiae Londino-Batavae*, 3, nos. 315, 420, 611 and Pettegree, *Foreign Protestant Communities*, 288, 139.

[50] *Ibid.*, 138–39 and O. Boersma, *Vluchtig Voorbeeld, de nederlandse, franse en italiaanse vluchtelingenkerken in London 1568–1585* (Kampen, 1994), 145, see also 134–6.

[51] A. J. Jelsma & O. Boersma (eds.), *Acta Nederlandse Gemeente London 1569–1585*, RPG, 76 (The Hague, 1993), no. 1147.

[52] *Ibid.*, no. 3395.

11 The politics of toleration in the Free Netherlands, 1572–1620

Andrew Pettegree

That the seventeenth-century Dutch Republic was a haven of toleration has become almost axiomatic in literature on the Dutch Golden Age. Indeed, this is one fact on which both modern scholars and contemporary commentators can be expected to agree. To an interested observer like Sir William Temple, a sage and discriminating commentator on Dutch society in the later part of the seventeenth century, the benign treatment of religious minorities was an important aspect of the peculiarity of the Dutch as their system of government, their efficient engrossment of the world's trade, and the freedom accorded their women in public places. 'The great care of this state', he wrote in his justly famous *Observations upon the United Provinces of the Netherlands*,

has ever been, to favour no particular or curious Inquisition into the faith or religious principles of any peaceable man, who came to live under the protection of their laws, and to suffer no violence or oppression upon any man's conscience whose opinions broke not out into expressions or actions of ill consequence to the state. . . . It is hardly to be imagined how all violence and sharpness which accompanies the difference of Religion in other countries, seems to be appeased or softened here, by the general freedom which all men enjoy.[1]

Temple wrote in 1673, a full century after the foundation of the new free state, but other earlier English travellers commented in much the same way: all appeared fascinated and curious at the way in which persons of different faiths coexisted in the Netherlands, in defiance of the conventional wisdom that the unity and security of a state demanded unity in one faith.[2] This was an image which the Dutch to some extent consciously cultivated. The formative years of the free northern state in the late sixteenth century saw the erection of a number of new statues to Erasmus, the great Netherlander who

---

[1] Sir William Temple, *Observations upon the United Provinces of the Netherlands*, ed. Sir George Clark (Oxford, 1972), 103, 106.

[2] As for instance Fynes Morrison (1592), Sir William Brereton (1634). See J. N. Jacobsen Jensen, 'Moryson's Reis door en zijn karakteristiek van de Nederlanden', *Bijdragen en Mededeelingen van het Historisch Genootschap*, 39 (1918), 214–305. *Travels in the United Provinces . . . by Sir William Brereton*, ed. E. Hawkins (1844).

had put the pursuit of scholarship above party divisions, and whose humane and rational spirit epitomised the cultural climate for which the rulers of the new state appeared to be striving.[3]

Yet in some respects the adoption of Erasmus as a cultural totem was disingenuous. In the context of its time it was less an indication of national spirit, than part of a more or less conscious effort to dress a young independent nation with a plausible historical heritage.[4] The question arises whether toleration was ever, as the Erasmus cult was intended to imply, an integral part of the intellectual warf of the Netherlandish character; or at least, any more so than in other countries. Rather toleration was a weapon, and in the sixteenth century it could be used as ruthlessly and cynically as persecution and intolerance to further particular political ends. In the particular circumstances of the early years of the emerging Dutch Republic toleration was quite specifically a party tool: less an axiom of political life, still less a principle, than a state of affairs which emerged out of a long and ultimately defining struggle over the religious character of the new state. The protagonists in this confrontation were the Calvinist ministers who gave direction to the dominant church in the new free state, and the city magistrates of Holland, and the spirit in which they explored their different conceptions of a proper religious settlement was very far from that of Erasmus. The status of other minority faiths was but one of the issues which divided them, but one which could be manipulated to advance, or control, the influence of the Calvinist church over other areas of life in Dutch society. In this atmosphere it is all too easy to see a yawning chasm between the high-minded arguments and the bitter partisan spirit with which each side strove for advantage.

From the very beginnings of the Revolt 'toleration' was always a slogan which could be exploited with a high degree of cynicism by different religious groupings. In his *Brief discourse addressed to Philip II* in 1566, the author, the Calvinist minister Franciscus Junius did not scruple to urge the king to extend religious freedom to his Calvinist subjects, citing among his reasons the obvious justice of the Calvinist cause, and the fact that persecution was damaging to trade.[5] This was the main thrust of Calvinist appeals for tolerance in these early years, proposing limited freedoms for themselves: essentially freedom from persecution in a Catholic state.[6] But

---

[3] See *Erasmus en zijn tijd* (Rotterdam, 1969), nos. 567, 568.

[4] On the Dutch search for a past see especially I. Schöffer, 'The Batavian Myth during the Sixteenth and Seventeenth Centuries', in J. S. Bromley and E. H. Kossmann (eds.), *Britain and the Netherlands*, vol. 5 (The Hague, 1975), 78–101. Simon Schama, *The Embarrassment of Riches* (London, 1987).

[5] Quoted in E. H. Kossman and A. F. Mellink, *Texts Concerning the Revolt of the Netherlands* (Cambridge, 1974), 56–9.

[6] Martin van Gelderen, *The Political Thought of the Dutch Revolt, 1555–1590* (Cambridge, 1992).

Junius also suggested, with no apparent irony, that once granted freedom of worship the Calvinists could assist in combating atheism and radical sectarian groups.[7] The true spirit of Dutch Calvinism was revealed in the events of the summer of this year, when, faced with an apparent loss of nerve on the part of Philip's governor, Margaret of Parma, the consistories moved swiftly to 'cleanse' the Catholic churches of their idolatrous images by swift and undoubtedly illegal unilateral action.[8] The subsequent effect of the iconoclasm on the shaky unity of the opposition movement later caused the more politically sensitive ministers to draw back and disassociate themselves from the destruction, but this was largely tactical.[9] The unyielding hostility to images manifested in the iconoclasm did demonstrate the real spirit of Reformed theology, as was comprehensively proven by their conduct when the revolt broke out again in 1572. By now conscious of their central importance to William of Orange's military effort, the Reformed moved swiftly to secure the best churches in those towns in Holland which had gone over to the Revolt.[10] If the magistracy prevaricated, the Reformed usually pre-empted further discussion by cleansing the churches in renewed and carefully orchestrated waves of iconoclasm.[11] This subsequent episode of church-breaking is much less well-known than the more spectacular events of the 'Wonderjaar', but, in the context of any discussion of the spirit of Dutch Calvinism, equally significant. By the end of 1572 the small Reformed congregations had successfully commandeered the best churches in the principal rebel towns. The following year they achieved a further milestone, persuading the States of Holland to ban the Catholic mass altogether in areas held by the rebels.[12]

In this they achieved a signal victory over William of Orange, whose initial intention had been to promote equality between the competing faiths in areas under his control: this, indeed, was a vital part of his strategy for drawing into the rebellion a patriotic Catholic wing to whom the struggle would be

---

[7]   Kossman and Mellink, *Texts*, 57–8.

[8]   J. Scheerder, *De Beeldenstorm* (Bussum, 1964). S. Deyon and A. Lottin, *Les Casseurs de l'été 1566: L'iconoclasme danse nord de France* (Paris, 1981).

[9]   See the transparently disingenuous explanations of Philip Marnix, who in his *True narrative and apology* blamed Catholic priests acting as agents provocateurs alongside 'women, children, and men of no authority'. Quoted Kossmann and Mellink, *Texts*, 79–80.

[10] Summarized in my recent article 'Coming to Terms with Victory: Calvinist Church-Building in Holland, 1572–1590', in Pettegree, Duke and Lewis (eds.), *Calvinism in Europe, 1540–1620* (Cambridge, 1994), 160–80. See also Alastair Duke and Rosemary Jones, 'Towards a Reformed Polity in Holland', in Duke (ed.), *Reformation and Revolt in the Low Countries* (London, 1990), 199–226.

[11] As for instance in Leiden, Haarlem, Gouda and Dordrecht. Duke, 206. C. C. Hibben, *Gouda in Revolt* (Utrecht, 1983).

[12] H. A. Enno van Gelder, *Revolutionnaire reformatie* (Amsterdam, 1943), 179. Duke and Jones, 'Towards a Reformed Polity', 203–7.

presented as a war of national liberation against a foreign tyrant.[13] But for the Calvinist ministers the struggle was at its core religious, as they made all too clear in letters to friends abroad. 'The Lord through his boundless mercy spreads out his light over our Fatherland more from day to day', wrote a grateful minister from Dordrecht in January 1573, a sentiment echoed many times over in these first heady days of apparently effortless advance.[14] And since it was they who provided much of the personnel and financial support for Orange's forces they were for the time being in a position to impose their will. Having secured the extinction of public Catholic worship in 1573, the pressure on the old faith was remorselessly maintained. A key ingredient of the Particular Union of Holland and Zealand of 1575 was the instruction to the Stadhouder to maintain the practice of the Reformed evangelical religion, ending and prohibiting the exercise of the Roman religion. The local coup in 1578 which brought Amsterdam belatedly into the rebel camp led automatically to the expulsion of the Catholic clergy and the suppression of Catholic worship.[15] Finally in 1581 the northern state enacted the first general placard against Catholicism. Catholics were now prohibited from assembling for worship in public or in private, on pain of substantial fines.[16]

The events leading to the enactment of this legislation may give some idea of the tenor of the debate which informed proscriptions of this nature. In 1579 the governor of Gelderland, William's brother Duke John of Nassau, expressed some concern at the systematic destruction of Catholic altars and statues in the region where there was not as yet an extensive Calvinist organisation to fill the resultant religious vacuum. He put his concerns to three of Orange's closest advisers, Philip Marnix, Jean Taffin, and Pierre de Villiers.[17] Not surprisingly, given their proximity to the thinking of the Prince, the three returned responses urging caution and restraint. But other bolder spirits now entered the fray. One such was the Calvinist preacher Jan Schuurmann. He had no doubt that measures against Catholics should be energetically pursued. Recalling the texts on the punishment of idolaters in Deuteronomy, he declared that it was a good and honest thing to break any oaths made with the Catholics. While he admitted that no one could be forced to believe, he

---

[13] On Orange's policy during three years see Koen Swart, *William van Oranje en de Nederlands Opstand, 1572–1584* (The Hague, 1994).

[14] J. H. Hessels, *Ecclesiae Londino-Batavae Archivum*, 3 vols. in 4 (Cambridge, 1889–97), III, nos. 201, 206, 207.

[15] R. B. Evenhuis, *Ook dat was Amsterdam*, 5 vols. (1965–78), I, 83–128.

[16] L. J. Rogier, *Geschiedenis van het katholicisme in Noord-Nederland in de 16de en 17de eeuw* 3rd edn, 5 vols (1964), II, 351.

[17] Letter in G. Groen van Prinsteren, *Archives ou Correspondance inédite de la Maison d'Orange-Nassau*, 9 vols. (Leiden, 1841–7), VII, 128–33. E. van Gelder, *Vrijheid en onvrijheid in de Republiek* (Haarlem, 1947), I, 135ff.

affirmed nevertheless that all subjects could be forced to listen to the pure Gospel, or even to frequent the sacraments. Another minister, Charles Galus of Arnhem, would only consent to peace with papists if one forbade them all public worship, dissolved their monasteries, and demanded they came to the sermons.[18] For many Reformed ministers such conclusions were self-evident. Reformed ministers could no more tolerate the public exercise of Catholicism than the Old Testament prophets could sanction the worship of Baal. The ministers believed whole-heartedly, as one anonymous minister told his congregation in Haarlem in 1577 'that he could not be expected to make much headway unless they only permitted one religion'.[19]

This then was one view of the proper relations between the faiths in the new state. It is important to understand that this was not a denial of freedom of conscience, seen through the particular prism of early Calvinist triumphalism. All sides in the developing debate acknowledged freedom of conscience fully: it could not really be otherwise in a movement which had emerged from the shadow of papal tyranny.[20] But to the Calvinist true freedom of religion was not synonymous with freedom of opinion. Freedom of conscience did not consist of allowing vicious sects to speak freely, thus seducing innocent hearts and creating discord. Rather the public authorities had a duty to silence those who undermined the true religion which they perversely refused to accept. Put another way, true freedom of conscience was to live in Christ, which in practice implied adherence to the Reformed Protestant faith.[21]

In the first years of the revolt, a time when religious differences were still sharpened by the ongoing military conflict with Spain, the leaders of the Calvinist church had considerable success in imposing this point of view on the rulers of the emerging free state. In the leading Holland towns the best churches were made over for Calvinist worship; other faiths were discouraged, and in the case of Catholicism, banned altogether. And all this with the apparent co-operation of the city magistrates, their allies in the struggle against Parma's armies. No wonder that in their publications and correspondence, the ministers gratefully celebrated this virtuous co-operation. 'I see that we have a more godly government than ever France or Germany have had', wrote Jan van der Beke from Delft in 1573.[22] Spurred by the hope of continuing good relations, the ministers pressed on with further steps aimed at the creation of a godly society, a society which would bring them closer to the circumstances they had enjoyed in their exile churches, or which they

---

[18] Joseph Lecler, *Toleration and the Reformation*, 2 vols. (London, 1955), II, 241–2.
[19] Quoted Duke and Jones, 'Towards a Reformed Polity', 226.
[20] A point made by Van Gelderen, *Political Thought of the Dutch Revolt*.
[21] Van Gelderen, *Political Thought*, 250, 257–8.
[22] Hessels, *Ecclesiae Londino-Batavae Archivum*, III, no. 226.

imagined to pertain in Geneva. But here they found the magistrates less and less co-operative; indeed the next years would reveal a whole series of issues where it was clear that the ministerial vision of a godly society and that of the magistrates diverged. It was in this context that the debate over toleration took on a wider social significance.

The first years of the new free state were in fact disfigured by a whole series of disputes between the ministers and magistrates which gradually eroded the generally harmonious co-operation of the initial revolt.[23] In broad terms, the ministers in these years, buoyed by their almost incredible progress from banned sect to public church, hoped now to build on their success by creating a national church, indeed a Calvinist society, in which they would exercise a preponderant influence over many areas of social life. These would include such important areas of social provision as poor relief and care for the needy; a dominant role in the education of the young through control of the appointment of schoolteachers; and through their preaching and church discipline, a determining influence over the general tenor of life in the state. Experience of life in the exile churches, where the community had exercised an almost total influence over the life of its members, had certainly prepared them for such a role. At the very minimum the ministers assumed that once the church was re-established in Holland, they would continue to exercise the basic church functions set out in their church orders: electing their ministers and church officials, and controlling access to the sacraments. However in the different circumstances of the Holland towns, the city magistrates were equally determined not to resign control over such wide areas of social life to the ministers. The outcome of this struggle was in some respects defining for Dutch Calvinism. It was certainly chastening for the church's ministers.

The first area of conflict concerned the ministry itself. As the new state had appropriated all the property of the old church in the first months of the rebel take-over, it was entirely appropriate that a portion of this booty should be laid out in providing salaries for the new Calvinist ministry. This was a solution which suited both parties. The congregations were freed from the necessity of raising a levy for this purpose on their members and the city population; the state, meanwhile, was able, given the substantially smaller numbers of clerical personnel employed *vis-à-vis* the old Catholic church, to appropriate a substantial surplus for its own purposes. This, particularly in the first years when war costs were pressing, it proceeded quite shamelessly to do.[24] And generally the system worked well enough, despite complaints in the first years that clerical salaries were often badly in arrears; at least by delegating this responsibility to the state the Dutch church was spared the

[23] These are described in my 'Coming to Terms with Victory'.
[24] W. van Beuningen, *Het Geestlijk Kantoor van Delft* (Arnhem, 1870).

frequent disputes over clerical pay and tithes which disfigured other Protestant cultures in this period.[25] But the system also had its drawbacks. Given
that they held the purse-strings the magistrates also expected to exert some
influence on who would be appointed to ministerial positions in their towns,
a demand which would be quite contrary to the principles enunciated in the
Dutch church orders adopted in their synods.

Here were two quite conflicting views of the role of the state in what the
church regarded as its own internal affairs; and this was an issue which
brought home to the ministers as no other the difference between the status
of a gathered church, in exile or 'under the cross', and the responsibilities
of a public church. In towns where the ministers enjoyed good relations with
the magistracy the matter could be swept under the carpet, but it came quite
acrimoniously to a head in a number of towns where the magistrates promoted the claims of ministers whom the orthodox ministers found quite unacceptable. A number of these cases produced significant writings on the theme
of church-state relations, in which the role of the state was unsurprisingly
championed by the unorthodox minister opposed by orthodox Calvinists. The
magistrates, whatever local compromises they made to settle particular disputes over ministerial appointments (and in the last resort it was well nigh
impossible to force on a congregation a minister they would not accept),
were not prepared to give ground on the general principle, that the churches
were public space and as such the property of the whole community rather
than one particular community. As such they must be open to all. Thus it
was swiftly made clear to the ministers that the role of public church carried
with it obligations as well as privileges. The ministers were expected to marry
or baptise any citizens who presented themselves, and in some towns it was
only with difficulty that the Calvinist consistories defended their right to
restrict access to the Lord's Supper to full members of their own church.[26]
This involved painful adjustment for many veterans of exile, since in the
churches abroad regulation of marriage and baptism were significant aspects
of the control the churches exercised over members' lives. And if the magistrates were expected to maintain the church space, they were not necessarily
prepared to allow the ministers to dictate to them on all aspects of their
internal decoration. Thus representations from the more precise ministers that
organs should be removed along with other 'idols', were generally ignored.
Organs belonged to the municipality or parish and could not be removed
without their permission, a circumstance which provoked some Calvinist
ministers almost beyond endurance. 'I really marvel', protested Jean Poly-

---

[25] Scott Dixon, 'Rural Resistance, the Lutheran Pastor and the Territorial Church in Brandenburg
Ansbach-Kulmbach, 1528–1603', in Pettegree (ed.), *The Reformation in the Parishes*
(Manchester, 1993), 85–112.
[26] Pettegree, 'Coming to Terms with Victory', 171–4.

ander in 1579, 'that when other idols were removed, this noisy idol was retained.'[27] But retained it was, despite frequent protests from the Calvinist national synod.[28] Here the Calvinist ministers tangled with the magistrate, but tangled in vain, a fact to which the apparently plainly descriptive church interior paintings of the mid-seventeenth century sometimes make subtle allusion. If one accepts, as many scholars now do, that even apparently realistic paintings may have an underlying moral agenda, it is surely not without significance how few of these paintings show a service in progress: most instead show the church with small groups of strolling citizens exercising their right to make use of this public space: talking, sight-seeing, even breast-feeding their babies.[29] Churches were frequently used for meetings or business transactions, though few would have been as lively centres of commerce as the New Church in Amsterdam, which functioned as the city's Bourse until the end of the century.[30] Other painters are at pains to show the despised and disapproved of organs with a demonstrative prominence, most notably the Catholic-sympathising Pieter Saenredam, who painted two particularly splendid pictures of the organ in the Haarlem Bavokerk at a time when the ministers and town authorities were at serious loggerheads over its use.[31] There was more than one way of making a pictorial ideological point to an audience sensitized to issues of this nature.

The disputes over the ministry and church space revealed seriously divergent views of the proper role that should be played by a public church in a pluralist society. That it remained so, owed something to the fact that the Calvinist consistories themselves adamantly defended their right to restrict full membership of their church to those who had made a full confession of faith: a distinction which inevitably led, even among those sympathetic to the Reformed, to a two-tier membership, with full members, the *lidmaeten*, who subjected themselves to the full disciplinary supervision of the consistory, being far outnumbered by *liefhebbers*, citizens who attended services

---

[27] Letter of Polyander to Cornelisz, 27 February 1579. Gemeentearchief Delft, 112, Colectie Cornelisz.

[28] F. L. Rutgers (ed.), *Acta van de Nederlandsche Synoden der Zestiende Eeuw* (Utrecht, 1889), 174, 253, 409.

[29] Walter A. Leidtke, *Architectural Painting in Delft* (Doomspijk, 1982). T. T. Blade, 'Two Interior Views of the Old Church in Delft', *Museum Studies*, 6 (171), 42. A nursing mother was often juxtaposed with an open grave, symbolizing the transitory nature of life.

[30] As Fynes Morrison observed in 1592: 'The Marchants in summer meet upon the bridge, and in winter they meet in the New Church, in very great number, where they walke in two rankes by couple, one ranke going up, and another going downe, and there is no way to get out of the Church, except they slip out of the doores, when in one of theose rankes they pass by them'. Jacobsen Jensen, 'Moryson's Reis', 223.

[31] Pictures in the Rijksmuseum, Amsterdam and National Gallery, Edinburgh. Gary Schwarz and Marten Jan Bok, *Pieter Saenredam: The Painter and his Time* (The Hague, 1990), 119, 124–9, 207.

but did not make the Confession of Faith which would have secured them admission to communion.[32]

This outer circle possibly amounted to a full 30 or 40% of the population of the major cities, a situation to which the ministers accommodated themselves, not least because the *liefhebbers* often included among their number most of the cities' ruling elites. This was, relatively speaking, the acceptable face of pluralism, and many of the ministers were able to adapt themselves to this situation. Less acceptable was the continuing more or less open existence of other competing religious groups. The extent of their freedoms was a hotly debated issue, in a context which brought the debate over religious toleration very much to the forefront. The freedoms afforded other religious groupings was obviously an issue on which Calvinist ministers felt strongly. With regard to suppression of Catholic services, they may be said, by and large, to have prevailed. The association of Catholicism with the enemy in the military struggle against Spain here greatly assisted their cause, and although the pressures on Catholics diminished as the military struggle receded, Catholics continued to enjoy only the most grudging freedoms, their gatherings sometimes winked at in return for cash payments to venal local officials.[33] With other dissident groups on the Protestant side the situation was somewhat different. Against these confessions it was impossible to raise the spectre of a potentially disloyal fifth column. Mennonites and other Anabaptist congregations had been brave early opponents of Catholicism, and resolute allies in the military struggle against Spain. This did not, however, diminish the determination of the Calvinist ministers to exclude them if at all possible from the religious freedoms enjoyed in the new northern state.

This was easier said than done. Anabaptist groups had a long history in the northern Netherlands, and in many places remained well entrenched alongside their younger competitor. Numerous congregations existed in Friesland and Groningen; and in Holland, in the country areas north of Amsterdam, in the islands of Voorne and Putten, and in most of the major cities. In the case of these dissident groups it was not easy to propose punitive measures. Since they had already separated themselves from the church the threat of excommunication meant little; since they did not come to the sermons they were not easily persuaded of the error of their ways. The synods had little choice but to appeal to the lay authorities for help. In 1574 the provincial synod of Dordrecht heard a recommendation from the classis of Walcheren that the authorities be moved to proceed against those who refused an oath of loyalty to the state, an attempt to exploit the Anabaptist prohibition

---

[32] A. Th. van Deursen, *Bavianen & Slijkgeuzen. Kerk en kerkvolk ten tijd van Maurits en Oldenbarnevelt* (Assen, 1974). Van Deursen, *Plain Lives in a Golden Age* (Cambridge, 1991), 260–79.

[33] Van Deursen, *Plain Lives*, 290–3.

of oathtaking to paint them as potentially disloyal subjects. In addition the synod recommended that Reformed ministers should take the fight to the enemy by infiltrating Anabaptist communities, so that they could confute their opinions face to face.[34]

But here they found the lay authorities strangely uncooperative. An ominous sign of things to come came in 1577, when William of Orange intervened to relieve the local Mennonite community from an oath imposed by the local powers in what was an important war zone. An appalled Gaspar van der Heyden appealed to Jean Taffin, William's court preacher, to have the decision reversed, but William was not to be moved: the progress of the military struggle on this occasion took precedence over Reformed sensibilities.[35] The Reformed did not lose hope that local magistrates might be persuaded to intervene to close down Mennonite assemblies, but more and more they were forced back on their own resources. The same synod of Dordrecht recommended a number of measures to limit the potential influence of Anabaptist beliefs within their own congregations. These went beyond mere exhortation from the pulpit. The ministers were also instructed to exercise vigilant oversight over what books members of the congregations possessed, if necessary confiscating books found during their house to house visits. A closer supervision was also to be exercised over printers and booksellers.[36]

In addition to limiting Mennonite access to public opinion, the Reformed preachers embarked on their own direct action to confront the sects. The National Synod of Dordrecht in 1578 recommended two initiatives. Firstly, they undertook to encourage the publication of a number of short, clear writings laying out the fundamental errors of Anabaptist beliefs. Secondly, they urged ministers of the public church to seek out opportunities to challenge the Anabaptist leaders to public disputations, where, it was hoped, the more educated Reformed would prevail.[37] Both strategies were energetically pursued. The years after 1578 saw a sudden flurry of anti-Anabaptist works, among them reprints of a number of the most important early Calvinist writings of Martin Micronius and Bernard Buwo, prominent figures from among the first generation of ministers who had been forced to pursue radical dissidents in the exiled churches abroad.[38] And in 1600 when the Holland synods

---

[34] Rutgers, *Acta*, 160–1, 213. See also F. S. Knipscheer, 'De Nedelandsche gereformeerde synoden tegenover der doopgezinden (1563–1620)', *Doopsgezinde Bijdragen* (1910), 1–40; (1911), 17–49.

[35] Pettegree, 'Coming to Terms with Victory', 175.

[36] *Acta*, ed. Rutgers, 140.

[37] *Ibid.*, 269.

[38] Marten Micron, *Waerachtigh verhaal der t'zamensprekinghen tusschen Menno Simons ende Martinus Mikron* (Antwerp, 1582), originally published Emden, 1556, modern edn ed. W. F. Dankbaar in *Documenta Anabaptistica Neerlandica*, 3 (Leiden, 1981). Bernhard Buwo, *Frundtlycke thosamensprekinge ... van de doop* (Ghent, 1580). Original edn Emden, 1556. On the campaign against Anabaptism more generally see Andrew Pettegree, 'The Struggle

decided the time had come for a new phase in the campaign they devolved this task, with quite unconscious irony, on a rising star of the new generation, the Amsterdam minister Jacobus Arminius.[39]

Public disputations were another favourite device of the Reformed ministers, never short of confidence that the superiority of their doctrines would be demonstrated in public debate. Nor did they totally abandon the hope that the lay magistrates would be recalled to their duty as protectors of true religion. Thus in 1595 the veteran Calvinist statesman Marnix de St Aldegonde set off a new round of polemical debate with his *Thorough Refutation of the teaching of the fanatics*, a work which specifically demanded that magistrates should intercede to exile Anabaptists and destroy their works. To allow them to spread their teachings freely, Marnix argued, would mean that the foundations of the faith would be completely destroyed, 'piety demolished, and God's authority over the human conscience completely smothered.'[40]

The Calvinist ministers' acute sensitivity to the Anabaptist challenge is hard to explain in purely numerical terms. Modern research has tended to cast doubt on the contemporary assumption, frequently reiterated in the Reformed synods, that Anabaptist numbers were constantly on the increase. Rather there is clear evidence that by the end of the sixteenth century the Mennonites were in retreat, both numerically and in terms of social influence.[41] Whether this was the result of the Calvinist onslaught or their own internal difficulties is hard to say. The Anabaptist movement in the Netherlands was never united, and by the mid sixteenth century even the most coherent group, the Mennonites, were split into three irreconcilable factions, the Waterlanders, Frisians, and Flemings. Dependent as they were on relatively uneducated leaders, Anabaptist churches in The Netherlands were always prone to further fissures and destructive quarrelling.[42] It is tempting to think that left to themselves they would in any case have declined into irrelevance, but for the Calvinist ministers their combination of wrong doctrine and an exemplary community life always touched an extremely sensitive nerve. For all their contempt, Calvinist ministers were forced to admit that the Mennonites did live an austere life of brotherly rectitude: a fact of which they received an occasional uncomfortable reminder when one of their own members abandoned the com-

---

for an Orthodox Church: Calvinists and Anabaptists in East Friesland, 1554–1578', *Bulletin of the John Rylands Library*, 70 (1988), 45–59. Carl Bangs, *Arminius. A study in the Dutch Reformation* (Abingdon, 1971), 166–7.

[39] Knipscheer, 'Synoden', 28.

[40] *Ondersoeckinge ende grondelijcke wederlegginge der geestdrijvische leere.* J. J. van Toorenenbergen, *Philips M. van Sint Alsegonde: godsdienstige en kerkelijke geschriften*, 3 vols. (The Hague, 1871–91), II, 1–240. Quoted in Lecler, *History of Toleration*, II, 288.

[41] Van Deursen, *Plain Lives*, 304–18.

[42] *Ibid.*, 310.

munity citing the worldliness or impurity of the Calvinist church as a reason.[43]

This was an insoluble dilemma for the Calvinist leadership, for as the privileged leaders of the public church they had to be in and of the world. But the criticism hit home. The south Holland synod of 1589 recommended that the Anabaptists should be combatted in two ways: a refutation of their writings should be reinforced by promoting in their own communities a way of life that was faithful and godly.[44] And it is tempting to argue that the ministers' attempts to urge the magistrates towards an enforcement of a more stringent public morality was in some measure stimulated by a consciousness of their own vulnerability to criticism on this score.

But here the ministers found the magistrates at their most unyielding. For all urgent polemicising about the low quality of public morals, thunderous sermons against abuse of the sabbath, and urgent synodical decrees urging closer control over licentious behaviour, the city authorities turned a determinedly deaf ear to all entreaties. There were many issues on which the more precise ministers felt very strongly: the popularity of taverns during the Sunday sermon, and the dangerous consequences of licentious dancing and theatricals, for instance, but in all cases the lay power declined to intervene.[45] Perhaps they understood better than the ministers that the delicate social consensus underpinning the church's place in the new state could not tolerate too fundamental an assault on traditional forms of popular sociability. But as ministerial opinion on such issues hardened towards the end of the sixteenth century so the danger of outspoken criticism of the lay authorities, so manifestly failing in their duty to uphold godly standards, increased.

For all that it achieved such limited success, the ministers' attacks on popular entertainment culture were still of some importance. The magistrates could hardly object to use of the pulpit to attack licentiousness, indeed they shared with the ministers a common interest in enforcing good standards of morality on their populations. But attacks on the entertainment culture of their own class, such as the theatre, brought home in a very direct way the dangers of uncontrolled clerical influence. So that when the magistrates took up the cause of well-known clerical dissidents, they were also engaging the Calvinist hierarchy on a wider front. In this context disputes over the election or deposition of a controversial minister who had fallen foul of the clerical hierarchy

---

[43] A. Th. van Deursen, *Bavianen en slijkgeuzen*, 152.
[44] J. Reitsma and S. D. van Veen (eds.), *Acta der Provinciale en Particuliere Synoden gehouden in de Noordelijke Nederlanden gedurende de jaren 1572–1620*, 8 vols. (Groningen, 1892–9), II, 348.
[45] For the ministers' campaign against popular entertainment culture see Pettegree, 'Coming to Terms with Victory', 176–9. For opposition to the theatre, Herman Roodenburg, *Onder Censuur, De kerkelijke tucht in de gereformeerde gemeente van Amsterdam, 1578–1700* (Hilversum, 1990), 321–0 336–8.

could serve a more general purpose, to remind the ministers that the magistrate retained ultimate control over the nature of the church settlement in Holland. Disputes over Church order and the toleration of religious minorities could thus become the means of articulating wider concerns about the nature of Dutch society and the respective influence of lay and clerical authority.

This can most conveniently be demonstrated by examining one or two of the more famous controversies surrounding the appointment of ministers in the principal Holland towns. Several such cases: that of Pieter de Zuttere at Rotterdam, Herbert Herbertsz at Gouda, and Caspar Coolhaes at Leiden, demonstrated that the first generation of ministers was not short of men prepared to make common cause with the magistrates against their own colleagues.[46] Caspar Coolhaes was one of those who discovered the virtues of religious toleration and the superior power of the magistrate in the context of the collapse of his own relationship with his ministerial colleagues.[47] When in 1578 the Leiden town council refused to ratify the recent elections to the consistory, Coolhaes had publicly supported their position, to the horror of his own colleagues who quickly moved to have him suspended from his post. The magistracy retaliated by dismissing Coolhaes's orthodox Calvinist colleague and a confrontation became inevitable. The resulting exchange of pamphlets produced some vigorous assertions of the magistrates' rights, none more so than Dirck Coornhert's *Justification of the Magistrates of Leiden*. As Coornhert put it, 'having been delivered from the yoke of Roman tyranny, there could be no question of putting another yoke on the community's shoulders.' The churchmen pretended to rule everything in the city. It was the duty of civil authority to maintain public authority, and to eliminate from the ministry those who were troublemakers and provoked disorder: meaning in this cased the orthodox Calvinist Cornelisz.[48]

The ministers had no sympathy for this view, but that it could even be stated so baldly explains why the question of who had final authority in the election of ministers remained so crucial. Not surprisingly, having taken diametrically opposing views on the principle of final authority over minis-

[46] On de Zuttere, H. ten Boom, *De Reformatie in Rotterdam, 1530–1585* (Amsterdam, 1987), 159–63. Christiaan Sepp, *Drie evangeliedienaren uit de tijd der Hervorming* (Leiden, 1879). On Herbertsz, Hibben, *Gouda in Revolt*, 120–9.

[47] H. C. Rogge, *Caspar Janszoon Coolhaes, de voorloper van Arminius en der Remonstranten*, 2 vols. (Amsterdam, 1856–8). Van Gelder, *Vrijheid en onvrijheid in de Republiek*, I, 245–9. Bibliography in H. C. Rogge, *Bibliotheek der Remonstrantische geschriften* (Amsterdam, 1863), 12–16. J. P. van Dooren, 'Caspar Coolhaes; het een en ander uit zijn leven voor en na de synode van Middelburg', in van Dooren (ed.), *De Nationale Synode te Middelburg* (Middelburg, 1981), 174–83.

[48] *Justificate des magistraets tot Leyden in Hollant* (1579). W. P. C. Knuttel, *Catalogus van de pamfletten-verzameling berustende in de koninklijke bibliotheek* (The Hague, 1889), I, no. 516. Lecler, *Toleration*, II, 264. B. Becker (ed.), *Bronnen tot de kennis van het leven en werken van D.V. Coornhert* (The Hague, 1928). Van Gelderen, *Political Thought*, 243–56.

terial appointments, neither ministers nor magistrates were prepared to give much ground. From the first years of the re-established church in 1572, the question of who should choose ministers in the new church was a source of protracted conflict. The early Reformed synods had merely restated the decision, taken in the Synod of Emden in 1571, that authority in such matters lay with the ministers and consistory, acting for the church community.[49] In the changed circumstances of the Holland towns this was clearly unacceptable to the lay authorities, and in 1576 the States of Holland proposed a radically different solution in their draft church order, that ministers should be chosen by the magistrates, with the other ministers acting in an advisory capacity, an inversion of their proposed relationship which the church not surprisingly emphatically rejected at the Synod of Dordrecht in 1578.[50] In 1583 the States of Holland proposed a compromise, whereby the appointment of ministers would be entrusted to a joint committee of burgomasters and church delegates. This was a system which in fact operated quite successfully in a number of towns where the magistracy was sympathetic to the church.[51] But hard-liners on both sides opposed the settlement, and the draft church order of 1583 was never adopted. The Holland towns continued to employ a wide variety of different practices for electing their ministers.

The question of ministerial appointments thus gradually came to play a central part in the wider discussions of toleration and the locus of authority within the Dutch state. By the time of the dispute surrounding Coolhaes in Leiden, the magistrates were well on the way to discovering that the defence of religious minorities within or outside the Reformed church was one way of challenging the orthodox ministers' claim to set the tone for the religious life of the new nation. The claim of freedom of conscience meant different things to a Mennonite, a Catholic, or a Reformed dissident like Coolhaes, but it was a slogan with which urban magistracy could increasingly identify, particularly when they saw that their own pretensions to be the final arbiters of religious life within their urban space was under threat. In this context religious toleration became as much a weapon as a statement of religious belief, a statement to the dominant religious confession that their role in Dutch society could go so far and no further. It is against this background that one must view the spate of Erasmus statues erected in the United Provinces at the end of the century, or the famous 'freedom of conscience' window added

[49] Rutger, *Acta*, 61–2.
[50] The various stages of this debate may be followed in the documents translated in Duke, Lewis and Pettegree, *Calvinism in Europe*, 175–89. Cf. J. C. Overvoorde, 'Advies van Burgemeesters en gerecht van Leiden aan de Staten van Holland over de Acta van de in 1578 te Dordrecht gehouden synode', *NAK*, 9 (1912), 117–49.
[51] Such as Dordrecht. John P. Elliott, 'Protestantisation in the Northern Netherlands, A Case Study: The Classis of Dordrecht, 1572–1640' (Columbia University PhD thesis, 1990), 196.

to Gouda's St Jankerk in 1598.[52] Given the Reformed aversion to such idolatrous decoration this was a particularly effective demonstration of the shifting balance of power in the towns.

But if the Gouda magistrates congratulated themselves on this subtle pictorial one-upmanship, they celebrated too soon. Even as the glaziers of Gouda
were at their work, a conflict was being prepared which would test most
severely the new state's capacity to deal with a major religious crisis within
the framework of divided responsibilities that had emerged in the years since
1572. This is not the place for a detailed examination of the Arminian crisis
of 1610–19, except to remark that it represents to a large extent the apotheosis
of both the strands of debate that have been examined thus far: the extent to
which conscientious scruples could be accommodated within a right religious
settlement, and the place of the state power as arbitrator between conflicting
religious groups.[53] Not surprisingly, it was again the dissident minority who
appealed to the state for protection. When in 1609 Arminius and Gomarus
both appeared before the States of Holland, Uyttenbogaert, leading spokesman of the Arminian side, had already proclaimed that the magistrate's rights
were supreme in religious matters. In his *Treatise of the function and authority of a superior Christian magistrate* he set out the developing Arminian
view with great clarity. 'Doubt not', he wrote to the States of Holland,

> that your authority comes from God, who has established you like gods over your
> people. Watch carefully over the teaching given to your subjects. Do not suffer idle
> disputes in the pulpit; do not allow precious hours to be wasted on lessons which are
> useless to the Christian way of life. Do not suffer your subjects to be disturbed,
> divided and torn apart by men that thrive on discord.[54]

It is interesting to compare these high-minded sentiments, and the long
tradition of appeals to toleration among those who elevated the authority of
the magistrates, with the actual conduct of urban regimes in the towns in
which the Remonstrants obtained an ascendancy. What is most striking, in
the increasingly polarised politics of the years before 1618, is the ruthlessness
with which the Remonstrant regimes drove home their advantage. In 1609
Oldenbarnevelt masterminded a blatantly irregular purge of the Alkmaar
vroedschap to remove hard-line Calvinists from the city council and restore
a Remonstrant assembly: in the following year troops were employed to

---

[52] See note 3 above. C. A. van Swigchem, *'Een goed regiment.' Het burgelijke element in het
vroege reformierte kerkinterieur* (The Hague, 1988), 27.

[53] Bangs, *Arminius*; Van Deursen, *Bavianen en Slijkgeuzen*, 227 ff. An excellent narrative survey
of the events leading to the crisis of 1618–19 can be found in Jonathan Israel, *The Dutch
Republic. Its Rise, Greatness and Fall, 1477–1806* (Oxford, 1995).

[54] Traectaet van't Ampt ende authoriteyt einer hooger christeliijcker overheydt in kerkelijke
saecken (The Hague, 1610). Knuttel, *Pamfletten*, nos. 1767–8. Quoted Lecler, *Toleration*, II,
303.

achieve the same end in Utrecht. From 1614, after the imposition of the decree of the States of Holland forbidding the pastors to treat controversial subjects from the pulpit, Counter-Remonstrant ministers could justly fear that this would be used to deprive them of their livelihoods; and indeed, deprivations began before the end of the year. In the years of their ascendancy the advocates of toleration pursued their goals with a single-minded ruthlessness which certainly deserves to be as well known as the high-sounding but partisan writings of Hugo Grotius. By 1616–17 the church was hopelessly split, with large numbers of people now demonstrating their opposition to the Remonstrant ascendancy by walking out of town each Sunday to attend Counter-Remonstrant churches in the countryside.

It would certainly do no justice to the complexities of this conflict to suggest that the failure of the Holland resolution of 1614, with its false, indeed illusory hope of reconciliation, made the downfall of Oldenbarnevelt inevitable. The complex political and economic crisis also played its part in finally inducing Maurice of Nassau to throw his weight behind the orthodox party, and mastermind the destruction of his great adversary.[55] But however affecting the picture of the old statesman going to his death may have been, it would be a gross distortion to see Oldenbarnevelt as a martyr for a liberal world view. In the last resort the Advocate paid the price for making toleration the party weapon of too narrow a faction among Holland's political and ecclesiastical elite.

The reversal of 1618–19 was not to prove decisive. The crisis of Arminianism settled the question that the Dutch Reformed would be permitted to set the limits of acceptable dissent within their own church, and that was a victory with which they would have to be content. On other questions which had exercised them in disputes of the first generation, control over schools and poor relief, control of access to their services, the appointment of ministers, there was to be no fundamental readjustment. Here the state had effectively already made good its claim to play a part, alongside the dominant confession, in the regulation of these important aspects of community life. The next thirty years of comparative theological calm allowed those so inclined time to rebuild the battered myth of religious toleration. A gradual slackening of the military conflict brought with it a loosening of pressures on other faiths, and the passing of years must also have accommodated the ministers of the Reformed church to their curious half ascendancy. Yet, this should not disguise the fact that the peculiar religious stand-off that so impressed Sir William Temple in 1673 was none of the Reformed church's making, and certainly none of their desiring.

[55] J. van Tex, *Oldenbarnevelt*, 2 vols. (Cambridge, 1973). There is a sympathetic treatment of Maurice in both Herbert Rowen, *The Princes of Orange* (Cambridge, 1988), 32–51, and Israel, *The Dutch Republic*.

All of these events do suggest some general, and generally sobering reflections about the nature of toleration in the sixteenth and seventeenth centuries. Even in a society so famously open-minded as the Dutch Republic, the argument for toleration served particular strategic ends. Often the objectives of those calling for toleration were no more high-minded than those who argued, rationally in the context of the early modern state, that religious solidarity was the essential glue of a godly society. The occasional visionary thinker such as Dirck Coornhert[56] should not disguise the fact that in the main, toleration in this period was only ever likely to be the party cry of the disappointed, the dispossessed, or the seriously confused. The development of a modern liberal society has taught us to admire tolerance above almost any other principle of social interaction. But in the early modern period it was only ever a loser's creed; and one which, if the Calvinist church leaders of the Dutch Republic were anything to go by, could easily be abandoned when yesterday's persecuted minority became the day's dominant elite.

[56] Ivo Schöffer, *Dirck Volckertszoon Coornhert* (Zutphen, 1989).

12 Archbishop Cranmer: concord and tolerance in a changing Church

Diarmaid MacCulloch

Let us begin by defining terms. Particularly helpful are recent discussions of toleration by Mario Turchetti and Malcolm Smith, which although directed towards the religious divisions of sixteenth-century France, have a wider application.[1] From Turchetti, we can draw the distinction between concord and tolerance: that is, refusal of diversity versus acceptance of diversity. With the help of friendly criticism of Turchetti's position made by Smith, we can refine this distinction still further. There are two sorts of concord or refusal of diversity: one can enforce concord and overcome diversity by coercion, prohibition and ultimately violence, or one can seek concord by discussion and persuasion, the spinning of formulae and the cultivation of generous vagueness in definition.[2] Naturally, it is possible to slide from one to the other: a famous example, one indeed much quoted in the Reformation, would be Augustine of Hippo's change of stance on the Donatists to 'compel them to come in', once conferences had failed. More happily, on occasion, coercion can move to discussion in the search for true concord.

Moving on from concord to tolerance: as Turchetti points out, tolerance implies the recognition of something which is forbidden and which remains forbidden. It involves concessions by an authority which remains in a superior position, in a society which has not fundamentally adjusted its structures or the ideologies which legitimises them, even though it is putting up for the time being with an alternative set of ideas. There is a stage beyond this tolerance: religious freedom – what Smith calls 'the right of individuals and of groups to hold any belief and express that belief publicly', or what Bob Scribner in chapter 3 above calls 'indifference to difference'.[3] So we can consider a four-fold range of possibilities in any society which takes

---

[1] M. Turchetti, 'Religious Concord and Political Tolerance in 16th and 17th Century France', *Sixteenth Century Journal*, 22 (1991), 15–26; M. C. Smith, 'Early French Advocates of Religious Freedom', *Sixteenth Century Journal*, 25 (1994), 29–51.

[2] Here I am moving on from the point made by Smith, 'Early French Advocates', 35 n. 13, to accept Turchetti's assumption that both these forms represent varieties of concord.

[3] *Ibid.*, 29.

religious practice seriously: concord by coercion, concord by discussion, tolerance and religious freedom.

How does this set of definitions apply to Thomas Cranmer, Primate of All England for twenty-three years from 1533? Straight away we can narrow down our discussion by removing the last of our four-fold categories from consideration. Cranmer had no interest in religious freedom. His mind was alert and outstandingly well-furnished, on the basis of what was probably the best scholarly library in the England of his day, but he was rarely an original thinker; it would have taken bold original thought in early Tudor England to conceive of publicly expressed freedom of belief. One original English mind, Thomas More, had indeed made the toleration of 'varied and manifold forms of worship' one of the founding principles of the commonwealth of Utopia. Yet Utopia was precisely that – nowhere – and More's persecuting practice while he held political power made it clear that he thought that the best place for religious freedom was nowhere.[4] Small wonder that a cautious, well-read humanist like Thomas Cranmer had no time for the idea. The most generous reflection which he made on the subject came in his 1549 adaptation of a medieval prayer for the conversion of non-Christians, derived from the Sarum Rite for use on Good Friday. Here he asked God to 'have mercy upon all Jews, Turks, infidels and heretics, and take from them all ignorance, hardness of heart and contempt of thy word'. His description was marginally more courteous than Sarum's '*pro heretics ... et pro perfidis iudeis ... et pro paganis*', but in the end the sentiment was the same.[5]

The aim of this chapter, therefore, will be to consider the place in Cranmer's thought and practice of three options for the English Church: concord by coercion, concord by discussion, and tolerance. However, by way of preliminary definition, we still need to clarify Cranmer's relationship first to the Reformations of Henry VIII, Edward VI and Mary I, and second, to the religious diversity which these Reformations faced. Cranmer was not the inspired, charismatic leader of a Reformation from below, as Luther was at first, as Müntzer was for a moment, and as John Knox remained; he was not even the inspired, charismatic leader of a Reformation from above, as Zwingli and Calvin discovered that they were. He was an agent, not an initiator, and that is how he wished it to be. Cranmer had a profound belief in the supposedly ancient truth which Henry VIII and Thomas Cromwell had discovered in the 1530s: the best form of government in the Church was through the sole authority of the anointed godly prince. From about 1531 until literally the last morning of his life, this remained Cranmer's guiding principle, even

---

[4] On this aspect of More's thought, see G. R. Elton, 'Persecution and Toleration in the English Reformation', in W. J. Sheils (ed.), *Persecution and Toleration* (Oxford, 1984), 164–71.

[5] F. E. Brightman, *The English Rite*, 2 vols. (London, 1915), 1, 372.

if on occasion he could feel deeply frustrated that God's anointed had not yet grasped the point of what God wanted.[6]

Cranmer took this belief to a remarkable extreme. In 1540, as a member of one of Henry VIII's interminable series of doctrinal committees, the archbishop answered a set of questions about the sacraments and the nature of the Church. One of these questions was 'whether the apostles lacking a higher power, as in both having a Christian king among them, made bishops by that necessity, or by authority given them by God?'[7] In the course of a lengthy answer, Cranmer pointed out that the apostles of the first century AD had lacked 'remedy then for the correction of vice, or appointing of ministers' and had to make do with 'the consent of christian multitude among themselves'. There is an unmistakable distaste in his use of the word 'multitude'; Cranmer would have sympathised with the dictum attributed to the Rev. Dr Jabez Bunting, a great autocrat of nineteenth-century Wesleyanism, that Methodism was 'as opposed to democracy as it is to sin'.[8] Far from holding any doctrine of apostolic succession, Cranmer viewed the first Christians as casting round to create makeshift structures of authority: 'they were constrained of necessity to take such curates and priests as either they knew themselves to be meet thereunto, or else as were commended unto them by other that were so replete with the Spirit of God . . . that they ought even of very conscience to give credit unto them'.

This view of church history is a consequence of a view of royal supremacy as the natural condition of the Church. It puts an interesting question-mark against a common assumption among humanist reformers: that the apostolic church of the first generation should be the ultimate court of appeal in all disputes about the nature of the contemporary Church. In this respect at least, Cranmer did show a certain originality among leaders of the Reformation: in his eyes, the apostolic church was an imperfect, incomplete model for the Church of the sixteenth century. One can express this in terms of one variant on the common Protestant Reformation sport of defining the marks of the true Church. If one takes three marks – first, true preaching of the Gospel, second, right administration of the sacraments, and third, discipline – then for Cranmer, the early Church was only normative for the first two: preaching

[6] On the dating of Cranmer's adoption of belief in the Royal Supremacy, see D. MacCulloch, *Thomas Cranmer: A Life* (New Haven and London, 1996), chs. 2–3. On his battles with Henry VIII over justification by faith alone, *ibid.*, chs. 6, 8.

[7] The questions and answers are to be found in Lambeth Palace MS 1108, ff. 69–141; Public Record Office, London (hereafter PRO), SP 1/160 ff. 2–5, PRO, SP 6/6/9, ff. 77–81; British Library (hereafter BL) MS Cotton Cleopatra E V ff. 38, 53, 113 (J. S. Brewer, J. Gairdner and R. H. Brodie (eds.), *Letters and Papers, Foreign and Domestic, of the Reign of Henry VIII*, 21 vols. in 33 parts (1862–1910) and revision of vol. 1, and 2 part addenda, by Brodie, 1920–32, 15 no. 826). Cranmer's replies are conveniently presented in J. E. Cox (ed.), *Works of Archbishop Cranmer*, 2 vols. (1846), 2, 115–17.

[8] Quoted by M. Brock, *The Great Reform Act* (London, 1973), 40.

and the sacraments, not for discipline. This view was liable to create a gulf between Cranmer and those reformers, both English and Continental, who took apostolicity as their criterion for discipline as well. From the early 1530s, the archbishop was familiar with the publications of Martin Bucer, who became his admiring correspondent, and he also quickly bought the first edition of Calvin's *Institutes* of 1536. Already Bucer and Calvin were wrestling with notions about church polity which would lead to Bucer's attempts to restructure the Church at Strassburg on scriptural lines; later Calvin would make an even more thorough-going claim that the Church of the New Testament was a clear and unequivocal guide to the perfect form of any Church of Christ.

Cranmer could not and would not go down the same path. What probably weighed more with Cranmer than the developing theories of these eminently respectable figures, was his wish to defend the true Church of which Henry was Supreme Head against a double threat: papistry and evangelical radicalism of many varieties. Between 1531 and 1533, Cranmer abandoned what had been a very conventional late medieval piety, not simply for a new belief in the royal supremacy, but also for a fairly complete identification with Lutheran theology.[9] During the course of the 1540s, he would drastically modify his Lutheranism, particularly under Bucer's influence, but this would not affect his sense of standing between two extremes which were both enemies of truth.

Perhaps at an even faster pace than Henry VIII, after 1531 Cranmer came to have a deep hatred for the papacy. By early 1536, he was publicly preaching that the Pope was Antichrist: a remarkable statement for a cautious, gentle theologian who was also Primate of All England. The only prominent English commentator previously to say the same thing was William Tyndale, and he was then lying in a Low Countries gaol awaiting death, with the connivance of Henry VIII.[10] At the other extreme from papistry was the multiform threat of Continental Anabaptism, which first seems to have caused the English authorities alarm in 1534–5. From the start, Cranmer was involved in the suppression of the Anabaptists.[11] We can point to his persistent hatred for

---

[9] For further discussion of Cranmer's changing theology, see D. MacCulloch, 'Two Dons in Politics: Thomas Cranmer and Stephen Gardiner, 1503–1533', *Historical Journal*, 37 (1994), 1–22, MacCulloch, *Cranmer*, and A. Null, 'Justification and Penance in the Theology of Thomas Cranmer' (PhD, University of Cambridge, 1994).

[10] W. D. Hamilton (ed.), *A Chronicle of England . . . by Charles Wriothesley, Windsor Herald*, 2 vols. (1875, 1877), 1, 33–4, and G. E. Corrie (ed.), *Sermons by Hugh Latimer . . .* (1844), 49. Cf. H. Walter (ed.), *An Answer to Sir Thomas More's Dialogue, the Supper of the Lord . . . and William Tracy's Testament expounded. By William Tyndale . . .* (1850), 102–10 (1530) and H. Walter (ed.), *Expositions and Notes on sundry portions of the Holy Scriptures together with the Practice of Prelates. By William Tyndale . . .* (1849), 183 (1532). For further comment on this sermon, MacCulloch, *Cranmer*, ch. 5.

[11] *Letters and Papers*, 8, no. 846; this refers to a 'Dr. Chramuel', but I think it likely that the Archbishop rather than Cromwell is intended, particularly since the Vice-gerency was not

the Anabaptists and other radical reformers, an echo of which we have heard in his fastidious choice of the word 'multitude'.

Cranmer and his circle had a useful rhetorical device for linking the two extremes: they referred to both of them as 'sects'. Papistry and the radicals had 'divided, rent and torn in pieces the quiet unity and friendly concord of the holy religion', as Cranmer's chaplain Thomas Becon informed God in 1550.[12] The various orders of monks and friars which were the chief source of the worst features of papistry could be listed in their diversity alongside the diversity of the radicals. Thomas Becon, for example, produced a splendid list of sects ten lines long, which begins with St Benedict and his rule and ends with sacramentaries and libertines – a combination which would not have pleased either end of this spectrum.[13] Cranmer's old friend Hugh Latimer preaching two years later in 1552, picked up another supposed common feature of the monastic orders and the Anabaptists: neither of them could 'abide the company of men' and so they forgot the 'commandment of love and charity' by quitting normal society.[14] Very precisely, then, papists and evangelical radicals broke concord in the Church.

If we return to Cranmer's distinctive historical relativism about the early Church, we may now appreciate how it was encouraged by his wish to defend the Church against the two-fold sectarian threat. With this aim in mind, he would be deaf to the attractions of Bucer's and Calvin's developing ecclesiology and their emphasis on recovering the structural forms of the apostolic church. The radicals' constant cry was for a return to the Church of the apostles; they perceived (in fact, perfectly correctly) that the apostolic church had been ambiguous in its attitude to civil government, and they were frankly hostile to what the Emperor Constantine the Great had down to Western Christianity. At the same time, against the other flank, Cranmer wanted to repudiate the false claims to authority by the traditional Church, with its constant defence of error by reference to 'unwritten verities', over against the authority of Scripture.

The neat solution was to kill these two birds with one stone, by denying any independent authority or identity at all to the Church, and this is what Cranmer did in his responses to the questions of 1540. Once this had been done, one was left with the authority of the Christian prince, who could be

---

fully developed at this stage. Cf. I. B. Horst, *The Radical Brethren: Anabaptism and the English Reformation to 1558* (Nieuwkoop, 1972), 59; P. L. Hughes and J. F. Larkin (eds.), *Tudor Royal Proclamations*, vols. 1, 2 (New Haven, 1964, 1969), 1, no. 155; MacCulloch, *Cranmer*, ch. 5.

[12] J. Ayre (ed.), *The Works of Thomas Becon*, 3 vols. (1843–4), 3, 41.

[13] *Becon*, 3, 40–1. For another list of Becon's, including simply 'papists' alongside varieties of radicalism, see *ibid.*, 401.

[14] G. E. Corrie (ed.), *Sermons and Remains of Hugh Latimer* (1845), 197. Cranmer himself in the Homilies, possibly assisted by Becon, referred to the religious Orders as 'sects', without making the comparison with radicals: R. B. Bond (ed.), *Certain Sermons or Homilies (1547) and A Homily against Disobedience and Wilful Rebellion (1570)* (Toronto, 1987), 110–12.

persuaded and educated in the right use of Holy Scripture in order to govern his kingdom correctly. Now it was no doubt apparent to Cranmer even in 1540 that there might be theoretical drawbacks to this scheme; he had just witnessed with deep distress Henry VIII's wrong turn in backing the passage of the Act of Six Articles in 1539, including the personal trauma of having to send off his clandestine wife Margaret to refuge in Germany. The draw-backs of the Supremacy would become even more painfully apparent with Mary's accession in 1553. It is likely, too, that the archbishop was later influenced by Martin Bucer's arrival in England in the reign of Edward VI, and by the face-to-face conversations which the two men were then able to have about the nature of the Church; this would give the archbishop cause to modify the stark version of Erastian belief which he had presented for the boisterous approval of Henry VIII at the beginning of the 1540s. Yet his basic trust in the royal supremacy in the Church remained.

The royal supremacy in England under all three sovereigns, Henry, Edward and Mary, involved concord by coercion, and there was little that Cranmer could do to stop this, even if he had wanted to. Once more, remember that he was an agent, not an initiator. Very precisely, he was an adviser: chaplain to Henry VIII, godfather to Edward VI. Henry VIII executed religious dissi-dents from both ends of the spectrum, famously illustrating the nature of his murderous ecumenism on 30 July 1540, when he killed three papalists and three evangelicals, the papalists for treason and the evangelicals for heresy. These executions revealed both the similarities and differences between the outlooks of the king and his archbishop. What they had in common was a passionately held view of the English Church as possessing a middle ground of truth which needed to be defended from two extremes of error, and they both frequently articulated this view, often in the same language.

However, Cranmer and Henry VIII never came to agreement on what made up the content of this middle ground; both men constructed their own package of truth, in the case of Henry a weird jackdaw's nest containing a jumble of theological ideas from traditionalist and evangelical sources.[15] Cranmer would never have considered Barnes, Garrett and Jerome, the evangelicals who died in 1540, as heretics; they were in fact his colleagues, representatives of the evangelical mainstream, Robert Barnes in particular being the most self-conscious Lutheran among leading English clergy. Their deaths came at a moment of unusual political mayhem and danger for the archbishop, who with a small change in the political equation at that moment might have shared their fate. To criticise Cranmer for standing aside while Barnes,

---

[15] For discussion of Henry's views and his rhetoric of the middle way, see D. MacCulloch, 'Henry VIII and the English Reformation', in D. MacCulloch (ed.), *The Reign of Henry VIII*, (Basingstoke, 1995), ch. 7.

Jerome and Garrett died is to be unrealistic about the brutal business of politics.

Cranmer's uneasy relationship to other Henrician executions has often been criticized. In particular, his attitude to the death of his friends and patrons Queen Anne Boleyn and Thomas Cromwell has been the source of much ill-directed sarcasm, but this is not an issue of religious toleration, and should not concern us here.[16] More relevant is to note that there were two executions of apparently mainstream evangelicals on heresy charges during the 1530s in which he was directly involved. One was the death of John Frith in 1533, the other, the death of John Lambert in 1538. Both died primarily because of the views which they had expressed on the eucharistic presence, views which were similar to those which Cranmer came to hold after 1546–7. This irony was already gleefully exploited at Cranmer's trial for heresy in 1555, and we need to consider these two cases carefully.[17]

Firstly, the case of John Frith. In his first few months as archbishop, Cranmer inherited this from his predecessor. Something would have to be done about Frith, who had already been arrested in 1532 on returning to England from work with William Tyndale in the Low Countries; in an orgy of writing while in prison in the Tower of London, he had spelled out his spiritualising views on the Eucharist, against Tyndale's explicit advice.[18] In June 1533 he was brought from the Tower first to Lambeth and then to Cranmer's Surrey palace at Croydon for several examinations about his 'sacramentarian' theology by a high-powered commission of bishops and aristocrats, before his final sentence of condemnation as a heretic in the consistory court of London. Cranmer reported on the proceedings to his friend and successor as Ambassador to the Emperor Nicholas Hawkins; he was quite clear that Frith was in serious error on the Eucharist:

whose opinion was so notably erroneous, that we could not dispatch him . . . His said opinion is of such nature, that he thought it not necessary to be believed as an article of our faith, that there is the very corporal presence of Christ within the host and sacrament of the altar, and holdeth of this point most after the opinion of Oecolampadius. And surely I myself sent for him three or four times to persuade him to leave that his imagination; but for all that we could do therein, he would not apply to any counsel.[19]

Martin Luther would have said no less. Cranmer already knew exactly what he was talking about when discussing variants on Swiss theology, and he was evidently prepared to spend a good deal of time to argue Frith out

[16] I consider these incidents in MacCulloch, *Cranmer*, chs. 5, 7.
[17] Cox (ed.), *Works of Cranmer*, 2, 218.
[18] G. Townshend and S. R. Cattley (eds.), *The Acts and Monuments of John Foxe*, 8 vols. (1837–41), 5, 133.
[19] BL MS Harley 6148 f. 25r; Cox (ed.), *Works of Cranmer*, 246 (17 June 1533).

of his views; but when he failed, the law must proceed. He saw no problem in moving from the concord of persuasion to the concord of coercion, and as he told Hawkins without especial drama, Frith now 'looketh every day to go unto the fire'. However, one notes that the archbishop had given the Basle Reformer Oecolampadius his latinised academic surname, so he recognized his status as an evangelical fellow-scholar. Most hostile Catholic English commentators referred to Oecolampadius (if they knew of him at all) only by his original German surname, Hussgen. It may also be significant that in this account written to an intimate friend, Cranmer did not use the word 'heretic' about Frith, a word which by contrast he habitually used about traditionalists of whom he particularly disapproved. Luther and Lutherans, having been so often called heretics themselves, tended to avoid this term as being tainted, and Cranmer after his experience of Lutheran Germany may have felt the same way.[20]

Frith was burned on 4 July 1533. His death was not of Cranmer's making; the situation was one which he had inherited, and he can hardly be blamed for not knowing in 1533 that he would change his mind on the question of the Eucharist thirteen years later. One also has to consider the politics of the Frith case against the general political background in the Church. It occurred in the course of a long-standing row about the preaching of Cranmer's close associate Hugh Latimer, which by summer 1533 was being gradually resolved in Latimer's favour. It would be a gift to Latimer's enemies if someone like Frith who could be associated with Latimer's evangelical circle, and who had gone so grievously off the rails in eucharistic theology, was seen to be let off the hook. As the breach with Rome widened, it was important to be firm against such 'sacramentaries' as Frith in order that Henry's regime did not lose the loyalty of conservative leaders like Bishop Stokesley of London, who continued to detest Latimer to the extent of forbidding him to preach in his diocese during autumn 1533.[21]

Nevertheless, the Frith affair is not a happy story, particularly since Frith's reputation remained high among evangelicals, and his writings and Catholic refutations of them continued to be printed right into the reign of Edward VI. John Foxe clearly found the whole business embarrassing; he first minimised Cranmer's role and later seized gratefully on a circumstantial account of one of Cranmer's household gentlemen vainly giving Frith the chance to escape in the woods around Brixton while they escorted him to Cranmer's palace at Croydon. However, honesty compelled Foxe to narrate the story in a way

---

[20] L. W. Levy, *Treason against God: A History of the Offense of Blasphemy* (New York, 1981), 124–30.

[21] On the Latimer affair at Bristol, see M. C. Skeeters, *Community and Clergy: Bristol and the Reformation c. 1530–c. 1570* (Oxford, 1993), 38–46, and discussion in MacCulloch, *Cranmer*, ch. 4. On Stokesley's prohibition, *Foxe*, 7, 459; appendix VII.

which made it clear that Cranmer was not involved in this abortive act of mercy to Frith. Foxe also tried to make the best of a bad job by suggesting that much later, in Cranmer's published *Answer* to Stephen Gardiner of 1551, Frith was the chief source of ammunition for the archbishop's assault on wily Winchester's eucharistic theology: 'I doubt much whether the archbishop ever gave any more credit unto any author of that doctrine, than unto this aforesaid Frith', he said.[22] It may be so, and in terms of common outlook, Cranmer's eucharistic theology did eventually settle down to be much like Frith's, but unless Foxe had information otherwise lost to us, Cranmer kept his revised opinion of Frith to himself.

The disaster which befell John Lambert in 1538 also well illustrates the English evangelical establishment's continuing hard line on the corporeal presence of Christ in the Eucharist. What is evident from the embarrassed account in Foxe's narrative on Lambert is that it was the evangelicals who caused his downfall. Lambert began by arguing about the Eucharist with John Taylor (who would become bishop of Lincoln under Edward VI); Taylor called on Robert Barnes to back him up on confuting Lambert, and Barnes in turn decided that Cranmer ought to be brought in; after the Archbishop had examined him, Lambert was confined in Lambeth Palace. Lambert is then said to have appealed to the king: a highly unwise move in autumn 1538, because Henry was then taking one of his occasional fitful but intense bursts of interest in his religious policy. The king decided to single out Lambert for destruction, by summoning a special heresy tribunal to Westminster, over which he would preside in person as Supreme Head of the Church.[23]

Since all the leading bishops were present at the tribunal, it was only natural that the king should ask Cranmer to take up the questioning when he himself had finished. Cranmer concentrated on putting arguments that the body of Christ could be in two places at once, on the analogy of Christ's appearance to Paul on the road to Damascus, an approach which would have drawn the approval of Martin Luther. There is one aspect of the subsequent discussions which is surely significant: their avoidance of the technical language of transubstantiation. If Foxe's summary of the proceedings is to be trusted, none of the first four interrogators, Henry, Cranmer, bishops Gardiner and Tunstall, used the word 'substance' in their arguments against him; it was only the ultra-conservative Bishop Stokesley, speaking fifth, who is recorded as bringing in this term and using it in a scholastic sense. Nor, perhaps even more significantly, had the word 'substance' appeared in the otherwise stridently conservative language about the sacrament of the altar in the king's proclamation against heresy issued that day; this was all the

[22] *Foxe*, 5, 11; 8, 697–9; 5, 9.
[23] See Foxe's account of these events, *Foxe*, 5, 227–36; all details are taken from there unless otherwise stated.

more remarkable because Lambert himself had used the scholastic language of substance fairly freely in previous arguments and in a eucharistic treatise which he had addressed to king from prison at Lambeth. At least one conservative spectator referred to the word 'substance' in his summary description of the trial.[24]

The primary eucharistic argument in the trial itself, therefore, could be regarded as being about presence and not about the scholastic definition of the eucharistic miracle as transubstantiation. Lambert's case was not like that of Adam Damplip of Calais earlier that same year: Cranmer had successfully defended Damplip although he denied transubstantiation, because he still upheld the 'truth' in the eucharistic presence.[25] The analogy for Lambert was rather the examination of John Frith in 1533; Lambert was going to die for his error in denying the truth of the presence, and that must have been consolation for Cranmer as the King pronounced sentence. More straightforwardly, it may be that John Foxe's account has suppressed other more unpalatable opinions of Lambert's which put him squarely in the radical camp, and which any evangelical would regard with horror: the chronicler Charles Wriothesley records Lambert facing charges of denying infant baptism, and of affirming that Christ took no human flesh of the Virgin Mary.

In the cases of both Frith and Lambert, then, Cranmer was being true to himself. A man should not be condemned for changing his mind at a later date. Indeed, when in 1546 there are signs that he had indeed begun to change his mind on the nature of eucharistic presence, he kept severely away from the persecutions of sacramentarian evangelicals which then took place, and which in fact was intended to endanger himself.[26] Nevertheless, one must admit that in the cases which we have just examined, we have had to tread carefully in order to guide Cranmer away from charges of hypocrisy and cowardice. Cranmer's record in relation to his conservative opponents is more straightforward.

The archbishop exhibited a remarkable forbearance towards intransigent Catholics; he hated the sin but loved the sinner. In fact, he was frequently criticised by his friends for doing so; no less a person than Henry VIII lost his temper with Cranmer when he asked a favour for a Kentish gentleman who had just been one of the ringleaders in a conservative plot to destroy the archbishop and all his evangelical associates.[27] His attitude is well illustrated by the case of two monks who were indeed executed for treason in

---

[24] John Husee said that Lambert denied the 'corporal substance' of the presence at his trial; that is not the same as addressing the question of transubstantiation. M. St. C. Byrne, *The Lisle Letters*, 6 vols. (Chicago, 1980), 5, no. 1273 (*Letters and Papers*, 13, ii, no. 854).

[25] PRO, SP 1/135 ff. 86–7 (*Letters and Papers*, 13, ii, no. 97).

[26] See MacCulloch, *Cranmer*, ch. 9.

[27] M. Parker, *De Antiquitate Britannicae Ecclesiae* . . . (1572), 396; this was after the so-called Prebendaries' Plot of 1543, on which see MacCulloch, *Cranmer*, ch. 8.

1535 for denying the royal supremacy; the Carthusian prior of Axholme and the Bridgettine monk of Syon Richard Reynolds. Even after their condemnation, Cranmer felt that they should not die for their initial resistance to instruction; he had a particular admiration for the scholarship and therefore for the possible convertibility of his old Cambridge acquaintance Reynolds. He pleaded that the two should be spared, to encourage 'the conversion of the fautors hereof' (i.e. papalists), and also so 'that their consciences may be clearly averted from the same by communication of sincere doctrine'; he offered to undertake the task of persuasion himself.[28]

There was only one exception to this general advocacy of concord by persuasion, though admittedly it is a very considerable exception: Cranmer bitterly hated the Observant Franciscans, and he was not merely a passive conniver at their destruction by Henry VIII. He played a major part in the horrible death of Friar John Forest, who was roasted alive in chains in 1538, and he personally hounded Friar Hugh Payne into a gaol where he died of illness in 1539; Cranmer recorded Payne's death with what can only be termed righteous relish.[29] This was hardly surprising. The Observants were the most effective and respected exponents of what the archbishop regarded as devilish error, not simply on questions of systematic theology, but in their opposition to his cherished royal supremacy. To adapt his phrase about a different aspect of Romish doctrine, they were 'the roots of the weeds'.[30]

Otherwise, those of a more coercive bent than Cranmer were bewildered by his mildness towards his enemies, as was recorded by his long-term servant and admirer Ralph Morice. Morice's elder brother William, a fervently evangelical courtier, tackled the archbishop because 'he always bare a good face and countenance unto the papistes, and wolde both in worde and dede do very moche for theym, pardonyng their offences ... encoraging therby the papistes, and also therby ... discoraging the protestants'. However William Morice also realised that this was 'not to be don but apon some purpose': it was a strategy, not simply a temperamental inclination to woolly liberalism. Cranmer explained his rationale at length, in relation both to traditionalists and to evangelicals. Let us consider what he had to say about the first category:[31]

What will ye have a man do to hym that ys not yet come to the knowledge of the trueth of the gospell, nor peradventure as yet callid, and whose vocation ys to me uncerteyne? Shall we perhaps, in his jorney comyng towards us, by severities and

[28] PRO, SP 1/92 f. 120; Cox (ed.), *Works of Cranmer*, 2, 303 (*Letters and Papers*, 8, no. 616).

[29] PRO, SP 1/143 ff. 30–1; Cox (ed.), *Works of Cranmer*, 2, 361 (redated to 1539 by *Letters and Papers*, 14, i, no. 244). On Forest and Payne, see MacCulloch, *Cranmer*, respectively chs. 6 and 5, and for comment on other Observants, *ibid.*, ch. 4.

[30] Cox (ed.), *Works of Cranmer*, 1, 6.

[31] The text is from J. G. Nichols (ed.), *Narratives of the Reformation* (1859), 246–7.

cruell behaviour overthrowe hym, and as it were in his viage stoppe hym? I take not this the way to alleure men to enbrace the doctrine of the gospell. And if it be a true rule of our Saviour Christe to do good for evill, than lett suche as are not yet come to favour our religion, lerne to folowe the doctrine of the gospell by our example in using them frendlie and charitablie.

The terms in which Cranmer discussed this problem reveals what is also apparent from recent research into his private notebooks: he was a convinced predestinarian.[32] For him, unenlightened conservatives still enmired among papist sects might well be part of the elect, who were simply awaiting the call of God in faithful preaching of the word: the only exception to this general principle would be the obviously incorrigible agents of Satan like the sect of Franciscan Observants. This being so, the imposition of concord by coercion could actually be an obstacle to the pilgrimage of the elect towards their consciousness of election. Let us turn now to Cranmer's opinion of radical evangelicals:

On thother side, such as have tasted of syncere religion, and as it were taken holde of the gospell, and seme in wourdes to maynteyne the true doctrine thereof, and than by the evill example of thair lyves moste pernitiously become stombeling blockes unto suche as are weake, and not attall as yet enterid into this voiage, what wolde you have me do with them? beare with them and wyncke at their faultes, and so willinglie suffer the gospell (by thair outeragious doinges) to be troden under our feete? neglecting herwith an other notable saying of our Saviour oute of our memorie, whiche saieth, 'The servante knowing his Lorde and Master's pleasure and comandement, yf he regardith not the same, is (as a man might say, of all other) wourthie of many plagues'.

Here, once again, the problem was election, but now an added dimension was justification. Justification, as Luther and Cranmer understood it, was a once-for-all act of God, but that was not to say that the elect could not temporarily stumble and fall away in this life from the subsequent process of sanctification. They needed sharp correction for this reason alone, for their own spiritual health; once justified, they were servants who knew their master's commands, and were therefore particularly worthy of punishment when they disobeyed, as Cranmer's quotation from Luke 12.47 made clear. Moreover, by the bad example of their sin, the elect could hinder the elect among the traditionalists who were making their painful journey towards consciousness of the truth. Committed evangelicals therefore bore a double responsibility in their errors: a much heavier responsiblity than traditionalists.

With this clarification of Cranmer's position in mind, it is interesting to note how it was mirrored in official policy in the reign of Edward VI. To begin with, no Catholic was executed solely for his or her belief by Edward's governments; indeed, even among the political executions, far more con-

---

[32] On this, see Null, 'Cranmer's doctrine of repentance'.

vinced evangelicals than Catholics were put to death. Even more to the point, there were two burnings at the stake for heresy of radicals or Anabaptists who had proclaimed unitarian views on christology. These and other Edwardian trials of Anabaptists took place in spite of the government's ostentatious repeal of all previous heresy legislation; the use of coercion reflected acute alarm at the rapid growth of radicalism in south-east England after Henry VIII's death.[33] There was little controversy about the principle of what happened. The blueprint for the reform of England written by Cranmer's friend Martin Bucer just before his death, *De Regno Christi*, defended the death penalty for heretics, and it was also proposed in the abortive reform of English canon law in 1553, the so-called *Reformatio Legum*.[34]

One of those who died was a long-standing spokeswoman of English radicals, Joan Bocher (1550), and the other was a Fleming, George van Parris (1551). For the moment we can postpone discussion of van Parris's case. Joan had been a noisy member of Cranmer's diocesan flock for a decade when she died, and she had more than a decade of evangelical activism elsewhere before that.[35] Her nickname 'the Maid of Kent' instantly recalls another strong-minded female who ten years before had also been called the Maid of Kent, the traditionalist visionary Elizabeth Barton: this is an example of the way in which the two extremes were given similar labels and could thus be yoked together by mainstream evangelicals. Cranmer's treatment of Joan aroused the indignation of John Foxe, who was very unusual among English evangelicals in deploring all executions even of those who were clearly in error. Foxe made his disapproval clear at length in the 1559 Latin edition of *Acts and Monuments*, in a passage reflecting on Cranmer's eventual death at the stake; he then decided that this was too controversial and deleted it from subsequent editions.

Even so, Foxe remained so upset by the Bocher affair that most uncharacteristically he continued to tell a disapproving story of his hero Cranmer: he said that the Archbishop bullied a reluctant Edward VI into signing Joan's death warrant. Moreover this story has subsequently been proved to be much exaggerated.[36] Yet even when one has corrected Foxe's facts, his main point

---

[33] For details of Anabaptist trials under Edward VI, see P. Ayris in P. Ayris and D. Selwyn (eds.), *Thomas Cranmer* (Woodbridge, 1993), 148–52. Corpus Christi College Cambridge MS 105, 233–4 is an interesting paper which appears to be a dialogue between Cranmer and an Anabaptist, probably as part of an examination for heresy.

[34] For a useful discussion of the relationship between the two documents, see L. R. Sachs, 'Thomas Cranmer's "Reformatio Legum Ecclesiasticarum" of 1553 in the Context of English Church Law from the Later Middle Ages to the Canons of 1603' (Catholic University of America JCD, 1982), 111–16.

[35] On Bocher, see J. Davis, 'Joan of Kent, Lollardy and the English Reformation', *Journal of Ecclesiastical History*, 33 (1982), 225–33.

[36] The omitted passage was printed by the nineteenth century editors as an appendix, *Foxe*, 5, 860. For discussion of Cranmer, Edward VI and Bocher, J. G. Ridley, *Thomas Cranmer* (Oxford, 1962), 291–3, and of Foxe on toleration, Elton, 'Persecution and Toleration', 171–80.

remains: the fate of Joan Bocher was a perfect example of concord by persuasion moving Augustine-like to concord by coercion. Cranmer's diocesan officials had examined Bocher in the early 1540s but had protected her from serious consequences; however, instead of returning to the central ground of the evangelical fold, she had become more radical, and by 1548 she was under arrest again. After that she showed herself a resourceful and sophisticated opponent, not scrupling to sneer at her principal judges' recent change of mind on the nature of the Eucharist; unlike the other Anabaptists put on trial by the Edwardian government in 1549, she would not give way. She was kept alive for a year before her imperviousness to argument led to the sentence being carried out on her. Cranmer would indeed have been the obvious person in persuading the young king of his duty to burn his first heretic in 1550.

Finally, the question of tolerance. Did Cranmer show any signs of enthusiasm for allowing religious diversity in the commonwealth of England? We can dismiss the case of the Lady Mary, who under Edward VI was granted a very temporary, grudging and sometimes interrupted permission to hear the traditional Latin mass, on account of her rank, and under extreme diplomatic pressure from the Holy Roman Emperor. More pertinent is the remarkable opportunity provided by the Edwardian regime for the establishment in London of a grouping of autonomous foreign congregations, collectively known as the Stranger Church; another specialised French congregation was set up at Glastonbury in Somerset. The London Stranger Church was a congregational organisation whose ministry and decision-making were organised on a different principle to the three-fold order of bishop, priest and deacon: that order had been officially reaffirmed for the Church of England in the same year by the issue of the Ordinal. The Strangers' anomalous status in relation to the royal supremacy was formalised by a royal grant of letters patent in July 1550.

There can be no doubt of Cranmer's direct involvement in the London initiative. The first general superintendent of the London church was the Polish evangelical Johannes à Lasco who stayed with Cranmer at Lambeth Palace all through the period in which the royal grant establishing the Church was in preparation.[37] Yet from the start there were tensions between the English evangelical establishment and à Lasco and his followers. It was clear that the model for the Stranger enterprise was the Church of Zurich, and it was equally clear that many English evangelical activists regarded the new congregations as models for a more drastic restructuring of the Church of England than Cranmer had countenanced. Only a few months after the grant-

---

[37] A. Pettegree, *Foreign Protestant Communities in Sixteenth Century London* (Oxford, 1986), 31, and for the general outline of what follows, *ibid.*, ch. 2.

ing of the letters patent to the Stranger Church, Cranmer was already showing himself unhappy about its usage of sitting to receive communion and its rejection of English clerical dress, and a tense correspondence began between him and à Lasco.[38] Worse still, à Lasco was quickly drawn into an internal power struggle in the English Church. In 1550–1 John Hooper tried to defy Cranmer and Bishop Ridley of London by refusing to wear the rochet and chimere (hardly very demonstrative episcopal vestments) when he was consecrated bishop of Gloucester; à Lasco proved to be Hooper's most prominent foreign supporter before Cranmer and Ridley forced Hooper to yield. Partly because of this row, Bishop Ridley was consistently more hostile than Cranmer to the Stranger Church, and he was still harassing it and trying to assert his jurisdiction over it when mutual disaster overtook them with the accession of Queen Mary in 1553.

The tensions between the Stranger Church and Cranmer and Ridley are easy to explain, given their commitment to uniformity in the practice of the English Church; one remembers that the essence of concord as defined by Turchetti is the refusal of diversity. What needs some explanation, therefore, is the tolerance which the Stranger Church initiative apparently represents. One motive for Cranmer in backing it will have been precisely the achievement of concord by discussion: the risky idealism of the hope that close contact between churches of different nationalities would promote useful dialogue, and that differences could thereby be reduced to unimportance. It is highly relevant that Cranmer was a lifelong enthusiast for councils of the worldwide Church to agree on doctrine. Even in the 1520s, when his theology was fully within the orbit of the traditional Church, he had shown a particular enthusiasm for the ideal of the General Council, and a particular detestation of Martin Luther because he felt that Luther had denigrated the authority of General Councils.[39] Later, his favourite Continental theologians would be successively Philipp Melanchthon and Martin Bucer, the two arch-exponents of the spinning of formulae designed to unite conferences of diverse theologians. After the Hooper vestments row was safely buried, Cranmer would put a good deal of vain effort in 1551–2 to secure a European-wide ecumenical conference of evangelicals to rival the false General Council of Trent.[40]

[38] A. Kuyper (ed.), *Joannis à Lasco opera tam edita quam inedita*, (2 vols., Amsterdam, 1866), 2, 655–62, where à Lasco's letter is dated to 1551, but it is more likely to be from autumn 1550.

[39] MacCulloch, 'Two Dons in Politics', 12–13, and MacCulloch, *Cranmer*, ch. 2.

[40] For this initiative, see Cox (ed.), *Works of Cranmer*, 2 431–3; *Epistolae Tigurinae de rebus potissimum ad ecclesiae Anglicanae Reformationem pertinentibus* ... (1848), 462–3, or H. Robinson (ed.), *Original Letters relative to the English Reformation* ..., 2 vols. (1846–7), 711); G. C. Gorham (ed.), *Gleanings of a few scattered ears, during the period of the Reformation in England* ... (London, 1857), 277; C. G. Bretschneider (ed.), *Corpus Reformatorum*, 42 (*Calvini Opera*, 14), col. 370.

However, there was more to the Stranger Church initiative than this. In his private journal, King Edward recorded that the motive for making what was a very generous financial grant of premises as well as legal status to the Strangers, was for 'avoiding all sects of Anabaptists and suchlike'.[41] Joan Bocher had only been executed two months before the royal letters patent; there was an obvious advantage to be gained in setting up a structure of authority and discipline to control radicals who could otherwise flourish in the middle of London protected by their alien languages and private support systems. Indeed, the second burning for heresy to take place under Edward VI shows that the mechanism of the Stranger Church could work for the suppression of radicalism. George van Parris was a member of the Stranger congregation, and he was excommunicated by them for his unitarianism. It is most likely that the Strangers themselves denounced him to Cranmer, who tried him under a royal commission for investigating heresy, before activating the traditional mechanism to hand him over to the secular power for burning. There is a notable silence in sources from the Strangers' Church itself on van Parris, no doubt reflecting their unease about what they had done. Heretic he might have been, but it did not reflect well on a church which consisted of refugees from persecution itself to initiate persecution.[42] The only convincing justification was that offered by Cranmer to William Morice: evangelicals in error did far more harm to God's purposes than traditionalists in error.

So even the one initiative of tolerance in which Cranmer played a definite part was directed rather to concord: both concord by persuasion and concord by coercion. Noticeably, when Cranmer found himself at the mercy of Mary's Catholic government which was determined to destroy him, he never challenged the government's right to treat him as it did; he made a careful distinction between Mary's legitimate powers as Supreme Head which she happened to be using in a bad cause, and the wholly illegitimate powers of the Pope.[43] His belief in the royal supremacy was so strong that in 1556 it combined with his sense of guilt at having betrayed Mary for Queen Jane, almost to shipwreck his evangelical faith in a series of steadily more abject recantations. Only on the last morning of his life did he finally reject more than two decades of obedience, and join the defiant martyrs whose deaths he had watched during his years as archbishop. The effect of this new departure on his views on concord and tolerance can only be known to the inhabitants of Paradise.

---

[41] Pettegree, *Foreign Protestant Communities*, 44, quoting W. K. Jordan (ed.), *The Chronicle and Political Papers of Edward VI* (Ithaca, 1966), 37.

[42] Pettegree, *Foreign Protestant Communities*, 65–6.

[43] Cf. especially his letter to the Queen, September 1555, Cox (ed.), *Works of Cranmer*, 2, 447–54.

Forty years later, the great Jesuit conspirator Robert Parsons produced a proposal for the aftermath of a Catholic victory in England. He was envisaging a situation in which English Catholicism would be in much the same position as the evangelicals of the reign of Edward VI: an active and victorious minority, facing a broad swathe of the confused and indifferent, and a committed minority of enemies. In this situation, he advocated dealing with obstinate Protestants by a cautious 'connivance or toleration of magistrates only for a certain time'. Superficially, this sounds more generous than Cranmer, but Parsons went to emphasise the very temporary nature of such a 'toleration' (in my terms, tolerance). Once more, his aim was concord by persuasion, or if necessary by coercion:

I do give notice that my meaning is not in any way to persuade hereby that liberty of religion, to live how a man will, should be permitted to any person in any Christian commonwealth, for any cause or respect whatsoever; from which I am so far off in my judgment and affection as I think no one thing to be so dangerous, dishonourable or more offensive to Almighty God in the world than that any prince should permit the Ark of Israel and Dagon, God and the Devil, to stand and be honoured together, within his realm or country.[44]

In this respect, at least, Archbishop Cranmer would have been happy to echo the words of a member of the Jesuit sect.

[44] Parsons, *Memoriall*, quoted by Elton, 'Persecution and Toleration', 183–4.

13   Toleration for Catholics in the Puritan revolution

Norah Carlin

Although later than most topics in this volume, the mid seventeenth-century English revolution must hold a significant place in any discussion of when the age of the Reformation, with its characteristic attitudes to tolerance and intolerance, came to an end. Fifty years ago, most historians would have agreed that the Puritan revolution opened a new epoch in the history of toleration and saw the first manifestations of modern liberalism. In recent decades, however, both revisionist and anti-revisionist historians have denied the modernity of tolerationist views in the revolutionary period, arguing that even the most radical thinkers belonged to the previous age and were limited by their theological inheritance to quite narrow views of who could be tolerated and why.

Such historians quite rightly point out that both Cromwell and Milton, the most ardent defenders of toleration among the Independents, explicitly excluded Catholics. Milton's *Areopagitica* may disappoint modern readers when he qualifies his apparently general arguments with, 'I mean not tolerated popery and open superstition . . .'[1] Cromwell's crisp reply to an official in Ireland may also look like a contradiction to modern eyes: 'I meddle not with any man's conscience', he wrote, 'but if by liberty of conscience, you mean liberty to exercise the Mass, I judge it best to use plain dealing, and to let you know, Where the Parliament of England have power, *that* will not be allowed of.'[2]

This may seem to us as much of a let-down as the later concept of universal suffrage for men only, but recent historians have stressed the gulf between the seventeenth-century context and modern liberal thinking. Blair Worden points out that many of those who advocated liberty of conscience did not advocate toleration, which they saw as dangerous licence rather than liberty, and a risk to the salvation of many souls in that it would allow 'a liberty to all men to deceive them' and to entice them to hell, as Richard Baxter put

[1] John Milton, *Areopagitica*, ed. George H. Sabine (Northbrook, IL 1951), 52.
[2] Thomas Carlyle, *Letters and Speeches of Oliver Cromwell* (London, 1888), V, 74.

it.[3] Cromwell believed in tolerating error but not heresy, and what mattered to him was liberty for 'God's peculiar people' and the distinction between the precious and the vile. Worden sees Puritan theological conservatism as dominating the Independents, especially policy-makers like Cromwell and John Owen, and considers that the gains made for toleration were purely pragmatic: toleration increased during the Interregnum, he argues, because of the difficulty of stopping it. Meanwhile, more liberal principles were emerging from circles of Arminian intellectuals standing in the non-Calvinist traditions of Christian Stoicism, Erasmian tolerance and the Laudianism of Great Tew. It is there if anywhere, Worden argues, that the evolutionary thread of liberal tolerationism can be picked out.[4]

Christopher Hill, on the counter-revisionist wing, has long been impatient with critics of Milton's 'normal English Protestant attitude' in refusing to tolerate Catholicism. Although he admits that there were some 'eccentric tolerationists' who would not have made this exception, 'None of them was a practical politician in the sense that Milton was, or ever associated with any government', he tells us.[5] With more patience, Hill has shown the enormous importance to radical political action of ideas such as the fear of Antichrist, the horror of idolatry, and the conviction that the English had been chosen by God as the Israelites had been chosen in the Old Testament.[6] No one could deny the necessity of understanding that such notions, which seem irrational and even reactionary to the modern observer, could play a revolutionary and progressive role in the seventeenth century. The problem is, however, that Hill seems increasingly to define such ideas as *necessary* to the revolutionary mentality: anti-Catholicism was 'part of the English revolutionary heritage', and he finds it 'easier to understand . . . why even some of the most tolerant of English Protestants . . . were not prepared to tolerate Catholics' than why there were exceptions such as Roger Williams. In this account, revolutionaries whose ideas were different are in danger of disappearing.[7]

William Lamont, on the other hand, does include Roger Williams in his re-examination of radicals' attitudes to toleration, but decides that the inspi-

---

[3] Blair Worden, 'Toleration and the Cromwellian protectorate', in W. J. Sheils (ed.), *Persecution and Toleration* (Oxford, 1984), 201.

[4] *Ibid.*, 211, 213, 223, 205–6.

[5] Christopher Hill, *Milton and the English Revolution* (London, 1979), 155–6. Roger Williams did, of course, set up and lead the government of Rhode Island, where toleration for Catholics was put into practice.

[6] Christopher Hill, *Antichrist in Seventeenth-Century England* (London, 1971).

[7] Christopher Hill, *The English Bible and the Seventeenth-Century Revolution* (London, 1993), 295–6. Roger Williams does find his way into this book, but in over a dozen references this is the only one to his toleration of Catholics (296), and there are none to his denial that the example of the Israelites was a model for the Christian state.

ration of all the Calvinist revolutionaries was 'the Book of Revelation, not the Petition of Right', and that like Cromwell's and Owen's, Williams's main goal was discipline, not liberty. Like Worden, Lamont finds the roots of toleration in Arminianism, but in the implicit Arminianism of the sects rather than in intellectual circles.[8]

Before this new consensus becomes historical orthodoxy, however, it is necessary to point out that in order to stay in the air it is throwing overboard a considerable weight of historical evidence as well as an outdated Whig interpretation. For there were radicals who advocated toleration for Catholics in the 1640s, and they were not individual eccentrics remote from practical politics, but a group of pamphleteers and activists clustered around the separatist churches and the Leveller movement. They did speak a primarily religious language, but they expressed a political theory significantly different from that of the Puritan mainstream, and an examination of their ideas may also serve to highlight the problems of meaning and understanding in history which are not always solved by ditching old evolutionary interpretations and replacing them with contextualising models which then come to be used as new paradigms.

I became aware of these radical tolerationists, as I will call them, when researching English attitudes to Ireland in the late 1640s. Toleration for Catholics was, of course, a central plank of the Irish Confederate platform from 1643 to 1649, and stood at the head of Owen Roe O'Neill's secret proposals for an alliance with the English Independents when the Confederacy broke up in 1649.[9] There were persistent allegations – and a few confirmations in print – that some of the soldiers and Levellers who opposed the English reconquest of Ireland believed that the Irish were wrongly being persecuted for their religion.[10] The Cromwellians' anxiety in 1649 to deny that they were carrying out a religious persecution was stimulated by taunts in the anonymous *Tyranipocrit Discovered* and the Leveller *Mercurius Militaris* that compared them to notorious Catholic persecutors such as Philip II of Spain.[11] I found that there was indeed an undercurrent of radical views in favour of toleration for all Christians or even for all religions, and that such ideas were

---

[8] William Lamont, 'Pamphleteering, the Protestant Consensus and the English Revolution', in R. C. Richardson and G. M. Ridden (eds), *Freedom and the English Revolution. Essays in Literature and History* (Manchester, 1986), 72–92.

[9] Thomas L. Coonan, *The Irish Catholic Confederacy and the Puritan Revolution* (Dublin, 1954), 292–3.

[10] Norah Carlin, 'The Levellers and the Reconquest of Ireland in 1649', *Historical Journal* 30 (1987) 269–88.

[11] Norah Carlin, 'Extreme or mainstream?: The English Independents and the Reconquest of Ireland, 1649–1651', in B. Bradshaw, A. Hadfield and W. Maley (eds), *Representing Ireland: Literature and the Origins of Conflict, 1534–1660* (Cambridge, 1993), 209–26.

being debated in the press at the time of Cromwell's preparations for invading Ireland in 1649.

The two most interesting and prolific writers in this group were Roger Williams and Henry Robinson. Although Williams had been in New England from 1631 and founded the new settlement of Providence in 1636, in 1643 he returned to England, where *The Bloudy Tenent of Persecution* was published in 1644. Although much of this work is a response to views put forward by John Cotton and other New England ministers, it also addresses English affairs directly.[12] Williams's stance on the necessity of toleration is uncompromising:

> It is the will and command of *God*, that since the coming of his Sonne the *Lord Jesus*, a permission of the most *Paganish, Jewish, Turkish* or *Antichristian consciences* and *worships*, be granted to *all* men in all *Nations* and *Countries*: and they are onely to be fought against with that *Sword* which is only (in *Soule matters*) *able* to *conquer*, to wit, the *Sword* of *God's Spirit*, the *Word* of *God*.[13]

Although for Williams the church is an enclosed garden from which all weeds must be rigorously removed, the world is the field in which the tares must be allowed to grow alongside the wheat, or alternatively the wilderness in which good seed grows along with the weeds, until the end of the world:

> A false religion out of the *Church* will not hurt the *Church* no more thaen *weeds* in the *Wilderness* hurt the inclosed *Garden*, or *poyson* hurt the *body* when it is not touched or taken, yea and *antidotes* are received against it.[14]

Toleration, moreover, is not simply putting up with what cannot be helped: it is 'not for hurt, but for common good, even for the good of the good wheat, the people of God'; and premature weeding may interfere with God's plans, for 'those who appear *Soule-killers* today, by the grace of *Christ* may prove (as *Paul*) *Soule-savers* tomorrow ...'[15]

The merchant writer Henry Robinson also argues repeatedly for a general toleration, both in *Liberty of Conscience* (1644) and in *A Short Answer to A. S.* (1645). The struggle against 'Papists, Jewes, Turkes, Pagans, Hereticks', he says, 'must be fought out upon eaven ground, on equall termes, neither side must expect to have greater liberty of speech, writing, printing ...' and even 'Jesuited Papists' must be tolerated because, 'Though a toleration of erroneous opinions may give some to Sathan, yet truth being therewith per-

---

[12] Roger Williams, *The Bloudy Tenent, of Persecution, for cause of Conscience, discussed, in A Conference betweene Truth and Peace* (London, 1644), e.g. 200, 243–7.

[13] *Ibid.*, sig. A2. All emphases are as in the original.

[14] *Ibid.*, 103.

[15] *Ibid.*, 53–7, 111; A. S. P. Woodhouse, *Puritanism and Liberty*, 2nd edn (London, 1974), 272.

mitted to be published and improved, will in all probability . . . gain so many to God.'[16]

Part of a sentence from Robinson's *Liberty of Conscience* has led Hill to claim that Robinson 'insisted' on denying toleration to Catholics. This is, however, part of an argument which may have been intended ironically, or even as a protection against censorship, since it can indeed be quoted out of context to give a misleading impression:

And because it may be objected that many places of Scripture herein alledged, may as well seem to speake for a tolleration of Popery, and my selfe therein to pleade for it, let such be pleased to rest satisfied, that though I cannot for the present make full discovery in the word of God, why, or how Papists should be forced by fines and other penalties to be of *our* Religion, yet I take not upon me to be a spokesman for a tolleration of *theirs*, by reason of their idolatry . . .

In the even longer and more complex sentence which follows, Robinson asks why, if Catholics may not be tolerated in England 'in a qualified and more moderate manner', as in parts of Germany where they are allowed private but not public worship, should English Protestant merchants be able to go, as they do, to Catholic services in Italy and Spain, even though they are not forced, or troubled by the Inquisition for not doing so.[17] Is he recommending such a moderate toleration in England, or criticising English merchants for their lax behaviour abroad? He may have intended his readers to be able to take it either way. From the similarity of his arguments to those of the other radial tolerationists, however, I am giving Robinson the benefit of the doubt and including him among them.

Three works appearing in 1649 which I would also include in this group are *Certain Quaeries concerning Liberty of Conscience* by Henry Danvers, a Staffordshire gentleman, officer in the New Model Army and later Fifth Monarchist member of Barebones Parliament; Edward Barber's *Answer to the Essex Watchmen's Watchword*; and the anonymous *Liberty of Conscience Asserted*, which briefly stated a selection of arguments used by Williams and Robinson: all these are unambiguously in favour of toleration for Catholics. I would also bring into consideration John Canne's *The Snare is Broken*, which puts many of the radical tolerationist arguments before partially backing down in favour of laws against 'publick and notable Idolatrie'. Canne

---

[16] William Haller (ed.), *Tracts on Liberty in the Puritan Revolution* (1965), III, 133; [Henry Robinson], *A Short Answer to A. S. Alias Adam Stewarts Second part of his overgrown Duply to the two Brethren* (London, 1644/5), 33. For the attribution of the second tract to Robinson, see Haller, *Tracts on Liberty*, I, 65–72, and W. K. Jordan, *Men of Substance. A Study of the Thought of Two English Revolutionaries* (Chicago, 1942), 38.

[17] Haller, *Tracts on Liberty*, III, 114. Cf. *Liberty of Conscience Asserted* (London, 1649), to which the government licenser Theodore Jennings added the proviso: 'Not assenting that visible Idolatry publikely manifested by prophaneness, and worshipping of God by images be tolerated by the Magistrate.'

also wrote a denunciation of the Levellers, but Barber's pamphlet argues in support of the *Agreement of the People*.[18]

Richard Overton, one of the leading Levellers, had advocated toleration for Catholics in *The Arraignment of Mr. Persecution* in 1645, and although there had long been considerable debate about this in the pages of the *Moderate*, it continued to be the Levellers' agreed position up to and beyond December, 1648, when they were involved in a long wrangle about toleration with the Independents in the committee for drafting a joint manifesto which met at Whitehall.[19] When the Council of Officers issued their own version of an *Agreement of the People* which inserted into the toleration clause a reservation concerning popery and prelacy, they were denounced by John Lilburne and others.[20] In the Levellers' own final version of the *Agreement*, in May 1649, the clause concerning freedom of religious belief and worship still contained no reservation, but a later clause proposed barring 'such as maintain the Popes (or other forraign) supremacy' from holding office in the commonwealth.[21] There is some doubt about the position of the Leveller William Walwyn, who in 1641 may have written in favour of toleration for Catholics and who in his writings on toleration at this time certainly did not explicitly exclude them.[22]

What is most interesting about these radical tolerationists, both Levellers and others, is the systematic and coherent nature of their ideas. Far from being a random eccentricity, their commitment to toleration for Catholics was based

[18] Henry Danvers, *Certain Quaeries concerning Liberty of Conscience* (London, 1649); Edward Barber, *An Answer to the Essex Watchmen's Watchword* (London, 1649); [Anon.], *Liberty of Conscience Asserted* (London, 1649); John Canne, *The Snare is Broken* (London, 1649); [John Canne], *England's Discoverer, or the Levellers' Creed* (London, 1649).

[19] Haller, *Tracts on Liberty*, III, 203–56; Jurgen Diethe, '*The Moderate*: the politics and allegiances of a revolutionary newspaper', *History of Political Thought*, 4 (1983), 247–79; Woodhouse, *Puritanism and Liberty*, 125–78.

[20] Woodhouse, *Puritanism and Liberty*, 342–67, 472–4; Don M. Wolfe, *Leveller Manifestoes of the Puritan Revolution* (New York, 1944), 304–10.

[21] Wolfe, *Leveller Manifestoes*, 405, 408.

[22] Jack R. McMichael and Barbara Taft, *The Writings of William Walwyn* (Athens GA, 1989), 15, 532. I find the editors' reasoning entirely circular: having decided that Walwyn wrote *A New Petition of the Papists* (55–61) in 1641, they judge all his later works as showing 'an unceasing commitment to absolute liberty of conscience', interpreting other passages in the light of this supposed commitment (cf. 15, 18, 81, 164, 239), and rejecting Walwyn as the author of *No Papist nor Presbyterian* (Wolfe, *Leveller Manifestoes*, 304–10) largely because it would tolerate only Christians. There is in fact one passage in *The Power of Love* (1643) which clearly does limit toleration to 'such opinions as are not destructive to humane society, nor blaspheme the worke of our Redemption', though in *Tolleration Justified* (1646), Walwyn argues that there should be no limits (McMichael and Taft, *Writings of Walwyn*, 94, 164). I am inclined to think that Walwyn wrote neither *A New Petition* nor *No Papist*, because both use the word 'religions' in the plural, even for Protestant sects. Both Williams and Robinson regularly do this, but Walwyn's acknowledged and probable writings (so far as I can find) never. Cf. John Locke, *A Letter Concerning Toleration* (Indianapolis, 1955), 59–62.

on a set of principles and attitudes which run through all the examples, though they are most clearly shown in the works of Williams and Robinson. Some of their attitudes, such as the necessity of freedom of conscience, they shared with Independents such as Cromwell and Milton; but some features of their thinking mark a decisive break with mainstream Puritanism and in some ways with the attitudes to tolerance which had prevailed since the Reformation.

Like some of the Independents, these thinkers stress that the individual conscience cannot be coerced by laws or punishments; but they carry this so far as to make conscience an extremely subjective experience, in which the truth may genuinely not be recognised. Robinson, for example, writes,

Though a man would use all the means which can be prescribed to him, and should even himself be contented, and desire that such a religion [as he is forced to follow] were the true one, yet it is not in his power to think so, and consequently to be the same in heart, until his reason and understanding be convinced thereof.[23]

Walwyn argues that 'every one ought to be fully perswaded in his owne minde of the lawfulnesse of the way wherein he serveth God ... because whatsoever is not of faith or full assurance of minde is sin'; he insists that 'before an opinion can properly be said to be mine, it must concord with my understanding.'[24] The author of *Liberty of Conscience Asserted* agrees that 'no man can without committing a damnable sin, relinquish those erroneous doctrines, or that erroneous Religion, which in his conscience he believes (upon a due examination) to be the right, no not to imbrace the true faith of Christ, until his conscience be convinced it is such.'[25]

This opinion that conviction is necessary for religious belief is not at all dependent on belief in free will, even though Walwyn was no Calvinist and the positions of other writers on this point are not always clear. Several stress that faith is a gift of God, and neither the individual nor any human authority can compel God to grant it.[26] But the most vehement on this point is Roger Williams, who argues that giving the magistrate power to constrain people in religious matters has 'an appearance of that Arminian Popish doctrine of Freewill, as if it lay in their owne power and ability to beleeve upon the Magistrates command'; as if God is to be forced or commanded to give faith, to open the heart or incline the will.[27] Historians who have identified tolerationist views with Arminianism are therefore quite mistaken: many Calvinists were intolerant, but Calvinism in itself was not a barrier to tolerationist views.

[23] Haller, *Tracts on Liberty*, III, 141–2.
[24] McMichael and Taft, *Writings of Walwyn*, 136, 158.
[25] *Liberty of Conscience Asserted*, 2.
[26] *Ibid.*, 3; Robinson, *Short Answer to AS*, 10; Barber, *Answer to the Essex Watchmen*, 14.
[27] Williams, *Bloudy Tenent*, 139.

Stressing the subjectivity of conscience led many of these writers to show, despite their strong Protestant convictions, a remarkable capacity for empathy. *Liberty of Conscience Asserted* argues that God may not count the papists guilty of idolatry if 'they are zealous in their way, and are verily persuaded in their conscience that they serve God aright'.[28] *No Papist nor Presbyterian* (1649) even points out that Catholics say 'they give not Pictures or such representations (as they call them) any Soveraigne honor, which is that that properly belongs to God, but an inferiour or relative kind of reverence or honor', and suggests that rather than idolaters they ought to be called 'superstitious and Popish persons'.[29] Robinson, though he vehemently objects, in his remarks on Catholic processions abroad, to 'the superstitious pageantry of their will-worship and idolatry', nevertheless argues that 'a Protestant sermon is as Idolatrous to a Papist, as a Popish Masse is to a Protestant; and neither of them can more judge with the understanding, than see with the eyes of the other'.[30] Canne makes similar remarks about the relativity of the concept of superstition.[31]

This imaginative reciprocity could be applied even to non-Christians. Robinson not only suggests that 'Turkes have as much reason to persecute Christians, as Christians have to persecute Turkes,' but goes on to argue that persecuting Christians are more guilty than the Jews who put Christ to death, because 'they knew him not to be Christ, and the Jewes had better ground and warrant to put a blasphemer to death, and such they accounted Jesus, than Christians have now'.[32] Overton points out, 'He that hangs a *Jew* because he will not be a *Christian*, would be loath a *Jew* should reward him in the same kind, because he will not be a *Jew*.'[33] Williams admits that the native Americans, who worship devils, nevertheless 'must judge according to their *Indian* or *American Consciences*, for other *consciences* it cannot be supposed they should have'.[34]

This is surely a psychological development of some significance, for it broke with a Protestant tradition, running from Luther to Cromwell and Owen, that saw opponents (once instructed by the true Protestant) as somehow knowing that they were wrong; as well as an even older Western European tradition that saw in religious difference a dangerous form of pollution inviting God's vengeance on the whole community. The construction and dismantling of such mental barriers are, as Bob Scribner has suggested,

---

[28] *Liberty of Conscience Asserted*, 5.
[29] Wolfe, *Leveller Manifestoes*, 309.
[30] Haller, *Tracts on Liberty*, III, 114; Robinson, *Short Answer to AS*, 36.
[31] Canne, *The Snare is Broken*, 22.
[32] Haller, *Tracts on Liberty*, III, 126, 148.
[33] *Ibid.*, 225.
[34] Williams, *Bloudy Tenent*, 102, 138.

appropriate topics for investigation by a historical social psychology which has as yet hardly begun to exist.

Roger Williams, who very frequently expresses a horror of idolatry and a belief in Antichrist more vividly than any of the other writers considered here, and who describes with apparent relish the future torments of the damned in hell,[35] nevertheless labours throughout *The Bloudy Tenent of Persecution* to express a distinction between the outer and inner person, the social and spiritual reality. He points out that St. Paul showed 'the lawfulness of conversation with such persons in *civill things*, with whom it is not lawful to have converse in *spirituals*'; and when he goes on to ask whether Jews, Muslims or Catholics may not be 'peaceable and quiet *Subjects*, loving and helpful *neighbours*, faire and just *dealers*, true and loyall to the *civill government*', he replies, 'It is clear they may from all *Reason* and *Experience* in many flourishing *Cities* and *Kingdomes* of the World . . . notwithstanding that in *spirituall* and *mystical account* they are ravenous and greedy *Wolves*.'[36] He argues that 'many glorious and flourishing *Cities* of the World maintain their *Civill* peace, yea the very *Americans* and wildest *Pagans* keep the peace of their *Towns* or *Cities*', though there is no true religion in such places, 'and consequently no spirituall and heavenly peace'. Many states have been peaceful and prosperous without true religion, as 'every *Historian*, *Merchant*, *Traveller*, in *Europe*, *Asia*, *Africa*, *America* can testifie'.[37]

This double vision of the world is certainly curious, and to a modern reader may even seem schizoid, but both perspectives must be taken into account by the historian, since they were both taken into account by Williams in his thinking. Perhaps it was his way of resolving the psychological tension between Calvinist beliefs and the necessary pragmatism of everyday life, and perhaps there were others who did likewise.

Other radical tolerationists handle the distinction between public and private life in a more formal way, as a question of roles rather than personalities. Robinson asserts that papists and Brownists may serve their country satisfactorily, 'as those thundering legions of Primitive Christians did the Heathen Emperors'. Danvers argues that 'an unbelieving Magistrate, Father or Husband, is not less a magistrate, father, husband than one that believes'; and Barber points out that taking religious authority away from the state would not hinder individuals from 'instructing, catechising and perswading their families, either Magistrates or private persons'. The idea of religion in itself as a separate sphere to be distinguished from public life is also expressed by Robinson when, discussing previous persecuting regimes, he suggests that 'it

---

[35] Worden, 'Pamphleteering, Protestant Consensus', 82, 86; Woodhouse, *Puritanism and Liberty*, 272–3.
[36] Williams, *Bloudy Tenent*, 51–2, 67.
[37] *Ibid.*, 25, 138.

was not their Popery or Prelacie (that was to themselves) which so much oppressed us, as their power . . .'[38]

This distinction between public and private spheres may be the reason for the popularity of gendered metaphors. Overton says that compelling religious observance against conscience is 'worse than to ravish the bodies of women and Maides against their wills', and Williams uses this metaphor of spiritual rape so often that I must confess to having lost count. Williams also compares the church to a chaste and loving wife, contrasts the modesty of a true church with the whoredom of public women (as does Robinson), and argues that the spouse of Christ does not use material weapons any more than does '*a chaste and modest Virgin* fight and scratch like *whores* and *harlots*'. These are not images of hierarchy and submission, since the church is not in these authors' view subject to any earthly power. The confinement of modest wives to the domestic sphere, which was a common theme in puritan advice books on family life, seems to be the more appropriate reference.[39]

The central political idea common to all these radical tolerationists, one which gave coherence and ideological meaning to their efforts to reconcile public and private spheres, inner and outer persons, secular and spiritual roles, was the separation of church and state. This was not only a matter of mutual non-interference, but a question of assigning very different natures and functions to the two types of institution. Explicit in Williams and implicit in Robinson's writings, we even find a distinction between the state and civil society similar to that which Locke was to make forty years later.

The Levellers' insistence that the magistrate can have no power in spiritual matters was central to the Whitehall Debates in December, 1648. Nothing would deflect them from it: neither Ireton's attempts to argue that some spiritual matters (such as idolatry and blasphemy) were within the magistrate's purview because they were matters of natural law; nor Hugh Peter's insistence that godly rule was on the agenda: 'the matter of England is religion'.[40] When the Council of Officers issued their own version of the *Agreement of the People*, adding that it was not intended 'that this liberty shall necessarily extend to popery or prelacy', three Leveller pamphlets quickly denounced them for it.[41] This insistent defence of toleration can only be understood by looking at the context of radical tolerationist writings.

[38] Haller, *Tracts on Liberty*, III, 108, 113; Danvers, *Certain Quaeries*, 2; Barber, *Answer to the Essex Watchmen*, 12.

[39] Haller, *Tracts on Liberty*, III, 118, 225; Williams, *Bloudy Tenent*, 20, 48–9, 100–1, 144, 191; Susan Cahn, *Industry of Devotion. The Transformation of Women's Work in England 1500–1600* (New York, 1987) 156–74.

[40] Woodhouse, *Puritanism and Liberty*, 138, 143–4, 154–6, 160–2. I cannot agree with Hill that the Levellers found Ireton's arguments hard to answer (*English Bible*, 410–11).

[41] Woodhouse, *Puritanism and Liberty*, 355–7, 472–4; Wolfe, *Leveller Manifestoes*, 304–10.

Nothing was so fundamental to these writers as their denial of spiritual power to the state – except perhaps the denial of temporal power to the church, which was not the main focus of these discussions.[42] Williams announced that in his book, 'All *Civill States*, with their *Officers* of *justice* in their respective *constitutions* and *administrations* are proved *essentially Civill*, and therefore not *judges*, *Governours* or *Defendours* of the *Spirituall* or *Christian state* and *worship*.'[43] If the civil magistrate has power to judge in spiritual matters, Danvers asks 'whether it will not necessarily follow, that every Common-wealth must have radically and fundamentally a power in it of true discerning the true Worship and fear of God ... But Christ says expressly ... *My Kingdom is not of this World*.' Barber and Robinson agree, and Williams comes back to the theme many times.[44]

What applies to any civil state applies to all, they insist, and allowing spiritual power to the magistrate in principle could have either of two unacceptable consequences. The first would be that all states would have the power to persecute, and then, as Danvers says, 'Queen Mary as well discharged her duty as Queen Elizabeth, who judged and punished according to her conscience'; and the same example is used by several other authors.[45] Even pagan rulers would be justified in persecuting Christians, suggests Williams.[46]

The second possible consequence would be that the legitimacy of a ruler could always be challenged on the grounds of religious error, which would bring a return to the papal practice of releasing godly subjects from obedience to a heretical ruler. We must beware of 'such infernal tenets', warns Robinson, 'according unto which there would be found no safety, neither for Prince nor Parliament.'[47] Not only could unbelievers not legitimately be magistrates and rulers; they could not exercise authority as husbands, fathers or masters, and there would be as a result no order in the world.[48]

All agree that the civil state exists for the sake of order, even though to Williams it is 'dead in sin'. The end of judicial power, says Barber, is to punish 'trespassers against men'; it is to ensure 'that there may be a generall comely demeanour as rationall creatures', according to Overton. For

[42] Haller, *Tracts on Liberty*, III, 240; Robinson, *Short Answer to AS*, 14–15.

[43] Williams, *Bloudy Tenent*, sig A2v.

[44] Danvers, *Certain Quaeries*, 1; Barber, *Answer to the Essex Watchmen*; Robinson, *Short Answer to AS*, 13.

[45] Danvers, *Certain Quaeries*, 1–2; Haller, *Tracts on Liberty*, III, 121, 178; Canne, *The Snare is Broken*, 8; Williams, *Bloudy Tenent*, 97.

[46] Williams, *Bloudy Tenent*, 137.

[47] Robinson, *Short Answer to AS*, 7–8; Barber, *Answer to the Essex Watchmen*, 17–18; Haller, *Tracts on Liberty*, III, 233.

[48] Williams, *Bloudy Tenent*, 188.

Williams, the 'Sword of *Civill Justice* exists 'for the *defence* of the *Persons, Estates, Families, Liberties* of a *City* or *Civill State*'.[49]

The fact that some of these writers, like the Levellers in the Whitehall Debates, derive civil power from the people, serves only to reinforce their distinction between the spiritual and temporal powers. For the people as a whole, being made up of saints and sinners, or (for the Calvinists) the elect and the unregenerate, can never be judge in spiritual matters.[50] To the question asked by a group of millenarians in 1649, 'How can the kingdom be the Saints', when the ungodly are electors, and elected to govern?' they reply that the kingdom never can be the saints', because it is a natural, civil institution, not a vehicle for godly rule on earth.[51]

In abandoning the idea of godly rule by the temporal state, the radical tolerationists had to repudiate the relevance of Israel in the Old Testament and the idea of a chosen people among Christians. That they did so explicitly, unanimously and without hesitation shows to me that they knew what they were doing in terms of having a consistent political theory. All agreed that the Gospel had brought a new dispensation and that the Christian church could not be 'national'; and the idea of the chosen people was not so difficult to dispense with as Hill has supposed.[52] Even in the Whitehall Debates, the Levellers and their opponents spent some time arguing about whether the Israelites in the Old Testament were a figure, or type, of the Christian state or the Christian church.[53]

For the other side of the coin was that although the state could not use physical weapons to punish dissent, the church was free to use spiritual weapons as harshly as it might choose in order to purify itself and separate the saints from the unregenerate, without putting anyone in danger of imprisonment, execution, or exclusion from the benefits of belonging to the civil community. It is one of the ironies of Williams's *Bloudy Tenent of Persecution* that the benign and orderly civil state is shadowed throughout by the narrow and spiritually vindictive church of the saints, using excommunication for 'spiritual killing by the most sharp two-edged sword of the spirit, in delivering up the person excommunicate to *Sathan*', and condemning the

---

[49] Barber, *Answer to the Essex Watchmen*, 13; Haller, *Tracts on Liberty*, III, 242; Williams, *Bloudy Tenent*, 57, 79–80.

[50] Danvers, *Certain Quaeries*, 1; Williams, *Bloudy Tenent*, 203–4, 210–11. Robinson also derives spiritual power from the people, in the conciliarist tradition, and believes it cannot be delegated (Robinson, *Short Answer to AS*, 28.)

[51] Woodhouse, *Puritanism and Liberty*, 246.

[52] Danvers, *Certain Quaeries*, 2; Canne, *The Snare is Broken*, 33; Barber, *Answer to the Essex Watchmen*, 4; Robinson, *Short Answer to AS*, 2–6; Williams, *Bloudy Tenent*, sig. A2v, 179–86; cf. Hill, *English Bible*, 295–6.

[53] Woodhouse, *Puritanism and Liberty*, 155–69.

damned to a punishment 'endless, easeless, in extremity, universality, and eternity of torments'.[54]

This is not a theoretical contradiction (and whether it is a psychological one I have discussed above). Liberty in civil society is the essential precondition for the functioning of exclusive churches as of all private societies, as Williams explains:

> The *Church* or *Company* of *worshippers* is like unto a body or Colledge of *Physitians* in a *Citie*; like unto to a *Corporation, Society or Company* or *East-India* or *Turkie-Merchants*, or any other *Societie* or *Company* in *London*, which companies may hold their *Courts*, keep their *Records*, hold *disputations*, and in matters concerning their *Societie*, may dissent, divide, break into *Schismes* and *Factions*, sue and implead each other at the *Law*, yea wholly breake up and dissolve into pieces and nothing, and yet the *peace* of the *Citie* not be in the least impaired, or disturbed; because the *essence* or being of the *Citie*, and so the *well-being* and *Peace* thereof is essentially distinct from those particular *Societies* . . . The *Citie* was there before them, and stands absolute and intire, when such a *Corporation* or *Societie* is taken down.[55]

This is a distinct foreshadowing of Locke's view on freedom of association in civil society in his 1689 *Letter on Toleration*, the main difference being that Williams's images of quarrelsome merchants/believers are far more lively than Locke's examples of dons and drinking clubs.[56]

Robinson also paints an attractive picture of the benefits of civil society, asking whether it is better for 'a thousand men and women of ten severall religions or opinions to assemble together every Sunday in a parish church for fear of imprisonment . . . or else that the same thousand men and women being permitted freely, may meet in a peaceable manner at ten severall places according to their respective differing opinions and religion . . .' He goes on to compare the liberty of Christians with that of the individual merchant, saying that 'we should think it a most grosse solecisme, and extravagant course in any State which did make Laws and Statutes, that the Subject might not goe about and despatch his worldly businesse, save in one generall prescript forme and manner.'[57]

The radical tolerationists of the mid- to late 1640s were not always the obscure and half-forgotten figures they now seem to have become. For historians of the mid-twentieth century such as William Haller and W. K. Jordan, these were progressive, modernising men who made important contributions to the development of modern liberal thought. But when Jordan wrote that their tolerationist views were a sign that 'the lay spirit had triumphed in England', or put Robinson, Walwyn and Overton, together with Winstan-

---

[54] Williams, *Bloudy Tenent*, 57, 99–100; Woodhouse, *Puritanism and Liberty*, 272–3.
[55] Williams, *Bloudy Tenent*, 25.
[56] Locke, *Letter concerning Toleration*, 20–1.
[57] Haller, *Tracts on Liberty*, III, 133–4, 155.

ley and Milton, in a chapter on 'Rationalists and Sceptics'; when Haller described Robinson's vision as 'a capitalist empire'; they were more than a little guilty of that 'historical foreshortening' condemned by more recent historians of ideas; of 'seeing far too readily the "modern" elements which the commentator has ... programmed himself to find'.[58]

The healthy and necessary reaction against such simplifications of history has tended to stress the context of past ideas which are unfamiliar and at first sight seem irrational to the modern observer. But are we perhaps in danger of thinking that too much was impossible for the seventeenth-century writer to recognise that he or she was doing? It was, it seems, perfectly possible for radical tolerationists to dispense with much of the 'normal English Protestant' mentality such as horror of idolatry or confidence in the God-given mission of the English people.

One of the reasons why the thought of writers such as Williams and Robinson can easily be misapprehended is a question of language. Although there is scarcely an argument in Locke's 1689 *Letter* which is not found somewhere in these writings, the language is so different that it comes as something of a shock to realise that the ideas are there.[59] The language of these earlier writers is sometimes simply described as 'theological', but would be recognised by a historian of early modern political thought as the *language of scholastic political theory*, still current in the seventeenth century.[60] For example, some of the ideas first suggested by late medieval thinkers such as Marsiglio of Padua and William of Ockham, which had served Luther and others to argue against the temporal power of the Catholic church, were turned around and used by these radical tolerationists to deny spiritual power to the state.[61] The point is that it is always possible to say new things in an old language, though in the end the new ideas may be taken in and expressed more clearly by a new language. This is what I think happened between the mid-century radicals and Locke, as the old language was discredited and marginalised by the reversal of political fortunes at the Restoration.

There is, of course, one idea in Locke's *Letter* which is not in any of the writings I have selected here: the exclusion of Catholics from toleration

---

[58] W. K. Jordan, *The Development of Religion Toleration in England*, vol. III, *From the Convention of the Long Parliament to the Restoration* (London, 1936), 33–4; vol. IV, *Attainment of the Theory and Accommodations in Thought and Institutions* (London, 1940), 15–17; Haller, *Tracts on Liberty*, I, 65–72; James Tully (ed), *Meaning and Context: Quentin Skinner and his Critics* (Cambridge, 1988), 45.

[59] Locke, *Letter concerning Toleration*, 16–18, 20–1, 23–4, 26, 33–4, 40–1, 42–3. All these can be directly compared with passages in the works of radical tolerationists referred to above.

[60] Antony Black, *Political Thought in Europe, 1250–1450* (Cambridge, 1992), 1–13, 42–84; Anthony Pagden (ed), *The Languages of Political Theory in Early Modern Europe* (Cambridge, 1987), 3–6.

[61] Quentin Skinner, *The Foundations of Modern Political Thought* (Cambridge, 1978), vol. II, *The Age of the Reformation*, 20–64.

altogether, on the grounds of their allegiance to a foreign power.[62] Why did Locke do this, when his political ideas were otherwise so consistent with what the radical tolerationists had argued? One reason might be that the revolution Locke was interested in supporting was a much less radical one than that of the Levellers and their associates.[63] But it may also be due to changes in the international situation. The late 1640s had seen a brief respite from major international conflicts involving religious alignments, and it had even been possible for English writers to describe some Catholic countries as more tolerant than England.[64] Between the winding down of the Thirty Years' War and the rise to power of Louis XIV, when the saints of Piedmont had not yet been slaughtered and toleration in Venice and Tuscany could overshadow reaction in Rome, a window of opportunity was presented for including Catholics in the tolerationist argument. The opportunity receded after 1660, and when it came again the arguments would be conducted in a different language – less theological, less passionate, and less revolutionary.

---

[62] Locke, *Letter concerning Toleration*, 51–2. They are thinly disguised as 'Mahometans', but the reference to royal supremacy makes it clear that Catholics are meant.

[63] David McNally, 'Locke, Levellers and Liberty: Property and Democracy in the Thought of the First Whigs', *History of Political Thought*, 10 (1989), 17–40.

[64] Haller, *Tracts on Liberty*, III, 147. Robinson had travelled to France and Italy himself. Jordan, *Men of Substance*, 38–66.

14 The question of tolerance in Bohemia and Moravia in the age of the Reformation

Jaroslav Pánek

In the lands of Bohemia, the problem of religious tolerance at the turn of the Middle Ages and the pre-modern age is indissolubly linked with Hussitism. In the peak period of its activities, between the years 1419 and 1434, this movement brought about an overthrow of the traditional political and ecclesiastical situation, living further on, in a moderate and transformed manner, up to the first quarter of the seventeenth century. Hussitism is justly referred to as the first, or Czech Reformation, as against the second, German or European Reformation, coping with similar problems as the Hussites within a much broader geographical range during the sixteenth century. Elaborating on the doctrine of John Wyclif and applying it in its social practice, Hussitism resolutely suppressed the Catholic Church and stripped it both of its landed property and of its political power in Bohemia and partly also in Moravia. The arguments of Hussitism were persuasive enough to win over an absolute majority of the country's population including major segments of the nobility and burghers. However, Catholicism managed to hold its positions in the border regions of Bohemia, partly in Moravia and, to retain a dominant position, in the remaining three lands of the Crown of Bohemia (Silesia and Upper and Lower Lusatia), throwing up a rampart which held back the onslaught of Hussitism. The population of the state of Bohemia split into two long-term confessional and political camps faced essentially with two possibilities – either to go on fighting until the total elimination of the weaker adversary or to seek a path towards coexistence and mutual tolerance.[1]

---

[1] For the most important introductory and general works on the Czech history of the fifteenth century, see F. M. Bartoš, *Čechy v době Husově* [Bohemia in the Age of John Hus], *1378–1415* (Prague, 1947); Bartoš, *Husitská revoluce* [The Hussite Revolution], vols. 1–2 (Prague, 1965–6); F. Hrejsa, *Dějiny křesťanství v Československu* [History of the Christianity in Czechoslovakia], vols. 2–4 (Prague, 1947–8); O. Odložilik, *The Hussite King: Bohemia in European Affairs 1440–1471* (New Brunswick, N. J., 1965); H. Kaminsky, *A History of the Hussite Revolution* (Berkeley, 1967); J. Macek, *Jean Hus et les traditions hussites* (Paris, 1973); Z. Fiala, *Předhusitské Čechy* [Bohemia in the pre-Hussite period], *1310–1419* (Prague, 1978); J. Kejř, *Husité* [The Hussites] (Prague, 1984); F. Šmahel, *La révolution hussite, une anomalie historique* (Paris, 1985); Šmahel, *Husitská revoluce* [The Hussite Revolution], vols. 1–4 (Prague, 1994); a German translation of this valuable work is being prepared by the Monumenta Germaniae Historica in Munich. Literature in Western languages can be found

In the initial stage the Hussite ideology was built up on the idea that the mission entrusted to the 'warriors of God' was to carry out an amendment of the Church and society both within and without the territories of the state of Bohemia. The zeal for religious reform and the outstanding success in war buttressed the Hussite conviction of the superior status of the Bohemian nation, supposed to have been called upon by God to carry out the amendment work, manifesting itself in a strong wave of Bohemian Messianism. In spite of the fact that nationalistic tones were not missing in this chorale, Hussite ideology was based on the primacy of religion and its essence put forward in the Four Articles of Prague of 1420.[2] The stipulations concerning the liberty of propagation of the divine message, the Eucharist (offering the communion cup to the laity), the obligatory apostolic poverty of the Church and the public punishment of sins (including those perpetrated by the clergy) meant a change of the tide which was utterly unacceptable to the Catholic Church.[3]

Not even repeated incursions from abroad managed to dislodge the Hussites from their public positions in Bohemia. From this and the fact that the movement's moderate version prevailed during the 1430s, there arose a need for negotiations and an interest in a certain compromise. This was acknowledged by the representatives of the church, then congregated at the Council of Basle, who for the first time in the history of western Christendom accepted heretics as partners in negotiations whose only criterion was to be the divine law and the acts of Jesus Christ, the Apostles and the pristine Church together with councils and doctors truly based on the former (the so-called Judge of Cheb/Eger of 1432). It emerged none the less during the ensuing disputations between Catholic and Hussite theologians at Basle that both sides lacked the will to compromise and that no solution on the level of the entire western Christendom could be reached.[4]

in J. K. Zeman, *The Hussite Movement and the Reformation in Bohemia, Moravia and Slovakia (1350–1650). A Bibliographical Study Guide* (Ann Arbor MI, 1977) and in the bibliographical notes to recent articles published in English: W. Eberhard, 'Bohemia, Moravia and Austria', in A. Pettegree (ed.), *The Early Reformation in Europe* (Cambridge, 1992), 23–48; F. Kavka, 'Bohemia', in B. Scribner, R. Porter, and M. Teich (eds.), *The Reformation in National Context* (Cambridge, 1994), 131–54.

[2] R. Kalivoda, *Husitská ideologie* (Prague, 1961); Kalivoda, *Revolution und Ideologie. Der Hussitismus* (Cologne and Vienna, 1976); F. Šmahel, 'The Idea of the "Nation" in Hussite Bohemia', in *Historica, Les sciences historiques en Tchécoslovaquie*, 16 (1969), 143–247; 17 (1969), 93–197; Šmahel, 'Primat des Glaubens im hussitischen Böhmen', in S. Tanz (ed.), *Mentalität und Gesellschaft im Mittelalter. Gedenkschrift für Ernst Werner* (Frankfurt on Main, 1994), 261–70.

[3] Edition of the Four Articles of Prague in R. Říčan et al. (eds.), *Čtyři vyznání* [Four Confessions] (Prague, 1951), 35–52. Cf. F. Šmahel, *Husitská revoluce*, vol. 3, 36ff.

[4] Recent summary of research in A. Molnár et al., *Soudce smluvený v Chebu* [The Judge of Cheb/Eger] (Cheb, 1982).

Another path, however, which was felt to be open was that of separate and by far more pragmatic contacts among politicians, namely between emperor Sigismund of Luxemburg, heir to the throne of Bohemia, but refused for years, and the moderate Hussite élites. These negotiations resulted in the conclusion of the so-called Compactata of Jihlava/Iglau of July of 1436, opening the way towards the restoration of monarchy in Bohemia and Moravia whose inhabitants were guaranteed communion in both kinds. This meant the renewal of peace and lawful recognition of two faiths of identical status (Utraquist and Catholic) within one state where both creeds vindicated their own ecclesiastical organisation. A situation full of paradoxes arose: only a minority of the country's population confessed the same faith as their sovereign (the only short-term exceptions having been the reigns of the Hussite George of Poděbrady, 1458–1471, and, later on, of the Calvinist Frederick of the Palatinate, 1619–1620) while the majority embraced a different confession, were ministered to by their own Church and took positions that were different from – or even conflicting with – those of the sovereign.[5]

Though the Compactata became the country's basic law for more than 130 years, they fell short of preventing periodically repeated clashes between the two confessions and power groups in which both the papal court and the adjacent Catholic states were delighted to interfere permanently. The Catholic sovereigns of Bohemia attempted to exploit their momentarily strong positions for re-conversion of the country to Catholicism but the Utraquists prevented all such efforts, for the last time in the uprising of the inhabitants of Prague in 1483 which managed to convince king Wladislaw of Jagiello of the futility of such undertakings.[6] The decades which followed the last Hussite battles witnessed the birth of several new generations. Unlike the revolutionary fervour of an earlier period, they grew up in a consolidated society of Estates divided into corporations in which Catholics and Utraquists worked together without any substantial limitations to their essential life interests. The more perceptive politicians accepted the existence of two creeds as a reality sanctioned by law and by the royal oath. This long-term custom, supported by a relative decrease of interest in religious questions in the second half of the fifteenth century, led to attempts at finding reasons for this unprecedented situation and, at the same time, at securing lasting peace between

---

[5] Z. Měřínský (ed.), *Sborník příspěvků k 555. výročí vyhlášení Basilejských kompaktát v Jihlavě* [Contributions to the 555th Anniversary of the Proclamation of the Basel Compactata in Jihlava/Iglau] (Brno and Jihlava, 1991); see also R. Urbánek, *České dějiny* [History of Bohemia], vol. III, 1. *Věk poděbradský* [The Age of King George], vol. 1 (Prague, 1915), 88–136; W. Eberhard, 'Der Weg zur Koexistenz: Kaiser Sigismund und das Ende der hussitischen Revolution', *Bohemia* 33 (1992), 1–43.

[6] F. Šmahel, 'Pražské povstání 1483' [The Prague Uprising of 1483], *Pražský sborník historický*, 20 (1986), 35–102.

the two confessionally different segments of both the privileged and the underprivileged population of Bohemia and Moravia.[7]

A remarkable reasoning in favour of this binarity of creed was put forward by a Catholic humanist from Bohemia named John of Rabštejn/Rabenstein (Iohannes Rabensteinensis, 1437–1473) in his treatise *Dialogus*. In this he opposed the views of radical Catholic aristocrats who rose against the rule of king George of Poděbrady, supporting the invasion of Bohemia proclaimed by the Pope and carried out by Matthias Corvinus, king of Hungary. Rabštejn, a doctor of canon law who had studied at Bologna and Padova, was a scion of a Catholic baronial family and a Catholic priest by profession. Nevertheless, he refused to put religious strife before the general welfare of his motherland, torn by confessional divisions. Becoming a diplomat loyal to king George, he attempted to prevent the outbreak of civil war. In 1470, only a year after the writing of *Dialogus*, he joined the Catholic grouping under threat of excommunication. In this treatise he did acknowledge a subordination to the Pope but he rejected explicitly the violent means by which the lands of Bohemia were to be brought back to Catholicism. He demonstrated that the struggle of Catholic nobility against the king was not motivated by religious but by power considerations. He fully recognized the reality of a land in which a majority of the population was to be exposed to violence and to be forced back into obedience to the Roman Church at the price of enormous sufferings. Rabštejn ultimately came to be convinced that 'in expulsion of heresy from such numbers of people the preference of giving way to sword and fire before reason and humaneness was wrong'. For this Catholic humanist the motherland and *bonum commune* incarnated values on which the real coexistence of two confessional and political parties, supposed to tolerate each other, was to be based.[8]

Though Rabštejn's treatise exercised no direct influence on the practical solution of the tolerance question, it did express general trends manifested both among the Catholics and Utraquists of Bohemia. Both parties clearly saw that short of introducing a religious peace, both internal wars and foreign

---

[7] J. Válka, *Česká společnost v 15.–18. století* [Czech Society from the fifteenth to the eighteenth Centuries], vol. 1 (Prague, 1972); Válka, 'Politická závěť Viléma z Pernštejna (1520–1521). Příspěvek k dějinám českého politického myšlení v době jagellovské' [The political testament of the Lord Vilém of Pernštejn (1520–1521). A Contribution to the History of Czech Political Thought in the Jagiellonian Age], *Časopis Matice moravské*, 90 (1971), 63–82; W. Eberhard, *Konfessionsbildung und Stände in Böhmen 1478–1530* (Munich and Vienna, 1981); J. Macek, *Jagellonský věk v českých zemích* [The Jagellonian Age in the Bohemian Lands], vols. 1–2 (Prague, 1992–4); J. Pánek, 'Proměny stavovství v Čechách a na Moravě v 15. a v první polovině 16. století', *Folia Historica Bohemica*, 4 (1982), 179–217; F. Šmahel, 'Obrysy českého stavovství od konce 14. do počátku 16. století' [The Development of the Estates in Bohemia from the End of the fourteenth to the Beginning of the sixteenth Century], *Český časopis historický*, 90 (1992), 161–87.

[8] A. Grund and K. Hrdina (eds.), *Jan z Rabštejna, Dialogus* (Prague, 1946), esp. 48, 64–72, 94.

interventions led to nothing but destruction. After the installation of the Polish Jagiellonian dynasty on the throne of Bohemia in 1471 and after the above-mentioned failure of the re-Catholicisation efforts of the sovereign and his Catholic partisans in 1483, the initiative was taken by Bohemian nobility which, in a reconciliatory mood, concluded peace fully respecting the real facts at the Kutná-Hora/Kuttenberg diet of 1485. Much as Rabštejn, the participants of this diet put peace and common welfare above all the relativised religious differences, giving this recognition the form of a compromise treaty. They were none the less not united as to how long the peace among both confessional and political groupings should last. The Catholics assumed a possible re-Catholicisation in the future while the Utraquists wished eternal peace. Ultimately, the peace was concluded for thirty years with the possibility of an extension. After this, it was actually proclaimed as an eternal peace in 1512.[9]

Both parties acknowledged the principles of freedom of conscience, recognised each other mutually and promised not to regard each other as heretics. This meant a most perceptive recognition of the status quo which was further concretised by a stipulation that every community and parochial church was to adhere to the confession which it professed at the moment, regardless of the confession of the overlord. This put a considerable limitation on the overlord's right to present priests to ecclesiastical benefices and excluded the possibility of imposing any religious change on the individual communities in dependence on the possible change of overlord. Not even the community, however, was to become a decisive administrative agency, as every subject's right to an individual choice of creed was acknowledged. Such an extensive confirmation of religious freedom was exceptional in pre-Reformation and Reformation Europe. It suffered none the less from being limited exclusively to the land's two creeds – Catholic and Hussite Utraquist. Other religious congregations which emerged in Bohemia in the meantime did not enjoy the privileges set forth in the Kutná-Hora peace treaty.[10]

The most important of the new churches was the Unity of Brethren, arising after 1450 as a radical current within Utraquism. In the intention of evading the ecclesiastical-administrative nebulosity and the theological and moral sterility of the Calixtines (another name for the Utraquists), its representatives established a fully independent church in 1467. The Catholics saw in the Brethren just another example of heresy but the Utraquists feared a split in their own ranks. For this reason the Brethren soon came under fire from both

---

[9] W. Eberhard, *Konfessionsbildung und Stände*, 56ff.; Eberhard, 'Entstehungsbedingungen für öffentliche Toleranz am Beispiel des Kuttenberger Religionsfriedens von 1485', *Communio viatorum*, 29 (1986), 129–54.

[10] Cf. W. Eberhard, 'Zu den politischen und ideologischen Bedingungen öffentlicher Toleranz: Der Kuttenberger Religionsfrieden 1485', *Studia Germano-Polonica*, 1 (1992), 101–18.

sides. Political practice showed that the mutual tolerance among Catholics and Utraquists was based on a recognition of political balance, not on a systematic respect for the freedom of conscience.[11]

The first persecution came under King George and after his death in 1471 again under the Catholic sovereigns. After a transformation in the 1490s the Brethren remained an exclusive Church but took a more conciliatory position on social life. This allowed admission of rich burgesses and noblemen which extended their support to the Unity in the decades to come. At that time it was essentially up to the overlords whether they would tolerate the Brethren on their domains or whether they would heed the draconic instructions of Wladislaw Jagiello. In 1503, this king declared the Brethren enemies worse than Turks and ordered that they be burnt at the stake. After several executions the territorial diet promulgated the St James's mandate in 1508 whereby the congregations of Brethren and the propagation of their books were forbidden, their clergy arrested and imprisoned, and lay members forced to convert either to Catholicism or to Utraquism. This course of action *vis-à-vis* the Unity of Brethren showed the limits of Bohemian tolerance in cases where the respective religious minorities lacked sufficient worldly power and influence. The St James's mandate was renewed several times and until 1609 the Brethren were in fact outlawed, being exposed to possible legal prosecution at any time. However, they managed to win strong support from the opposition nobility groups, so that their persecution was neither systematic nor too vigorous. The range of political forces was thus enriched by another component which gradually came into position to command respect for its existence and expanded the tolerance radius from Catholic–Utraquist dualism to trialism or even to pluralism.[12]

In Bohemia and Moravia, the beginning of sixteenth century saw the emergence of a system of three parallel and competing confessional groupings enjoying varying degrees of legal protection. This situation acquired a measure of complexity after 1517 when the lands of Bohemia felt the impact of the German and later the Swiss Reformation. The border regions and Moravian royal towns, Catholic up to that time, partly accepted Lutheranism and another Church was thus born under a strong influence of Saxon ecclesiastical administration. Moreover, Utraquism crumbled under the action of

---

[11] A. Gindely, *Geschichte der Böhmischen Brüder*, vols. 1–2 (Prague, 1861–2); J. Th. Müller, *Geschichte der Böhmischen Brüder*, vols. 1–3 (Herrnhut, 1922–31); P. Brock, *The Political and the Social Doctrines of the Unity of Czech Brethren in the Fifteenth and Early Sixteenth Centuries* (The Hague, 1957); R. Říčan, *Die Böhmischen Brüder* (Berlin, 1961); M. L. Wagner, *Petr Chelčický – A Radical Separatist in Hussite Bohemia* (Scottdale, PA, 1983).

[12] A. Molnár, 'Luc de Prague édifiant la communauté (1498–1502)', *Communio viatorum*, 5 (1962), 189–200; Molnár, 'Autour du mandat royal. Luc de Prague entre 1504 et 1509', *Communio viatorum*, 6 (1963), 39–46; J. Glücklich, *Mandát proti Bratřím z 2. září 1602* [The Decree against the Unity of Brethren from 2 September 1602] (Prague, 1904).

Lutheranism: the more radical Neo-Utraquism incorporated many elements of Luther's doctrine while the conservative Old Utraquism dropped innovation and drew closer and closer to Catholicism. Finally, even the Brethren harked to the clarion-call of Lutheranism but ultimately gave preference to the voice of John Calvin and absorbed a considerable measure of his teachings in the second half of the sixteenth century. These innovations were followed by other radical Reformation trends invading Bohemia such as Anabaptism, anti-Trinitarianism, etc. The adherents of all these doctrines lived side by side and had to cope with the problem of mutual tolerance. The usual practice was that when a threat of persecution was imminent, all non-Catholics declared themselves Utraquists and took refuge under the land's laws.[13]

The enthronement of Ferdinand I and the unification of Bohemian, Austrian and Hungarian lands in the central European Habsburg monarchy brought about a threatening situation of conflict. Obliged to respect religious freedom for Utraquists by his electoral agreement, Ferdinand I was ready to extend legal protection to the Old Utraquist minority only. The king professed the idea of the necessary unity between the religious creed of a sovereign and his people and he even attempted to bring the Utraquists back into the Catholic fold. In addition he missed no opportunity to attack the Unity of Brethren and other illegal Churches. Twenty years of such molestations brought the Estates of Ferdinand's empire to the battlefield against their sovereign in the first anti-Habsburg uprising of 1546–1547. Taking advantage of a temporary weakening of Habsburg power during the Schmalkaldic War in the Holy Roman Empire, the Fraternal and Lutheran nobility attempted to contain Ferdinand's onslaught against religious liberties and those of the Estates.[14]

Unfortunately, Habsburg victories in the Empire and capitulation of the Bohemian rebels had quite different results. While Ferdinand had earlier manifested his intolerance *vis-à-vis* the non-Catholics by imposing on them

[13] R. Říčan, 'Melanchthon und die böhmischen Länder', *Philipp Melanchthon: Humanist, Reformator, Praeceptor Germaniae*, vol. 1 (Berlin, 1963), 237–60; F. G. Heyman, 'The Impact of Martin Luther upon Bohemia', *Central European History*, 1 (1968), 107–30; A. Molnár, 'Luther und die Böhmischen Brüder', *Communio viatorum*, 24 (1981), 47–67; W. Eberhard, *Konfessionsbildung und Stände*, 121ff.; Eberhard, 'Die deutsche Reformation in Böhmen 1520–1620', in H. Rothe (ed.), *Deutsche in den böhmischen Ländern* (Cologne, Weimar, and Vienna, 1992), 103–23.

[14] B. Bretholz, *Neuere Geschichte Böhmens*, vol. 1, *Der politische Kampf zwischen Ständen und Königtum unter Ferdinand I. 1526–1564* (Gotha, 1920); F. Hrejsa, *Dějiny křesťanství v Československu* [History of Christianity in Czechoslovakia], vol. 5 (Prague, 1948); J. Janáček, *České dějiny. Doba předbělohorská* [History of Bohemia, 1526–1547], vol. I, 1–2 (Prague, 1968–84); K. J. Dillon, *King and Estates in the Bohemian Lands 1526–1564* (Brussels, 1976); P. S. Fichtner, *Ferdinand I of Austria: The Politics of Dynasticism in the Age of Reformation* (New York, 1982); W. Eberhard, *Monarchie und Widerstand. Zur Ständischen Oppositionsbildung im Herrschaftssystem Ferdinands I. in Böhmen* (Munich, 1985).

a legally fossilized situation (the pretence of identity with Utraquists), in 1547 he initiated a full-scale persecution. Property confiscations, house arrests for the Brethren nobles and eviction of Lutheran preachers had none the less conflicting consequences. Though they slowed down the onset of the Reformation and facilitated consolidation of Catholic ecclesiastical administration, they considerably enhanced the coherence and solidarity of Bohemian non-Catholics in the long run. The idea that the adoption of one single religious confession and that a firm organisational structure of Evangelic Churches was imperative, gradually gained ground in spite of minor divergences. After the accession of Maxmillian II to the throne of Bohemia (1564–1576), non-Catholics attempted to shed the Compactata, now a dead letter no longer corresponding to the religious and political realities, and achieved their abolition in 1567. This happened none the less with the proviso that only Christians participating in the communion *sub una* and *sub utraque specie* and not erring sects were to enjoy the protection of the law. A wide range of Protestants attempted to implement the recognition of the *Confessio Augustana*. The Austrian nobility succeeded in this in 1568. This was none the less not a real success, because it took no account of the very different Reformation tradition of the Bohemian lands. A realistic solution could only be achieved by the acceptance of a new confession and of an ecclesiastical order that reflected the results of the long-term plurality of Reformation communities in Bohemia.[15]

A most precious compromise among the non-Catholic churches was reached in 1575, at a time when both the Lutheran–Calvinist fronts and the lines of internal conflict within the Lutheran camp bristled with weapons. The initiative was taken by politicians and moderate theologians from among the Neo-Utraquists, the interlinked Lutherans of the Melanchthonian orientation and the Brethren who understood the necessity of common action for the securing of religious liberty. The theologians worked out the Bohemian Confession (*Confessio Bohemica*), based on Lutheranism but respecting the peculiarities of Bohemian Hussitism as well as the doctrines of the Unity of Brethren. Far from a single compilation, this text aimed to express the common traits of the Protestants of Bohemia on as general a level as possible,

[15] F. Hrejsa, *Dějiny křesťanství v Československu*, vol. 6 (Prague, 1950); F. Kavka and A. Skýbová, *Husitský epilog na koncilu tridentském a původní koncepce habsburské rekatolizace Čech* [The Hussite Epilogue to the Council of Trent and the Original Conception of the Habsburg re-Catholicization of Bohemia] (Prague, 1969); J. Pánek, *Stavovská opozice a její zápas s Habsburky 1547–1577* [The Estate Opposition in Bohemia and Moravia and its Struggle against the Habsburgs 1547–1577] (Prague, 1982); Pánek, 'The Opposition of the Estates in the Beginnings of the Habsburg re-Catholicization of Bohemia', in J. Purš (ed.), *History and Society* (Prague, 1985), 353–80; Pánek, 'Maximilian II. als König von Böhmen', in F. Edelmayer and A. Kohler (eds.), *Kaiser Maximilian II. Kultur und Politik im 16. Jahrhundert* (Vienna and Munich, 1992), 55–69.

representing a clear manifestation of their wide tolerance. This was visible especially in the clause permitting the Brethren (with the consent of the other partisans of the Bohemian Confession) to retain internally their own specific Fraternal confession even demonstrated their understanding of weaker confessional groupings by purging their work of any denigrations of Calvinism, Zwinglianism, Anabaptism or Arianism. Readiness to coexistence and to tolerance in the plurality of confessions was thus incarnated in a most authoritative document of the Bohemian non-Catholics. This was the more important as the Bohemian Confession and the interdependent ecclesiastical order were no mere theoretical proclamations, having been backed by the political and economic power of the Evangelical Estates. As the diet went on, the Bohemian Estates community split into two wings: a Protestant, containing Neo-Utraquists, Lutherans and Brethren, and a Counter-Reformation wing in which the declining Old Utraquists clung to the Catholics.[16]

Though the Protestants did not manage to put the Bohemian Confession into practice as the legal basis for one of the land's religions in 1575, they built up a solid theoretical and organizational base to achieve this goal at the earliest opportunity. This occurred during the Habsburg dynastic crisis when Rudolph II and his brother Matthias competed for the monarchy at the beginning of the seventeenth century. At the time the Protestant Estates' opposition put the emperor under enormous pressure – they nominated their own government (*Directorium*), mustered their own army and negotiated with the Estates of the neighbouring lands for mutual help. The Emperor, afraid to meet the Estates in a battle for which he was ill prepared, signed the Letter of Majesty guaranteeing religious liberty. This charter of 9 July 1609 and the interconnected agreement between the Protestant and compromising Catholic Estates meant legalization of the Bohemian Confession as a fully privileged religion of the land. An independent church came into being headed by a corps of Defensors (elected protectors from among the nobles and burgesses) and with a Neo-Utraquist (Lutheran)–Fraternal consistory as an administrative and judiciary centre with the University of Prague as the spiritual centre of Bohemian non-Catholics. Two centuries after the beginning of the Bohemian Reformation, the non-Catholic nobles, burgesses and serfs, making up some 85–90 per cent of the population of Bohemia, obtained complete religious liberty and legal protection. The formula proposed for the 1609 solution to the question of coexistence and mutual tolerance developed the principle of individual choice of confession, anchored as early as the Kutná-Hora

---

[16] F. Hrejsa, *Česká konfesse* [The Bohemian Confession] (Prague, 1912); Hrejsa, 'Die Böhmische Konfession, ihre Entstehung, ihr Wesen und ihre Geschichte', *Jahrbuch der Gesellschaft für die Geschichte des Protestantismus in Österreich*, 35 (1914), 81–123; 37 (1916), 33–54; 38 (1917), 96–174; A. Eckert (ed.), *Die Böhmische Konfession 1575. Confessio Bohemica MDLXXV* (Wolfach and Kirnbach, 1976).

religious peace, but was much more elaborate and took account of the transformation of the one-time confessional dualism into a pluralism.[17]

The legislative act of 1609 made the long-term solution to the problem of multi-confessional coexistence foreseeable both from the theoretical and the organisational points of view. The internal and especially international political situation none the less did not favour any growth of mutual tolerance between the Catholics and Protestants. Though the radical Catholics who held the key appointments in the Bohemian administration refused to acknowledge the Letter of Majesty, they were not dismissed from their offices. Nor did the Habsburgs object to subversion of the peaceful coexistence of religious communities, nursing their hopes for the re-Catholicisation of the lands of Bohemia. Finally, even on the Protestant side the radicals who opposed the *de facto* political preference of the Catholic party were listened to more and more favourably. Institutionally, the growing contradictions undermined the political system of the state of Bohemia. Confessionally and politically, they led to the flareup of the second Estates anti-Habsburg insurgence in 1618–1620.[18]

This event constituted one of the decisive conflicts between Catholic and Protestant forces in Europe which resulted in the beginning of the Thirty Years' War. The Estates of Bohemia took care not to proceed in an isolated fashion. Winning support of the Estates of the incorporated lands of the Crown of Bohemia, Austria and Hungary, and to a very limited extent that of their co-religionists in western Europe, they attempted to reorganise the Habsburg monarchy into a confederation of central European lands under the sway of the Wittelsbach dynasty and with decisive influence of the Estates. The proposed solution to the religious questions was outlined in the constitutional charter of the Bohemian confederation of 31 July 1619. This envisaged the regulation of Catholic-Protestant relations in all lands including

[17] A. Gindely, *Rudolf II. und seine Zeit 1600–1612*, vols. 1–2 (Prague, 1868); Gindely, *Geschichte der Ertheilung des böhmischen Majestätsbriefes von 1609* (Prague, 1859); K. Krofta, *Majestát Rudolfa II.* [The Majesty Letter of Rudolf II] (Prague, 1909); R. J. W. Evans, *Rudolf II and his World: A Study in Intellectual History* (Oxford, 1973); Evans, 'Rudolf II and his Historians: the Nineteenth Century', *Prag um 1600. Beiträge zur Kunst und Kultur am Hofe Rudolfs II.* (Freren-Essen, 1988), 4–50; K. Vocelka, *Rudolf II. und seine Zeit* (Vienna, Cologne, and Graz, 1985); J. Janáček, *Rudolf II. a jeho doba* [Rudolf II and his Age] (Prague, 1987).

[18] P. Chlumecky, *Carl von Zierotin und seine Zeit 1564–1615* (Brünn, 1862); J. B. Novák, *Rudolf II. a jeho pád* [Rudolf II and his Downfall] (Prague, 1935); H. Sturmberger, *Georg Erasmus Tschernembl* (Linz, 1953); Sturmberger, *Kaiser Ferdinand II. und das Problem des Absolutismus* (Vienna, 1957); J. Franzl, *Ferdinand II. Kaiser im Zwiespalt der Zeit* (Graz, Vienna, and Cologne, 1978); J. Pánek, 'The Religious Question and the Political System of Bohemia before and after the Battle of the White Mountain', in R. J. W. Evans and T. V. Thomas (eds.), *Crown, Church and Estates, Central European Politics in the Sixteenth and Seventeenth Centuries* (London, 1991), 129–48; J. Válka, 'Moravia and the Crisis of the Estates' System in the Lands of the Bohemian Crown', in *ibid*, 149–57.

Moravia which until then had enjoyed a peculiar tradition, an unwritten law code sanctioned by usage, on the principles of the 1609 Letter of Majesty. Henceforth the relations of tolerance among the adherents to various confessions were to be codified not only by the goodwill of aristocratic overlords but, first and foremost, by legal clauses and relevant institutions. A good intention was, in fact, defiled by acts of partial discrimination, especially in the sphere of Catholic access to political influence. This can be understood with reference to the dramatic situation of a threat of war to the country from Catholic enemies, as well as by the fact that Catholics made up a minority of the population. Nevertheless, even the confederation charter eloquently illustrates the difficulties experienced by the Protestants with recourse to tolerance of the Catholic confessional-political minority at a moment in which they held all the power of the state.[19]

It is very difficult to estimate the course of Catholic-Protestant relations if the confederation had lasted longer. The Bohemian insurgents succumbed to the far stronger enemy armies as early as November 1620 and all their projects thus lost any practical importance. Treating Bohemia and Moravia as conquered lands, the victorious Habsburgs turned them into part of their dynastic lands and unilaterally transformed their legal system. A series of draconic measures wiped out the Protestant Estates opposition both physically and economically, and included the imposition of Catholicism as the only state religion. The process of violent re-catholicisation proceeded at lightning speed, starting with the 1621 eviction of non-Catholic clergy, then by that of their lay followers and ending with the promulgation of the *Obnovené zřízení zemské*, the Renewed Land Ordinance for Bohemia and Moravia in 1627 and 1628. Though of necessity superficial at the onset, it gradually penetrated deeper, resulting ultimately in a conversion of the overwhelming majority of the country's inhabitants to Catholicism.[20]

Although tiny groups of clandestine Protestants survived as late as the eighteenth century, the entire period between the years 1621 and 1781, the

---

[19] A. Gindely, *Geschichte des Dreißigjährigen Krieges*, vols. 1–3 (Prague, 1869–82); R. Stanka, *Die böhmischen Conföderationsakte von 1619* (Berlin, 1932); J. Válka, 'Morava ve stavovské konfederci roku 1619 (Pokus o vytvoření paralelních církevních a politických struktur v Čechách a na Moravě)' [Moravia in the Estates' Confederation of 1619 (An attempt to create parallel church and political structures in Bohemia and Moravia)], *Folia Historica Bohemica*, 10 (1986), 333–44. The Constitution of the Bohemian Confederation has been published by F. Kameníček, *Zemské sněmy a sjezdy moravské* [Moravian Territorial Diets and Congresses], vol. 2 (Brno, 1902), 649–69.

[20] A. Gindely, *Geschichte der Gegenreformation in Böhmen* (Leipzig, 1894); Z. Kalista, 'Die katholische Reform von Hilarius bis zum Weißen Berg' [The Catholic Reform within period ca. 1460–1620], in F. Seibt (ed.), *Bohemia Sacra. Das Christentum in Böhmen 973–1973* (Düsseldorf, 1974), 110–44; W. Eberhard, 'Entwicklungsphasen und Probleme der Gegenreformation und katholischen Erneuerung in Böhmen', *Römische Quartalschrift für christliche Altertumskunde und Kirchengeschichte*, 84 (1989), 235–57; J. Francek (ed.), *Rekatolizace v Českých zemích* [The re-Catholicization in the Bohemian Lands] (Jičín, 1995).

promulgation date of the Act of Toleration by Emperor Joseph II, may be termed a period of confessional absolutism. Any tolerance *vis-à-vis* non-Catholics was unthinkable: declared enemies of the Catholic Church and the state, they found themselves prosecuted both as heretics and as political criminals. This was the tragic end to efforts to stake out a Bohemian way to religious tolerance over more than two centuries. The buildup of conditions for tolerance and co-existence between the Catholic or religiously indifferent majority and the surviving and re-constituted Protestant minority had to wait until the emergence of the Enlightenment concepts of government.[21]

In terms of the history of the Bohemian struggle for religious freedom and tolerance the problem of the acceptance of foreigners and especially of dissidents of foreign origin, settling in the territory of Bohemia and Moravia merits a particular attention. This extraordinary test of tolerance was undergone by the Estates society of the lands of the Crown of Bohemia in the course of the sixteenth and at the beginning of the seventeenth century in connection with the advent of new population groups, especially from German- and Italian-speaking territories. Germans, mostly of Lutheran persuasion, felt close to the Neo-Ultraquists of Bohemia while the Catholic Italians clung to the imperial court and to the Catholic nobility. In spite of minor fits of xenophobia and recurrent fears of predominance of the Czech language in Bohemia and in Moravia, where this Slavic idiom constituted the exclusive means of communication in the diets and courts of justice, ethnic tolerance always prevailed, especially in the cooperation between the newcomers and their autochthonous co-religionists.[22]

A much more complex affair is represented by the cases in which the territory of the Bohemian state was chosen by immigrant groups markedly different from the home population, religiously, ethnically and even socially. Minorities with atypical religious and ethnic traits included the anti-Trinitarians, penetrating the Bohemian and Moravian territories in the six-

[21] M. Chr. A. Peschek, *Geschichte der Gegenreformation in Böhmen*, vols. 1–2 (Dresden and Leipzig, 1844–50); T. V. Bílek, *Reformace katolická v Království českém po bitvě bělohorské* [The re-catholicization in the Kingdom of Bohemia after 1620] (Prague, 1892); H. Opočenský, *Protireformace v Čechách po bitvé na Bílé hoře* [The Counter-Reformation in Bohemia after the Battle of White Mountain 1620] (Prague, 1921); E. Winter, *Die tschische und slowakische Emigration in Deutschland im 17. und 18. Jahrhundert* (Berlin, 1955); A. Molnár, 'Das Toleranzpatent und der tschechische Protestantismus', *Im Zeichen der Toleranz* (Vienna, 1981), 324–99; J. Mikulec, *Pobělohorská rekatolizace v českých zemích* [The re-Catholicization in the Bohemian Lands after 1620] (Prague, 1992).

[21] J. Klik, *Národnostní poměry v Čechách od válek husitských do bitvy bělohorské* [Relations between nationalities in Bohemia between the Hussite Wars and the Battle of White Mountain, 1420–1620] (Prague, 1922); A. Míka, 'Národnostní poměry v českých zemích před třicetiletou válkou' [Relations between Nationalities in the Bohemian Lands before the Thirty Years' War], *Československý časopis historický*, 20 (1972), 207–33; J. Janáček, 'Les Italiens a Prague a l'époque précédant la bataille de la Montagne Blanche (1526–1620)', *Historica. Les sciences historiques en Tchécoslovaquie*, 23 (1983), 5–45; T. Pěkný, *Historie Židů v Čechách a na Moravě* [History of Jews in Bohemia and Moravia] (Prague, 1993), 38ff.

teenth century mainly from Italy and Poland. These none the less constituted a marginal phenomenon, though extremely interesting both from the religious and ideological viewpoints.[23] A conspicuously deeper trace was left in the social context of the lands of the Crown of Bohemia by the advent of the Anabaptists after the defeat of radical Reformation in German and Tyrolean territories. The period between 1526 and 1622 when Anabaptists from a number of European countries were active in Moravia constitutes a 'golden age' in the history of this remarkable movement which later retreated before the onslaught of intolerance into southeastern Europe and Russia, ultimately finding a new home in the North American colonies.[24]

The first Anabaptist wave reached Bohemia and Moravia in 1526, where they were safe from persecution, in consequence of the defeat in the Peasants' War in Germany and Tyrol. The lands of Bohemia, by then characterised by pluralism of confessions, lacked any repressive apparatus which would have systematically operated against persons of different faith. The fairly weak rule of the Jagiello dynasty over the Bohemian lands allowed a measure of internal strife in which the individual overlords felt free to choose their own strategy of conduct. In these chaotic circumstances affecting both politics and ecclesiastical administration Anabaptists were accepted by Leonhard von Liechtenstein, who even underwent a second baptism in accordance with their doctrine and who provided a refuge for them in his Mikulov/Nicolsburg residence. Setting up a printing shop there, Anabaptists issued editions of their treatises.[25]

The Anabaptists retreated into Bohemia and Moravia from the west and south without any major disturbance up to 1527 when the land's new king, Ferdinand I of Habsburg, who had recently suppressed the Anabaptist movement in Tyrol, chose to step in. Unlike the tolerant domestic population, royal policy persecuted Anabaptists in a systematic fashion not only as an erroneous sect but also as potential spies for the Ottoman empire, menacing the eastern frontier of the nascent Habsburg monarchy.[26] This point of view

[23] W. Urban, *Der Antitrinitarismus in den Böhmischen Ländern und in der Slowakei im 16. und 17. Jahrhundert* (Baden-Baden, 1986).

[24] C.-P. Clasen, *Anabaptism. A Social History, 1528–1618. Switzerland, Austria, Moravia, South and Central Germany* (Ithaca and London, 1972); H.-J. Goertz (ed.), *Umstrittenes Täufertum 1525–1975. Neue Forschungen* (Göttingen, 1977); Goertz, *Die Täufer, Geschichte und Deutung* (Berlin, 1988); G. H. Williams, *The Radical Reformation* (Kirksville, 1992).

[25] J. Loserth, *Doctor Balthasar Hubmaier und die Anfänge der Wiedertaufe in Mähren* (Brünn, 1893); L. Müller, *Der Kommunismus der mährischen Wiedertäufer* (Leipzig, 1927); W. Wiswedel, *Balthasar Hubmaier, der Vorkämpfer für Glaubens- und Gewissensfreiheit* (Kassel, 1939); Th. Bergsten, *Balthasar Hubmaier. Seine Stellung zu Reformation und Täufertum 1521–1528* (Kassel, 1961); Ch. Möhl, 'Die Herren von Liechtenstein und die Wiedertäufer in Mähren', *Jahrbuch des historischen Vereins für das Fürstentum Liechtenstein*, 77 (1977), 119–71.

[26] A. Gindely *et al.* (eds.), *Sněmy české – Die böhmischen Landtagsverhandlungen und Landtagsbeschlüsse*, vol. 1 (Prague, 1877), 270, 381, 385, etc.; J. Pánek, 'Die Türkengefahr und die böhmische Gesellschaft im 16. und zu Beginn des 17. Jahrhunderts', *Rapports, co-rapports,*

heralded the essential position of confessional absolutism, seeing in a non-Catholic believer an enemy of the state. After 1535, arrest and execution of the Anabaptists in Bohemia resulted in their migration to Moravia, where they enjoyed a greater measure of autonomy and became more successfully integrated into the society of Estates.

The land of Moravia offered exceptionally favourable conditions for the reception of new settler groups. Large tracts still remained waste after the holocaust of the Bohemian-Hungarian wars of the second half of the fifteenth century. As well as being capable of nourishing many more inhabitants, especially in its fertile southern segments, it stood on the threshold of an era which saw remarkable unfolding of the potential of aristocratic landholdings. This made the nobility eager to welcome new-comers regardless of their confession, although burghers of the royal towns rejected them as serious economic competitors. In addition to socio-economic and political-administrative conditions, a major role was played by the practical application of confessional pluralism, unlimited by the written laws which inhibited it in Bohemia. An overwhelming majority of Moravian overlords staunchly professed the belief that even the king had no right to interfere on their estates and that their serfs received their faith as a gift of God. They thus assumed the role of *de facto* defenders of religious liberty within their domains, including the Anabaptists. Of course, all this with the tacit condition that the newcomers complied with the given social order, becoming industrious providers and taxpayers to their overlords.[27]

All these conditions were met by the Moravian Anabaptists. Among these, partisans of the Tyrolean reformer Jacob Hutter, pacifists who renounced any violent action in favour of the 'Kingdom of God', gradually prevailed. In 1535 and 1545, the Hutterites issued a statement to the effect that they repudiated any connection with the Münster commune as the 'Devil's work', and wished only to serve their lords in peace.[28] They proved their words by industrious and peaceful work, bringing profits both to the nobility and to the

commmunications tchécoslovaques pour le IVe Congres de l'Association internationale d'Etudes du Sud-Est européen (Prague, 1979), 139–68.

[27] J. Beck (ed.), *Die Geschichts-Bücher der Wiedertäufer in Oesterreich-Ungarn* (Wien, 1883); R. Wolkan (ed.), *Geschicht-Buch der Hutterischen Brüder* (Standoff-Colony, 1923); F. Hrubý, *Die mährischen Wiedertäufer* (Leipzig, 1935); J. Válka, *Hospodářská politika feudálního velkostatku na předbělohorské Moravě* [The Economic Policy of the Feudal Estates in Moravia before 1620]; (Prague, 1962); Válka, 'K otázkám úlohy Moravy v české reformaci' [On the Role of Moravia in the Czech Reformation], *Studia Comeniana et historica*, 30 (1985), 67–80; Válka, *Stavovská Morava* [Moravia in the Age of Estates], *1440–1620* (Prague, 1987); J. Janáček, *České dějiny* [History of Bohemia], vol. I, 1, 218–21.

[28] J. Beck (ed.), *Die Geschichts-Bücher*, 169ff.; R. Wolkan (ed.), *Geschicht-Buch*, 107, 110ff.; F. Kameníček, *Zemské sněmy* [The Moravian Territorial Diets], vol. 3 (Brno, 1905), 472ff.; F. Hrubý, *Die Wiedertäufer in Mähren*, 7ff.

whole land. Introducing technological innovations from countries extending from northern Italy to the Netherlands, the Anabaptists surpassed domestic craftsmen in a number of arts, especially in pottery-making and metallurgy, and their artfully decorated faience, showy daggers and carriages for the nobility became luxury goods sought after eagerly. Agricultural specialists found employment as reliable managers of estate farms and as skilled vintners, orchard keepers and cattle breeders. After several decades, those overlords who offered hospitality to the Anabaptists justly declared that they could not imagine running their estates without them.[29]

Economic symbiosis opened for the Anabaptists the path to complete integration into Moravian society of Estates. Far from surrendering their own particular character, they adhered to their religion, though members of the Unity of Brethren offered them shelter within one unified confession in times of persecution. Unfortunately, even friendly discussions led to the conclusion that the differences in perception of baptism, and of the Eucharist, as well as anthropological, ethical and social questions constituted an unbridgeable gap.[30] In the Czech-speaking environment the Hutterites clung to German as a language for daily communication and their liturgy and only some of their preachers mastered Czech sufficiently to allow them missionary activities among the indigenous populations.[31] Social integration took place in a sphere in which every inhabitant had to fulfil his or her tasks towards the country, namely that of taxation. From 1570 the territorial diet decided to levy regular taxes from the Anabaptists. This meant an essential change in their status: ceasing to be tolerated out of charity, they became fully fledged citizens of the Margraviate of Moravia. The Estates did not require the sovereign's consent for this unilateral decision, implementing it under the terms of the extensive Moravian autonomy. Fearing that their contributions would serve to support military activities, the Hutterites refused to pay taxes, passively allowing their financial obligations to be discharged by confiscation of part of their property by taxation officials. As recognition of this religiously inspired attitude, the Moravian Estates promised to use the collected money exclusively for peaceful purposes. In 1585,

---

[29] F. Hrubý, 'Nové přispěvky k dějinám moravských novokřtěnců. Jejich význam na poli hospo-dářské a průmyslové výroby' [Recent Contributions to the History of Moravian Anabaptists. Their Role in the Field of Economy and Industrial Production], *Českou minulostí. Sborník k 60. narozeninám Václava Novotného* (Prague, 1929), 213–39; Hrubý, *Die Wiedertäufer in Mähren*, 23ff.; J. Kybalová and J. Novovtná, *Habánská fajáns* [The Fayance produced by the Anabaptists], *1590–1730* (Prague and Brno, 1981); *Die Hutterischen Täufer, Geschichtlicher Hintergrund und handwerkliche Leistung*, ed. Bayerisches Nationalmuseum München (Bolanden, 1985).

[30] J. K. Zeman, *The Anabaptists and the Czech Brethren in Moravia, 1526–1628* (The Hague and Paris, 1969).

[31] J. Beck (ed.), *Die Geschichts-Bücher*, 300ff.; R. Wolkan (ed.), *Geschicht-Buch*, 131, 329, 361; F. Kalesný, *Habáni na Slovensku* [The Anabaptists in Slovakia] (Bratislava, 1982), 19, 119.

for instance, they were used to secure the financial position of the chief physicians of the land.[32]

Regardless of the sovereign's wrath, the Moravian aristocrats displayed maximum tolerance towards the Anabaptists, securing for them the best conditions under the circumstances. Enjoying their own ecclesiastical administration and educational facilities, the Hutterites were able to live in accordance with the principles of production- and consumption communism in their communities and communal dwellings (*Haushaben*). Around 1600 there were 45 communities numbering around 20,000 souls, amounting to 2.75 per cent of the population of Moravia and about one-tenth of the population of the southeastern part of the Margraviate in which the Hutterites were concentrated.[33] Aware of the fact that their religious liberty was conditional upon the generous tolerance of the nobility and especially of its Protestant majority, the Anabaptists respected this in their behaviour in the critical period of the society of Estates, during the Moravian anti-Habsburg Estates rebellion of 1619–1620. Putting at the disposal of the rebel leader, Ladislav Velen of Žezotín, their extensive network of covert contacts with a number of western European lands, they helped the newly elected king Frederick of the Palatinate in much the same friendly manner.[34]

In this particular instance the Anabaptists transgressed the borders of their systematic avoidance of political action, entering the power struggle for the survival of the dualistic constitution and for religious tolerance in the lands of Bohemia. Helpless to avert the crushing defeat of the Estates in 1620 and the triumph of confessional absolutism, they became one of its first victims. The victorious Habsburgs ordered them to leave the land as early as 28 September 1622. This onset of intolerance drew the curtain over the 'golden age' of the Anabaptists, sending them off to a long search of new homeland and religious freedom.[35]

In the Reformation period, the Bohemian lands, and especially Moravia are summarily referred to as model territories of religious freedom and tolerance. To a certain extent this is true for the sixteenth century, especially

---

[32] F. Kameníček, *Zemské sněmy* [The Moravian Territorial Diets], vol. 3, 483ff.; F. Hrubý, *Die Wiedertäufer in Mähren*. 47, 52ff.; see also R. Wolkan (ed.), *Geschicht-Buch*, 399, 415, 431.

[33] F. Hrubý, *Die Wiedertäufer in Mähren*, 107ff.; J. K. Zeman, 'Historical Topography of Moravian Anabaptism', *The Mennonite Quarterly Review*, 40 (1966), 266–78; 41 (1967), 40–78, 116–60; J Pánek, 'Die Täufer in den böhmischen Ländern, insbesondere in Mähren, im 16. und 17. Jahrhundert', *Der Schlern. Monatszeitschrift für Südtiroler Landeskunde*, 63 (1989), 646–61.

[34] K. Tieftrunk (ed.), *Pavla Skály ze Zhoře Historie česká* [History of Bohemia by Pavel Skála of Zhoř], vol. 3 (Prague, 1867), 444f.; F. Hrubý, *Die Wiedertäufer in Mähren*, 81ff.

[35] F. Hrubý, *Die Wiedertäufer in Mähren*, 92ff.; Hrubý, 'Karel st. z Žerotína a moravští novokřtěnci' [Charles Senior of Žerotín and the Moravian Anabaptists], *Český časopis historický*, 43 (1937), 68–72; P. Balcárek, 'Kardinál František z Ditrichštejna' [Cardinal Franz of Dietrichstein] (Kroměříž, 1990), 65f.

because unlike the rest of Europe, Bohemia and Moravia had by then lived within a Reformation tradition for a century. Religious plurality thus had a chance to sink roots in the mentality of several generations and was firmly established at a time when this problem was only appearing elsewhere. I hope I have demonstrated sufficiently by this brief review of developments between the fifteenth and the beginning of the seventeenth century that such tolerance fell short of being universal and unlimited. The sovereigns, some of their officials and municipal councils, especially in Moravia where the aristocrats displayed such tolerance sometimes proceeded in a most authoritative manner resulting in waves of evictions, imprisonments and even executions of people of different faith.

The chances of tolerance decreased considerably in periods of open conflict between religious and political interests. On the other hand, after the clash of arms had died down and in times of social consolidation the amount of mutual understanding grew. Even in these circumstances, however, the key role was played by political considerations based on the recognition of the fact that the adversary was simply too strong to be defeated by violent means. In such situations the voices of humanists were heard, who preferred values such as 'motherland', 'culture' or 'humanity' to religious strife. Political and possibly economic interests defined by the pluralistic foundations of the society of Estates, linking the Estates' privileges with religious liberty and defying the principle of unlimited power of a monarch to impose a single confession on the entire population of the state, remained of decisive importance. The conjunction of political interests, the principles of Estates' liberties and personal piety resulted in a conviction of a part of the Estates' élites that faith is the gift of God and that conflicts and wars could be prevented by assuming a Christian attitude above confessionalism. In Bohemia and Moravia and coexistence of adherents of various confessions grew out of respect for realities and the projection of the material interests of noble overlords towards their subjects. The further blossoming of tolerant relationships among people was conditioned by humanism and the depth of personal religious belief.[36]

[36] Cf. F. Hrubý, 'Zápas Čechů s Habsburky o náboženskou toleranci' [The Struggle of Czechs against Habsburgs for the Religious Tolerance], *Co daly naše země Evropě a lidstvu* (Prague, 1940), 156–67; A. Míka, 'Z bojů za náboženskou toleranci v 16. století' [Struggles for Religious Tolerance in the 16th Century], *Československý časopis historický*, 18 (1970), 371–82; F. Seibt, 'Das Toleranzproblem im alten böhmischen Staat', *Bohemia*, 16 (1975), 39–50; J. Macek, ' "Bonum commune" et la Réforme en Bohême', *Histoire sociale, sensibilités collectives et mentalités. Mélanges Robert Mandrou* (Paris, 1985), 517–25; W. Eberhard, 'Der Legitimationsbegriff des "Gemeinen Nutzens" im Streit zwischen Herrschaft und Genossenschaft im Spätmittelalter', in J. O. Fichte *et al.* (eds.), *Zusammenhänge, Einflüsse, Wirkungen. Kongressakten zum Ersten Symposium des Mediävistenverbändes in Tübingen 1984* (Berlin and New York, 1986), 241–54; J. Válka, 'K otázkám úlohy Moravy v české reformaci' [On the Role of Moravia in the Czech Reformation], *Studia Comeniana et historica*, 30 (1985),

Far from being the fruit of agnosticism or syncretism, tolerance in the lands of Bohemia during the Reformation period was also not the tolerance of a modern enlightened relativism. It ultimately emerged as the result of practical experience of several generations who had spent their lives seeking to perfect the principles of the society of Estates, defending them against autocratic sovereigns. This type of tolerance could live only as long as its defenders wielded enough power to counterbalance royal autocracy. Once they lost their struggle with the Habsburgs, their approach to religious pluriformity had to give way to the resolutely intolerant 'confessional absolutism'.

Translated by Petr Charvát

67–80; Válka, 'Tolerance, či koexistence? (K povaze soužití různých náboženských vyznání v českých zemích v 15. až 17. století)' [Tolerance or co-existence? (On the Character of the Common Life of Different Religious Confessions in the Bohemian Lands from the fifteenth to the seventeenth Centuries)], *Studia Comeniana et historica*, 35 (1988), 63–75.

15   Tolerance and intolerance in sixteenth-century Hungary

Katalin Péter

I should like to begin by making two observations concerning the method and substance of my contribution. Firstly, this chapter is bound to give the impression of being circuitous and based on inappropriate evidence. Hungarian history of the early modern period, especially concerning non-economic and non-political matters, tends to generate this impression in scholars used to the quantity and quality of sources available in Western European countries. Compared with such countries, Hungary is short of sources illustrating local and personal history. Thus, the matriculation of Hungarian students at universities abroad is well documented in the matriculation lists, most of them published, of the respective institutions, but we can only surmise that these students had experienced primary and secondary schooling, since sources relating to schools and schooling in Hungary are conspicuous by their absence.

Two explanations for the shortage of sources to early modern Hungarian history have become prevalent among historians. One emphasises the backwardness of sixteenth- and seventeenth-century Hungary, claiming that very few written sources were produced. The other points out that, though Hungary was not the Netherlands, it still produced the records of a kind characteristic of most Western European countries of this period, but most were destroyed by the wars and the political upheavals in the early modern period. I belong to the latter school of thought and regard my view as confirmed by much of the surviving evidence. A case in point is the early modern central government of Transylvania, in whose archives no government sources from this period have survived. Thus, all government activity from these years have to be reconstructed on the basis of documents issued by the government, but extant only in copies preserved by the recipients.[1] I have personally encountered this problem on the local level, in the case of Sárospatak, a middling market town. While researching the modern history of the town I discovered a list, from the 1570s of fees paid for documents issued by the local

[1] This reconstruction has been done by Zsolt Trócsányi in *Erdély központi kormányzata 1540–1690* (Budapest, 1980).

magistrate.[2] However, neither I nor anybody else has ever found a single such document issued by the Sárospatak magistrate: evidently such documents have perished. Under these circumstances, we have to rely on what little material has survived. Research based on a direct approach is thus made impossible by lack of the relevant sources: instead we have to conduct our inquiries in a circuitous manner, relying on meagre source material.

My second observation concerns the substance of my contribution, which might after all be approached in a number of ways. With regard to tolerance and intolerance one might for instance focus on famous or notorious persons as examples of such attitudes. Or one might concentrate, in pursuing the issue of tolerance, on the extensive contacts some internationally renowned advocates of tolerance had with Hungarians. This volume, however, is particularly concerned with tolerance and intolerance in the Reformation. In dealing with Hungary, I do not intend to discuss theories of toleration or their intellectual implications. Such an approach would, in my opinion, prove unrewarding, since the introduction of Protestantism, and the history of tolerance and intolerance in the Hungarian Reformation has very little to do with such attitudes.

I am of the opinion that both Catholic and Protestant secular authorities exercised some degree of tolerance regardless of their beliefs, and that such tolerance was generally dictated by political considerations. Later in the seventeenth century it was political considerations of like kind which brought about a change in the general attitudes of secular government and led to the violent Counter-Reformation of the country in the 1670s. These events however, will not be treated here. Instead I shall concentrate on the sixteenth century. In what follows I shall focus on two important incidents in sixteenth-century Hungary which throw some light on the significance of the political considerations involved when questions of religion and tolerance or intolerance were tackled by central government.

The first event to which I should like to draw attention to occurred in Sárospatak in 1537, on the estate of Péter Perényi. Towards the end of that year Johan Wese, former archbishop of Lund in Denmark, now envoy of Emperor Charles V, arrived in Hungary to negotiate peace between the country's two rival kings, Ferdinand I brother of the emperor, and John I Szapolyai.[3] Both kings had been elected eleven years earlier, and from the outset their supporters had waged war against each other, interrupted only by brief intervals dedicated to peace negotiations. Until Wese's arrival Charles V

---

[2] The unregistered material of the town is kept by the Tiszáninneni Református Egyházkerület Gyüjteményei, Levéltár in Sárospatak.

[3] His travel diary had been published in Bunytay Vince, Rapaics Rajmund, and Karácsonyi János (eds.), *Egyháztörténelmi emlékek a magyarországi hitújítás köréből, II (Budapest, 1904). (Hereafter EEH, with several volumes).*

had not shown much interest in the conflict, so the appearance of an embassy led by Wese indicated a change of imperial policy and enhanced the importance of the peace-talks which had started in the summer of 1536. Péter Perényi however, appears to have been unimpressed. He had been a key figure in Hungarian politics for decades and in 1537 was a leading figure in the camp of John I. That he did not deign to participate in the main meetings must have been a blow to the emperor's envoys. His aloofness forced Wese to seek a personal meeting and for this purpose the archbishop was actually obliged to travel to Sárospatak.

Here Perényi proved remarkably inhospitable. The lodgings provided for the archbishop and his entourage proved far from satisfactory, and Péter Perényi left them to attend regular services in the parish church without joining them. Even on Christmas Day he absented himself from mass. Wese would not have been surprised when a Hungarian representative in the peace negotiations confidentially informed him 'Petrus sit Lutheranus'.

A second incident characteristic of these events also most probably took place in Sárospatak, in 1540 and Péter Perényi was once again the central figure. On this occasion he was negotiating a return to Ferdinand's camp to which he had twice previously belonged. The talks were led by Elek Thurzó a personal and political friend of Perényi. Indeed, these two magnates had remained close friends although they had pursued different policies. Thurzó had remained loyal to Ferdinand from the outset and never wavered throughout the repeated upheavals of Hungarian politics. He seems, nevertheless, to have sympathised with Perényi's repeated changes of allegiance. In this respect, I consider the friendship between the two men to be proof of Perényi's sincerity in his negotiations with Thurzó, and moreover to be a guarantee of Thurzó's honesty when informing Ferdinand of the talks. The negotiations had in all probability been initiated by Ferdinand, since they began with Perényi announcing his terms. The first reference can be found in a note by Thurzó, confirmed by another two documents, which shows that the talks were concerned with religious issues. Thurzó informed the king: 'First of all my lord Péter would like an assurance from Your Majesty that he will never be forbidden his faith because he declares himself to be a good Christian and he knows the Christian faith through Christ and according to the Gospel.'[4]

In his reply Ferdinand responded 'to the first article where he asks His Majesty to guarantee that he will not be forced to abandon his faith', by granting his request in a decidedly pre-Tridentine manner. According to the surviving draft document, Ferdinand admitted – ('concedit Majestas Sua') – that Perényi was a good Christian who conducted himself as required of

[4] Franz Bucholtz, *Geschichte der Regierung Ferdinand des Ersten. Urkundenbuch* (Vienna, 1838), 323–4.

everybody by 'piety towards God and our true and Catholic faith'.[5] The word 'concedit' can only mean that Ferdinand was fully aware of Perényi's evangelical orientation. It would otherwise have been absurd for a devout Catholic monarch to allow him to remain a Catholic. But the pre-Tridentine atmosphere of these negotiations must be emphasised. Ferdinand summed up his expectations in a manner acceptable to nearly every Christian of the age, since to observe the Catholic faith was a non-committal condition in 1540, when all denominations still considered themselves to be Catholic. This view appears to have been particularly popular in Hungary where it remained so pervasive that even the first evangelical church ordinance published in 1562, and heavily influenced by the Swiss Reformation, was entitled *Confessio Catholica*.

Perényi's reaction corresponds neatly to this view. According to the response noted by Thurzó, he pronounced himself satisfied with Ferdinand's declaration. The reason was again pre-Tridentine in character. Perényi did not want to nourish or establish some new sect.[6] This was the core of the matter. He had only sought a guarantee that he could remain a Christian according to the Gospel, and as the king had not condemned him as a heretic, the matter was satisfactorily concluded.

These two events, which I see as characteristic of the circumstances in sixteenth-century Hungary, demonstrate the existence of tolerance on two levels. The first level can be typically in the relationship between church patrons and their parishes, the second in the relations between kings and Estates.

With regard to the first, it is clear that, according to Archbishop Wese, Catholic services were celebrated regularly in the parish church of Sárospatak despite the non attendance of the patron of the church, who was, as the archbishop's informer puts it, 'Lutheranus', a view confirmed by other sources. In a letter of 1539 to Pope Paul III, a papal nuncio labelled Perényi the most apostate Lutheran, while István Gálszécsi, a graduate of Wittenberg University, in 1536 dedicated an evangelically-inspired hymnal to Péter Perényi. Even more telling was the fact that another Wittenberg graduate, Mihály Siklósi, officiated as a chaplain on Perényi's estate from around 1532 onwards. Yet there is no indication whatsoever that Siklósi preached in any of the parish churches on Perényi's vast domains. This means that this evangelically minded, 'Lutheran' patron of numerous parish churches for many years worshipped privately on his estates while Catholic services continued undisturbed in the churches under his patronage.

[5] *EEH* III, 470.
[6] *EEH* III, 478–9.

Perényi was never accused of intolerance by the serfs on his estates. This is evident from a wide-ranging inquiry into the management of his estates conducted by royal officials some years after his death. The final report certainly blackened Perényi's reputation, presenting him as one of the worst landlords of his age. The serfs voiced numerous grievances especially about the heavy feudal duties they were forced to pay during Perényi's time, but no complaints about religion were ever advanced. Considering that the royal officials were Catholics, the serfs would have been guaranteed a positive hearing had they wished to voice any complaint about religious intolerance on Perényi's part.[7]

Clearly, Perényi had no hesitation in exploiting his serfs economically, yet did not seek to impose his faith on them. This was an inclination shared by most Hungarian church patrons in the sixteenth century. In general the Reformation was introduced in Hungary without the use of coercion. This is confirmed by the proceedings of trials and investigations against people accused of being adherents of 'Luther's plague' in the 1520s.[8] The accused were charged with reading prohibited books, with non-attendance at mass, with breaking fasts or with breaking secular and ecclesiastical laws but never, to my knowledge, with physically attacking members of the clergy, monks, friars or any other Catholics.

In Hungary spontaneous outbursts of popular anticlericalism were extremely rare. On the one hand, this was undoubtedly due to the fact that the number of friars and monks was extremely low by the beginning of the sixteenth century. Thus, people were unlikely to be confronted by the monastic way of life in practice. On the other hand, a considerable and conspicuous part of the Church's representatives joined the Reformation. Thus, it is a commonplace in Hungarian historiography, for instance, to emphasise the role of the Franciscans in the establishment of the Reformation.

The stance of many Catholic clerics in these matters is also reflected in the above-mentioned documents relating to the trials and investigations against the followers of Luther, in which priests and monks constitute most of the accused. This, however, was not peculiar to Hungary. All the reformers of the first generation had, after all, originally begun as Catholics, and it is no surprise that priests, monks and nuns were prominent among the first propagators of the new faith in Hungary.

It strikes me that the Hungarian Reformation was characterised by a tendency to lampoon rather than resort to physical confrontation. The reformers used laughter rather than violence. In this regard it is most telling that the

---

[7] This document is kept in the Országos Levéltár, Urbaria et Conscriptiones 40/35.
[8] These documents are published in *EEH* II.

most frequent accusation was the charge that an offender had made fun of the cloth. The form taken by such ridicule is seldom described in the documents, but what little we know shows that it often consisted of publicly chanting derogatory rhymes at female and male representatives of the Church. Such lampooning could also begin with the secret dissemination of satirical songs which were then sung openly, as occurred in Brassó and Szeben where a prolonged investigation into such deeds was conducted in 1524. This attitude towards Catholicism or its representatives is further reflected in the satirical plays about the clergy enacted in town squares, Two written by the eminent Protestant man of letters, Mihály Sztárai, also appeared in print in the 1550s. One ridiculed celibacy and the other, called *Comoedia lapidissima*, the haughty manners of priests. Such plays were by all accounts very popular.

The relative peace that prevailed in Hungary during the Reformation era was closely related to the restrained behaviour of the church patrons. However, as I have mentioned above, this was not the result of conscious confessional preference. To sum up, an important behavioural determinant was the special relationship between patrons and their parishes. This meant that the owners of the estates, whether private individuals or whether magistrates exercised the *ius patronatus* over the churches on their estates without taking into consideration either party's religious leanings.[9]

This flexible principle in matters of religion already had a fairly long history at the time of the Reformation. It had emerged in the thirteenth century when Greek Orthodox Romanians began to emigrate to Hungary from neighbouring territories. These were usually organised settlers, invited, so to speak, to take up residence by different landlords. At no stage in the immigration process was any mention of them changing their religion. The Romanian communities were granted the right to build churches and to conduct their own worship without restrictions.[10] The Greek Orthodox lived under Catholic patronage, but their church buildings bear witness to an excellent and tolerant co-operation. Thus, some of the most beautiful medieval frescoes in Hungary were painted by Orthodox churches. The only medieval fresco depicting together the first saints of the House of Arpád, Saint Stephan, Saint Emeric and Saint Ladislas, has been preserved in the Greek Orthodox church in Kristyán, Criçior, part of present day Romania.

It would be difficult to prove that sixteenth century Hungarians perceived the relationship between Catholics and Orthodox, on one hand, and Catholics and Protestants, on the other, as similar. The practice, however, of being

---

[9] The inter-dependence of *ius patronatus* with land-owning differed in Hungary from the western European practice: Kolláni Ferenc, *A magán Kegyúri jog hazánkban* (Budapest, 1906), 13–15.

[10] Makkai Lásló, 'Görögkelelti román papok és templomok', in Köpeczi Béla (ed.), *Erdély Története*, I (Budapest, 1986), 394–400.

impartial patrons of an alien denomination was well-established by the time of the Reformation. It was shared thereafter by both Catholics and Protestants. My interpretation runs contrary to the established view of this matter. The Reformation in Hungary is usually described as the consequence of the conversion of the lay patrons and it is assumed that the churches were automatically turned over by force of the *ius patronatus*, to the denomination chosen by the patron.

This is a natural supposition, and I would not claim that changes in religion were not forcibly introduced during the Reformation period. There is, however, good reason to argue that changes in the religious orientation of the parish churches was assisted by the secular authorities out of their desire to oblige their evangelically minded subjects.[11] It would appear that church patrons, individual or collective, who had the last word in these matter, usually consented to the new form of worship rather than forcing the parishes to accept Protestantism. This must have been the normal procedure. Contemporary assessment of the situation supports this interpretation. Significant in this regard was the position taken by the Hungarian Diet. When, in 1548, it prohibited the activity of lay preachers it accused some lords and noblemen of tolerating them as priests in the churches.[12]

Similarly, the generally peaceful atmosphere of the Reformation in Hungary does not testify to any intolerance on the point of the landowners or the town magistrates as patrons. I have dealt with the case of Péter Perényi in some detail in order to provide a convincing example of the typical behaviour, and mentioned the relationship of Greek Orthodox and Catholic believers, which has not hitherto been taken into consideration in Hungarian historiography, to show that precedents existed well before Reformation. The most striking consequence, however, of the *ius patronatus* over alien denominations seems to be the fact that town magistrates often tolerated the exercise of several faiths, that is, churches of different denominations co-existed in many towns. As for the villages, in many of them churches were used in turn by different faiths according to prior agreement.[13]

How typical the practice I have labelled *cuius patronatus, eius religio* was is also reflected in the attitude of the rulers of Transylvania. This province had been separated from the rest of the country and assigned to the infant-successor of John I by Sultan Suliman in 1541. It was ruled throughout the sixteenth century except for seven years, by devout Catholics. Nevertheless, these rulers were accepted as the supreme secular authority by all Protestants. This practice was introduced by the dowager queen of John I, Izabella Jagel-

---

[11] Katalin Péter, 'Hungary', in R. W. Scribner *et al.* (eds.), *The Reformation in National Context.* (Cambridge, 1994), 159.

[12] *Corpus Juris Hungarici 1526–1608* (Budapest, 1899), 226.

[13] Benda Kálmán, *A felekezeti kisebbségek jogainak biztosítása* (Budapest, 1991), 35–40.

lon who headed the regency. As a ruler she was far from impressive, but in matters of religion she proved fortunate. Instead of confronting her subjects, the majority of whom were already evangelically inclined by the 1540s, the queen began to act as their patron. At first, in 1543, disregarding the protests of the Catholic clergy she assented to the new evangelical church ordinance of the Saxons. Then, during the delicate negotiations at the 1557 Diet, she declared: 'By our Royal station and office we are obliged to protect all Churches'.[14] This meant, that the dowager Queen sought to stay out of religious conflict by taking on the role of defender of all denominations represented in Transylvania. The Estates concurred in the queen assuming this role, and her successors had only to imitate her gesture by endeavouring not to alienate their subjects on religious matters.

Indeed, the Catholic patrons of the Protestant Churches in Transylvania occasionally demonstrated a willingness to accept highly unorthodox developments. Thus, it was Stephen Báthori, the later king of Poland, who in 1571 as ruler of Transylvania consented to the election of the first anti-Trinitarian superintendent. Historians tend to forget that Transylvania under Catholic rulers became a haven for freethinkers and radical reformers from all over Europe. The most commonly known fact in this connection is the shameful persecution of the above-mentioned first anti-Trinitarian superintendent, Ferenc Dávid, after he had openly declared his christological views. However, I am not sure that the case of Dávid should not be seen, as far as Báthori is concerned, as an example of toleration of intolerance within the anti-Trinitarian church.[15]

The Habsburg kings who ruled the rest of the kingdom were not faced with similar problems and did not establish any contacts with Protestant groups or individuals. The second episode I described at the beginning of this chapter illustrates the role religion played in the relationship between king and Estates. The circumstances in which Perényi demanded freedom of conscience were indeed typical. To switch from the camp of one king to that of another was an action often repeated and highly rewarded from 1526 until around 1570. Such cases generally followed a similar pattern. The nobleman about to change his allegiance was approached by royal representatives at which point he stated his terms and made it clear the rewards he expected by joining or rejoining the monarch. If the terms were accepted the change of allegiance occurred, and the whole procedure might begin again, in reverse.

What was significant in Perényi's case was that his demand for religious freedom featured prominently in the negotiations. In other instances the main objectives were purely secular, such as the approval of otherwise dubious

---

[14] Szilágyi Sándor (ed.), *Erdélyi Országgyülési Emlékek, II* (Budapest, 1877), 78.
[15] Mihály Balázs has recently dealt with this delicate case in *Defensio Francisci Davidis* (Budapest, 1983), vii–xxxviii.

inheritance or marriage contracts; mostly the negotiations were simply and unashamedly concerned with substantial rewards in money and land. Such grotesque bargaining, in a country on the brink of total collapse, was regarded by most outsiders with severe distaste. The proceedings, and the disgust of the disinterested observers is described in an excellent play, (by an anonymous author) *The Treason of Menyhárt Balassi*, published in 1569.

Perényi, incidentally, having secured his freedom of worship, then joined his peers in the traditional bargaining. A draft of his original demands has been preserved. In it his religious demands occupy eighth place, sandwiched between traditional claims for awards, titles and possessions. However, what matters in this context is not Perényi's ethical standards or religious commitment, but that his case is an illustrating example of the relationship between the king and the Estates in matters of religion.

Perényi's demand for freedom of worship in negotiations about renewed allegiance to Ferdinand might easily lead to the assumption that Catholicism in its papalist form served as a boundary marker for the king's party. That, however, was hardly the case, even if the traditional view of Hungarian historiography has been to portray the Habsburg monarchs as the natural protectors of Catholicism and consequently as the enemies and persecutors of Protestants, unwilling to tolerate evangelically-minded people in their lands. I do not dispute that their natural inclination may have been to act in this way, but I must emphasise that I am concerned with political actions, not with spiritual preference. Bearing that in mind it is reasonable to assume that Ferdinand should have been inclined to show tolerance in the case of Perényi. Undoubtedly Perényi would have been aware that by 1540 the Hungarian nobility, who supported both kings, was 'Catholic' in the sense he considered himself to be, according to the Gospel.

Despite his open sympathy for the Reformation, Elek Thurzó had been chosen as the leading member of Ferdinand's party to negotiate with Perényi. It was no secret that he belonged to a circle of courtiers in Buda who had been attracted to Luther from the early 1520s. A decade later it was on his estate in Pápa that Bálint Eck, a pastor who had refused holy orders, officiated and was employed as a schoolmaster. Probably around the same time a group of ministers in the northern part of the country, on an estate belonging to Thurzó, decided to interpret the Gospel 'in accordance with Doctor Luther and Philip Melanchton'.[16] This could hardly have happened without Thurzó's tacit consent.

Another evangelical sympathizer within Ferdinand's camp in 1540 was Ferenc Révai, who two years earlier had corresponded with Luther on ques-

---

[16] The canons are published in *Magyar Protestáns Egyháztörténeti Adattá*, VII, 1–11. The date assumed here, however, is erroneous.

tions of evangelical doctrine. Not only did he enjoy the king's confidence, but in 1542 he was appointed palatine-lieutenant. We should also mention Tamás Nádasdy who had held high offices at Ferdinand's court since 1536. Moreover, Ferdinand's court was a famous meeting place for Erasmian and Lutheran intellectuals. Later, in 1554, Tamás Nádasdy was elected palatine of the country, with the consent of the Habsburgs. The first Protestant theological work in Hungarian appeared bearing the coat-of-arms and evidently with the financial assistance of Ferenc Frangepán, one of Ferdinand's councillors. There is no evidence of Ferdinand trying to interfere with the religious views of his vassals in Hungary or trying to isolate the Protestants among them.

Throughout his reign, and under his successors up to the turn of the century, the religious question caused no strain in the relationship between king and Estates. This did not mean that total harmony prevailed, but that the conflicts centred on other issues. The mines, which were in a state of exhaustion like elsewhere in Europe, caused much strife, as did the budget, primarily because the Estates suspected that the Habsburg kings spent incomes from Hungary in the other territories under their rule. Then there was the often repeated reproach of non-residence since the kings lived in Vienna. The Diets passed tax-bills describing in detail the obligations of the different social strata. They took complicated decisions as to who were obliged to serve in person in the army, who had to supply armed men and in which circumstances everybody had to serve, such as in a general mobilisation. The kings' property transactions were examined in detail, although the Estates had no rights in such matters. Nor did they have the authority to declare anybody guilty of high treason, but the Diets nevertheless often requested such powers. Religious irregularity, however, was never among the grievances, and the issue of religion in general did not arise in the negotiations of the Estates.

It could be said there was no reason to turn the matter of religion into an issue of debate with the kings as there was no need to seek the secularisation of church property. In a fateful battle at Mohács in 1526 nearly the entire bench of Bishops had fallen and the possessions of the Catholic Church had been expropriated by the king and the nobility. The monarchs used church property to placate and reward their capricious followers, and were not keen to re-establish the proprietorial rights of the Catholic Church. The Catholic kings of the sixteenth century had been so thorough in their distribution of church property to secular landowners that the struggle of the ecclesiastical authorities of the Counter-Reformation to regain them after the turn of the century took decades.[17] Even then the Catholic Church never fully regained its former glory.

---

[17] Péter Pázmány, the head of the Catholic Church between 1616 and 1637, was famous for his obduracy in this matter.

Such concerns contributed to the fact that the issue of religion, continued to be regarded a private matter in the sixteenth century. This is exactly why the case of Perényi so effectively illustrate the relationship between the kings and the Estates in the matter of religion. Perényi chose not to confront the Diet, and did not demand freedom of conscience for his peers or for anybody else, but only for himself. Ferdinand reacted as we might expect. He rewarded Perényi richly when he renewed his allegiance. In Ferdinand's eyes, and in the eyes of his successors for the rest of the century, the matter of religious worship had no public consequence.

In the 1520s when evangelical ideas first reached Hungary the situation had been different. The first law dealing with the new religion issued in 1523 declared it no duty of the king to punish the Lutherans and their protectors.[18] It was a tricky situation, as the hatred of the lesser noblemen who demanded this sanction, had been prompted by the courtiers of Queen Mary, mentioned above in connection with the case of Thurzó. Nevertheless, Louis II, who was himself no fervent Catholic, took the necessary steps. He was forced to take action by the presence of several papal nuncios at his court who had been deeply alarmed by Queen Mary's Lutheran sympathies.

The dramatic change in royal attitude to religious matters followed the young king's death in 1526 and is illustrated by the events of the Diet of 1548. Under the influence of the Council of Trent, the reformation of the Catholic Church was put firmly on the agenda. The Diet passed a bill concerned with Catholic reforms, but rejected another ordering the punishment of Lutherans: only non-Lutheran Protestants were condemned.[19] The votes show the majority of the Estates either considered themselves to be Protestant or wanted to avoid a confrontation with the Protestants. However, the king's duty was not mentioned, and Ferdinand ignored the rejection of the second bill. He indicated that he was not concerned with religion as a matter of public interest, and so acted wisely, in Hungary at least. In his own hereditary lands, however, he behaved rather differently.

It was Rudolph II, Ferdinand's successor after next, who destroyed the religious equilibrium in Hungary. He was undoubtedly encouraged by some of his Counter-Reformation clerical advisers who lured him into attacking the royal free towns in 1604.[20] Some church buildings were confiscated from the Protestants and Catholic priests were installed. These measures, however, did not affect all Protestant churches in these towns. Nevertheless, they succeeded in enraging Protestant burghers, noblemen and magnates all over Hungary, becoming one of the causes of the Bocskai War of Independence.

The argument of Rudolf and his advisers was that since the royal free towns belonged to the king, he had the right to decide their religious

---

[18] *Corpus Juris Hungarici 1000–1526*, 825.
[19] *Corpus Juris Hungarici 1526–1606*, 226.
[20] R. J. W. Evans, *Rudolf II and His World* (Oxford, 1973), 26.

allegiance. However, this reasoning was alien to the Hungarian Estates. The interpretation of the *ius patronatus* itself did not become part of the debates. The conflict revolved around the status of the royal free towns. According to the Estates they were properties of the Crown, but the Crown rested in the hands of the Estates, so that the king was in no position to exercise a *ius patronatus* over them.[21] This debate served to bring to the fore the issue of religion. In the course of the War of Independence all the grievances against the king were summed up in the accusation of having violated the country's religious liberty.

Finally, to explain further the role of tolerance in Reformation Hungary, I shall turn to a third event. It concerns the above mentioned Perényi, who had left his young son, Ferenc, in Turkish hands as a hostage, only himself to endure detention some years later, in 1542, after being accused by Ferdinand of complicity with the enemy. Many contemporaries ascribed his dealings with the Turks to his endeavour to have his child returned from Constantinople. It is far from certain, that Perényi did not have illicit dealings with the Ottoman authorities and we do not know whether Ferenc ever returned home.[22] Only one thing seems definite, that his fate and the fate of his family was determined by the Turks. That this particular enemy was seen to lurk everywhere and behind everything was characteristic of the Reformation period in Hungary.

After decades of more or less unsuccessful attacks, the Ottomans finally took Belgrade in 1520, as contempories saw it the gate to Hungary. In that year the first evangelical books were brought to Hungary. In 1541, when the first complete translation of the New Testament appeared, the sultan divided the country, ceding the western section to Ferdinand I and the eastern to the infant heir of John I, while the middle part was incorporated into the Ottoman Empire.

Further parallels, however, exist between the events of the Reformation and those of the Turkish conquest. Here I should state that I do not intend to argue that the presence of the Ottomans proved advantageous to Protestantism. That would only serve to repeat a rather tired and dated historiogaphy. Traditionally, church historians have ascribed the victory of the Reformation in the Ottoman occupied territory to Ottoman sympathies for Protestantism, by contrast to their hostility to the Catholics who were allegedly regarded as representatives of the Ottoman's main enemy, the Catholic Habsburg kings.

A fairly recent study into the exact relationship between the Ottomans and the Protestants has reached a totally different conclusion and brought to light

---

[21] The document relating to this debate is published in *Magyar Országgyűlési Emlékek*, X, 86–7.
[22] The story told by Mihály Sztárai had been published by Imre Téglássy in *Irodalomtörténeti Közlemények* (1984), 463–70.

significant new evidence.[23] It now appears that the Turkish authorities did not in general distinguish between Catholics and the various Protestant denominations. Nevertheless, and this is noteworthy, there were attempts by the Turkish authorities to establish contacts with Protestants. These attempts, however, were explicitly rejected. It could not have been easy to resist the temptation to seek favour with an otherwise dreaded infidel enemy.

I should also like to call attention to the obvious fact that, as far as the spread of the Reformation was concerned, there was no significant difference between the three parts of the country. The same developments took place in the Habsburg kingdom, in Transylvania, and in the territory under Turkish occupation. By the 1670s roughly 80–85 per cent of the Christian inhabitants belonged to one of the Protestant churches.

The continued presence of the enemy in my opinion had a different effect. I tend to see the generally tolerant attitude of successive secular authorities in Reformation Hungary as dependent on the Ottomans' presence. As contemporaries put it, they were in the jaws of the Turk. In this atmosphere of continued uncertainty, no ruler wished to antagonise his subjects. That was the rule, of course, with some exceptions, but the secular authorities seem to have been generally determined not to swim against the rising tide of the Reformation. In this situation the Catholic Church remained powerless.

This statement may seem to suggest that later events were determined by the ability of Catholics to win secular support. This, however, was far from the case as the Catholic Church only managed to ally itself with the supreme and lower secular authorities in the kingdom during the seventeenth century. In Transylvania a series of princes belonging to the Reformed Church ruled until 1690, and the territory in the middle of the country remained under Turkish occupation for a similar period. This has to be said, since it is a well-known fact that the predominance of Protestantism in Hungary vanished at some point in the country's history and this change is generally seen to have been caused by the post-Tridentine activities of the Catholic Church.

In my opinion the decisive moment came with the expulsion of the Turks. Until then neither Catholic proselytising nor Counter-Reformation initiatives had really been successful. Catholic dominance was not achieved until the regions devastated by the wars were repopulated with settlers from Catholic countries.

[23] Ferenc Szakály, 'Türkenherrschaft und Reformation in Ungarn', in *Etudes Historiques Hongroises* (Budapest, 1985), 437–59.

16   Protestant confessionalisation in the towns of Royal Prussia and the practice of religious toleration in Poland-Lithuania

Michael G. Müller

Within the history of toleration the case of Poland presents a somewhat reverse chronology compared with developments in the rest of early modern Europe. The famous Polish culture of tolerance was essentially a phenomenon of the late Middle Ages and the sixteenth century. It had developed in the context of the construction of a multinational monarchy under the Jagiellonian kings, and it offered a legal and ideological framework that was able fairly easily to accommodate the Reformation once it gained massive support among the Polish and Lithuanian nobility from the 1550s onwards.[1] The subsequent period instead saw tolerance in decline. From roughly the mid seventeenth century onwards religious tension both between Christians and non-Christians and among the Christian confessions seemed to grow steadily, finally culminating in a series of violent conflicts over the so-called 'dissident' question that immediately preceded the partition of 1772. In short: the Poles seem to have 'invented' tolerance well before it became an issue of humanistic and proto-enlightened debate; but they apparently abandoned it precisely at the time when elsewhere religious tolerance became part of a commonly shared European culture.

This chapter offers some tentative explanations of this phenomenon, focusing mainly on what seems to have been the turning point in this long-term development: the period of confessionalisation. In this context three points will be argued.

1. The history of the legal and constitutional framework for religious toleration in Poland-Lithuania has to be clearly distinguished from the parallel developments on the levels of religious culture and popular religiosity, since the turn towards intolerance in Poland-Lithuania from the mid-seventeenth century onwards seems to have been essentially a phenomenon of the latter levels.

2. The roots of an increasingly intolerant religious culture in Poland-Lithuania can be traced to the process of confessionalisation as such, and

---

[1] For a reliable outline of the history of toleration in Poland-Lithuania see Janusz Tazbir, *Dzieje polskiej tolerancji* [A History of Polish Tolerance] (Warsaw, 1973).

confessional Protestantism as a theological and political factor appears to have had a substantial share in bringing about such effects.

3. What resulted in intolerance, as an outcome of confessionalisation, could be identified as a 'nationalisation' of religiosity – nationalisation here understood as a territorialisation of religious identities in the context of political developments, but also the implementation of certain patterns of religious values and religious practices specifically representing the political, cultural, and social profile, and self-perception, of elites in what was to become the Polish-Lithuanian 'Republic of Nobles'.[2]

In order to substantiate these claims three sets of questions will be re-examined. We shall start with an overview of how the legal and constitutional framework for the policies of toleration in the Polish-Lithuanian Commonwealth had developed and how the system reacted to, and was affected by, the impact of the Reformation. We shall then examine the patterns of confessional relations in post-Reformation Poland with particular emphasis on those factors in the process of confessionalisation that could primarily be held responsible for the decline of tolerance. Finally we shall discuss, very briefly, the circumstances under which, from the early seventeenth century onwards, the confessional issue entered into a context of territorial identity building, thus leading to the 'nationalization' of religion.

The discussion of the second and the third issue is largely based on source material that stems from a regional study on the history of the Reformation in Royal Prussia.[3] Since Poland's Prussian province was in many respects, at least after the 1580s, the theological and institutional centre of Polish-Lithunian Protestantism, the events within the region certainly reflected, and were immediately linked with, the major developments in confessional relations on the 'national' level. Yet the Prussian experience does not deserve to be generalised in every respect, and it obviously does not cover the whole panorama of confessional phenomena represented in the Polish-Lithuanian Reformation.

Considered in a broader European context of constitutional solutions to the problem of toleration, the case of Poland-Lithuania might appear to be less exceptional than is often claimed. Indeed the Jagiellonian monarchy did develop patterns of religious cohabitation at a very early stage, but these patterns reflected essentially the same logic as the concepts of religious toler-

---

[2] This issue is most recently addressed by Janusz Tazbir, *Szlachta i teologowie: Studia z dziejów polskiej kontrreformacji* [Nobles and Theologians: Studies in the History of Polish Counter-Reformation] (Warsaw, 1987).

[3] Michael G. Müller, *Zweite Reformation und städtische Autonomie im Königlichen Preußen: Danzig, Elbing und Thorn in der Epoche der Konfessionalisierung 1557–1660* (Berlin forthcoming).

ance later implemented elsewhere in Europe. It was the logic of having to react to major challenges of dynastic state-building that, in the Polish case, occurred more or less simultaneously after the fourteenth century. The implementation of the Polish-Lithuanian Union and the subsequent expansion of Jagiellonian rule to large territories east and south of the core lands of Piast Poland rapidly produced the necessity of providing a basis for religious coexistence that would allow for the integration into the dynastic state of the feudal elites from territories as religiously diverse as White and 'Red' Russia, or the Tartar and Cossack dominated regions of the Ukrainian South. Besides, the issue of toleration was to acquire an economic dimension in the context of 'colonial' settlement and urbanisation – a process that in its later stages, and predominantly in the eastern and south-eastern lands of the monarchy, increasingly involved non-Christian population, namely Jews. Last but not least, the problem presented itself also as a political challenge, since the Hussite movement had threatened the existing order in East Central Europe on religious grounds, thus producing a necessity to define more explicitly the range of religious toleration in order to exclude potentially dangerous heresies.

The practice of religious toleration in the Polish-Lithuanian lands that emerged under these circumstances, however, far from represented a coherent model. Toleration was obviously not conceived as a matter of theological, or constitutional, principle; rather than addressing the problem in a general way, the policies of the crown and the Estates reacted specifically, and with different concepts, to individual challenges. While the Jews had to rely entirely on local and regional privileges to guarantee their religious freedom, the rights of the 'dissidents' of noble status were formalised in the constitutional contracts which established, and consolidated, the Polish-Lithuanian union, and also in the various collective privileges for the nobility that were to create a system of fundamental laws for the emerging Republic of Nobles.[4] Other groups, like the Orthodox peasantry and clergy, or the Muslim and Karaim Tartars, ultimately obtained no formal recognition of their religious status other than in a local or regional context, but they were tolerated *de facto*; the Orthodox church organisation with its nine dioceses under the metropolite of Kiev remained intact under Jagiellonian rule, and the question of their re-Catholicisation was only raised after the religious freedom of the Orthodox nobility had been solemnly confirmed by Sigismund II.[5] In any

---

[4] The most recent discussion of the specificity of the constitutional model of the Polish-Lithuanian Republic of Nobles is Klaus Zernack, *Polen und Rußland: Zwei Wege in der europäischen Geschichte* (Berlin, 1994), 188–208.

[5] Confirmations that the Orthodox szlachta should benefit from full noble privileges were issued in 1563 and 1568; this has to be seen against the background of the rapid breakthrough of

case, the most prominent feature of the Polish pattern of tolerance in the Jagiellonian period appears to be that it distinguished between two social models of religious toleration: the aristocratic model on the one hand, based upon an essentially 'modern', i.e. individualistic concept of noble citizenship including the idea of individual freedom of faith, and, on the other hand, a much less clearly defined model of toleration, that collectively applied to certain groups of non-noble status and provided for pragmatic arrangements and where the degree of the religious freedoms granted, including the question of non-Catholic church organisations, ultimately depended on the very size as well as the social weight of the given group within the very much 'multi-cultural' society of the Polish-Lithuanian Commonwealth.

It seems important to bear this is mind, if one wants to understand the somewhat contradictory developments in the period of Reformation. Because it depended, once again, primarily on the social context whether the Protestant movement stood a chance to develop a certain dynamic and to consolidate itself in institutional terms. Thus the history of urban Reformation in Poland-Lithuania was, in most parts of the Commonwealth, bound to come to a rapid end as the Protestant burghers lacked the legal and political instruments to enforce an interconfessional consensus even on a provisional basis and Counter-Reformation action found no institutionalised resistance. The aristocratic Reformation instead could rely on long established constitutional practice of toleration in the Jagiellonian tradition and was therefore able to consolidate the principle of 'dissident' rights so that it remained intact well beyond the success of the Counter-Reformation.

For the fate of the urban Reformation it proved decisive that the status of the *Confessio Augustana* was indeed never legally formalised beyond mere toleration of the Protestant Eucharist. The royal mandates and privileges issued for a number of royal towns, starting with Danzig in 1557, in most cases stipulated no more than that senate and burghers should have *liberum usum Coenae Dominicae sub utraque specie* until a further decision had been taken by the Diet[6] *vel ad celebrationem concilii generalis vel nationalis.*[7] No mention was made of a right to build, and institutionally to consolidate, urban church organisations. The question of Catholic property claims on parish

---

the Protestant movement, and in the context of the political preparations for the renewal and revision of the Polish-Lithuanian Union implemented in Lublin in 1569. The issue of integration of the Orthodox church organisation was raised by the synod of Brest (Litovsk) in 1590 as a result of which four Orthodox dioceses acceded to the Greek Catholic church whereas the others rejected the proposed union.

[6] Royal manadate for Danzig of 5 July 1557, Archiwum Państwowe Gdańsk (APGd.) 300 D/ 5b, 543.

[7] Privilege for the city of Thorn, 22 December 1558, Archiwum Państwowe Toruń (APT) Kat. I. 3008.

churches and monasteries in Protestant use remained unsettled – and was to be successfully instrumentalised by the episcopate in due course.[8] And, perhaps most importantly, the crown had nowhere obliged itself to defend the integrity of the Protestant 'burgher'-churches against the Counter-Reformation pressure that was soon brought to bear from both inside and outside the towns; on the contrary, as Protestant magnates started, after 1573, to exercise what they interpreted as a *ius reformandi* over the towns on their private domaines, the crown claimed the same rights with respect to the royal towns and openly supported anti-Protestant action.[9]

As a result, despite the legal recognition of Protestantism, the fate of the urban Protestant communities depended entirely on the social and political power they represented or could mobilise in their support. For the great Prussian towns, having an overwhelmingly Protestant population and representing a major economic and military factor in the power structure of the monarchy, the ambiguous legal situation in fact proved to be an advantage; the Prussian burghers not only resisted the challenge of the Counter-Reformation, but they were also successful in autonomously establishing and consolidating a church organisation that was soon to acquire the function of an institutional and theological centre for the major Protestant communities in Poland-Lithunia as a whole. Where instead the urban population remained confessionally divided and the Catholic party, including the royal administration, maintained a strong presence, the Protestants soon found themselves on the defensive. The capital of Cracow was the first major royal town to experience violent anti-Protestant action as the joint mobilising efforts of the court and the bishop, supported by the resident nobility and the university, resulted in riots against Calvinist burghers in 1574/75.[10] Many similar incidents were to follow as the conflict in Cracow rapidly escalated, and a generation later, after the Jesuits had taken the lead, the popular movement against the toleration of Protestants also swept on to Protestant strongholds like Poznan or Wilna.[11] Simultaneously a 'quiet' Counter-Reformation took place in many minor royal towns; having, in most cases, been deprived of the use of the parish churches after the 1590s and facing strong pressure from royal administrators

---

[8] For a detailed (although highly biased) account of the conflicts over Catholic claims in the Prussian towns see Hans Neumeyer, *Kirchengeschichte von Danzig und Westpreussen in evangelischer Sicht*, Vol. 1 (Leer, 1971), 109ff.

[9] The issue of urban Reformation in a broader perspective discussed by Wladyslaw Krasiński, *Zarys dziejów Reformacji w Polsce*, vol. 2/I (Warsaw, 1903).

[10] Gottfried Schramm, 'Reformation und Gegenreformation in Krakau', *Zeitschrift für Ostforschung*, 19 (1970), 11–28.

[11] Krasiński, *Zarys*, vol. 2/II, 126; Gottfried Schramm, 'Protestantismus und städtische Gesellschaft in Wilna: 16. und 17. Jahrhundert', *Jahrbücher für Geschichte Osteuropas 17* (1969), 128–49. See also Wladyslaw Sobieski, *Nienawiść wyznaniowa tlumów za Zygmunta III* [Popular Confessional Hatred Under the Rule of Sigismund III] (Warsaw, 1902).

and Jesuits, Protestant communities here often simply ceased to exist as councils no longer recruited Protestant ministers and teachers.[12]

If the legal concessions made to the Protestants thus fell clearly short of providing the basis for an Interim in the towns, the opposite was true for the inter-confessional relations on the level of the nobility.[13] Here too, of course, the question of the social and political power behind the Protestant movement was most relevant, namely in the period immediately preceding the constitutional settlement of 1573; the very success of the Protestants in raising the issue of toleration on the constitutional level and imposing a debate over it on the king and the Catholic estates would probably have been unthinkable without a political movement that, at the time, had the support of no less than half of the country's nobility, including a strong magnate faction. The difference, however, was that the cause of the dissident nobility could easily be accommodated within the existing legal framework: the claim for a constitutionally consolidated Interim could be justified not only with reference to the Commonwealth's tradition of pragmatic toleration, but also in the logic of the concept of noble citizenship in which the principle of the individual's freedom of belief was already implied. Furthermore, given the unionist structure of the Polish-Lithuanian monarchy and the ethnic diversity of its feudal elites the problem of how to reconcile political unity with religious diversity, so difficult for the jurists and politicians of the Holy Roman Empire to solve, did not occur. Finally, once the consensus over an Interim was approved by the Estates and formalised in the act of the Warsaw Confederation, the established constitutional practice offered sufficient guarantees for its implementation; it automatically became part of the canon of fundamental laws that defined the civic status of the individual nobleman.

The political process that led to the Interim therefore proved remarkably smooth. Although Catholic mobilisation against the advance of Protestantism was well under way by 1573, the Catholic Estates themselves advocated a constitutional solution to be implemented by the Convocation Diet after the death of king Sigismund Augustus. This was of course largely due to the fact that the Catholic party had, at the time, at least as much reason as the 'dissident' nobility to worry about the political risks involved with the Interregnum and the election of a new king. However, it seems to be symptomatic that the leaders of the Catholic Estates left the political initiative in this crucial matter to their Protestant counterparts, thus allowing for a toleration act to be put in place that clearly went beyond that of Catholic interests in

---

[12] For an overview of the developments in the minor towns see Stanislaw Salmonowicz, *Konfederacja warszawska 1573 r.* [The Warsaw Confederation of 1573] (Warsaw, 1985), 8ff.; with a perspective on Royal Prussia Neumeyer, *Kirchengeschichte*, vol. 1.

[13] The best analysis of the problematic, although not based on archival research, is still Gottfried Schramm, *Der polnische Adel und die Reformation* 1548–1607 (Wiesbaden, 1965).

an Interim along the lines of the German solution. Apparently the cautious tactics of Catholic action were dictated by the understanding that the prospects of opposing a straightforward constitutional solution were poor; any alternative proposal short of full recognition of the individual's freedom of faith would, in the Polish-Lithuanian context, probably have provoked major disputes over the nature of the Commonwealth's fundamental laws and the question of constitutional legitimacy.

Nevertheless the *pax dissidentium* implemented by the Warsaw Confederation Act of 6 January 1573 could, in retrospect, appear ambiguous in several of its legal and religious implications.[14] The written document neither referred explicitly to the question which of the confessions should benefit from the declared peace among the *dissidentes in religione christianae*, nor did it offer any clear definition of who the 'other Estates' were that, alongside with the *szlachta*, were granted protection against offence and discrimination on religious grounds. It seems, however, noteworthy that these fundamental issues were not at all raised in inter-confessional dispute over the interpretation of the Confederation act that was to start almost immediately after its proclamation. Major conflicts arose over the question whether some kind of *ius reformandi* with respect to not only the peasants but also the urban subjects of magnate, and royal, rule could be deduced from the Warsaw Confederation, whereas the confessional aspect became an issue primarily in the context of Catholic attempts at embarrassing the Protestant party by insisting on the letter of the *Consensus Sendomirensis*. But apparently none of the parties involved questioned the fact that the *pax dissidentium* was to be understood as referring to the Protestant movements united by the *Consensus Sendomirensis* of 1570 as well as to the Orthodox dissidents, thus excluding the anti-Trinitarians,[15] and that, in social terms, it was primarily concerned with the privileges of the nobility.[16]

In a comparative perspective, the Polish-Lithuanian model of inter-confessional toleration as developed on the basis of the *Consensus Sendomir-*

[14] The text of the confederation act published in *Reformacja w Polsce*, vol. 1, 316–19; for a thorough interpretation see Salmonowicz, *Konfederacja*, also Gottfried Schramm, 'Ein Meilenstein der Glaubensfreiheit. Der Stand der Forschung, über Ursprung und Schicksal der Warschauer Konföderation von 1573', *Zeitschrift für Ostforschung*, 24 (1975), 711–36, and Miroslaw Korolko/Janusz Tazbir, *Konfederacja warszawska 1573 r. Wielka karta polskiej tolerancji* [The Warsaw Confederation of 1573. The Magna Carta of Polish Tolerance] (Warsaw, 1980).

[15] For a different reading Salmonowicz, *Konfederacja*, 22, who claims that only the formal exclusion of the Antitrinitarians by a decision of the Diet of 1658 limited the scope of toleration in this sense. However, the very context in which the Confederation act emerged seems to indicate that the *Consensus Sendomirensis* was generally regarded as defining the legitimate protestant confessions.

[16] The most convincing interpretation of the mention of 'other estates' seems to be that it refers to the major Royal towns, namely in Prussia, that, in constitutional terms, were still considered as having seats and votes in the Diet although they did not exercise this right.

ensis, and implemented by the Warsaw Confederation, thus presents itself in the following way. It was clearly an outcome of 'late Reformation' in that it took account of the beginning confessional diversification of Protestantism and therefore carefully avoided theological commitment, namely with respect to the competing interpretations of the *Confessio Augustana*; even the *Consensus Sendomirensis* as such, designed as a *fraterna coniunctio* between the followers of the 'Augsburg, Bohemia, and Swiss confessions' in the 'evangelical churches' of Poland and Lithuania, referred to theological matters only in the context of confirming the 'essential truths' of the gospel, and of banning mutual polemics over the Eucharist.[17] At the same time the model of the Warsaw Confederation was very much in line with a specifically Polish-Lithuanian tradition in that it was orientated towards a broad consensus among Christian churches – a fact that proved important when, after the 1580s, the increasing pressure of the Counter-Reformation gave rise to closer 'inter-dissident' cooperation including the Orthodox church. But above all, the Polish-Lithuanian model represented a specific alternative to the German solution of the *cuius regio* formula. Being based on the concept of protecting the individual's freedom of belief, it had essentially no territorial component. This makes the Polish solution appear, on the one hand, more consistent and more 'modern' than the German one; on the other hand, the lack of territorial institutionalisation rendered the Protestant position much more vulnerable.

Considering the effects of the pragmatic consensus established in 1573, one thus has clearly to distinguish between its constitutional implications and its impact on confessional relations. While the principle of individual freedom of belief as an attribute of noble citizenship indeed remained unchallenged until at least the mid eighteenth century, the *pax dissidentium* had only marginal effects on the fate of confessional pluralism as such. It was ultimately the institutional power behind the competing confessional churches alone that was to decide over their future, and in this respect neither the individual efforts of Protestant magnates nor those of the remaining Protestant towns could in any way compete with the highly organised and well directed action of an essentially undamaged Catholic church. In confessionally divided areas and communities the Protestants were already on the retreat in the 1590s. Not much later many of the original strongholds of rural and urban Reformation had to surrender to the Counter-Reformation as, after 1600, a rapidly growing number of Polish-Lithuanian nobles rejoined the old Church, and as the institutional infrastructure of the Protestant church eventually became

---

[17] The most comprehensive study is Karl Eric Jørgensen, *Ökumenische Bestrebungen unter den polnischen Protestanten bis zum Jahre 1645* (Kopenhagen, 1942); the most recent interpretation is Janusz Tazbir, 'Die Religionsgespräche in Polen', in G. Müller (ed.), *Die Religionsgespräche der Reformationszeit* (Gütersloh, 1980), 127–44.

reduced to some magnate-protected rural enclaves as well as the church organisations of the Prussian towns.

If the decline of the 'dissident' churches can be analysed in the context of institutional, and social, developments, the decline of religious tolerance as such requires, however, an explanation that also accounts for the internal dynamics of confessionalism and religious practices in the period of Reformation. The following discussion of the process of confessionalisation in Royal Prussia focuses primarily on this aspect. The study of a regional case of Protestant confessionalisation is expected to shed some light on how 'religious culture' changed under the impact of Reformation, and to which extent the changes affected intra-Protestant relationships. It is also meant to contribute to explaining why Protestant-Catholic relations in Poland-Lithuania deteriorated in the context of a polarisation of 'national' religious cultures.

The case of Royal Prussia is not an exception to the rule that the dynamic of tolerance and intolerance did not so much depend on the confessional configuration as such, but rather on the social and political contexts in which the fact of confessional division became relevant. The political perspectives for the preservation of religious peace in the province initially appeared most favourable. Good neighbourly relations across confessional borders were long established with the bishops of Ermland maintaining friendly contacts with the Protestant Hohenzollerns in Ducal Prussia,[18] and Protestant Prussian magnates peacefully cooperating with the remaining Catholic towns on the Prussian Council. And once the *Confessio Augustana* was formally recognised in the province after 1557, a pragmatic consensus was easily reached that the troubles of confessional conflict as experienced in France and the Holy Roman Empire should by all means be avoided.[19]

Much depended in this respect on developments in the major towns. Since Danzig, Elbing and Thorn were the only territorial entities in the province to establish autonomous Protestant church organisations and to provide substantial political backing for the Protestant movement, the towns were bound to take the lead in shaping its confessional profile. At the same time, the risk of confessional tension grew much higher here than elsewhere as the newly emerging urban churches inevitably became an object of fierce competition between Protestant theologians from many parts of Central Europe seeking

---

[18] Most telling in this respect is the following recently edited correspondence *Herzog Albrecht von Preußen und das Bistum Ermland: 1525–1550* (Cologne, 1991).

[19] Stanislaw Salmonowicz, 'Preußen Königlichen Anteils und das Herzogtum Preußen als Gebiet der Begegnung zweier Kulturen vom 16. bis 18. Jh.', *Schlesien und Pommern in den deutsch-polnischen Beziehungen vom 16. bis zum 18. Jh.* (Braunschweig, 1982), 66–86; for the political context see also *Historia Pomorza* (History of Pommerania), vol. 2/I (Poznań, 1976).

employment and protection with the wealthy German burgher communities. Town councils were thus confronted with the delicate task of implementing a confessional policy that would satisfy both the religious expectations of their communities and the political requirements evolving from the towns' specific status within the province and the monarchy. On the one hand, they had carefully to avoid 'importing' inner-Protestant conflict by openly siding with one of the emerging confessional churches in the West. On the other hand, it seemed vital to integrate the Prussian churches into the framework of religious co-existence that was beginning to take shape in the Polish-Lithuanian Commonwealth.

Although it is quite obvious that confessional sympathies among the Prussian patricians rapidly turned towards Calvinism, the official position of the town councils remained far more cautious.[20] Councils insisted that a 'non-confessional' interpretation of the *Confessio Augustana* could, and should, provide a common theological basis for the Protestant Prussian churches irrespective of theological dispute elsewhere, namely the 'foreign German quarrels' (*'frembde teutsche streitsachen'*).[21] In order to commit the local ministers to respecting this position, the towns issued their own *notulae concordiae* that were drafted by jurists in the service of the councils, and designed to regulate confessional relations primarily in a pragmatic way rather than to define a confessional profile in theological terms: While the *essentialia* of the *Confessia Augustana* were mentioned in the most general terms possible, much emphasis was put on the towns' commitment to church unity as well as on the theologians' obligation to refrain from polemics and as on the theologians' obligation to refrain from polemics and 'arbitrary explanations' of Scripture.[22] Moreover, tight control over the very recruitment of ministers was of major concern to the councils. Although officially no other requirement was stated than that ministers should stand firm in the defence of the *Confessio Augustana* and be 'learned and peaceful' men, the practice of recruitment reflects marked preferences for specific confessional profiles, or at least specific academic affiliations. All three towns clearly favoured Saxonian Philipists who, as it seemed, ideally represented the mediatory interpretation of the *Augustana* supporting the confessional compromise

---

[20] The most prominent source of information about the ecclesiastical policies of the towns is Christoph Hartknoch, *Preußische Kirchen-Historia* (Frankfurt on Main and Leipzig, 1686). His reading of the events, however, is strongly biased in favor of the Lutheran view. For an alternative interpretation see Reinhold Curicke, *Der Stadt Dantzig historische Beschreibung*, (uncensored 2nd edn) (Amsterdam, 1652), and, closest to the events, the manuscript of a history of confessional relations in Danzig written around 1602 by the Calvinist theologian Jacob Fabricius, 'Historia Notulae', APGd. 300 R/Pp 2.

[21] APGd. 300, 53/434, 9–11.

[22] 'Notula Concordiae' for Danzig of 1562, APGd. 300 R/Pq 1, 3r–21v; for Thorn 'verfaßte Ordnung' of 1569, Acta consularia APT Kat. II, II–1, 95r–95v. In the case of Elbing the respective document has not been preserved.

envisaged for the Prussian churches. Thorn also relied on theologians recruited among the Bohemian Brethren, and the Elbing church benefitted from the immigration of Scottish Presbyterians.[23]

In the course of the 1560s and 1570s a particular Prussian model had thus taken shape. Having maintained their 'supra-confessional' status, the Prussian churches represented a remarkable exception from what might be perceived as a universal dynamic of confessional polarisation of Protestantism in the German speaking world. It was only in Prussia that a consensual interpretation of the Eucharist in the Melanchtonian tradition still provided a basis however fragile for theological coexistence of Lutheran and Calvinist affiliations – despite steadily rising confessional pressure from Lutheran churches and universities in the *Reich*. At the same time, the supra-confessional model allowed for the integration of the Prussians towns into the broader framework of dissident politics in the Polish-Lithuanian Commonwealth. Having avoided siding with Lutheran orthodoxy, Prussian Protestantism fitted into the pragmatic 'national' consensus of Sandomierz and thus qualified as a potential ally of the Protestant and Orthodox communities in other parts of the Commonwealth. In any case, the Prussian development in the first two decades after the recognition of Protestantism was clearly part of, and contributed to, a process of consolidating toleration along the lines defined by the *Consensus Sendomirensis* and the Warsaw Confederation.

Before the end of the 1570s, however, signs of a destabilisation of the urban model of religious co-existence had already become visible. Rapidly escalating confessional disputes challenged the inner-urban *pax dissidentium*. At the same time, religious issues gave rise to external conflicts undermining the consensual relations between the towns and their Polish-Lithuanian hinterland. This was due to a number of reasons, both social and political, that will be discussed below.

One source of conflict was that the secular authorities of the towns had clearly overestimated their capacity to retain full control of ecclesiastical life. Despite a harsh regime of all three councils in matters of church discipline, confessional rivalry among local ministers developed a dynamic of its own that gradually undermined the pragmatic consensus imposed in the 1560s. This was partly due to the fact that not even the most thoroughly supervised procedure for the recruitment of ministers could provide for theological uniformity. Having a high demand for qualified theological personnel for their churches and schools, the towns had to rely, until the 1590s, primarily on external recruitment, and the German universities that were usually asked for recommendations could neither provide a sufficient number of candidates,

---

[23] For detailed biographical information Danziger Presbyteriologie, APGd. 300 R/Pp 85 and 300 R/Pp 93; Wernicke, Thornische Presbyteriologie, APT Kat. II, X–27; Fuchs, Ecclesiastica Elbingenses, APGd. 492/495.

nor were their judgements with regards to the candidates' confessional profile in all cases trustworthy. Having thus to rely ultimately on a theological 'examination' of the candidates by the Senior Minister and the town's jurists, a certain degree of uncertainty remained. No wonder therefore, that all three towns eventually counted among the ministers a number of theologians who were more committed to their 'confessional field' outside Prussia than to the pragmatic consensus of the local churches, and who more or less openly contested the right of lay authorities to 'rule over the souls' by deciding over theological *essentialia* according to political convenience. Usually Lutheran ministers with an orthodox background were the first to make this an issue of public controversy,[24] but ex-Philipists and Calvinists soon joined in as Lutheran propaganda raised anxieties that the process of 'completing the Reformation' along the lines of moderate change might be reversed.[25]

Yet not only the weaknesses of recruitment procedures can be held responsible for the confessional polarisation. At least equally important was the fact that the theological factions among local ministries constantly realigned, following the dynamic of a gradually escalating confessional conflict. Factors to be mentioned in this context are:

the impact of an increasingly fierce confessional controversy in the Protestant German territories that was obviously closely followed by theologians in neighbouring Royal Prussia;

the problem of conflicting loyalties as ministers recruited from outside Prussia remained attached to their respective confessional networks in Germany as well as to their region of origin and their *alma mater*;

a sense of frustration among both Lutherans and Calvinists over having to compromise with a politically imposed theological consensus with which they felt increasingly uncomfortable;

frequent conflict over the 'tyrannic' regiment of councils over the churches, being perceived by Lutherans as arbitrary curtailment of ecclesiastical autonomy as defined by Luther's 'two-kingdoms doctrine';[26]

finally, social competition between an 'inner' and an 'outer' circle of local ministers whose status, and career opportunities, at least

---

[24] In Danzig Dr Johannes Kittel and Clemens Friccius who, by starting a public debate over the Lutheran Formula Concordiae in 1580, triggered off a major conflict over both the theological foundations and the civic status of the ministry; APGd. 300 R/Pp 85, 4–19, 33, 83–4.

[25] About the considerations among the Calvinist ministers in Danzig after 1584 to finally abandon the defensive strategy for the sake of a more explicitly Calvinist course see Fabricius, Historia Notulae, APGd. 300 R/Pp 2, 125v–29r.

[26] For an early example of such Lutheran criticism see Franz Burchard's 'advice' to his former parish in Danzig in 1560, APGd. 300 R/Pp q. 1, 23r–43v.

partly depended on their relationship with the urban elites, namely the pro-Calvinist patricians.[27]

Some of the ecclesiastical conflicts that seemed to virtually explode from the 1580s onwards were thus immediately related to theological issues, and reflected the general tendency towards confessional polarisation of Protestantism, whereas others had rather a local and non-theological context. A clear distinction between matters of principal and contextual issues, however, cannot be made, since almost every conflict over ecclesiastical relations was, after 1580, almost automatically 'translated' into confessional categories.

Inevitably the confessional split within the urban churches therefore became more and more visible, and took finally the form of a 'schism'.[28] In Danzig this happened as early as 1586, and once again the magistrates intervened immediately by issuing a mandate *de non calumnando*.[29] At that stage, however, attempts at settling theological dispute by administrative enforcement of church discipline were bound to fail. Members of both factions in the ministry now insisted on their right and obligation to condemn false doctrine by virtue of the theological *Strafamt*, and to 'explain' the Gospel to the faithful.[30] Furthermore, both factions now explicitly repudiated the hitherto respected non-confessional consensus as a precarious practice of 'syncretism', thus depriving the magistrates' ecclesiastical position of its theological justification.

Subsequent attempts by the Danzig Council at reactivating the town's *Notula Concordiae* of 1562 in fact only accelerated the process of delegitimisation. Even Jacob Fabricius, hitherto the most loyal defender of the magistrates ecclesiastical policies and the town's leading Calvinist theologian, was now forced to denounce the *Notula* on confessional grounds. In his response to the Council he characterised it as 'grossly Flaccian' (*gut grob Flaccianisch*), and he added that, in the light of the devastating effects of Lutheran radicalism, it appeared to have been a grave mistake that the more prudent ministers had 'apparently been all too patient until now, allowing for the common cause to suffer irreparable damage, and depriving ourselves of all honor and respect.'[31] As a result, the magistrates of all towns indeed tried to readapt their ecclesiastical policies to the new situation. They still

[27] A good example is the case of Dr Jacob Fabricius, son of a Danzig patrician, who, immediately after graduating from the university of Basel, was appointed rector of the Danzig gymnasium and theological adviser to the council in 1580, and was soon to become the object of fierce attacks by his less privileged Lutheran colleagues; APGd. 300 R/Pp 85, 83f.

[28] The term 'schism' was used by the Lutheran ministers who, in 1586, refused to participate in the ordination of an allegedly Calvinist theologian; APGd. 300 R/Pp 15, 219f.

[29] 23 October 1586, APGd. 300, 10/9, 302r–304r.

[30] A comprehensive theological discussion of the issue in a Lutheran perspective was published in Danzig in early 1587: APGd. 300 R/Pp 31, 18–23.

[31] APGd. 300 R/Pp 2, 181r–84r.

hoped to maintain the link with the model of the *Consensus Sendomirensis*. Yet, they could no longer ignore the fact that the reality of supra-confessional co-existence had *de facto* been overtaken by multi-confessionalism.

The second challenge to the elitist concept of confessional coexistence arose from the dynamics of popular religiosity. It cannot, of course, be denied that in the context of daily urban life a certain 'tolerance of practical rationality' might have developed in Prussia as well, and that, in principle, the necessity to accommodate not only other Protestant confessions but also Catholics supported the permissive approach of the magistrates at some stage. Ultimately, however, the particular circumstances in Prussia seem to have favoured quite the opposite: rather than positively responding to mediatory efforts by the magistrates, the 'common man' proved most receptive to exclusionist confessional propaganda, namely in its Lutheran variant.

This can partly be explained by the fact that the Prussian towns had a long record of latent conflict between German-speaking burghers and non-German potential competitors, and also that religious diversity had always played a role in underpinning this conflict. In the past this had been primarily an issue of Christian-Jewish relations. After the Reformation the problems of course multiplied as Poles and Czechs, Dutchmen and Scots became identified as religiously 'alien'. Indeed, in all these cases the burghers' fears seemed justified in economic terms. The magistrates tended to encourage foreign competition, and this happened not only for the sake of stimulating commodity production and trade, but also in order to undermine the political power of the guilds. The latter, in turn, had their own political reasons to raise the confessional issue. It not only served as a pretext to stigmatise economic competitors – like the Dutch Calvinists whom councils were eager to tolerate despite their outspokenly anti-Lutheran attitude – but it also provided suitable arguments for political action of the guilds against the magistrates: while any kind of straight-forward opposition against the legitimate urban authorities involved the risk of being stigmatised as 'rebellious', the legitimacy of claims in defence of the 'true faith' could hardly be questioned. In fact, this was tested in the course of a number of limited conflicts after the 1560s, and at least with respect to their economic objectives the guilds were often successful.[32]

If after the 1570s, the 'common man' also engaged in confessional disputes between the towns' theologians, different reasons will have to be considered, however. One explanation lies in the phenomenon that as a rule congregations only very reluctantly accepted changes of ritual practices eventually implemented as a result of the Reformation; almost everywhere the less edu-

---

[32] See H. G. Mannhardt, *Die Danziger Mennonitengemeinde. Ihre Entstehung und ihre Geschichte von 1569 bis 1919* (Danzig, 1919); Ludwig Neubauer, 'Mährische Brüder in Elbing', *Zeitschrift für Kirchengeschichte* (1912) 447–59.

cated among the faithful seem to have, in this respect, preferred the moderate Lutheran to the much more rigid Calvinist approach. Yet, the events in Danzig seem to suggest that popular mobilisation in the defence of traditional rites was, at least partly, a result of manipulation: apparently the Lutheran ministers consciously, and most skillfully, exploited the conservatism of popular religiosity in order to put pressure on the magistrate, and to provoke public unrest against their Calvinist opponents.

Reports on religious riots in Danzig in the 1580s reflecting the mechanisms of popular mobilisation indeed provide strong evidence for this assumption.[33] Not only did popular unrest always break out as an immediate consequence of conflicts between the magistrates and Lutheran ministers, and in situations where administrative sanctions against disobedient theologians were pending. But it can also be proved that the followers of the Lutheran faction were directly 'instructed' by the ministers − be it in the context of the sermon or, as in 1584, through public appeal to the crowd that had gathered in front of the town hall. Both the specific cause of popular resistance, and the 'enemy' had to be clearly indicated by the Lutheran leaders before 'spontaneous' protest could come to bear.

The success of Lutheran strategies of popular mobilisation had mainly to do with the capacity to play on specific rhetorics, and symbols. Obviously genuine theological reasoning played no major role in this − at least not until translated into an extremely simplified language of confessional dispute. In fact, Lutheran polemics initially operated on the basis of a simple equation of Calvinist with the 'diabolical', the conspiratorial, but also associating it with tyrannic rule (*Hispanica Inquisitio*), without the substance of confessional controversy at all becoming an issue. As the Lutherans mobilised forces against the Calvinist rector of the Gymnasium in 1584, their primary allegations was that, by 'seducing' his pupils with Calvinist ideas, he had made himself guilty of a 'Massacre of the Innocent'; and when warned to refrain from 'personal condemnations' the responsible Lutheran ministers publicly declared that they refused to be made 'dump dogs and forced idly to watch the crimes of ravening wolves, thieves, and murderers'.[34] Later, as Calvinists took more determined steps after 1586 towards abolishing the 'papal relics' in their churches, the issue of rites and visual symbols came to the fore. Calvinists tried to ridicule the Lutheran habit of wearing the traditional surplice as making ministers look like 'butcher apprentices or brewers', and they severely criticised the use of 'many wafers' for the ceremony of the Eucharist instead of 'plain bread' as prescribed in the Scrip-

---

[33] On riots in 1584 and 1587 Curicke, *Stadt Dantzig*, 332 and 342–44, APGd. 300 R/Pp 25, 162 and 562–64, 300 R/Pp 2, 116r–19r and 198r–200r.

[34] APGd. 300 R/Pp 2, 110rff.

ture.[35] Much more successful, however, were the Lutherans, calling for resistance against the 'cleaning of altars' on the grounds that Calvinist reforms were to 'deprive the Savior of His power', and denouncing the new habit of breaking the bread as a profanation of the Eucharist.[36] Finally, magic beliefs also seem to have played a substantial role in motivating action by the 'common man'. In fact, almost every incidence of public unrest over religious matters was reported to have been accompanied by supra-natural events making strong impressions on the faithful. Such events were: the allegedly 'unnatural' death of the Crypto-Calvinist minister Peter Praetorius in 1588 who was said to have fallen victim of a 'miraculous disease' that made his body dissolve, and eventually vanish; the appearance of a 'blind prophet' who claimed to have had a vision of Calvinist patricians burning in hell; or, on the eve of the riots of 1587, the apparition of a strange light 'as clear as sunshine' during late-night deliberations of the guild masters over possible action in defence of a suspended Lutheran minister.[37]

In any case, the dynamics of popular involvement in the confessional controversy clearly worked in favour of Lutheran exclusionism. Once the confessional frontlines had become 'visualised', and the dispute had turned into a conflict over the symbolic practices of popular religiosity, the project of supra-confessional toleration seemed no longer defendable. After 1590 the ecclesiastical profile of the Prussian towns became perceived as multi-confessional, and pressure to abandon the principle of pragmatic coexistence, or 'syncretism', for the sake of confessional unity rapidly increased.

The third factor, finally, to challenge the policies of toleration were the attempts by the Crown to instrumentalise the confessional issue as a political weapon against the largely autonomous Prussian towns. Remarkably enough, this factor came to bear only after the mid 1590s, and in the context of rising inner-Protestant tension rather than of Catholic-Protestant conflict.

Until then, the towns' cautious strategy of integration into the 'dissident' movement among the Polish-Lithuanian nobility had indeed protected them efficiently against any kind of political interference on religious grounds. Since the three towns had declared their adherence to the *Consensus Sendomirensis* in 1595, the position of the Prussian churches within the constitutional framework defined by the Warsaw Confederation seemed ultimately consolidated. The law against religious 'unrest' passed by the Diet of 1593 had served as an efficient instrument to deal with occasional clashes between Catholic noblemen and Protestant burghers. Even the attempts of the episcopate to re-establish Catholic presence by reclaiming church property in the towns had finally come to a deadlock as, in the case of Prussia, the outposts

---

[35] APGd. 300 R/Pp 13, 165–8.
[36] APGd. 300 R/Pp 25, 164f.
[37] Curicke, *Stadt Dantzig, passim*; for the events of 1587 APGd. 300 R/Pp 25, 161f.

of urban Counter-Reformation remained utterly isolated within the large Protestant communities.

The prospects for external interference improved, however, as the religious division of urban society deepened, and the question of the towns' confessional status eventually became an issue of internal political struggle. In the case of Danzig a critical point was reached when, at the end of the 1590s, the antipatrician faction in the town's Broader Council uniting the most influential guild masters and merchants stood up in defence of the Lutheran cause. In a series of petitions to the town's mayors they requested the immediate 'restoration' of the 'privileged Confession of Augsburg',[38] and since the magistrates – quite expectedly – failed to react, the representatives of the Council's 'Third Order' eventually, in 1605, proceeded to appealing to the king: By tolerating, and encouraging 'Calvinist abuse' in the town's churches, the 'protesting party' claimed, mayors and Council members had deliberately violated royal privileges issued in favour of the 'pure *Confessio Augustana*'; the king was therefore requested to restore religious peace in his town – and to replace the disobedient patricians in the Council by 'pious and trustworthy men'.[39]

In juridical terms this was clearly a weak case. The very mention of the *Augustana* in the respective royal privileges could hardly be regarded as a valid argument against the legitimacy of the moderate Calvinist profile of Prussian Protestantism. And the fact that all privileges contained a clause prohibiting any 'alteration of ceremonies'[40] in the Protestant churches was not to be understood, as the Lutheran party argued, as a provision against Calvinist reform but much rather as a royal guarantee that the churches in Protestant use should not be returned to the Catholics. Nevertheless the king was most eager to endorse the Lutheran interpretation as providing a suitable pretext for political intervention. Other than the inner-urban opposition expected the objective of the king's initiative was, however, not actually to overthrow patrician rule but to undermine the towns' alliance with the Calvinist magnates, and to establish a position that would allow to exploit politically the ambiguous ecclesio-political status of the towns in the future. The investigations by royal commissioners in Danzig as well as the trial against the accused council members at the royal court in Cracow lasted two years without producing any conclusive results. Still, the political pressure resulting from formal legal action against the magistrates was strong enough finally to convince the urban elite that the development towards Lutheran confessionalisation could not be reversed, and that the supra-confessional model

---

[38] The first formal complaint to the Danzig Council was filed in 1601; APGd. 300, 10/198, 109.
[39] Text of the official 'protestation' submitted to the king in February 1605: APGd. 300 R/Pp 1, 573–86, also Curicke, *Stadt Dantzig*, 366–70.
[40] See Stefan Bathory's 'cautio religionis' for the city of Danzig of 1577: 'Nec volumus ut in templis ritus caeremoniarum ullo pacto immutentur . . .', APGd, 300 D/5c, 24.

of religious toleration had to be ultimately abandoned. In 1606 the Danzig Council co-opted a number of new Lutheran members and, at the same time, declared their firm intention to restore religious peace on the basis of strict observance of the *Augustana*.[41] Thorn and Elbing hesitated slightly longer, but ultimately followed the example of Danzig.

The events that resulted in the Prussian towns opting in favour of Lutheran confessionalism, and withdrawing from the pragmatic consensus among the Polish-Lithuanian Protestant churches were to have far reaching consequences. They not only marked the ultimate failure of the attempts at containing the dynamics of confessional exclusionism in the urban context. But they also contributed to the decline of religious toleration on a national scale. The fact that the remaining Protestant communities in Poland and Lithuania lost the institutional support of the Prussian churches clearly accelerated the advance of the Counter-Reformation in the other provinces of the Commonwealth. More importantly, as the Prussian churches now loosened their ties with the Polish hinterland, and became instead part of an essentially German confessional network, the religious issue gradually acquired a 'national' dimension. In the Polish perspective, not only the Lutheran faith as such but Protestantism in general was, after the beginning of the seventeenth century, increasingly identified with the milieu of the German-speaking Prussian burghers – thus underlining the social and cultural 'otherness' of the province. And since these developments coincided with the emergence of a new, proto-national ideology of 'Polishness' based on Catholicism and nobilitarian tradition, the question of religious diversity now inevitably entered into a context of political demarcation, and mutual exclusion.

Compared with the situation before, and around, 1600 this was indeed a dramatic shift. As we have seen, the 'German origins' of urban Reformation in Prussia had created no obstacle for the towns' integration into the constitutional framework provided by the Warsaw Confederation. On the contrary: the Melanchthonian model had served as an ideal basis for ecclesiastical cooperation with the Polish-Lithuanian 'dissidents' – and this, in turn, had enabled the towns to play a much more active role than previously in the political system of the Commonwealth. When, in 1595, the Prussian patricians had expressed their willingness to adhere to the *Consensus Sendomirensis*, it had seemed perfectly normal that they addressed the dissident magnates as their 'brothers in faith' (*Konfessionsverwandte*), members of the same aristocratic estate, and natural political allies in the defence of Republican rights against 'papal tyranny'.[42] And the response by the Senatorial and

---

[41] APGd. 300 R/Pp 19, 216.
[42] APGd. 300 R/Pp 54, 169ff.

noble Estates had always been a positive one: throughout the 1590s, they had eagerly supported the towns' appeals to provincial diets and the Sejm, and still in 1603 the Wojewoda of Brest formally declared that the dissidents would not hesitate to 'risk their blood' in order to assure that the Prussian Protestants would freely benefit from the rights granted by the Warsaw Confederation.[43]

Relations started to change in the aftermath of the Danzig conflict. This was, to some extent, due to the fact that, almost simultaneously, the political movement behind Polish-Lithuanian Protestantism suffered a major defeat in the unsuccessful revolt of the lower nobility against the Crown in 1607/8.[44] But frictions between Prussian and Polish-Lithuanian Protestants had already become visible earlier. When the question of Danzig's confessional status was raised dissident leaders proved somewhat reluctant to support the magistrates in what was perceived as 'unnecessary' religious quarrels with disobedient ministers and rebellious subjects,[45] and as Danzig in the end formally withdrew from the supra-confessional Protestant consensus relations clearly cooled off.

The crucial factor in the development leading to the ideological and political marginalization of the Prussian towns within the Polish-Lithuanian Commonwealth was, however, the influence of the Polish-Swedish wars between 1617 and 1660.[46] The involvement of the towns in the conflict over the possession of Livland and the rights of the Polish Vasa-dynasty to the Swedish succession was, in fact, of an entirely passive nature. Remaining perfectly loyal to the Polish crown throughout the conflict, they suffered substantially from the economic repercussions of the war at sea, and were exposed to siege and occupation by foreign troops when the Swedes invaded Prussia in 1626 and in 1655. The very fact, however, that Danzig had eventually opened its port to the enemy fleet, and that Thorn and Elbing had not been able to defend their walls against a besieging Swedish army, was soon turned into an ideological argument against the Prussian burghers. In attempts at explaining the military successes of the Swedish invasion Polish leaders claimed that the towns had hastened to collaborate with the foreign invaders – and since Prussians and Swedes shared the Lutheran faith, the motivation for such disloyalty seemed obvious. But Swedish propaganda also contributed to the dissemination of such views. Swedish diplomats left out no occasion to stress the king's commitment to the Lutheran 'brothers' across the Baltic Sea. And Swedish administrators in occupied Thorn and Elbing made a point

---

[43] APT Kat. II, XIII–10, 176–9.

[44] Krasiński, *Zarys*, Vol. 2/II, 113–19.

[45] APT Kat. II, XIII–10, 190ff.

[46] For the major events of the war, and its political repercussions see *Historia Pomorza*, Vol. 2/I, 487–507.

of actively 'defending' the Lutheran cause by tightly controlling, and openly discriminating against, Catholic activities.

By the end of the Swedish wars the process of alienation had, in any case, become irreversible. Not only the Polish-Lithuanian nobility considered the Lutheran milieu from now on to be excluded from both the religious and political culture that was understood essentially to constitute 'Polishness'. But the Prussian burghers themselves also started to develop a particularist identity for which the Lutheran faith functioned as one of the central markers; a re-integration into the civic society of the Commonwealth seemed neither politically feasible nor even desirable.

At that stage, at the latest, the point was reached where the constitutionally implemented model of religious toleration in Poland-Lithuania ultimately ceased to be politically operational. The dynamics of confessional demarkation, both in the Protestant and the Catholic context, had resulted in a 'nationalisation of religion', and with the Protestant community withdrawing, and being excluded, from citizenship in the seventeenth century 'Republic of Nobles', the concept of a civic *pax inter dissidentes* lost its relevance. Of course, Prussian Protestantism maintained its autonomy nevertheless. But rather than being a positive consensus over the principle of toleration, this was due to the existence of a relative balance of economic and political power between the semi-autonomous Prussian towns and their Polish-Lithuanian hinterland.

Index